1995

BASIC READINGS
IN ANGLO-SAXON ENGLAND
VOL. 2

ANGLO-SAXON
MANUSCRIPTS

GARLAND REFERENCE LIBRARY
OF THE HUMANITIES
VOL. 1434

Basic Readings in Anglo-Saxon England

CARL T. BERKHOUT, PAUL E. SZARMACH, AND JOSEPH B. TRAHERN, JR.
General Editors

OLD ENGLISH SHORTER POEMS
Basic Readings
edited by Katherine O'Brien O'Keeffe

ANGLO-SAXON MANUSCRIPTS
Basic Readings
edited by Mary P. Richards

BEOWULF
Basic Readings
edited by Peter S. Baker

ANGLO-SAXON MANUSCRIPTS

Basic Readings

edited by

Mary P. Richards

GARLAND PUBLISHING, INC.
New York & London / 1994

Library of Congress Cataloging-in-Publication Data

Anglo-Saxon manuscripts : basic readings / edited by
Mary P. Richards.
    p.   cm. — (Basic readings in Anglo-Saxon
England ; vol. 2) (Garland reference library of the
humanities ; vol. 1434)
    Includes bibliographical references and index.
    ISBN 0–8153–0100–6 (alk. paper)
    1. Manuscripts, English (Old)   2. English litera-
ture—Old English, ca. 450–1100—Criticism, Textual.
3. Paleography, English.   I. Richards, Mary P.
II. Series.   III. Series : Garland reference library of
the humanities ; vol. 1434.
Z105.A54   1994
411'.7—dc20   94–12990
                                                       CIP

Printed on acid-free, 250-year-life paper
Manufactured in the United States of America

Preface of the General Editors

Basic Readings in Anglo-Saxon England (BRASE) is a series of volumes that collect classic, exemplary, or ground-breaking essays in the fields of Anglo-Saxon studies generally written in the 1960s or later, or commissioned by a volume editor to fulfill the purpose of the given volume. The General Editors impose no prior restraint of "correctness" of ideology, method, or critical position. Each volume editor has editorial autonomy to select essays that sketch the achievement in a given area of study or point to the potential for future study. The liveliness and diversity of the interdisciplinary field, manifest in the annual bibliography of the *Old English Newsletter* and in the review of that bibliography in the *Year's Work in Old English Studies*, can lead only to editorial choices that reflect intellectual openness. BRASE volumes must be true to their premises, complete within their articulated limits, and accessible to a multiple readership. Each collection may serve as a "first book" on the delimited subject, where students and teachers alike may find a convenient starting point. The *terminus a quo*, approximately the 1960s, may be associated with the general rise of Anglo-Saxon studies and a renewed, interdisciplinary professionalism therein; other collections, particularly in literature, represent the earlier period. Changes in publication patterns and in serial-acquisitions policies, moreover, suggest that convenient collections can still assist the growth and development of Anglo-Saxon studies.

In this second volume of the series, *Anglo-Saxon Manuscripts*, Mary P. Richards selects classic essays from a field of study fundamental to the understanding of Anglo-Saxon culture. Taking an interdisciplinary, editorial point of view, Richards provides a collection that fulfills the series mandate to offer a "first book" that introduces the subject of research as well as suggests some of the newer directions and potential developments. Some of these essays show how approaches from manuscript study can affect our understanding of the production and history of key manuscripts. Peter Clemoes, for example, shows how an understanding of technical manuscript features sheds light on the compositional methods Ælfric of Eynsham followed in that most rare example in Anglo-Saxon England, an author-authorized manuscript (B.L. Royal 7.C.xii, fols. 4-218). Text and image, a standard theme in the study of illustrated manuscripts, receives an exemplary treatment when Barbara C. Raw discusses how Oxford, Bodleian Library Junius 11, was planned to include illustrations for more than just *Genesis*. That many Anglo-Saxon manuscripts are some form of a "whole from recognizable parts" has likewise been a theme in recent studies. Donald G. Scragg explains how the Vercelli Book is a compilation and, by implication, how one cannot speak of the unity of the Vercelli Book from any formalist perspective. And in this connection P.R. Robinson shows how to understand the idea of the "booklet," which stands behind many a compilation. These contributions cited here indicate in part how "basic terms, techniques, resources, issues, and applications" form the theme of this book. For this collection Richards commissioned three studies: Alexander Rumble's distillation of his introductory course in Palaeography at Manchester, Richard W. Pfaff's remarkable sketch of N.R. Ker in the context of Ker's indispensable *Catalogue*, and Kevin Kiernan's leading-edge overview of the developments in technology that may very well usher in a new age of manuscript study, wherein Anglo-Saxonists will surely play a major role.

The General Editors would like to thank Professor Richards for her willingness to organize this volume and to join her work with Peter Baker's edited collection on *Beowulf* and Katherine O'Brien O'Keeffe's edited collection on shorter Old English poems to launch the series. At this writing other volumes are in preparation or in planning.

Carl T. Berkhout
Paul E. Szarmach
Joseph B. Trahern

Contents

Acknowledgments

Among the many individuals who have given encouragement to the present collection over the past two years, Joyce M. Hill, Patrick W. Conner, Kevin S. Kiernan, and William P. Stoneman merit special mention. The general editor, Paul E. Szarmach, generously provided guidance and enthusiastic support. Robert G. Netherland patiently prepared camera-ready copy for a difficult set of materials, while Martha Carothers provided artwork for the charts and figures.

My thanks are due to those authors—Rumble, Kiernan, and Pfaff—who contributed new essays for the benefit of this collection. Blockley, Lapidge, Dumville, Scragg, and Clemoes revised and updated their essays at considerable effort. I am indebted further to all of the contributors excepting the late Kenneth Sisam for their patient proofreading and support of the present volume. Journals and presses, as follows, have given permission to reprint, often without charge:

P. R. Robinson, 'Self-Contained Units in Composite Manuscripts of the Anglo-Saxon Period'. Reprinted from *Anglo-Saxon England* 7 (1978), 231-8, by permission of the publisher. Copyright ©1978 Cambridge University Press.

Mary Blockley, 'Addenda and Corrigenda to N.R. Ker's "A Supplement to *Catalogue of Manuscripts Containing Anglo-Saxon*"'. Reprinted from *Notes and Queries* ns 29 (1982), 1-3, by permission of the publisher. Copyright ©1982 Oxford University Press.

Michael Lapidge, 'Surviving Booklists from Anglo-Saxon England'. Reprinted from *Learning and Literature in Anglo-Saxon England*, ed. Michael Lapidge and Helmut Gneuss, by permission of the publisher. Copyright ©1985 Cambridge University Press.

David N. Dumville, 'English Libraries Before 1066: Use and Abuse of the Manuscript Evidence'. Reprinted from *Insular Latin Studies. Papers on Latin Texts and Manuscripts of the British Isles: 550-1066*, ed. Michael W. Herren (Papers in Mediaeval Studies 1), pp. 153-78, by permission of the publisher. Copyright ©1981 Pontifical Institute of Mediaeval Studies, Toronto.

Introduction: Basic Readings in Anglo-Saxon Manuscripts

Mary P. Richards

The past fifty years have seen remarkable advances in the study of Anglo-Saxon manuscripts. Neil Ker, T.A.M. Bishop, M.B. Parkes, Helmut Gneuss, and P.H. Sawyer are examples of leaders in the field who have provided research tools for their many colleagues in scholarship. The work of cataloging, describing, and interpreting manuscripts is now well underway, and offers opportunities for sound analysis as never before. Because the study of manuscripts is fundamental to the appreciation of Anglo-Saxon texts and culture, the present volume seeks to provide a collection of materials covering basic terms, techniques, resources, issues, and applications. Drawn from a variety of published sources and new writings commissioned specifically for this collection, the essays are intended to give a thorough background in principles and practices, along with up-to-date coverage of new developments in paleography.

This volume begins with Alexander R. Rumble's 'Using Anglo-Saxon Manuscripts', a codification of lecture notes and handouts from his introductory course in paleography taught at the Manchester Centre for Anglo-Saxon Studies. He begins with lists of basic readings, provides detailed guidance for describing a codex, gives additional advice on describing manuscript fragments and single-sheet documents, and outlines procedures for transcribing and editing texts. One important aspect of codicology, or the description of a manuscript book, is the 'booklet', so termed and analyzed by P.R. Robinson in 'Self-Contained Units in Composite Manuscripts of the Anglo-Saxon Period'. Citing examples from a number of codices in British libraries, Robinson establishes nine features that characterize 'booklets' in Anglo-Saxon manuscripts and shows how to identify them. Her pointers are useful additions to the paleographer's repertoire of descriptive tools.

In 'Old Manuscripts/New Technologies', Kevin S. Kiernan reviews advances in manuscript study accomplished with the aid of various technological devices made for other purposes. He credits the British Library for having investigated the potential of new equipment to help us see and record writing that is obscured or invisible to the unaided eye. Kiernan points out that paleographical problems often require unique and imaginative solutions, and gives examples of discoveries made by a variety of means. He further describes the capabilities of tools such as fiber-optic light, the Video Spectral Comparator, and digital image processing, and predicts that these and other technologies will revolutionize manuscript study in the future.

Richard W. Pfaff provides interesting biographical detail and a succinct guide to major resources for manuscript study in his new essay, 'N.R. Ker and the Study of English Medieval Manuscripts'. Not only do we learn about the achievements of Ker and his contemporaries in Britain, but we also discover the genesis of Ker's works, their purposes and limitations. Pfaff rightly extols, for example, Ker's introduction to his *Catalogue of Manuscripts Containing Anglo-Saxon* as a handbook to paleography in itself. In a valuable and now updated supplement to Ker's *Catalogue*, Mary Blockley records sixteen items added over the past decade to the addenda and corrigenda provided by Ker in his own 1976 supplement to the 1957 *Catalogue*. Ker's supplement has been reprinted in a new issue of the *Catalogue* in 1991 by Clarendon Press. Blockley's work illustrates that 'new' discoveries can be scratched glosses (some now visible through the application of technological aids such as described by Kiernan), fragments, and jottings.

A major research tool first published in 1985 and updated in the present collection is Michael Lapidge's 'Surviving Booklists from Anglo-Saxon England'. The thirteen inventories recorded here represent the contents of Anglo-Saxon libraries or the gifts of donors to such libraries, and therefore comprise an invaluable source of information about books known to the Anglo-Saxons. Lapidge edits the booklists and provides detailed commentary on each, identifying the items listed where possible. In an appendix, he provides an alphabetical list of those identifications that may be regarded as certain, a reference-point for further work on books and authors available in Anglo-Saxon England.

The value of Ker's and Lapidge's work, among others, becomes clear in David N. Dumville's revised version of 'English Libraries before 1066: Use and Abuse of the Manuscript Evidence'. First, Dumville reviews the current state of manuscript research and defines the need for a bibliographical hand-list of Anglo-Saxon manuscripts. He then reviews what can be learned from evidence provided by the physical existence of manuscripts, evidence offered by texts preserved in these manuscripts, and evidence for lost or unidentified manuscripts and their contents. From there Dumville considers the difficulties in knowing just how many manuscripts have survived from English libraries prior to 1066, and of attributing provenance and/or origin to them. New evidence of a royal writing office in the Anglo-Saxon period casts doubt on many of our working assumptions about scribes and scriptoria. He concludes with an appendix listing books written prior to c. 1100 and assigned by Ker to specific provenances.

Beginning with Katherine O'Brien O'Keeffe's essay 'Orality and the Developing Text of Caedmon's *Hymn*', we move to specific considerations of texts and major codices preserving Old English materials. O'Keeffe studies variations in the copying of Caedmon's *Hymn* into the Latin and Old English versions of Bede's *Historia ecclesiastica* in order to discover elements of written and oral culture preserved within the manuscript context. The *Hymn*, she learns, travels as a gloss to the Latin text, and shows little significant variation from copy to copy, though it is not punctuated as thoroughly or presented as strikingly as are Latin poems and the Latin paraphrase of the *Hymn* within the same manuscript. In the Old English version of Bede, however, the *Hymn* is incorporated as part of the main text, is punctuated inconsistently, and preserves formulaic variations indicative of oral transmission and reception. Her observations suggest that Caedmon's *Hymn* represents a transitional state between pure orality and pure literacy conveyed by clues in the formatting conventions, pointing, and variants of its multiple copies.

Through analysis of physical features such as the collation, stitching, binding, pricking and ruling, Barbara C. Raw demonstrates what can be learned regarding the production and history of an important collection of Old English poetry, in 'The Construction of Oxford, Bodleian Library, Junius 11'. Raw argues that the codex as planned initially was to include illustrated versions of *Genesis*, *Exodus*, and *Daniel*. Additional leaves were inserted into the last gathering when the decision was made to add *Christ and Satan* with illustrations. By showing how the manuscript was re-stitched and re-bound in the early 13th century, Raw further indicates that *Daniel* probably is missing its conclusion. Her work provides an excellent sense of the original and then expanded conception of the codex, along with an account of the subsequent events leading to its current state.

The past decade has seen major advances and debates in the study of the *Beowulf* manuscript, London, British Library MS. Cotton Vitellius A.xv, precipitated largely by Kevin S. Kiernan's 1981 book. His essay reprinted in the present collection, 'The Eleventh-Century Origin of *Beowulf* and the *Beowulf* Manuscript', summarizes the paleographical and codicological arguments supporting his theory that the poem is contemporary with its extant manuscript. Kiernan believes, for example, that folio 179 is a palimpsest giving evidence of revision in progress. He further argues that the two scribes collaborated in proofreading, correction, and revision, even to the point of developing an episode (Beowulf's Homecoming) to join separate versions of the poem from other manuscripts. In another provocative article about a major poetic codex, Patrick W. Conner uses paleographic and codicological evidence to propose that the Exeter Book is a compilation of three manuscript booklets. His essay reprinted here, 'The Structure of the Exeter Book Codex (Exeter, Cathedral Library, MS. 3501)', covers evidence such as soiled first folios, different grades of membrane, auxiliary rulings, ornamentation, drypoint drawings, and scribal practices in support of Conner's thesis.

Donald G. Scragg analyzes the earliest of the four extant poetic codices and the earliest surviving collection of vernacular homilies in an updated version of 'The Compilation of the Vercelli Book'. In particular, he seeks to shed light on the book's origin by attempting to determine the number and nature of the sources used by the scribe, and by considering the distribution of distinctive linguistic forms in the manuscript. Scragg finds that the collection was not planned in advance, nor was it organized around a clear principle, although certain groups of texts seem to have been drawn from single sources, at least one from the south-east. The linguistic evidence is equally complex but seems to indicate that the scribe worked in Kent.

Introductory material excerpted from the facsimile edition of London, British Library, MS. Royal 7.C.xii, fols. 4-218, allows the editor Peter Clemoes to acquaint us with the unique witness to the earliest version of Ælfric's First Series of *Catholic Homilies*. Clemoes details the evidence of Ælfric's revisions in progress and sheds light on his process of composition, which included adding illustrative material to develop points already drafted. In addition, Clemoes analyzes Ælfric's system of punctuation as reflected in this early example of his work. In material excerpted from his contributions to the facsimile edition of *The Old English Illustrated Hexateuch*, a work with Ælfrician connections, Clemoes describes in detail how an artist would have chosen scenes from the Bible to illustrate, and how he planned the codex so as to leave room for pictures at the appropriate points in the text. Interestingly, chapter divisions in the Latin Vulgate seem to have influenced the plan of the Old English manuscript.

Finally, in Kenneth Sisam's seminal essay, 'The Publication of Alfred's *Pastoral Care*', appears a case study for the dissemination of manuscripts from a royal scriptorium of the Anglo-Saxon period. Sisam shows how Alfred's prefaces were added to the copied texts of the Old English translation of Gregory the Great's famous treatise, after which the codices were circulated according to strict directions. Both Sisam and Clemoes provide insight into the authorial and artistic practices reflected in surviving manuscripts, and open a window on the life that informs those monuments of the period.

List of Abbreviations

AAe	*Archaeologia Aeliana*
AB	*Analecta Bollandiana*
ABR	*American Benedictine Review*
ASE	*Anglo-Saxon England*
BHL	*Biblioteca Hagiographica Latina*
CCSL	*Corpus Christianorum Series Latina*
CSEL	*Corpus Scriptorum Ecclesiasticorum Latinorum*
EEMF	Early English Manuscripts in Facsimile
EETS	Early English Text Society [cited in the various series: OS, Original Series; ES, Extra Series; SS, Supplementary Series]
EHD	*English Historical Documents*
EHR	*English Historical Review*
HBS	Henry Bradshaw Society
JBAA	*Journal of the British Archaeological Association*
MGH	*Monumenta Germaniae Historica*
PL	*Patrologia Latina*
OED	*Oxford English Dictionary*
OEN	*Old English Newsletter*
RB	*Revue bénédictine*
RHE	*Revue d'histoire ecclésiastique*
ZDA, ZfdA	*Zeitschrift für deutsches Altertum und deutsche Literatur*

Anglo-Saxon
Manuscripts

Using Anglo-Saxon Manuscripts

Alexander R. Rumble

1. Palaeography, Codicology and Anglo-Saxon Studies

The Anglo-Saxonist should be able to both read and describe not only manuscripts written in the period but also those containing Anglo-Saxon texts copied and recopied in subsequent centuries. Only by so doing, whether in the original manuscripts themselves or merely in microform or photographic facsimile, can the character and difficulties of the primary written witnesses for the literature and history of the Anglo-Saxons be appreciated and enjoyed.

The aim of this essay is to provide some guidance to modern users of such manuscripts, primarily for those reading texts composed in Old English but also for Anglo-Latinists. It relates both to the recognition and the recording of those features which are of significance to the origin (the place of writing), the provenance (recorded associations with particular collections or owners) and the users of manuscripts containing Anglo-Saxon texts. The study of these features encompasses two interrelated disciplines: palaeography, the classification and description of former styles of handwriting; and codicology, the examination of the physical characteristics of the manuscript book or codex.

Further reading:

M.P. Brown, *Anglo-Saxon Manuscripts* (London, 1991).

N.R. Ker, *Catalogue of Manuscripts Containing Anglo-Saxon* (Oxford, 1957, reprinted 1991), Introduction.

A.J. Petti, *English Literary Hands from Chaucer to Dryden* (London, 1977), Introduction.

B. Bischoff, trans, D.Ó Croínín and D.Ganz, *Latin Palaeography: Antiquity and the Middle Ages* (Cambridge, 1990).

L.E. Boyle, *Medieval Latin Palaeography: A Bibliographical Introduction* (Toronto, 1984).

2. *Catalogues of Manuscripts*

It is essential to make a careful study of any published bibliographies or catalogues which may relate to the manuscripts one wishes to read before visiting the libraries in which they are now kept. This saves the time, energy and patience of both the reader and the various librarians involved. Above all, it is vital to be able to find out the precise press-mark or call-number (e.g. London, British Library, Cotton MS. Vitellius A.xv) of the item concerned in the library or collection where it is at present preserved. This differs from any customary name of the manuscript volume (e.g. the Nowell Codex) or the name of individual textual items within the volume (e.g. 'Beowulf' or 'Judith'), neither of which are of help to the librarian in locating the manuscript on its shelf.

2.1 *GENERAL BIBLIOGRAPHIES*

Some general bibliographies have been produced which are of great help to the user of Anglo-Saxon manuscripts. The catalogues of Anglo-Saxon manuscripts made in the eighteenth century by Humfrey Wanley (*Librorum veterum septentrionalium ... Catalogus Historico-Criticus*, Oxford, 1705) and in the twentieth by Neil Ker (see 1, above) are essential reading. Both provide a descriptive overview of the corpus, library by library, Wanley dealing with both vernacular and Latin manuscripts, Ker only with the Old English ones but in more detail. A summary list of the whole corpus, library by library, is also provided by Helmut Gneuss in 'A Preliminary List of Manuscripts Written or Owned in England up to 1100', *Anglo-Saxon England* 9 (1981), 1-60. A categorisation of the surviving Old English material, arranged text by text and with notes of printed editions, is provided by A. Cameron, 'List of Old English Texts', in R. Frank and A. Cameron, eds, *A Plan for a Dictionary of Old English* (Toronto, 1973), 25-306. For documents from the Anglo-Saxon period dealing with land tenure one must consult P.H. Sawyer, *Anglo-Saxon Charters: An Annotated List and Bibliography*, Royal Historical Society (London, 1968), whose arrangement is partly typological and partly chronological. For the context of those documents which have been copied into books or cartularies, one should also consult G.R.C. Davis, *Medieval Cartularies of Great Britain: A Short Catalogue* (London, 1958).

2.2 THE CONTENTS OF INDIVIDUAL LIBRARIES

Both modern and medieval libraries have had their contents described from time to time in specific lists or catalogues. These also should be studied and any relevant items compared to the descriptions contained in the books mentioned in 2.1. For the present location of surviving books from medieval British libraries one should consult N.R. Ker, *Medieval Libraries of Great Britain: A List of Surviving Books*, Royal Historical Society (2nd ed., London, 1964) and the *Supplement* by A.G. Watson (London, 1987). These include references to the known catalogues, medieval and later, of the books in each of the libraries concerned. An edition and discussion of all known Anglo-Saxon book-lists is provided by M. Lapidge, 'Surviving Booklists from Anglo-Saxon England', in M. Lapidge and H. Gneuss, *Learning and Literature in Anglo-Saxon England* (Cambridge, 1985), 33-89, reprinted in the present volume.

3. Describing a Codex

Manuscript volumes should be described as fully and accurately as possible, since each is a unique artefact with its own personal story to be discovered. Besides the intrinsic interest and importance of studying the physical context of any surviving ancient text, there is also the consideration that in the event of future loss of the manuscript, or damage to it, future researchers would at least have a good idea of its current appearance and character.

3.1 BIBLIOGRAPHICAL DETAILS

Much time can be saved by researchers if full and accurate notes are taken as work on a codex proceeds. The following should be discovered at an early stage of work: the present location of the manuscript, its present call-number and volume title (see 2, above); the *secundo folio* reference, i.e. the first word on the second folio of text in the manuscript, a significant feature for the identification of a particular volume; known previous call-numbers as part of earlier collections (cf. below, 3.3.1 and 3.3.4); references to previous catalogue descriptions and to any articles which have been written about its palaeography. In particular the detailed descriptions in Ker, *Catalogue* (see 2.1) should be studied, as also where applicable those in E.A. Lowe, *Codices Latini Antiquiores: A Palaeographical Guide to Latin Manuscripts prior to the Ninth Century*, 12 vols (Oxford,

1934-72) and T.A.M. Bishop, *English Caroline Minuscule* (Oxford, 1971).

3.2 THE TEXT

Individual textual units or articles in a book should be numbered and the following information given, where present, *for each article*:

3.2.1 *Folio numbers* (or page numbers if appropriate, see 3.3.6).

3.2.2 *Title of work* as given in the text.

3.2.3 *The incipit*: the first few words of the text of the article in the particular manuscript studied.

3.2.4 *The colophon, if present*: a statement added at the end of the text of the article, often by the text-scribe, stating information such as the name of the work, its author, the name of the scribe and the date and place of inscription. Care should be taken however to find out whether the colophon refers to the particular manuscript under examination or has been copied wholesale from the exemplar containing the main text. A collection of colophons has been made by the Benedictines of Le Bouveret, Switzerland and is published as *Colophons des manuscrits occidentaux des origines au XVIe siècle*, 6 vols (Fribourg, 1965-82).

3.2.5 *Reference to printed editions of the article that have been published to date*. Besides the bibliographies mentioned in 2.1, above, use should also be made of S.B. Greenfield and F.C. Robinson, *A Bibliography of Publications on Old English Literature to the End of 1972* (Toronto and Manchester, 1980), supplemented by the annual bibliographies in *Anglo-Saxon England* (1972-).

3.2.6 *A summary of the textual content*; the known or presumed date of composition; the language used; whether in prose or verse (with type of metre); whether there are any internal subdivisions (into books, chapters or fitts).

3.3 EXTERNAL FEATURES OF THE CODEX

All aspects of the appearance and structure of the codex need to be observed and recorded in a consistent fashion. The following order proceeds from outside in (3.3.1-12) and then from the writing of the main text to various additions made to it (3.3.13-18).

3.3.1 *Binding(s)*

The volume may be in a contemporary, later medieval, or modern binding; bindings of early date may give clues about the origin or provenance of the manuscript not contained in the text itself. The materials and the methods used in the binding should be described, e.g. wooden boards covered with decorated or stamped leather and/or metal and jewels; or covers made of stiff parchment or pasteboard. The number and arrangement of the leather bands to which individual quires (see 3.3.8) were sewn should be noted. Differing methods of attaching the boards to the sewn quires by means of the bands were used at various times in the medieval period and these can be used to give an approximate date to a particular binding, see G. Pollard, 'Describing Medieval Bookbindings', in M.B. Parkes and A.G. Watson, *Medieval Scribes, Manuscripts, and Libraries: Essays Presented to N.R. Ker* (London, 1978), 50-65. Some medieval bindings have the title (and sometimes the press-mark) of the volume on a parchment slip pasted to the outside cover. A previous owner's badge, coat of arms or initials may appear on the cover (cf. 3.3.4).

3.3.2 *Pastedowns*

A piece of parchment or paper was usually gummed on to the inside of each of the two boards of the cover in order to hide the grooves into which the ends of the bands (see 3.3.1) were channelled; such pastedowns were sometimes made from fragments of books which had been dismembered, study of which may reveal information about the provenance of the codex (cf. 4, below).

3.3.3 *Flyleaves*

Between the pastedowns and the leaves containing the text extra leaves were normally added in order to act as a protective buffer between the text and the cover. The parchment or paper used as flyleaves may be blank or again be fragments of dismembered manuscripts (cf. 4, below); if originally blank, they were often written upon by later owners or users (cf. 3.3.4).

3.3.4 *Marks of previous ownership*

Both institutional and individual owners often marked their books with an inscription, occasionally including an anathema against thieves. The signatures of owners, or donors, of manuscripts may also be found, usually on a flyleaf (see 3.3.3) or a pastedown (see 3.3.2), but also sometimes in the margin of the text itself. Similarly, badges and coats of arms also appear. Library press-marks were sometimes added to a flyleaf or a pastedown, or written on a parchment slip on the cover (see 3.3.1) and may correspond to a surviving library catalogue (see 2.2). Some libraries have used a proprietary stamp to safeguard their property rights, often in former times adding it rather obtrusively to the leaves containing the text or illustrations, a practice now generally discontinued. Details about the acquisition of the volume by a particular owner are also sometimes written within it and may include the date of purchase, the price paid, and the provenance. The personal marks used by various early modern and modern private collectors of manuscripts are described and illustrated in S. De Ricci, *English Collectors of Books & Manuscripts (1530-1930) and Their Marks of Ownership* (Cambridge, 1930) and *Hidden Friends: The Comites Latentes Collection of Illuminated Manuscripts*, Sotheby's Exhibition Catalogue (London, 1985).

3.3.5 *Table of contents or Index*

Internal finding-aids were added to codices from time to time in the form of a table of contents or an index. A table of contents consists of a summary of contents in the order of their occurrence in the volume, usually with folio or page references given (cf. 3.3.6). A medieval index will usually be only in rough alphabetical order of names or subjects, with folio or page or section references given. Either type of finding-aid may provide evidence of an earlier ordering of the contents of a volume or of the loss of items from it.

3.3.6 *Foliation(s) or Pagination(s)*

Individual leaves within a codex may be identified by a sequence either of folio or of page numbers. Foliation, the name given to the former of these methods, is the standard one used in manuscripts. In this, each leaf is numbered once, with the addition of *v* for 'verso' to refer to the back of the leaf, and sometimes of *r* for 'recto' to refer to the front. A pagination, in contrast, numbers each side of the leaf separately, as in modern printed books. Such numbers are added to the leaves in ink or pencil; earlier medieval ones will be in roman numerals, later ones in arabic numerals. Some foliations or paginations can be related to the construction of a table of contents or index; see 3.3.5.

3.3.7 *Quire-numbers or Quire-signatures*

It was often the practice to add a sequence of numbers or letters at the foot of the last folio verso (but occasionally the first folio recto) of each quire (see 3.3.8) in order to show to the binder of the volume the correct sequence of the quires. Later addition or insertion of quires into a volume, or the re-ordering of quires, can sometimes be detected from their lack of appropriate numbers or letters. Unfortunately, however, such quire-numbers or signatures are often now missing, having been lost when the leaves were trimmed as the last part of the binding process.

3.3.8 *Collation*

The internal make-up of individual quires (groups of leaves, usually consisting of sheets of parchment or paper folded into pairs of conjoint folios, but often with associated half-sheets) should be recorded. The number of pairs used per quire is usually consistent within a period; the normal number in the Anglo-Saxon and medieval period is four, but five, six, or more, occur. The abbreviated formulas commonly used in the recording of the collation of a manuscript volume assumes an ideal quire of several paired folios to which modifications may be made by the addition or omission of half-sheets. Examples are as follows:

2^8. The second quire (eight leaves) is made up of four conjoint pairs.

4^8 3 and 6 are half-sheets. The fourth quire (eight leaves) consists of three conjoint pairs, with the third and sixth leaves being half-sheets.

7^6 + 1 leaf after 3. The seventh quire (seven leaves) consists of three conjoint pairs, with a half-sheet used by the original scribe after the third leaf.

8^6 + 1 leaf inserted after 3. The eighth quire (seven leaves) is similar to the preceding, but the half-sheet has been added at a date later than that of the main text.

9^{10} wants 4. The ninth quire (nine leaves) contains a gap in the text which shows that the fourth leaf is now missing.

9^{10} wants 10, probably blank. As preceding, but the loss of a leaf is suggested by the fact that the scribe finished writing his text at the ninth leaf.

10 nine. The tenth quire consists of nine leaves but its make-up is uncertain.

In Anglo-Saxon manuscripts up to the beginning of the eleventh century the leaves were normally arranged within each quire so that all the hair sides faced outwards, thus giving a hair-flesh arrangement to all the openings (two facing pages) within a quire, except for that in the middle, but giving a hair-hair one where quires met. Later on, the internal arrangement was changed so that hair faced hair and flesh faced flesh, as it had from earlier times on the Continent.

3.3.9 *Catchwords*

A few words of the text were often written at the foot of the final folio in a quire, being an anticipation of those on the first line of the following quire. This was done to preserve the correct sequence of quires before or during binding. Catchwords were also used within quires to preserve the correct sequence of individual folios prior to binding, preceding the addition of a foliation or a pagination to the whole codex (see 3.3.6). They are often now missing, however, having been on that part of the leaf trimmed by the binder.

3.3.10 *Leaves*

Anglo-Saxon texts surviving in contemporary manuscripts and in most medieval copies are written on treated animal skins, the generic term for which is 'parchment'. The better type (vellum) was made from calf or lamb skin, the less fine from that of sheep or goats. The method of preparation of the skin included cleaning in a solution of lime, eradication of the animal's hair or wool by shaving, smoothing the skin with a knife or plane, whitening it with chalk, and cutting it to the required size. Despite the best efforts of the parchment-maker, there usually remains a discernible difference between the hair and the flesh sides of a parchment leaf, the former being darker in colour than the latter and often less smooth. There is also a difference, in the early Anglo-Saxon period of literacy, between the parchment produced in the British Isles and that produced on the Continent, the former being darker in colour, thicker and more velvety than the latter.

Anglo-Saxon texts surviving in early modern copies will usually be written on hand-made paper rather than parchment and will often have watermarks by which it may be possible to date and locate the place of production.

With both types of writing surface, the following details should be recorded: the nature, texture, and colour of the material; the outside dimensions of the leaves, height x width in millimetres; the presence of holes, tears or repairs (and whether these were made before or after the writing of the text).

3.3.11 *Pricking and Ruling*

Before any writing was added to a page its layout (see 3.3.12) was planned and marked out by means of ruled lines guided by patterns of prickings made in the margins with a sharp point. Sometimes a pricker in the form of a wheel was used in order to get an even distribution of pricks. A few lines, often in pairs, were ruled vertically in order to mark the sides of the intended text-block. Many more were ruled horizontally as a guide to enable the scribe to keep each line of text even across the page. Before the mid twelfth century it was normal to use a hard point, of metal or bone, to make the ruling; later, lead (plummet) was used. There was a short transitional period in the mid to late twelfth century when both hard point and lead were used together. By the late medieval period, ruling in ink is also found, but often merely as a frame for an internally unruled text-block. The presence in a manuscript of one of these methods of ruling rather than another may thus be used as a rough dating feature.

3.3.12 *Page-layout*

The outside size of the space taken up by the text on each page should be measured and recorded, height x width in millimetres. It will normally be found that the outside height of the text-block approximates to the width of the actual leaf. The shape of the text-block in Anglo-Saxon manuscripts for most purposes is usually a rectangle whose height is greater than its width. Double columns are unusual in vernacular manuscripts of the Anglo-Saxon period, but are more common in Latin and bilingual texts, particularly glossaries (where triple columns also occur); when they are used they are normally of equal width. A single wide column of long lines is usual for vernacular texts; it should thus be noted that poetic lines are not used in the manuscripts of Old English verse, despite their appearance in printed editions, though they are used in Latin verse of the period.

An allowance of blank space within the text-block was often left by the scribe for the subsequent insertion of coloured initials, rubrics, line drawings, music, or interlinear glosses. Full-page illustrations or miniatures, however, were sometimes added on half-sheets within or at the beginning of quires.

3.3.13 *The Writing of the Text*

The text was often written in an acidic ink intended to burn into the surface of the page just enough to give it permanence, but not enough to burn right through and cause irreparable damage. Recipes consisted of various mixtures of oak galls, iron sulphate, gum, and water, wine or vinegar. Other types of ink contained ingredients such as carbon and thorn branches.

The ink was added to the surface by means of a quill pen, usually made from the tail feather of a goose, its thicker end cut to shape and re-sharpened as necessary during the course of the writing. Marked changes within a text, both in the colour of ink and in the width of the nib, should be noted as they may be preliminary indicators relevant to the distinction between the work of different scribes.

The various types of script used (both for the text and for headings, glosses, rubrics or initials) should be described by their respective standard names. Those to be expected in contemporary Old English manuscripts are *insular minuscule* or *pointed*, *square* and *round Anglo-Saxon minuscule*. Latin texts of the Anglo-Saxon period were written in the same scripts as Old English ones until the mid tenth century after which *caroline minuscule* was adopted for Latin (but not vernacular) texts. Bilingual texts were thus subsequently written in two different scripts, one for each language. In early Middle English manuscripts some form of *protogothic minuscule* was used with varying ranges of Anglo-Saxon letters being retained. From the thirteenth to the sixteenth centuries some form of *gothic minuscule* will be found: formal *textura, cursive anglicana* or *cursive secretary*. In later transcripts *italic, round* or *copperplate* scripts were used.

A date should be assigned to the writing, using the standard formula where 's.' stands for 'from the ... th century' (Latin *saeculo*) and a roman numeral with an added modifier indicates a sub-division of a particular century. For example, the sequence of possible dates within the tenth century runs as follows:

s.ix/x	= c.900	
s.x^{in}	= 900 x 920	[^{in} = Latin *ineunte* 'at the beginning of ...']
s.x^1	= 920 x 940	
s.x^{med}	= 940 x 960	[^{med} = Latin *mediante* 'in the middle of ...']
s.x^2	= 960 x 980	
s.x^{ex}	= 980 x 1000	[^{ex} = Latin *exeunte* 'at the end of ...']
s.x/xi	= c.1000	

It should be noted that palaeographical dating is subjective and can only be periodic rather than annual. Particular scripts remained in use for several generations and individual scribes tended to stick fairly closely throughout their career to the styles in which they were first trained. The broad succession of scripts used in Anglo-Saxon England is however established, as are some modifications within them (e.g. the addition of a horn on the left shoulder of *e* in Anglo-Saxon minuscule from the tenth century). Characteristic features of each of the scripts need thus to be studied.

Some attempt should be made to distinguish between the work of different scribes within a manuscript. The key to this is the accurate description of the hands involved. The distinctive characteristics of the hand amount to consistent slight modifications of shape of letter-form from a norm to be expected within the type of script used.

The features of each hand should be described in the following order:

(i) *The treatment of ascenders*: their height in relation to that of minims; whether clubbed at the top, or curved, or notched, or looped;

(ii) *The treatment of descenders*: their length in relation to the height of minims; whether they end in a point, or curve in one direction or the other;

(iii) *Minims*: their width (reflecting the width of the nib); whether they have feet or not, and, if so, are these horizontal or oblique?

(iv) *Individual letters*. Where any letter-forms seem to be made in a consistently idiosyncratic fashion these should be described (in alphabetical order) as succinctly as possible. The terminology used in describing letter-forms is often taken from that for parts of the human body, e.g. 'head', 'shoulder', 'waist', 'back', 'neck', 'arm', 'leg', and 'foot'; but terms like 'tail', 'cross-bar', and 'bowl' also occur. Whatever terms are chosen, it is important that they should be applied in a consistent fashion. There is no need to mention letters whose appearance is not unusual within the context of the type of script being used. The shape given to the following letters is most often significant in distinguishing between hands: *a, d, e, g, r, s, t, y, æ, ð*. Note should also be made of the usage of particular forms of a letter where more than one was available, e.g. normal instead of '2-shaped' *r* after *o*; low, long, and round forms of *s* (particularly in relation to -*ss*-); and the three forms of *y*.

(v) *Ligatures*. Any deliberate union of neighbouring letters should be noted, e.g. that of *e* with the following letter, *c* + *t* or *s* + *t*.

(vi) *Abbreviations*. In order to save both space and time, Latin texts were normally heavily abbreviated by the omission of letters from within or at the end of words. The general stability of Latin inflexions and the frequent occurrence of certain groups of letters allowed a large body of accepted abbreviation-symbols to be developed by the early medieval period.   Old English texts, being less consistent in orthography, are much less abbreviated than their Latin counterparts. The most frequent ones are the following: 7 = *and/ond* (to be left unextended in transcripts and editions, see 6.2.6); æft̄ = *æfter*; f̄ = *for*; ḡ = *ge*; ł = *oððe*; sc̄e = *sancte*; þ̄ = *þæt/þet/þat* (to be left unextended; see 6.2.6); þoñ = *þonne*; -ū = -*um* or -*un*.

(vii) *Punctuation*. Although often internally consistent, the systems of punctuation used by Anglo-Saxon and medieval scribes differed from modern ones. It is therefore most important to study the system in operation within a particular text, in order to distinguish the scribal usage of the various symbols in relation to minor and major pauses in the text, the usage of accents (marking either vowel-length or word-stress), word-division, and the sorts of hyphen used to indicate the breaking of a word at a line-end.

(viii) *Orthography.* Scribal preferences should be noted as regards a range of possible variations in spelling in both Latin and Old English. In the latter, one should in particular look for the usage in relation to *an-/on-*, *æ/e/ea/a*, *b/f/u/v*, *eo/io*, *y/i/e/u*, *ð/þ* (in later copies *y*)/*th*, *u/uu/wynn* (in later copies *w/wu/gu*). In Latin texts, usage as regards *ae/ę/e* and *s/ss* should in particular be noted. Such spelling preferences may at least be significant for determining the place at which the scribe was trained, if not necessarily for deciding the place of origin of the manuscript.

Further reading:
Ker, *Catalogue*, xxv-xxxvi.
E.A. Lowe, *Codices Latini Antiquiores*, vol. 2, *Great Britain and Ireland* (2nd ed., Oxford, 1972).
T.A.M. Bishop, *English Caroline Minuscule* (Oxford, 1971).
D.N. Dumville, 'English Square Minuscule Script: The Background and Earliest Phases', *ASE* 16 (1987), 147-79.

3.3.14 *Rubrics and Running Headings*

Rubrics, as their name implies, were normally written in red ink, but occasionally occur in ink of another colour or in the ink of the text. They are short headings at the beginning and/or within texts, introducing the textual unit about to begin. They are usually slightly later additions made in spaces left by the scribe of the text, so that all the writing in red or coloured ink might be done at the same time. If written by someone other than the scribe of the text, they may have differences of letter-form, spelling or wording and so amount to a sub-text of the main work. It is therefore important in a transcript to distinguish them by a note (see 6.2.2) and in an edition by either footnotes or the use of a different typeface.

Running headings, often in red or coloured ink, are found in later medieval manuscripts, being a title given in the upper margin of each page, either the title of the whole work or the title or number of the chapter within it whose text appears on that particular page.

3.3.15 *Contemporary Glosses or Commentaries*

The text of some works, particularly religious ones, was sometimes explained by means of words or whole sections of commentary written either between the lines of the main text or in an adjacent margin.

These are distinguished as either 'interlinear' or 'marginal' glosses. They are sometimes in a language different from that of the main text and can develop into a continuous translation of it and provoke a double-column arrangement of the page. The longer commentaries sometimes were or became separate works and then followed their own individual manuscript tradition.

3.3.16 *Alterations or Corrections*

Where possible, a distinction should be made between alterations made en passant by the scribe of the text and corrections effected as a separate process in the production of a book or document.

Whether alteration or correction is involved, the methods used were more or less the same: either erasure (by scratching away the ink) of the incorrect letters or words and rewriting; or deleting, underlining or subpuncting of the mistake and writing of the correct version adjacent or interlineally. The second of these methods was the more common since the other often caused damage to the surface of the parchment and made rewriting impossible without blotting. Occasionally a serious copying error such as the repetition of a whole page of text caused a folio to be scrapped and this would be reflected by the collation (see 3.3.8).

3.3.17 *Decoration*

Note should be taken of the type of decoration found within a manuscript, and of its location in relation to the text. Styles of decoration may provide clues as to the origin of a manuscript.

Many of the surviving vernacular manuscripts from the Anglo-Saxon period are quite plain, with only minimal decoration in the form of large initials, often in the ink of the text but sometimes in one or more coloured inks. In some manuscripts, however, the construction of the initials is intricate, being made up of biting beasts (e.g. Oxford, Bodleian Library, MS. Tanner 10, the Old English translation of Bede's *Historia ecclesiastica*; see Ker, *Catalogue*, plate I) or ending in foliate terminals. The illustrated *Hexateuch* (London, British Library, MS. Cotton Claudius B.iv) has coloured drawings illustrating the text, added in specially reserved spaces in the text-block, while the *Paris Psalter* (Paris, Bibliothèque Nationale MS. lat. 8824) has little drawings placed in the column containing the Latin version, whose text is shorter than that in the parallel column containing the vernacular translation. In general, the line-drawings in coloured inks found in Anglo-Saxon manuscripts in either language are of high quality, with good attention to details of anatomy, expression and dress. As might be expected, however, manuscripts of Latin texts belonging to the liturgy or teachings of the Christian church throughout the Anglo-Saxon and medieval periods are much more sumptuous, with the use of gold leaf, whole pages carpeted with decoration or containing coloured miniatures.

Further reading:

Descriptive terms: L.N. Valentine, *Ornament in Medieval Manuscripts* (London, 1965).

Drawings: F. Wormald, *English Drawings of the Tenth and Eleventh Centuries* (London, 1952).

Illumination: J.J.G. Alexander, *Insular Manuscripts from the 6th to the 9th Century* (London, 1978); E. Temple, *Anglo-Saxon Manuscripts 900-1066* (London, 1976).

Subjects: T.H. Ohlgren, *Insular and Anglo-Saxon Illuminated Manuscripts: An Iconographic Catalogue, c. A.D. 625 to 1100* (New York and London, 1986).

3.3.18 *Non-contemporary Marginalia and Glosses*

Words or text were sometimes added to a manuscript by its readers, either between the lines as a gloss or in the margin as notes. A series of these in the same hand can provide a clue as to the purpose or main interest of one particular user of the manuscript. It is thus of importance both to read and to be able to date such notes. It is sometimes possible to identify their author if he or she has a distinctive hand and has written in other surviving manuscripts. It is sometimes possible to identify a user with a distinctive hand who has written in other surviving manuscripts. Such notes have proved to be helpful in studying the use of Anglo-Saxon manuscripts by early antiquaries such as Archbishop Parker, whose distinctive underlining and notations in red crayon in manuscripts now at Cambridge and elsewhere have provided much evidence about his interests and activity as a scholar-collector.

Further reading:

C.E. Wright, 'The Dispersal of the Monastic Libraries and the Beginnings of Anglo-Saxon Studies', *Transactions of the Cambridge Bibliographical Society* 1 (1949-53), 208-37.

3.4 BOOKLETS

The examination of the external features of a codex in the manner described above (3.3) may sometimes lead to the conclusion that within what is now treated as a single volume there exists more than a single unit of production. In these cases we may be dealing with a collection of structurally (and textually) independent booklets, each with its own physical history, which should be treated and described as separate entities, under the relevant headings.

Further reading:

P.R. Robinson, 'Self-contained Units in Composite Manuscripts of the Anglo-Saxon Period', *ASE* 7 (1978), 231-8, reprinted in the present volume.

4. Describing Manuscript Fragments

Throughout the medieval period it was common practice to dismember books that were no longer of interest or whose script was old-fashioned and difficult to read. The parchment of individual leaves was then re-used as pastedowns (see 3.3.2) or, often cut into strips, as stiffening within new bindings. The identification of the text contained in such manuscript fragments is sometimes a difficult task. The origin and provenance of the original codex from which they have come is even more difficult to ascertain, but a careful record of the discernible external features is important as it may lead to the discovery of other fragments from the same book elsewhere. Similar problems are encountered with the many fragments surviving in a charred and shrunken state from the fire in the Cotton Library in 1731, now kept together in boxes in the British Library.

Further reading:

M.P. Brown, 'A New Fragment of a Ninth-Century English Bible', *ASE* 18 (1989), 33-43.

R. Watson, 'Medieval Manuscript Fragments', *Archives* 13 (1977), 61-73.

5. Describing Single-Sheet Documents

Besides the intrinsic historical and linguistic interest of their text, those Anglo-Saxon documents which survive written in contemporary scripts are of importance to the palaeographer as dated manuscripts whose features may be compared to those in undated ones. Thus a careful record should be made of the appearance of their leaves, any pricking and ruling, their page-layout, the character of the writing, alterations or corrections, and any marks or notes associated with later owners or users (cf. above, 3.3.4, 3.3.10-13, 3.3.16, 3.3.18). In addition, a description should be made of any seal (on writs or letters) present now or any indication of past sealing, of any folds in the parchment, and of any endorsements.

Further reading:
   A. Bruckner and R. Marichal, eds, *Chartae Latinae Antiquiores,* III, *British Museum, London* (Olten and Lausanne, 1963).
   T.A.M. Bishop and P. Chaplais, eds, *Facsimiles of English Royal Writs prior to A.D. 1100 presented to Vivian Hunter Galbraith* (Oxford, 1957).
   S. Keynes, ed., *Facsimiles of Anglo-Saxon Charters*, British Academy (Oxford, 1991).

6. *Making Transcripts and Editions of Manuscript Texts*

6.1 THE USE OF FACSIMILES

It is sensible to be as proficient as possible in the reading of Anglo-Saxon and later scripts before one visits libraries in order to see the manuscripts themselves. It is important to remember that librarians cannot be expected to read the text for you but that they will often advise in cases where a manuscript is damaged, if only by the provision of aids such as cold light-sources or magnifying glasses.

The general availability of facsimiles of manuscripts has provided the student with the essential tools needed for home practice in transcription and description. Such a need was recognised by the palaeographers of the eighteenth century such as Thomas Astle, George Hickes and Humfrey Wanley who included engraved facsimiles of handwritten texts in their publications. More recently photography has provided the student with more extensive and more accurate reproductions of the manuscripts. Photographs of specific pages of manuscripts for private study may usually be ordered from the libraries where they are now preserved, unless the physical state of the manuscript does not allow this. Many of the most important surviving contemporary manuscripts from the Anglo-Saxon period have now however been published in facsimile and should be available in major libraries around the world. The student may thus consult the following:

-The series *Early English Manuscripts in Facsimile* (Copenhagen and Baltimore, 1951-), 23 vols to date; giving complete reproductions of whole codices, with detailed introductions.

-The Early English Text Society's useful (and reasonably priced) facsimiles of *Beowulf* (Original Series, vol. 245; 2nd ed., 1959) and *The Parker Chronicle and Laws* (Original Series, vol. 208; 1941).

-E.A. Lowe, *Codices Latini Antiquiores* (Oxford, 1934-72), 12 vols; giving palaeographical commentary and sample photographs from Latin manuscripts written before A.D. 900; some manuscripts with vernacular glosses are included.

For documents, see the works listed in 5, above. Also: E.A. Bond, *Facsimiles of Ancient Charters in the British Museum* (London, 1873-8), 4 vols; W.B. Sanders, *Facsimiles of Anglo-Saxon Manuscripts*, Ordnance Survey (Southampton, 1878-84), 3 vols.

6.2 TECHNIQUES OF TRANSCRIPTION

A distinction needs to be made between the facsimile reproduction of a manuscript, as an engraving or in print (see above, 6.1), and the making of a transcription. The latter is the rewriting of a text in one's own handwriting, rather than being an attempt to imitate the precise shape of the letter-forms in each word of the particular manuscript concerned. [A single facsimile alphabet can be made as a useful tool, however; see below.] Nevertheless, a transcription must entail the accurate recording of features of the manuscript which concern the scribe's preferred orthography. In particular it must be stressed that there is a need for strict consistency in the methods used to make a transcription, in order to minimise the amount of checking back to the manuscript at a later stage.

Before starting to transcribe, it is best to read right through the text at least once and to make preliminary notes on the punctuation and abbreviation. At this stage it is also helpful to make a facsimile alphabet of the letter-forms used by the scribe, or each scribe of several, concerned in the writing of the text.

The following rules are recommended for the use of transcribers:

6.2.1 Transcriptions should be written legibly, in ink or pencil, on lined paper, writing only on alternate lines, so that, if present, interlinear glosses may be transcribed in their actual position.

6.2.2 So long as rubrics, new columns, or new pages, are indicated in bracketed notes (see 6.2.9, below) there is no need to imitate the niceties of page-layout of the original. Old English verse should be kept in long lines however, as in the manuscripts. Line-ends should be indicated by the use of an oblique line [*freond/scipe*]. Word-division should be modernised, but notes may be made on the system used by the scribe(s).

6.2.3 All words should be spelt, letter for letter, in the transcript as they occur in the manuscript.

6.2.4 All Old English letters (ash, eth, thorn, and wynn) should be retained in the transcript (and in an edition, see 6.3, below) wherever they occur in the manuscript. The letter *g* in Old English texts, even though it is the formal ancestor of Middle English yogh, should always be transcribed as modern *g*, since it has both palatal and velar sounds, not just the velar one of yogh. In Middle English texts, yogh (having the value of either *y* or *ogh*) should be retained wherever it occurs.

6.2.5 The usage of the manuscript should be retained in the transcript for the following:

capital letters
numerals [e.g. roman as opposed to arabic]
punctuation, accents, hyphens

ae/œ/ę and *AE/Æ/Ę*
i/j and *i/y* and *u/v*
uu/w and *Vu/VV/W* and wynn
þ/ð/th

However, the occurrence of ligatures between letters such as *c* + *t*, *r* + *t*, *s* + *t* need not be indicated in the transcript but should be mentioned in the notes to the alphabet of letter-forms made as a preliminary to the transcription (see above).

6.2.6 The following abbreviations should not be expanded in the transcript, as the contemporary form of the expansion would have varied according to local convention or to dialectal spelling:

7 = OE *and* or *ond* 'and'; also in the compound 7lang = OE *andlang* or *ondlong* 'along'

þ = OE *þæt* or *þet* ME *þat* or *þet* 'it, that, which'.

iħs xp̄s. In the abbreviation for 'Jesus Christ', words which by custom were seldom written out in full, Greek letters were retained by Anglo-Saxon and medieval scribes writing texts in Latin scripts. As there is some uncertainty about what would have been the accepted extension of this abbreviation, in particular whether *cristus* or *christus* would have been thought more correct by any particular scribe, it seems best to leave it unextended in a transcript. See P. Chaplais, 'The Spelling of Christ's Name in Medieval Anglo-Latin: "Christus" or "Cristus" ?', *Journal of the Society of Archivists* 8 (1987), 261-80.

6.2.7 All other abbreviations should be expanded in the transcript, unless there is real ambiguity as to the scribe's intention.

Unambiguous expansions should be indicated by underlining the added letter or letters with a straight line: þonn̲e̲

On the rare occasions where there is some ambiguity as to the spelling intended by the scribe in the expanded word, a wavy underline should be used under the part that is in doubt: eallun

On the even rarer occasions where extension is impossible given the available information, e.g. with some names, a single inverted comma should be placed to show where the abbreviation was marked in the manuscript: Lond'

6.2.8 Interlineations (i.e. words or letters added between the lines of text) should be shown by caret-marks \ / :   dri\h/ten

                                                           Cnut \cing/ gret

6.2.9 All incidental notes or comments of one's own should be placed within square brackets and underlined, cf. 6.2.10.

6.2.10 Where a word has been altered in the manuscript by the original scribe, or has been corrected by a contemporary corrector, the altered or corrected reading should be given in the transcript, but precise details of what has occurred should be added within square brackets:

friond [freond, e *subpuncted*, i *written above*]

6.2.11 Where a scribe has inadvertently omitted a letter or word and the missing text is known then it may be supplied in angle brackets:

f < r > eond

Cnut cing < gret > Lyfing arcebisceop

6.2.12 Where damage to the manuscript has caused irretrievable loss of text, this should be indicated in the transcript by the use of square brackets containing a space or, where possible, a dot for each letter calculated to be missing:

[   ] or [.....]

If it is possible to reconstruct such damaged words with certainty this should also be done within square brackets:

f[r]eo[n]dscipe

The above rules are for the making of transcripts and are to be distinguished from those for editing (cf. 6.3). They are intended to record as much as possible of the external character of the text of individual manuscripts, for the future use and convenience of the transcriber, without going to the extreme of creating an imitative facsimile. Frequently they can save the researcher from the need to make a return visit to a library to check a doubtful or unusual reading.

6.3 FROM TRANSCRIPTION TO EDITION

Some conventional editorial interventions are usually carried out as a secondary stage in the scholarly transmission into print of texts from manuscripts. Simplifications and emendations have to be made to the text as first transcribed (see 6.2), both for reasons of economy, given the modern cost of printing, and in order to standardise the conventions of the manuscript for a wider readership, one used to the orthographic conventions of modern printing. Such modifications should however be kept to a minimum if the character of the original is not to be obscured. Where the edition being produced is part of an ongoing series (such as that of The Early English Text Society) there will naturally have to be conformity with the conventions laid down by the editorial committee of the series. With independent editions however there is more scope for decisions to be made which are particularly appropriate to the characteristics of a specific manuscript. Ideally, editorial modifications of the character of a manuscript for the reproduction of its text in print should be made sparingly. Justifiable ones include the following: not indicating the extension of standard and non-ambiguous abbreviations; not indicating line-endings; the rearrangement of poetry into verse lines and the addition of line-numbers; modern usage as regards capital letters; the addition of footnotes.

Otherwise, however, the manuscript should be followed as regards the usage of all Old and Middle English letters (including wynn), and medieval punctuation should be reproduced wherever a consistent pattern can be discerned. All such decisions will need to be justified in the editor's introduction.

Further reading:

A.G. Rigg, ed., *Editing Medieval Texts: English, French, and Latin, Written in England* (Toronto, 1977).

Careful attention to the recording of all external features of manuscript books, fragments, and single-sheet documents, as well as to the accurate transcription of the texts they contain, will assist the editor in his or her task. For all those using Anglo-Saxon manuscripts, for whatever purpose, physical clues exist as to the date and provenance of the manuscripts concerned, as well as sometimes to the origin of the text itself. There is a great deal of information on the manuscript page besides the actual words of the text, if it can be interpreted. It cannot even begin to be useful however until it is first noticed and then carefully recorded in ways similar to those suggested above.

Self-Contained Units in Composite Manuscripts of the Anglo-Saxon Period

P.R. Robinson

Many medieval manuscripts are composite volumes, made up of a number of self-contained units which elsewhere I have called 'booklets'.[1] Such a unit originated as a small but structurally independent production containing a single work or a number of short works. Two of the earliest surviving examples, dating from the late eighth century, were produced on the continent. Each is a single gathering now bound with other gatherings into a codex: Merseburg, MS. Stiftsbibliothek 105, fols. 85-105, containing Alcuin's *Vita S. Vedasti* and some of his homilies, and St Gall, MS. Stiftsbibliothek 567, pp. 135-53, containing a *Vita S. Lucii*.[2] There is a fold in the centre of every page of both these quires, made after the text had been copied and not present in the other quires with which they are now bound. In both instances the completed quire was folded so that the verso of its last leaf became the outer pages or 'cover' of the resulting booklet. This 'cover' is more soiled than the other pages in the quire, suggesting that the booklet once circulated independently of the other quires in the manuscript into which it is bound. Two such folded booklets have survived from eleventh-century England: Oxford, Bodleian Library, MS. Hatton 115, fols. 140-7, containing a vernacular

---

[1] P.R. Robinson, 'The "Booklet": a Self-Contained Unit in Composite Manuscripts', *Codicologica* 3, ed. A. Gruijs and J. P. Gumbert, Litterae Textuales (Leiden, 1980), 46-69.

[2] Bernhard Bischoff, 'Über gefaltete Handschriften, vornehmlich hagiographischen Inhalts', *Mittelalterliche Studien* 1 (Stuttgart, 1966), 93-100.

homily describing hell, which was folded across the middle,[3] and
Bodleian Library, MS. Auct. F.4.32, fols. 10-18, containing a
vernacular homily on the Invention of the Cross, which was folded
down the middle.[4]

The word 'booklet' should not be taken to suggest only a very
small unit such as a single quire of tiny format. The booklet may
consist of several quires and these may be either large or small in
dimension. For instance, the different booklets which between them
form the Parker manuscript of the *Anglo-Saxon Chronicle*, laws and
Sedulius, vary in length from one quire (booklets 2 and 4) to four
quires (booklet 5);[5] the size of the leaves is approximately 287 x 206
mm. A booklet has no standard length because what determined its
size was its content and there was no optimum length for a text.

Nowadays a booklet is usually in a collection with other booklets,
and I have tried elsewhere to establish features which may serve to
identify such a booklet in a composite volume.[6] For convenience I list
here those criteria that apply to Anglo-Saxon manuscripts.[7]

---

[3] N.R. Ker, *Catalogue of Manuscripts Containing Anglo-Saxon*
(Oxford, 1957) no. 332, art. 34: a quire of eight leaves; most of the
last page (147v) is blank.

[4] Ker, *Catalogue*, no. 297: a quire of eight leaves+one; the scribe
misjudged the length of his text and needed to add a single leaf (fol.
18) to complete it. For a facsimile of this booklet see *Saint Dunstan's
Classbook from Canterbury*, ed. R.W. Hunt, Umbrae Codicum
Occidentalium 4 (Amsterdam, 1961). The central fold is visible
throughout fols. 10-18.

[5] M.B. Parkes, 'The Palaeography of the Parker Manuscript of the
Chronicle, Laws and Sedulius, and Historiography at Winchester in the
Late Ninth and Tenth Centuries', *ASE* 5 (1976), 149-71.

[6] Robinson, 'The "Booklet"'.

[7] I omit catchwords—which may run only within a booklet, there
being no catchword at the end of the last quire of one booklet to link
it with the first quire of the next—because the system of catchwords
was not generally adopted before the twelfth century; see Jean Vezin,
'Observations sur l'emploi des réclames dans les manuscrits latins',
Bibliothèque de l'École des Chartes 125 (1967), 5-33.

1. The beginning and end of a booklet always coincide with the beginning and end of a text or group of texts.
2. The dimensions of its leaves may differ from those of other parts of the manuscript. This phenomenon does not often occur because a binder has usually cropped all the leaves in a codex to a uniform size.
3. Its handwriting may differ; where its handwriting is contemporary with other handwriting in the manuscript, differences in habits in setting out text on the page may help to distinguish one booklet from others in the same volume.
4. Its style of decoration may differ.
5. It may have its own series of quire signatures.
6. Its outer pages may be soiled or rubbed.
7. Its number of leaves to a quire may differ from the number(s) in other parts of the manuscript.
8. A scribe may have had difficulty in fitting a text into the quire structure of a booklet and, consequently, have modified that structure. The booklet's last gathering may be smaller than its preceding ones, because the scribe did not need a quire of the normal length to complete the text, or the gathering may have an extra leaf (or leaves) in order to accommodate the conclusion of the text.
9. The last page (or pages) of a booklet may have been left blank because the text did not fill the booklet. A booklet in which the concluding text is complete may lack its last leaf (or leaves), suggesting that a blank endleaf (or leaves) has been cut away when the booklet was bound up with others. Sometimes text has been added on an originally blank endleaf (or leaves).

It must be emphasized that the existence of a booklet is established only if its content forms a self-sufficient unit. For example, changes in handwriting may coincide with divisions between quires without this essential condition being fulfilled. The Leningrad Bede,[8] written by four scribes, is a case in point: scribe 1 wrote the first four quires, scribe 2 the next four, but their division of labour ignored the division

---

[8] *The Leningrad Bede*, ed. O. Arngart, EEMF 2 (Copenhagen, 1952), 18.

of the work into books. More often the stint of a scribe who was
sharing in the copying of a long work did not correspond with quire
boundaries; like the other two scribes of the Leningrad Bede, scribes
usually began their stints in mid-quire. A correlation between scribal
stints, quire boundaries and content in a copy of Cassian's *De
Institutione Monachorum* (Oxford, Bodleian Library, MS. Auct. D.
infra 2.9), of the second half of the tenth century, is exceptional.
Possibly the exemplar had been divided by books to facilitate
simultaneous production of this text. The text, consisting of twelve
books, was written on fourteen quires by ten scribes, six of whom have
been identified in a number of manuscripts from St Augustine's,
Canterbury.[9] The first scribe wrote the first quire containing book I
(spreading his handwriting towards the end of his stint so that his
conclusion coincided with the end of the quire), the twelfth quire
containing the conclusion of book XI and the thirteenth and fourteenth
quires containing book XII. The second and third scribes collaborated
in the second quire containing book II and the third scribe collaborated
with the tenth scribe in the tenth quire containing book VIII. The
fourth scribe wrote the third quire containing book III and collaborated
with the eighth scribe in the eighth quire containing most of book VI.
Three scribes wrote the four quires containing books IV and V: the
fifth scribe wrote one quire (the fourth) containing the opening of book
IV, the sixth scribe wrote the following quire (the fifth) containing
more of book IV, and the seventh scribe wrote the next two quires (the
sixth and seventh) containing the conclusion of book IV and book V.
The ninth scribe wrote the ninth quire containing the conclusion of
book VI and book VII. The tenth scribe, as well as collaborating with
the third scribe in the tenth quire containing book VIII, wrote the
eleventh quire containing books IX and X and part of book XI. Since,
however, an individual book in this work has no status independent of
the whole, no unit in this manuscript can be regarded as a booklet.

It follows that, even where there is an exact correspondence
between content and quire boundary, the criteria for identifying a

---

[9] T.A.M. Bishop, *English Caroline Minuscule* (Oxford, 1971), pl.
5, and the same author's 'Notes on Cambridge Manuscripts, part IV:
MSS connected with St Augustine's Canterbury', *Trans. of the
Cambridge Bibliographical Soc.* 2 (1954-8), 327-9.

booklet have to be applied with caution and the likely independence of the content has to be taken into account. In the case of gospel books this is a complicated question. In many early gospel books each gospel was copied in its own separate series of quires and sometimes this entailed adjusting the length of the last gathering of a series. The practice was still occasionally followed in later gospel books.[10] Four of the five codices of the West Saxon translation of the gospels were produced in this way.[11] However, although a gospel could be regarded as an independent text, usually all four gospels were transmitted together and four of the five manuscripts of the West Saxon gospels were each written by a single scribe. In the exception, Cambridge, Corpus Christi College, MS. 140, the gospels of Matthew, Luke and John were each copied by one scribe, but the scribe who copied Luke wrote Mark XII.26-38 as well, thus assisting another who copied the rest of Mark. In a case like this, where the scribe of a quire or group of quires collaborated elsewhere in the manuscript with another scribe, the divisions are more likely to represent scribal stints than independent booklets.[12]

A booklet may have been bound with others at any time, even long after the Anglo-Saxon period. Archbishop Wulfstan owned a legal collection[13] which is now bound with two booklets which formed another collection of laws.[14] Because of the similarity of their contents these two collections may have been put together as early as

---

[10] Patrick McGurk, *Latin Gospel Books from A.D. 400 to A.D. 800*, Les Publications de Scriptorium 5 (1961), 8-9.

[11] Ker, *Catalogue*, nos. 35, 245, 312 and 325. No. 20 is the exception.

[12] See below, p. 38.

[13] London, British Library, MS. Cotton Nero A.i, fols. 70-177; see *A Wulfstan Manuscript Containing Institutes, Laws and Homilies*, ed. Henry R. Loyn, EEMF 17 (Copenhagen, 1971). Wulfstan's ownership of this collection has recently been challenged by C.E. Hohler, 'Some Service-Books of the Later Saxon Church', *Tenth-Century Studies. Essays in Commemoration of the Millennium of the Council of Winchester and 'Regularis Concordia'*, ed. David Parsons (London and Chichester, 1975), p. 225, n. 59.

[14] Fols. 3-41 and 42-57.

the mid-eleventh century, but there is no certain evidence of their association before the sixteenth.[15] The folded booklet in the so-called 'Dunstan Classbook' (Oxford, Bodleian Library, MS. Auct. F.4.32, fols. 10-18) may not have been bound with the other booklets in that collection until the late fifteenth century or the early sixteenth.[16]

However, the practice of assembling booklets into compilations was already well established in the Anglo-Saxon period when many different types of compilation were formed. London, British Library, MS. Harley 585 is made up of two early-eleventh-century booklets, fols. 1-129 containing a translation of the pseudo-Apuleius *Herbarium* and fols. 130-93 containing the so-called 'lacnunga' (medico-magical recipes) and the 'Lorica' of Gildas;[17] the collection was perhaps intended for a practising leech. Archbishop Wulfstan's collection of ecclesiastical institutes, laws and homilies was made up of four booklets.[18] Other compilers put together booklets containing Latin verse and so formed anthologies useful for teaching the *ars poetica* in monastic schools. Cambridge, University Library, MS. Gg.5.35 consists of four booklets of poetry, the last of which contains the 'Cambridge Songs'.[19] Another schoolbook, Oxford, Bodleian Library, MS. Auct. F.2.14, is also made up of four booklets, containing Wulfstan the Cantor's *Narratio metrica de sancto swithuno* and various other works.[20]

In this article I am chiefly concerned with those booklets which were assembled to form collections of vernacular homilies. For example, a tall narrow booklet (fols 138-60) which contains homilies for Advent, Easter Day and the Assumption was added to a Worcester

---

[15] *A Wulfstan Manuscript*, p. 31.

[16] *Saint Dunstan's Classbook*, ed. Hunt, p. xv.

[17] Ker, *Catalogue*, no. 231.

[18] London, British Library, MS. Cotton Nero A.i, fols. 70-96, 97-108, 109-21 and 122-77.

[19] A.G. Rigg and G.R. Wieland, 'A Canterbury Classbook of the Mid-Eleventh Century (the "Cambridge Songs" Manuscript)', *ASE* 4 (1975), 129.

[20] Fols. 1-50, 51-89, 90-110 and 115-28 respectively. See R.W. Hunt et al., *The Survival of Ancient Literature* (Bodleian Library Exhibition Catalogue, 1975), no. 120 and pl. xx (a).

volume, Oxford, Bodleian Library, MS. Junius 121.[21] London, Lambeth Palace Library, MS. 489 consists of two small booklets written at Exeter; the first (fols. 1-24) contains homilies for Christmas, Easter and All Saints days, while the second (fols. 25-58) contains a Sunday sermon, a sermon on the Lord's prayer and three homilies suitable for the anniversary of the dedication of a church.[22] Booklets such as these contain three or four sermons which may have served for the various liturgical seasons or have been adapted for particular occasions.[23]

Hatton 115 is a collection of five booklets containing miscellaneous homilies without rubrics to appoint them to specified occasions.[24] Three of them (fols. 1-64, 68-94 and 95-139a) were written in the second half of the eleventh century by the same scribe. He also wrote a homily on St Alban on two singleton leaves (fols. 66 and 67) bound between the first and second booklets. The collection also includes one of the folded booklets already mentioned (fols. 140-7),[25] a leaf (fol. 65) containing two short pieces written at the end of the eleventh century by one scribe each, and a twelfth-century booklet (fols. 148-55) containing various prognostications. This collection could not have been bound together until some time after its component parts were copied. The booklets were written at different times and the folded booklet (fols. 140-7) was clearly once independent of the others. It may have been the practice to keep a collection of homiletic booklets loose in a wrapper rather than sewn into a binding.[26] This is suggested too by the apparent ease with which additional booklets were incorporated into existing collections, as in Cambridge, Corpus Christi College, MSS. 198 and 421. In CCCC 198 one booklet (fols. 150-9), containing two additional Lenten homilies, and another (fols. 218-47),

---

[21] Ker, *Catalogue*, no. 338, arts. 31-5.

[22] *Ibid*. no. 283, arts. 1-3 and 4-8.

[23] The existence of such booklets was postulated by Éamonn Ó Carragáin, 'The Vercelli Book as an Ascetic Florilegium' (unpublished Ph.D. thesis, The Queen's University of Belfast, 1975), p. 199.

[24] Ker, *Catalogue*, no. 332.

[25] Above, pp. 31-32.

[26] Several later medieval manuscripts survive in wrappers; see Robinson, 'The "Booklet"', pp. 52-3.

containing homilies for Easter and the common of Saints, were interpolated into the original collection without disturbing the order of the church year in which that series had been arranged.[27] In CCCC 421 two booklets (pp. 3-98, containing homilies for Pentecost and the common of Saints, and pp. 209-24, containing two homilies for unspecified occasions), written at Exeter, were added to two earlier booklets written elsewhere.[28]

The piecemeal growth of CCCC 198 suggests that its scribes did not collaborate according to a preconceived plan but made individual contributions to form an enlarged homiliary. In the early eleventh century the collection contained an ordered series of thirty-two homilies for the temporale and sanctorale from Christmas to the beginning of May (now fols. iii, 1-149 and 160-217). These homilies formed a homogeneous set, essentially the same as the one in a contemporary homiliary from Rochester, now Oxford, Bodleian Library, MS. Bodley 340.[29] In CCCC 198 three scribes (Ker's scribes 1-3) copied twenty-two of these thirty-two homilies within nineteen quires (fols. iii and 1-149) and scribes 2 and 3 copied the other ten homilies within another seven quires (fols. 160-217). Within these two groups of quires each scribe copied by the quire, but their stints do not correspond with the beginnings and ends of homilies. The division into two groups of quires does not seem to have had any functional intention originally.[30] However, these groups were a little later treated as self-contained units when three further booklets (fols. 150-9, 218-47 and 248-87) were inserted into the series. The earliest of them (fols. 248-87) contains eleven homilies copied by scribe 4, who left the last of these homilies incomplete, and the other two booklets were added by scribe 5. He also provided the essential rubrics to convert the collection into a homiliary, assigning each of the original homilies as well as each of the

---

[27] Ker, *Catalogue*, no. 48.

[28] *Ibid*. no. 69.

[29] See Kenneth Sisam, 'MSS Bodley 340 and 342: Ælfric's *Catholic Homilies*', *Studies in the History of Old English Literature* (Oxford, 1953), pp. 153-6.

[30] See above, p. 35. The unity and independence of this series is confirmed by the original list of contents on fol. iii which lists only arts. 1-32.

additions by scribe 4 and himself to a specific occasion. Soon after, four more scribes (6, 7, 7a and 8) contributed to the growing collection. Scribe 6 copied three booklets (now fols. 328-59, 360-6 and 378-85), which were originally arranged consecutively[31] to form a short orderly series of homilies for saints' days in August, September and November. He was assisted by scribe 7, who wrote the last homily in the first of these three booklets, and scribe 7a, who wrote the last twenty-one lines on 366v in the second booklet. Scribe 8 worked independently. He completed the homily which scribe 4 had left unfinished at the end of his booklet (fols. 248-87), and then supplemented the booklet with six further homilies in four extra quires.[32] Scribe 8 also produced another booklet (fols. 386-94) which contains a homily on St Andrew.[33] In the second half of the eleventh century a further booklet (fols. 367-77) was added by scribes 9 and 11 who each copied a homily in it. Scribe 9 also began to copy a homily on St Bartholomew on leaves (321v-7v) which scribe 8 had left blank at the end of his extension of scribe 4's booklet; this was completed by scribe 10.

The composite nature of manuscripts like Hatton 115 and CCCC 198 raises the question of how such collections were used. If a collection of booklets were kept loose in a wrapper, a single booklet could be borrowed from that collection for copying as an exemplar or for use in preaching.

The possible use of a booklet as an exemplar is of significance for the textual critic. A collection of homilies, although copied consecutively by a single scribe, may contain items derived from different sources. The Vercelli Book, containing a collection of

---

[31] According to the list of contents brought up to date by the 'tremulous hand'; the third of these booklets is now separated from the other two by fols. 367-77.

[32] Scribe 4 had left art. 43 incomplete at the end of quire xxxvi (287v); scribe 8 later concluded the unfinished homily in quire xxxvii and extended the booklet by adding Ker's arts. 58-63 in quires xxxviii-xli.

[33] Another homily originally began on 394v but has since been erased.

miscellaneous homilies and religious poetry, consists of three booklets.[34] The two smallest of these, the first (fols. 1-24) and the third (fols. 121-35), each contain a homogeneous group of texts, while the second, largest one (fols. 25-120) contains material which, from differences in scribal lay-out and language, can be recognized to come from various sources. There are several signs that these sources were probably different booklet exemplars; for instance, homilies VI-X are linked by numeration (II-VI) and homilies XI-XIV are linked by use of red ink for the headings and capitals which begin each homily. Transmission in booklet exemplars would help to explain why a manuscript containing items from a series such as Ælfric's *Catholic Homilies* may exhibit one set of textual relations in some of these items and another (or others) in others.

The format and appearance of most manuscripts containing Old English homilies suggest that they were intended as lectern books. They are large codices requiring to be supported on a desk. The homilies could easily be read aloud: they are usually written in a large clear script, with generous spacing between lines and wide margins, and they were well pointed. It would be easy to find one's place in the book: each homily begins with a large coloured initial and is generally provided with either a rubric or heading in red ink. A manuscript providing a full set of homilies for liturgical use would doubtless have remained where it was used. But the evidence of manuscripts such as CCCC 198 suggests that some of the bigger collections may have been drawn on in a different way. Although the present weight of CCCC 198 would prohibit its being carried around, a single booklet from it would be easily portable. Some booklets were obviously so carried. Hatton 115, fols. 140-7, containing an anonymous vernacular homily on hell, became pocket-sized when folded across the middle and Auct. F.4.32, fols. 10-18, containing an anonymous vernacular homily on the Invention of the Cross, when folded down the middle would have fitted into a satchel or sleeve. The rubbing undergone by the outer leaves of these two booklets testifies to such use. A small booklet, Oxford, Bodleian Library, MS. Junius 85, fols. 18-24, containing

---

[34] D.G. Scragg, 'The Compilation of the Vercelli Book', *ASE* 2 (1973), 189-207; see further *The Vercelli Book*, ed. Celia Sisam, EEMF 19 (Copenhagen, 1976), and Ó Carragáin, 'The Vercelli Book'.

Ælfric's homily for the first Sunday in Lent from the second series of *Catholic Homilies*, is now part of a collection of four homily booklets, all of tiny format;[35] each of them has soiled outer pages suggesting that it once circulated independently. A further three small, portable booklets were written by various scribes at Exeter in the third quarter of the eleventh century: London, Lambeth Palace Library, MS. 489, fols. 1-24 and 28-58, and their companion booklet, now London, British Library, MS. Cotton Cleopatra B.xiii, fols. 2-58.[36] Booklets such as these could have been used in preaching. A monk and mass-priest who was a member of a monastery such as Worcester, from which both Hatton 115 and CCCC 198 survive,[37] and who had the cure of a parish outside the monastery, could have borrowed a relevant homily to preach to his parishioners.[38]

---

[35] Ker, *Catalogue*, no. 336: the outside limits of the collection represented by Junius 85 and 86 are 160 x 115 mm. The leaves of Junius 85, fols. 18-24 are of slightly wider dimensions than those of the other booklets.

[36] Ker, *Catalogue*, no. 144.

[37] Both manuscripts were at Worcester by the early thirteenth century when the 'tremulous hand' glossed them; see N.R. Ker, 'The Date of the "Tremulous" Worcester Hand', *Leeds Stud. in Eng.* 6 (1937), 28-9.

[38] I am grateful to Professor P.A.M. Clemoes, Dr M.R. Godden, Dr A.J. Minnis, Professor É.Ó. Carrigáin and Mr M.B. Parkes, all of whom read drafts of this article and made helpful comments and criticisms. I am solely responsible for the errors and omissions and for the views expressed.

Old Manuscripts / New Technologies

Kevin S. Kiernan

It is well to keep some things in focus, if not all things in perspective: there are no new technologies specifically designed to improve the legibility of Old English manuscripts. We can none the less borrow various devices made for other purposes to help read and represent manuscripts uniquely obscured by such things as soil, discoloration, fading, off-printing, shine-through, deliberate erasure or accidental abrasion, dampness, alcoholic and non-alcoholic liquids, fire-damage (and the paste, paper, and tape of modern bindings), chemical reagents, censorship, and other forms of hap, vandalism, or conservation. The devices range from the ordinary light bulb, not always near at hand in the great reading rooms, to digital image-processing hardware and software, which are staples in crime laboratories, but have yet to find a secure home among medieval manuscripts.

Recent advances in industry, medicine, forensic science, the space program and, above all, computer technology, have provided lots of expensive new equipment most manuscript repositories have yet to see, much less own. Among places of preeminent importance to Anglo-Saxonists, however, the British Library during the 1970s and 1980s has followed these remarkable developments at a safe distance and investigated their applications to manuscript studies.[1] In the 1970s the Conservation Studio of the Department of Manuscripts acquired, for example, binocular and trinocular microscopes, a cold light source with appropriate fiber-optic cables and beam spreaders, two beta radiography sources, an active infra-red pistol, and a specially adapted electronic camera, the Video Spectral Comparator, capable of seeing and

---

[1] There are of course other repositories, such as the Bodleian Library, Oxford, with organized and well equipped conservation studios.

recording writing in manuscripts that for one reason or another is obscured or even invisible to the naked eye. In the 1980s, moreover, much of this kind of equipment made its way into the Students Room. The pre-World War II ultraviolet lamp was replaced with a new model, and an illuminated binocular microscope, electro-luminescent screens, and a fiber-optic light source with cables and beam spreaders were all newly introduced.[2]

The usefulness of all (and some) of this impressive-sounding gadgetry depends on the resourcefulness of scholars trying to read illegible texts. In the Students Room of the Department of Manuscripts scholars work in an unspecified mixture of overhead artificial lighting and natural illumination, daylight, which by itself might theoretically show an object in its 'true' colors. However, atmospheric conditions such as rain and humidity, both notoriously prevalent in London, as well as refraction through remote windows with blinds, affect this source of illumination in unpredictable and as yet unmeasured ways. For this reason it is preferable to control a visual examination by using, first of all, a high-intensity 'daylight' lamp when studying obscure or questionable details in a manuscript.

But each paleographical problem, like the manuscript in which it occurs, is bound to be unique and is likely to require inventive solutions. Daylight, even artificial daylight, does not always illuminate things. Because they evenly transmit light from a broad, flat surface, electro-luminescent screens, like the beta radiography sources, are typically used to examine paper watermarks. Yet, after all the more obvious methods failed, Simon Keynes successfully used this form of transmitted light to read a murky fragment from a gospel-book once belonging to King Athelstan. By trial and error Keynes eventually discovered that 'reading the text by transmitted light proved rather more effective in this instance than the ultra-violet lamp or the Video Spectral Comparator' (p. 172, note 143). By arrangement with the Photographic Service, moreover, he was able to acquire a permanent

---

[2] I am indebted to A.E. Parker, chief conservation officer in the Department of Manuscripts, for information about purchases of equipment since World War II.

record of his visual examination in a photograph taken under the same conditions in which he successfully read the text.[3]

The fiber-optic setup at the British Library was developed by its manufacturers for applications using microscopes, cameras and computers in everything from Agrostology to Zoology. A standard usage combines fiber-optics with a microscope, with the results either photographed or digitized for later image enhancement. Fiber-optic light is another excellent source of transmitted light. Applied in the most rudimentary ways to the visual examination of a manuscript, it is unsurpassed for reading the letters covered by the paper frames of so many damaged Cotton manuscripts.[4] As a 'cold' or remote light source, moreover, it may be safely placed immediately behind a covered reading without in any way endangering the manuscript. Unfortunately, the extremely localized nature of the transmitted light makes photographing the results rather impractical, except perhaps in controversial cases calling for illustration. There are many other applications, too. By providing variable, low-level lighting with or without a microscope, fiber-optics are excellent for reading scratched glosses, detecting abrasions associated with erasures, studying drypoint rulings, and determining the hair and flesh sides of vellum in collations.

The purpose of a microscope in manuscript studies is perhaps self-evident. It is good for looking at little things. Cautioning that it should not be too powerful 'or its detail obscures general shapes', Raymond Page uses a binocular microscope (in addition to various hand-held lenses) with fiber-optic lighting, scanning the surface of the parchment from various directions, to study scratched or dry-point glosses. Phillip Pulsiano found a microscope very helpful while studying the interlinear glosses in Cotton Otho E.i, a text rendered nearly microscopic from shrinkage caused by the 1731 fire. Like Page, he too warns that the highest magnification is not always the best, sometimes hiding rather than revealing details by enlargement. The

---

[3] See 'King Athelstan's Books', *Learning and Literature in Anglo-Saxon Literature*, ed. Michael Lapidge and Helmut Gneuss (Cambridge, 1985), pp. 143-201, Plate VIII. The fragment is in London, British Library, MS. Cotton Otho B.ix, folio 1v.

[4] See Kevin S. Kiernan, 'The state of the *Beowulf* manuscript, 1882-1983', *ASE* 13 (1984), pp. 23-42.

study of hidden glosses has probably remained a fairly well concealed subject in Anglo-Saxon studies because of the difficulty of seeing and then illustrating them. Microphotography may yet open this interesting field to a much larger group of scholars.

Victor Carter, Lotte Hellinga, Tony Parker and Jane Mullane, of the British Library, have recently combined the use of a microscope with fiber-optics and microphotography to produce splendid microphotographs of manuscript problems.[5] Although not drawing examples from Old English manuscripts, their collaboration is a model of the kind of cooperation among scholars and technical experts needed to produce excellent photographs of manuscripts. Following a list of her illustrations, Mullane identifies the specific equipment she used, and then describes the method in detail: 'The camera was coupled to the photo-tube of the microscope by using an adaptor which replaced the camera lens', she explains. 'The ring flash unit was clamped underneath the objective lens of the microscope in order to give a flat, even light which was triggered from a flash meter'. This method was not appropriate for all pictures, however. She goes on to say that, 'When an oblique light was required a different approach was used. The volume from which the photograph was to be taken was placed below the camera microscope as usual, but instead of the flash unit, up to three variable light sources with fibre optic cables attached were used, so that (due to the flexibility of the cables) the light could be moved around to obtain the best angle for illuminating the leaf ...' (p. 11). It is rare, of course, for scholars to have the opportunity to oversee the photographing of manuscript problems, but the quality of facsimiles would be immeasurably improved by similar collaboration.

An ultraviolet lamp will frequently reveal readings that for one reason or another are no longer visible in ordinary light of whatever intensity.[6] Light itself is composed of visible and invisible

---

[5] 'Printing with Gold in the Fifteenth Century', *British Library Journal* 9 (1983), 1-13.

[6] See *Ultraviolet and Fluorescence Photography*, Eastman Kodak Publication no. M-27 (Rochester, N.Y., 1968) and *Applied Infrared Photography*, Eastman Kodak Publication no. M-28 (1977). One of the best introductions to the use of ultraviolet with literary manuscripts remains R.B. Haselden's *Scientific Aids for the Study of Manuscripts*,

wavelengths, the visible waves of different length appearing to the eye as different colors, from deep red at one end of the visible spectrum to violet at the other. Beyond these points on the spectrum, the invisible waves, known respectively as infrared and ultraviolet, can be photographically and electronically recorded. Moreover, some substances, including both the parchment and the iron-based inks used in Anglo-Saxon manuscripts, sometimes absorb the rays of an ultraviolet lamp and emit radiation that fluoresces in the visible range of the spectrum. When fluorescence is excited in one or the other, creating a contrast, we can suddenly read something that was, for example, deliberately erased by a scribe a thousand years ago. The use of iron-based inks in Anglo-Saxon manuscripts makes ultraviolet fluorescent techniques among the most fundamental ways of improving illegible manuscripts.

The Video Spectral Comparator, or VSC as it is called, is a specially designed electronic camera comprising a highly sensitive video camera, a powerful zoom lens and a high-resolution video monitor. This bulky contraption combines many of the features and advantages of the other equipment. Not as restricted as a human eye, the 'eye' of an electronic camera, like a conventional camera, can register and record wavelengths outside the visible spectrum without having to worry about exposure times. The VSC has some advantages over a conventional camera, as well. Without having to wait for film to develop, a researcher can immediately see on a video screen the way a manuscript responds under ultraviolet, infrared, or high-intensity white light, while, for example, experimenting with a wide range of light filters to intensify or suppress different generations of ink.[7] At the same time the operator can block off and enlarge a particular section of text; enhance the contrast by adjusting the levels of

---

The Transactions of the Bibliographical Society, Supplement 10 (London, 1935), which is still cited by manufacturers of ultraviolet lamps.

[7] See Haselden for a useful discussion of light-filters (41). Although ultraviolet and infrared were unhelpful, Raymond I. Page discovered that 'good negatives were made using a tricolour red filter' (p. 36): 'A Note on the Text of MS CCCC 422 (*Solomon and Saturn*)', *Medium Ævum* 34 (1965), 36-39.

brightness or darkness, or by comparing positive with negative images; and examine off-prints and shine-through with mirror images of the text. Depending on the type of equipment attached to it, moreover, the VSC can store any or all of these results on a video tape, in a conventional photograph, or in a digitized file on a computer disk.

The most effective technology applied to Old English manuscripts prior to World War II was ultraviolet fluorescence photography,[8] first used in Anglo-Saxon studies in the early 1930s by E.N. da C. Andrade, a distinguished professor of physics at University College, London. A.H. Smith, his colleague in the English Department, published the results of some of Andrade's work in his 1933 edition of the Leiden Riddle.[9] Five years later, just before the war, Smith used two more of Andrade's photographs among his own illustrations from four famous manuscripts in his ground-breaking article on 'The Photography of Manuscripts'.[10] These same manuscripts—the Leiden Riddle, the Exeter Book, *Beowulf*, and Alfred's *Boethius*—usefully illustrate some common paleographical problems and the technological solutions open to scholars from the time of Smith and Andrade to the present.

In the early 1930s the Leiden Riddle was brought to University College, London, where Smith used it in preparing his edition. The manuscript had been disfigured in 1864, when the Leiden librarian, W.G. Pluygers, applied a reagent of ammonium sulfide in an effort to improve its legibility.[11] With the help of Andrade's special expertise

---

[8] After the war the use of ultraviolet became increasingly common, if not routine, in the study of Anglo-Saxon manuscripts. Thus, in his *Catalogue of Manuscripts Containing Anglo-Saxon*, N.R. Ker often mentions his use of it with manuscripts at the British Museum (*e.g.* items 153, 154, 157) and every now and then at the Bodleian Library too (*e.g.* 291 and 323); (1957: Oxford, 1990).

[9] A.H. Smith, ed., *Three Northumbrian Poems: Cædmon's Hymn, Bede's Death Song and the Leiden Riddle* (1933: London, 1968).

[10] *London Mediaeval Studies* 1 (1938), plates IIB, the ultraviolet photograph of the Leiden Riddle, and IXA, the ultraviolet photograph of fol. 8r from the Exeter Book.

[11] Pluyger's 'transcript was inserted at the end of the manuscript with the note *Descripsi in Novembr. 1864 Medicinam adhibui: sulphuret. ammonii. W.G.P.*' (Smith, 9). Early nineteenth-century

and the most advanced equipment for examining and photographing manuscripts, Smith was able to acquire strikingly effective photographs of the riddle, one in ordinary light and one showing ultraviolet fluorescent effects. The superior contrast of the ultraviolet photograph is partly vitiated, however, because the areas treated by the reagent are covered by an opaque film that shows up in the black and white photograph as dark stains eclipsing any vestiges of letters beneath them.

Forty years later, recognizing the drawbacks of an ultraviolet print, Malcolm Parkes achieved good contrast without the stains by enhancing an old photograph taken in ordinary light.[12] His photographer produced 'a series of very hard prints' from the original photograph, some of which heightened the contrast in the damaged areas, 'thus emphasizing very faint traces obscured beneath only a light film of reagent'.[13] Parkes has explained to me in correspondence that 'The readings were not, as I recall, visible to the naked eye on the photograph from which the negative was made (or rather the naked eye could not distinguish the marks as readings). It was only when the printing made them more obtrusive, at the expense of almost all the rest of the image, that one could recognize them as traces of strokes forming letters'. These photographic techniques for improving the contrast in old photographs anticipate the comparatively new field of digital image processing. What was actually needed to address this

---

transcripts show, however, that the text was already as illegible before Pluygers made his potentially disastrous experiments as it is today.

[12] Parkes simply identifies it as a 'photograph available in Oxford' in 'The Manuscript of the Leiden Riddle', *ASE* 1 (1972), 207. He informs me that he thinks he got the print from Norman Davis who got it from R.W. Zandvoort. For Zandvoort, see 'The Leiden Riddle', *English and Germanic Studies* 3 (1949-50), 42-56, reprinted in *Collected Papers* (Groningen, 1954). According to J. Gerritsen, 'Two of Smith and Andrade's u.v. prints are at Leiden. The lighter of these supplied the plate in Zandvoort's two publications, of which the earlier shows the best contrast'. 'The Text of the Leiden Riddle', *ES* 50 (1969), 529. Parkes' mysterious photograph may therefore go back to the series produced by Smith and Andrade.

[13] P. 207 and note 3. These faint traces are also likely to show up more clearly in a color photograph taken in strong light.

paleographical problem was an ordinary photograph for the stained areas, but an ultraviolet one for the rest. Image processing programs are now designed to frame or isolate specific areas of an image, improve their legibility without obscuring areas that are already legible, and then produce a photograph or printout of the entire improved image. Image processing can also combine the best features of two different images, in this case the best results of an ordinary and an ultraviolet photograph.

At about the same time that he was helping Smith with the Leiden Riddle, Andrade successfully used ultraviolet on some damaged pages in the Exeter Book, which had been brought to the British Museum in 1930 to prepare the facsimile edition.[14] Freed of its old binding, the manuscript had already revealed some letters previously hidden by binding strips and opaque tape. Yet Andrade's 'ultra-violet ray apparatus' was even more revealing, uncovering many additional letters not visible in natural light. The timing of his work, however, was unfortunate, for photographs of his discoveries were not ready in time to be included in the facsimile. They would have been worth waiting for. R.W. Chambers and Robin Flower had previously examined the same pages under ultraviolet, but with far less successful results, as they prominently acknowledged in their facsimile.[15] Even though Andrade's results were better than the new facsimile for these pages and undermined the accuracy of his own transcriptions, Chambers provided a copy of Andrade's photograph of fol. 8r to Neil Ker, who

---

[14] See Max Förster, Chapter V, 'General Description of the Manuscript', *Chapters on the Exeter Book*, eds. R.W. Chambers, Max Förster, and Robin Flower (London, 1933), p. 55.

[15] On the page facing the table of contents they cite some of his readings and add: 'Since this book was passing through the press at the time, it was not possible to include these readings obtained under Prof. Andrade's apparatus in the notes to Chapter VI ['Transcription of the Damaged Passages of the Exeter Book'], where the results of an earlier examination under ultra-violet rays are recorded'. They fail to make clear, however, that their results were far inferior to Andrade's.

was then reviewing the facsimile.[16] Chambers later gave Smith a copy of this photograph, too, for use as an illustration in his article.

Despite the relative availability of this ultraviolet photograph in the 1930s, it took nearly fifty years before a complete copy of it was published. Smith furnished only a cropped version of it, cutting off the right side, including some readings ultraviolet alone had brought to light. Fortunately, Ker later made a copy of his print for John Pope, who published the first uncropped version in 1981.[17] Pope's copy, however, was a photograph taken of Ker's photograph at the Bodleian Library in May 1979 (p. 142, note 22). Not entirely satisfied with these second-generation images, Pope points out that 'the Andrade ultra-violet photograph [is] best represented by Dr Ker's copy, the slightly clearer source' of the two plates Pope used for his illustrations.[18] New photographs are not always the answer, however. Pope in fact had acquired new ultraviolet photographs in Exeter, as well, but they were, he says, 'much inferior, largely because of the poor conditions under which they had to be taken but partly because the hole at the end of line 12 has once more been covered and transparent strips have been glued over some of the darkest parts of the surface' (p. 142 note 21).

---

[16] *Medium Ævum* 2 (1933), 224-231. Ker duly cited the photograph in pointing out some shortcomings in the new facsimile and in the editor's transcriptions (p. 225).

[17] 'The text from a damaged passage in the Exeter Book: *Advent (Christ I)* 18-32', *ASE* 9 (1981), 137-156 (and Plates V and VI following p. 118).

[18] P. 143. 'The reader should be able to identify most of the letters for himself in pl. VI', Pope says later on, 'but the Ker copy from which the plate is derived, the facsimile and the manuscript itself are the primary witnesses behind the present study' (p. 154). Unfortunately, Ker's copy has disappeared. Andrew Watson, Ker's literary executor, has not been able to locate it after several thorough searches among Ker's papers. He did find some of the ultraviolet photographs taken by Andrade and Smith of the Leiden Riddle, however, among papers left at University College by the late Professor Dodgson.

In another important study involving the Exeter Book, Pope explored with the technological aid of a photocopying machine the possible ways of filling the textual lacunae left by a hole in the vellum in the poem known as 'The Husband's Message'.[19] His first illustration is a plate from the facsimile, which he describes as 'a better guide for most purposes than the manuscript itself, because the edges of the hole are now slightly obscured by a protective covering' (p. 44). His second illustration is a 'conjectural restoration' of the same page, 'made by cutting out words and letters from photocopies of other pages of the facsimile and pasting them onto a photocopy of fol. 123' (p. 44). Pope was of course aware of the highly conjectural nature of his restorations, freely admitting that 'I am far from satisfied with some of my conjectures, yet I hope that even the worst of them will give a clearer idea of the problem than a mere blank would do, and may lead others to propose something better' (p. 56).

In fact, the same laborious and time-consuming, cut-and-paste technique Pope used can now be easily carried out with the help of an optical scanner and a computer with a good graphics editor. An optical scanner reproduces a facsimile by dividing it into a microscopic grid and numbering each element of the grid according to its relative brightness on a black-to-white scale of 0 to 255. The results are of course read as numbers by a computer, but are displayed as a high-resolution facsimile on a computer screen. A graphics editor, in the same way as a word-processor, can move parts of a text from one document to another, in this case from one scanned image to another. A scanned facsimile of folio 123 will faithfully reproduce the damaged text of 'The Husband's Message', including the great gap in the middle of the page. Anyone using the graphics editor can then provide conjectural restorations to complete the text, just as Pope did, by moving appropriate letters and words that fit the available space in the lacuna from other parts of the Exeter Book. Like Pope's restored text, the new 'restored' image of folio 123 can also be laser-printed or photographed in a new facsimile.

---

[19] John C. Pope, 'Palaeography and poetry: some solved and unsolved problems of the Exeter Book', *Medieval Scribes, Manuscripts and Libraries: Essays Presented to N.R. Ker*, eds. M.B. Parkes and Andrew G. Watson (London, 1978), 25-65.

The danger of this process, as Pope recognized in his photocopying version of it, is that it produces visually convincing results that may in fact be partly or even completely wrong. Similar dangers have always existed in modern printed editions, which often include 'authoritative' conjectural restorations that have taken precedence over contradictory manuscript evidence. The biggest danger now is that a computer can remake the manuscript evidence. In his scrupulous use of the methodology, Pope took great care to make sure that his conjectural restorations were paleographically feasible, both in terms of manuscript spacing and meaning. No proposed reading ignored any fragments of letters surviving along the damaged edges of the great hole. Still, the photographic restoration he provides makes it appear as if the manuscript has not suffered any losses, that his conjectural restoration is authentic.

Pope in this article also anticipates two other emerging computer fields, rather whimsically known as letterology and lacunology.[20] These new processes help identify possible reconstructions that are textually plausible and paleographically feasible. Letterology creates a databank by recording all instances of letter-forms in a particular manuscript. Scholars can then search the databank for characteristic letter-forms to match the vestiges of letters in damaged parts of the same manuscript. When a convincing match is found, identifying for example the remnants of an ascender as most likely part of a thorn, rather than some other letter with an ascender, an editor can with some confidence make conjectural restorations of a damaged text. Lacunology, on the other hand, first creates a databank of texts (the entire corpus of Old English, say), which editors can then search for appropriate strings of text to fill a lacuna. For example, a search for a string filling in '..c..o..g' would locate the word 'lacunology' in the data provided by this article.[21] The databank of Old English texts

---

[20] See Marcello Gigante and Mario Capasso, 'Papyrology and Computers', in *Rediscovering Pompeii* (Rome, 1990), pp. 55-61.

[21] By a technique related to lacunology Biblical scholars who had been denied direct access to the Dead Sea Scrolls were recently able to produce a renegade edition of them using only the published concordances.

might contain printed editions, diplomatic transcriptions, or even scanned manuscripts.

Many technological aids have helped uncover or decipher illegible parts of the *Beowulf* manuscript. Fiber-optic light is especially useful. The 1731 Cotton Library fire destroyed nearly 2000 letters along the outer edges of the vellum leaves. When the manuscript was rebound in 1845, each vellum leaf was individually mounted in paper frames. The retaining space of these frames, and the paste and tape used to secure the vellum to them, covered up or obscured many letters and bits of letters along the damaged edges of each manuscript page. Julius Zupitza did a painstaking job of deciphering what was covered by holding each manuscript page up to the light, but in 1882 he did not have the rudimentary technological help of bright, focussed, artificial lighting. A hundred years later, fiber-optic light easily disclosed hundreds of letters and parts of letters that Zupitza was unable to see beneath the paper frames.[22]

As might be expected, ultraviolet helps us read the *Beowulf* manuscript in a variety of ways. Because it sometimes fluoresces erased readings, ultraviolet is often useful for investigating the nature of scribal corrections. It reveals, for instance, that the first scribe started to omit part of the copytext on fol. 147A(131)r6, writing *he on* from the next line instead of *ræhte*; it also shows, with less certainty, however, that the scribe began to use a synonym for *medoheal*, either *medosele* or *medosæl*, on fol. 140v19.[23] In both cases ultraviolet confirms the attentiveness of the scribe, who in these instances made mistakes and fastidious corrections in the course of copying.

---

[22] Compare the notes in Julius Zupitza, ed., *Beowulf: Autotypes of the Unique Cotton MS Vitellius A. xv in the British Museum, with a transliteration and notes* (London, 1882) with 'The state of the *Beowulf* manuscript' (see note 4 above).

[23] Like Zupitza and most editors of *Beowulf*, I adhere to the foliation written on the manuscript leaves, but with two slight modifications. Two leaves, including 147A(131), were misplaced when the foliation was written; the double citation provides the present, correct location preceding fol. 147, and (in parentheses) the former, incorrect location preceding fol. 132.

Ultraviolet has been used most prominently, however, on two notorious folios, a palimpsest that begins the dragon episode (fol. 179), and the last page of *Beowulf* (fol. 198v). Both cases illustrate the kind of difficulties that can attend the indiscriminate use of technology to manuscript problems.

Ultraviolet is indispensable on the last page of the *Beowulf* manuscript, which suffered from wear in Anglo-Saxon times and was freshened up, apparently by the same scribe at a later time. Smith provides four separate plates of this page, three of them showing the effects of different filters in daylight, and the fourth showing fluorescent effects by ultraviolet. The ultraviolet photograph clearly shows several readings that do not show up in ordinary light nor in photographs taken in ordinary light. For example, the word *werudes* at the beginning of line 4 can be read in the ultraviolet photograph, whereas only *des* and the uncertain traces of a preceding *o* or *u* appear in ordinary light.[24] Why, then, do *both* facsimiles of *Beowulf* use a photograph taken in ordinary light for this page? According to Norman Davis, 'the photographer found after long experiment [that the last page] gave better results by ordinary light'.[25] This decision was

---

[24] The confusion in ordinary light is underscored by Zupitza's note: '*metodes?* I thought I saw all those letters pretty distinctly (except the two first strokes of *m*) on the tenth of September 1880, but on no other day. On the 12th of Sept., 1882, I thought I was able to read [*w*]*igendes*'. Davis, without the benefit of ultraviolet, says 'the faint traces before *des* look more like *o* than *u*', in Zupitza, *Beowulf: Reproduced in Facsimile from the Unique Manuscript, British Museum MS. Cotton Vitellius A.xv*, 2nd ed., EETS 245 (1959), xi. Malone, also without ultraviolet, says 'I cannot read the first three letters of the line but Smith's photographic text has *wer* and this reading must be accepted'. *The Nowell Codex (British Museum Cotton Vitellius A. xv. Second MS)*, EEMF 12 (1963), 106.

[25] 'Preface to the Second Edition' (v); Malone implies that he may have made the choice himself when he says that the page 'was photographed by both [ordinary and ultraviolet] lights but the photograph chosen for reproduction was the one done by ordinary light, since on the whole it seemed the better of the two', 'Note on the Photographs' (120).

probably correct for the folio as a whole, because large stains on the page, invisible in ordinary light, strongly fluoresce under an ultraviolet lamp.[26] But the ordinary photograph deprives us of the readings that are invisible except in ultraviolet. Today it is no longer necessary to make such self-defeating choices, for image-processing programs can produce a single photograph or laser-printed image combining the best features of the ordinary and the ultraviolet photographs.

Ultraviolet is not only useless, but actually detrimental, on fol. 179, particularly on the recto. It does not disclose any readings on the folio that cannot be seen in strong natural light. It is significant that Smith, who was aware of the illegibility of fol. 179 recto, does not furnish an ultraviolet photograph of this page (p. 220). Although the entire folio was erased and rewritten, the most obscure sections on the recto were deliberately erased a second time when the vellum was wet, leaving a grey residue in these areas that fluoresces slightly under ultraviolet. In a black and white photograph this fluorescence makes it almost impossible to distinguish the vestiges of letter-forms here. The photographer nonetheless chose an ultraviolet photograph for the facsimiles for this page, presumably because it achieved to his eye a better overall contrast. In fact, the best view of the folio is in strong daylight, that is, with the help of a stable, high-intensity, daylight lamp. The best way to reproduce these effects is in a color print.[27]

Apart from high-intensity light and color photography, the most effective technological aids on this difficult folio are an electronic camera (the VSC) and an image processor. I first experimented with the VSC in the early 1980s in an effort to improve the legibility of several problematic readings on the recto. After several trips and numerous experiments, I eventually acquired a videotape of the results

---

[26] Smith alludes to these stains when he mentions his unsuccessful use of infra-red photography, which produced, he says, 'photographs of the stains and little else' (p. 199). In my experience infra-red light is of no value in studying manuscripts written with iron-based inks.

[27] See the frontispiece to Kiernan, *Beowulf and the Beowulf Manuscript* (New Brunswick, N.J., 1981). Readers have often observed that Zupitza's *Autotypes* facsimile is in some ways superior to the new facsimiles in Davis and Malone. The reason is that the contrast is better in ordinary light than in ultraviolet on this page.

and then worked with a digitized version of the tape on a dedicated image-processing microcomputer at the University of Kentucky.[28] In the late 1980s, with the extraordinary cooperation of the British Library and a British computing firm, the manuscript, the VSC, and the microcomputer were all brought together in the Conservation Studio of the Department of Manuscripts, where I acquired a first-hand digitized image of the folio.[29] The results, while not as spectacular as the Magellan images from outer space, do conclusively show that some 'received' parts of the text of *Beowulf* are not right, and do give us new data to assess in reconstructing more likely readings. In this process, both letterology and lacunology, as well as other pattern-recognition programs, are likely to help solve lingering mysteries on the folio.

The biggest paleographical problem in all of the manuscripts discussed here, however, is the version of King Alfred's prosimetrical translation of Boethius' *Consolation of Philosophy* in London, British Library, MS. Cotton Otho A.vi. Anyone who visually examines this important 10th-century manuscript will see why it has been edited only once since it was damaged in the fire of 1731.[30] Fire and presumably the water used to extinguish it have rendered much of the text quite unreadable even in strong daylight or with the help of high-intensity artificial light. This manuscript exemplifies the kind of problem that can be approached only through modern technology. Here is a text we have in effect lost, unless we find some means of restoring it. As Smith observed in 1938, 'The ink has run and it is only with the greatest difficulty that one can sort out letters on the *a*-side [or recto] of a folio from those shining through from the *b*-side [the verso]. It is

---

[28] The Mipron-D by Kontron Electronics is a medical image processor used to enhance X-rays in the Cardiology Laboratory. It is well suited for paleographical study because it runs global algorithms and does not permit the kind of invasive editing techniques characteristic of new desktop software for PCs. If an X-ray shows a bad artery, a doctor wants to know how bad it is, not how good it can be made to look.

[29] See Kiernan, 'Digital Image Processing and the *Beowulf* Manuscript', *Literary and Linguistic Computing* (1991), 20-27.

[30] By Walter J. Sedgefield, *King Alfred's Old English Version of Boethius De Consolatione Philosophiae* (Oxford, 1899).

in fact a manuscript which is generally illegible by ordinary means' ('Photography', p. 198). In 1899, long before the extraordinary help of an ultraviolet lamp was available, Walter Sedgefield could only say that, 'By taking advantage of the rare intervals of London sunshine during the winter and spring months, I found much decipherable which in ordinary light would have remained hidden' ('Preface', p. vii). It is likely that the ultraviolet waves present in strong sunlight enhanced the contrast for him, but much stronger concentrations of ultraviolet are needed to produce truly revealing fluorescent effects. Sedgefield not surprisingly made lots of mistakes in his transcription, but in fairness they must be seen in the context of the horrors he bravely faced alone in this paleographical nightmare.

Smith decisively showed forty years later that ultraviolet fluorescence photography would reveal far more of the text than Sedgefield was able to record in his edition. The importance of his discovery was perhaps not immediately recognized because Smith used a fairly well preserved folio in his illustration,[31] noting that he would publish 'similar photographs of the rest of the manuscript ... and a diplomatic text ... in the course of a year or so' (p. 198 note 2). The outbreak of World War II a few months later presumably kept him from fulfilling his intention. Just last year Fred Robinson and Eric Stanley finally filled part of this void by furnishing ultraviolet photographs of all of the metrical sections, about 30 percent of the entire manuscript.[32] We now have new tools to repair old manuscript problems like these. In a process that once required hours and days in a darkroom and lots of wasted film and time, the VSC can quickly test a wide range of filters and determine, page-by-page, whether ultraviolet is in fact necessary on a particular page. Once a new image is acquired, moreover, the computer itself can serve as a

---

[31] Smith's Plate VIII does confirm, however, many of the uncertain readings for fol. 20r in Sedgefield's edition (33).

[32] *Old English Verse Texts from Many Sources*, EEMF 23 (Copenhagen, 1991). There are 78 plates of pages containing the meters out of a total 258 pages (or 129 folios). As they point out as an example in their introduction, 'All the text that Sedgefield and Krapp italicize as unreadable in *Meter* 25, vv. 12-24 can be read in the facsimile, and virtually all in *Meter* 21, vv. 36-44' (p. 21).

digital darkroom, separating problem areas of a page and instantly changing the contrast, for example, or experimenting with different levels of brightness to bring out underexposed parts of the text.[33] Image-processing routines can be written that might successfully restore to their former size and shape sections of the text shrunken by fire-damage. Other programs can eliminate obfuscating shine-through, which has made it so difficult to decipher the original text. Ten years ago, one had to have connections with rocket scientists or government sleuths to work with astronomically or criminally expensive, state-of-the-art, digital image processing equipment. Personal computers are now fast and powerful enough to run bigger and better image-processing software in a twinkling of an eye, provided they have enough memory and storage space for the gigantic graphics files.

Today the photographic services of manuscript repositories still fill orders for ordinary, ultraviolet, and infrared photographs, slides, and microfilms,[34] and some, like the British Library, accept special orders involving less conventional techniques, such as video tapes from the VSC. But a rapidly growing number of scholars will begin converting these analogue representations of manuscripts to digital formats for archiving, indexing, searching, editing, linking in hypertexts, image processing, and desktop publishing. In due course, all of the major repositories will begin to provide their own scanned images, including CD-ROMs or equivalents of entire manuscripts, as part of their service. The future of manuscript studies will include a major role for computers. By providing new access to formerly inaccessible manuscripts, they will bring about a revolution in manuscript studies.

---

[33] See James Marchand, 'The Computer as Camera and Darkroom', *Offline* 37 (1992), and the discussions of the subject in August 1991 on the electronic list, MEDTEXTL@UIUCVMD.BITNET ('Medieval Text—Philology, Codicology, and Technology'). The creators of image-processing software, such as Gray F/X by Xerox Imaging Systems, consciously try to incorporate all of the advantages of a darkroom.

[34] Already on the agenda of the new project 'Anglo-Saxon Manuscripts in Microfiche Facsimile', which intends to make available all of the approximately 420 manuscripts containing Old English, is the feasibility of transferring microfilm images to CD-ROM.

It is time for medievalists who work with manuscripts to embrace the many virtues of this new technology,[35] while learning to avoid its many wayward vices.

AFTERWARD/FOREWORD, DECEMBER, 1993

In the months between the completion of this article and its publication, the predictions of my closing paragraph have come to pass. As part of its strategic objectives for the year 2000, the British Library will increase access to its collections by use of imaging and network technology. In the summer of 1993, it announced a number of 'Initiatives for Access', including an ambitious 'Electronic *Beowulf*' project, which will make a full-color electronic facsimile of Cotton Vitellius A.xv available to readers in the British Library in early 1994. As editor of the facsimile, I am endeavoring to disclose as well the hundreds of letters covered by the paper frames of the nineteenth-century binding leaves and all scribal erasures that show up under ultraviolet. As this electronic archive grows, it will include electronic facsimiles of many ancillary texts. Plans are underway to digitize the Thorkelin transcripts of *Beowulf* at the Royal library in Copenhagen and other early collations and editions of *Beowulf*. Thanks to a generous gift by Whitney Bolton, one of the first additions will be J.J. Conybeare's 1817 collation of G.J. Thorkelin's 1815 *editio princeps*. A CD-ROM version of the archive is also planned. The academic directors of the project are Paul Szarmach and myself. The British Library Digital and Network Services Steering Committee oversees the project and has funded the equipment purchases. The staff most closely involved with the project have been David Hart and Charles Fischer of the University of Kentucky, John Bennett, an outside consultant, and from the British Library, Michael Alexander, Dave French, Ann Gilbert, and Andrew Prescott.

---

[35] In the context of the virtues, I wish to acknowledge help while writing this essay from Janet Backhouse, Patrick Conner, John Block Friedman, the Image Processing group at the IBM-United Kingdom Scientific Centre, Simon Keynes, James Marchand, Joe Nickell, R.I. Page, A.E. Parker, Malcolm Parkes, John C. Pope, Phillip Pulsiano, and Andrew Watson.

N.R. Ker and the Study of English Medieval Manuscripts

Richard W. Pfaff

The contribution of Neil Ripley Ker (1908-82) to the study of Anglo-Saxon manuscripts cannot be separated from his work with English medieval manuscripts as a whole, nor that work from the tradition of scholarship which he both inherited and greatly furthered.[1] The tradition is rooted in two institutions, a school and a university, which were Ker's own: Eton and Oxford; and though he was in no sense narrow or provincial in his outlook as a scholar, he was gratefully conscious of the debt he owed to both of those contexts of learning.

Eton College, the largest, greatest, and probably most peculiar of English 'public' schools, possesses both a fine collection of medieval manuscripts and the constitutional oddity of a Provost who is the resident head of the ancient foundation (established by Henry VI in 1441) but does not actually run the school, which is in the charge of

---

[1] A full memoir of Ker for the *Proceedings of the British Academy* is being prepared by Ian Doyle; Teresa Webber has published a brief notice in the *Dictionary of National Biography 1981-1985* (1990), 221-2. For sensitive insights, see Julian Brown's address at Ker's memorial service, later published in *Scrittura e Civiltà* 7 (1983), 265-70, and C.R. Cheney's 'Introduction' to *Medieval Manuscripts and Libraries. Essays presented to N.R. Ker*, ed. M.B. Parkes and Andrew G. Watson (London, 1978), xi-xv. A bibliography of Ker's published writings to 1978, by Joan Gibbs, appeared in that Festschrift volume, pp. 371-9; a supplement in his collected papers, *Books, Collectors and Libraries. Studies in the Medieval Heritage*, ed. Andrew G. Watson (London, 1985), xiii-xiv. Kevin Kiernan details Ker's accomplishments in his article 'Neil R. Ker' for *Medieval Scholarship*, v. 2, ed. Helen Damico and Joseph B. Zavadil (New York: Garland, in press).

the Head Master. The Provost's job is therefore pretty much what he wishes to make it, and the Provost in the years when Ker was a schoolboy at Eton (1921-27) had as his twin priorities getting to know many of the boys and continuing the activities which by that time had made him perhaps the best-known student of medieval manuscripts in the world. This was Montague Rhodes James (1862-1936), Provost of King's College, Cambridge from 1905 to 1918 and of Eton from 1918 to his death.

By the time Ker first encountered the Provost, James had published catalogues of the Western medieval manuscripts of all save one of the colleges at Cambridge (including the massive collection at Trinity, in four volumes, 1900-5, and that at Corpus Christi, superlatively important for Anglo-Saxon studies, in two volumes, 1909-12), the Fitzwilliam Museum, the John Rylands [University] Library at Manchester (Latin MSS only), and the Pierpont Morgan Library, as well as several smaller and private collections.[2] In his later years he turned increasingly to the study of medieval libraries, largely through their surviving booklists,[3] and to investigations of individual manuscripts, frequently in connection with publication by the Roxburghe Club.

While it would be an exaggeration to maintain that Ker came to feel that he knew the Provost well (as was the case with a few of his contemporaries),[4] he was without question influenced by a policy which James himself as a schoolboy seems to have been responsible for getting started: that pupils of unusual promise could be allowed access to the College Library (i.e., that of the Fellows, as distinct from the well-stocked School Library), a magnificent collection housed in rooms

---

[2] Richard W. Pfaff, *Montague Rhodes James* (London, 1980), *passim*. Of James's major catalogues, only that of the Lambeth Palace MSS was still to be published, after many delays, in 1930-2.

[3] For example the York Austin Friars, the Hereford Franciscans, Peterborough, Bury St. Edmunds, Norwich, the Leicester Augustinians; his pioneering work in this area was *The Ancient Libraries of Canterbury and Dover* (1903).

[4] For an account from Ker's schoolboy diary of an evening spent with James, see Pfaff (note 2), pp. 348-9.

of the utmost eighteenth-century elegance.[5] James had been allowed access to the manuscripts, and the descriptions in his first published catalogue, that of the Eton collection (1895), are based on notes he had taken as a teenager there. These descriptions are, not surprisingly, among the least polished and expert of the thousands he made; a new edition was long mooted but never accomplished. So when Ker took up the challenge of compiling revised descriptions of the Eton manuscripts as a very large component of volume II of his *Medieval Manuscripts in British Libraries*,[6] he concluded the first paragraph of the preface to that book by saying 'I can only hope that pp. 628-798 are a worthy contribution to the history of the library which he knew best and loved best and in which I spent happy Sunday afternoons some forty-five years after James, K.S. Unlike James, I did not see the manuscripts'.[7]

Where Ker first encountered manuscripts was instead at Oxford. Under the influence of his father, Ker entered Magdalen College in the autumn of 1927 purposing to devote himself to the most modern option then in the undergraduate Oxford curriculum, a combined subject called Philosophy, Politics, and Economics. After a few not very happy months he decided to switch to the Honours School (in Oxford parlance) of English Language and Literature—the teaching for which at Magdalen was largely in the hands of C.S. Lewis, a Fellow there since 1925. It seems that even as an undergraduate Ker preferred to get his hands on manuscripts whenever possible. After taking his B.A. degree in English in 1930, he earned an intermediate research degree, that of B. Litt., three years later, with a thesis on palaeographical aspects of Ælfrician manuscripts; as with many Oxford academics of

---

[5] For some idea of the riches contained therein, see Paul Quarrie, *Treasures of Eton College Library. 550 Years of Collecting* (catalogue of an exhibition at the Pierpont Morgan Library; New York, 1990).

[6] II: *Abbotsford-Keele* (Oxford, 1977), pp. 628-798. This work is discusssed at length below.

[7] Page v. 'K.S.' means King's Scholar, one of the seventy Foundation Scholars at Eton; Ker was an Oppidan, an ordinary Eton boy who lived in a School 'house' as opposed to the ancient accommodation in College.

his generation (and before), the notion of going on to get a Doctorate in Philosophy apparently never came up.

Indeed, for someone in Oxford in the 1930s who had developed an interest in medieval manuscripts, further formal training would have perhaps been otiose; simply to be working among the galaxy of scholars there at that time would have been worth several doctorates. Of these, the most influential older figure was E.A. Lowe (1879-1969), Reader in Palaeography from 1926—a position in which he was to be succeeded by Ker in 1946—who was beginning to produce his monumental *Codices Latini Antiquiores*.[8] Others, somewhat younger, included V.H. (later Sir Vivian) Galbraith (1889-1976), Reader in Diplomatic 1928-37; C.R. Cheney (1906-88), his successor in that post from 1937 to 1945; and R.W. (later Sir Richard) Southern (b. 1912), a don at Exeter and then Balliol from 1933 on. Two contemporaries in particular became lifelong friends and colleagues, and therefore require more than passing mention.

Richard William Hunt (1908-79) entered Balliol the same term as Ker went up to Magdalen, and in several respects their careers ran parallel. Hunt (who did take a D. Phil. degree) lectured in palaeography at Liverpool in the late thirties and forties but worked a great deal in Oxford, to which he returned in 1945 as Keeper of Western Manuscripts at the Bodleian—a position from which he exercised an enormous amount of beneficent influence on the world of manuscripts for thirty years. Though the output of work published under his name is much smaller than Ker's, he had a hand in several of the most substantial scholarly enterprises of the period, above all the *Summary Catalogue of Western Manuscripts in the Bodleian Library at Oxford*, of which volume I (1953), the historical introduction, is by him.[9]

---

[8] Vol. I, covering the Vatican Library, appeared in 1934; vol. II, for Great Britain and Ireland, the next year (second edition 1972); vol. III, Italy from Ancona to Novara, in 1938. See Julian Brown, 'E.A. Lowe and Codices Latini Antiquiores', *Scrittura e Civiltà* 1 (1977), 177-97.

[9] A bibliography of his writings to 1975 by S.P. Hall is printed in his Festschrift, *Medieval Learning and Literature*, ed. J.J.G. Alexander and M.T. Gibson (Oxford, 1976), 423-9; a supplement is in the

If Ker was nominally a student of English Language and Literature and Hunt of Modern History, Roger A.B. (later Sir Roger) Mynors (1903-89) was most definitely a Classicist. The purest product of the Eton and Oxford tradition of classical learning, he was successively Fellow and Tutor at Balliol and Professor of Latin first at Cambridge and then at Oxford. But he also had, partly through close ties with M.R. James, a lifelong involvement with manuscripts—one which is evident in two great works of medieval scholarship, *Durham Cathedral Manuscripts to the End of the Twelfth Century* (Oxford, 1939) and *Catalogue of the MSS of Balliol College, Oxford* (Oxford, 1963). An achievement of equal magnitude was his long-term co-editorship of the Medieval Texts series begun by Nelson's of Edinburgh and taken over by Oxford; the distinction of his contributions to numerous volumes in that series would in itself amount to an important scholarly career (which however in his case includes also standard editions of half a dozen basic Latin authors, from Virgil on).[10]

The most palpable evidence of this heady atmosphere of stimulating collaboration is a card-file case in a cupboard at the entrance to Selden End of Duke Humfrey's Library (where manuscripts held by the Bodleian are consulted): the cards which are the nucleus of the first edition (1941) of Ker's *Medieval Libraries of Great Britain*.[11] The preface to this work provides at once the best introduction to Ker's approach and best explanation of his subsequent achievement.

---

catalogue of his memorial exhibition, *Manuscripts at Oxford*, ed. A.C. de la Mare and B.C. Barker-Benfield (Oxford, 1980), 147-8. His 1937 doctoral thesis was published only in 1984, edited and revised by Margaret Gibson, as *The Schools and the Cloister: The Life and Writings of Alexander Nequam (1157-1217)*.

[10] A memoir by Michael Winterbottom is forthcoming in the *Proceedings of the British Academy*.

[11] Royal Historical Society Texts and Handbooks no. 3, 1941; all reference will be to the second, much expanded edition of 1964, which is the one possessed by most libraries and scholars. Here the preface to the first edition is printed in a slightly revised form.

This recounts how Ker, Hunt, Mynors, Cheney, and a fifth collaborator, J.R. Liddell,[12] began to record on cards 'the actual words of inscriptions of ownership, some details of the evidence for provenance, if there is no inscription, medieval pressmarks, the dates and positions of inscriptions and pressmarks, names of individual owners and the survival of medieval binding' (p. viii). Though many of the cards are written by Hunt and Mynors as well as by Ker, it seems to have fallen to the latter to organize them into a format which resulted in one of the basic tools for the study of English medieval manuscripts. The method of organization, and the way in which the work has come to influence subsequent investigations in the entire area it covers, will be discussed below; at this point it should be noticed that the cast of mind exhibited by the thirty-two-year-old author of this 1941 Preface was in a way to shape much of his life's work. If, as has been maintained, M.R. James came to carry in his mind a kind of *bibliothèque imaginaire* of the books of medieval England,[13] the same could be said of Ker after spending a good deal of his apprenticeship years (so to speak) putting the *MLGB* enterprise into publishable form.

Not that the entire energies of the young scholar were taken up with this project; for several of his smaller pieces of the greatest interest to students of Old English date from this period. The primary vehicle for their publication was *Medium Ævum*, the journal of the Society for the Study of Medieval Languages and Literature in Oxford, begun in 1932. Ker contributed notes, short articles, or reviews to each of the first five volumes of this new periodical, the longest being a seven-page review of the 1933 facsimile publication, by R.W. Chambers and others, of *The Exeter Book of Old English Poetry*;[14] and in 1939, as well as reviewing Dobbie's work on *Caedmon's Hymn and Bede's Death-Song*, published there his discovery of a Hague MS (Koninklijke Bibliotheek 70.H.7) containing Cuthbert's Letter on the

---

[12] He did not remain in medieval studies, but taught English literature at Cairo and Alexandria and wrote novels and literary criticism.

[13] Pfaff (note 2), p. 172.

[14] *Medium Ævum* 2 (1933), 224-31.

Death of Bede which provides the base text for the now standard edition (by Roger Mynors) of that work.[15]

The value of *MLGB* for students of Anglo-Saxon matters is immense, even if arguably not quite as great as for those concerned with later MSS—simply because information about the 'libraries' that pre-Conquest books belonged to is somewhat less likely to have been preserved than about those holding later codices (not to mention that the great majority of the 'libraries' of medieval England were founded after the Conquest). For establishments with a good deal of post-Conquest self-consciousness about their earlier existence, however, such as Exeter, Worcester, Rochester, both Christ Church and St Augustine's at Canterbury, and in a slightly different way Durham, the meticulous assemblage of evidence in *MLGB* provides the essential starting point for relating the collections of, say, the late eleventh century with what remains identifiable at the present day.

So, for example, by the time Ker and his collaborators had finished their work, they had identified some 145 surviving books which had belonged to Exeter Cathedral; as is pointed out in the Preface (p. xiv), this includes 101 out of the 387 books listed in a catalogue of the cathedral library drawn up in 1506, ninety of which are now in the Bodleian.[16] But whoever drew up the early sixteenth-century list omitted all the books in Old English, including the Exeter Book itself;[17] whereas *MLGB*, which gives the predominant language of a manuscript where this is not Latin, notes fourteen wholly or significantly in the vernacular and a further eleven Latin books as (probably) among the gifts of Bishop Leofric (d. 1072). Thus in a very few minutes a student can put together from *MLGB* a succinct hand-list of what survives of the Exeter library as it existed by the end of the Anglo-Saxon period, while careful use of the highly condensed but

---

[15] *Bede's Ecclesiastical History of the English People*, ed. B. Colgrave and R.A.B. Mynors (Oxford, 1969), p. 579. Ker's note is in *Medium Ævum* 8 (1939), 40-4, his review of Dobbie pp. 76-9 of the same volume.

[16] This catalogue is printed in G. Oliver, *Lives of the Bishops of Exeter* (Exeter, 1861), 301-10.

[17] Perhaps because, as Ker quotes the earlier Exeter catalogue, '*nullius valoris reputantur*' (p. xiv).

intensely informative headnote material[18] makes it possible to ascertain
what can be known about that library before the Reformation.

A word should be added here about the *Supplement* to *MLGB*
edited by Andrew Watson and published in 1987.[19] Watson notes that
when Ker died in 1982 the typescript addenda and corrigenda of the
Supplement were on his desk, so to a considerable degree this must be
counted as one of Ker's works. As for quantitative change, 'The
present supplement adds, or occasionally reassigns, 451 MSS and 82
printed books, the largest single group being one of 34 manuscripts
owned by the Cambridge friars, the outcome of Ker's research in the
Vatican Library in the 1970s'.[20] More important even than these
changes, however, is the complete revision by Alan Piper of the section
on Durham, which had been the longest single section of *MLGB*: 34
books are added and 128 corrections made to previous listings. This
is the only part of the *Supplement* that can be used by itself; for all
other medieval libraries it has to be, as it were, interleaved with the
main work. In the case of Exeter (to return to the previous example),
four manuscripts wholly or partly of the eleventh century are added in
the *Supplement* (plus a fragment)—one being an Ælfric Grammar and
Glossary (Cambridge, University Library, MS. Hh.1.10) which in
earlier editions had merely been rejected as a Canterbury book without
being assigned positively. In short, *MLGB* is now properly used only
as a two-volume work, and indeed should best be regarded as a tool in
progress (even if no further supplements or versions are ever
published); for, as Watson stresses in his preface to the *Supplement*,
users 'should be aware that they may have to go behind the printed
texts, as it were, and consult the record cards on which these are
based .... Many of the cards bear all the facts necessary for making
an assessment of the evidence, for on them one can see the doubts,

---

[18] 'The smaller print below the heading refers to special studies of
each medieval library, medieval book-lists ..., [and] notes of books in
the library by John Leland and John Bale about the time of the
Dissolution ... ' (p. ix).

[19] As Royal Historical Society Guides and Handbooks 15; both first
and second editions counted as no. 3 in the series.

[20] Preface, p. vii.

hesitations and changes of mind from which the editors suffered and one can weigh the pros and cons' (pp. viii-ix).

In the same year as the first edition of *MLGB* was published, 1941, there was discovered a catalogue of the very important library at Worcester Cathedral made in 1622-3 by Patrick Young, Librarian to James I; this was edited and published, with a lengthy introduction, three years later by (Sir) Ivor Atkins and Ker.[21] Unfortunately, there is no preface, and no indication what each editor's share of the work was; but it is reasonable to infer that most of the information about Worcester itself—the personnel of the Chapter, the circumstances in which the books were housed—fell to Atkins, at that time Librarian there, while facts about the manuscripts themselves were mostly supplied by Ker.[22] Since Worcester was in the eleventh and twelfth centuries among the principal repositories of Anglo-Saxon learning, and since the library of the cathedral priory seems to have held, until the Dissolution (and even largely after, when the cathedral became one of the New Foundation), one of the richest collections of pre-twelfth century English manuscripts, a source which helped to make plain the condition of this collection in the early seventeenth century would have been welcome even if presented in simple transcript form. Treated as Ker and Atkins did, it becomes both a tool for the tracking down of individual Worcester books and a window into the antiquarian scholarship of the period between Matthew Parker and Humfrey Wanley (of whom more later).

The value of the work can be seen most succinctly in the table of manuscripts which, listed by Young, have since been alienated from Worcester (pp. 5-7). This indicates at a glance twenty-two MSS shown for the first time to be from Worcester, seven of which are of the Anglo-Saxon period. Perhaps the most important of these is Oxford, Bodleian Library, Hatton MS. 48, an eighth-century copy of the Rule

---

[21] *Catalogus librorum manuscriptorum bibliothecae Wigorniensis...* (Cambridge, 1944).

[22] Atkins (1869-1953), however, was himself a considerable scholar as well as a distinguished musician (Organist and Master of the Choristers at Worcester 1897-1950). He published several articles on eleventh-century subjects.

of St. Benedict on which Ker published in 1941 a strikingly laconic note.[23] Here, in under a thousand words, he demonstrates that an eleventh century binding leaf on which his argument hinges (the binding itself is of the twelfth or thirteenth century) is almost certainly to be assigned to Worcester on palaeographical grounds, and in showing this gives a summary impression of a Worcester MS of the time: 'At Worcester the scribes, when writing Latin, tended to make the belly of *a* fat and the neck short, and to finish off the end of a descender (*p*, *q*) with a heavy, short cross-stroke. The top of an ascender is much thicker than the shaft and forms a sort of blob: it is not split, as it often is in Exeter and Canterbury manuscripts'. The language is quite plain, but the impression conveyed is vivid; an illustration is less necessary than it would have been had the description been more technically couched.

Though much more could be said about the value of this collaborative undertaking, as about *MLGB*, we must pass on to one of Ker's greatest solo achievements, the appearance of which in 1957 was the mature product of much of his detailed investigations of the previous two decades: the *Catalogue of Manuscripts Containing Anglo-Saxon* (hereafter *CMCAS*).[24] It needs to be stressed at once that this is a book which can be disappointing if the title is not construed literally and frustrating unless the work is used with meticulous care. These two caveats aside, it becomes one of the greatest treasures for a student of things Anglo-Saxon.

The potential disappointment is clearly evident from a glance at the *CMCAS* entry for the MS just referred to, the Hatton 48 Rule of St.

---

[23] 'The Provenance of the Oldest Manuscript of the Rule of St. Benedict', *Bodleian Library Record* 1 (1941-9), 28-9. A partial facsimile had been published by E.A. Lowe in 1929: *Regula S. Benedicti. Specimina selecta e Codice Antiquissimo Oxoniensis*. For more recent discussion, and a possible wider context, see Patrick Sims-Williams, *Religion and Literature in Western England, 600-800* (Cambridge, 1990), 203-5.

[24] *CMCAS* was reprinted by Oxford University Press in 1990, with some supplementary material by Ker first published in *ASE* 5 (1977), 121-31. Addenda and corrigenda by Mary Blockley published in 1982 are reprinted and updated in the present volume.

Benedict. The total entry for this codex of major importance runs to seven lines and is headed 'Scribbles' followed by the date 's. ix or x': by which is meant, of course, that the only Old English words in the MS are scribbles in the margins, 'cnih' on f. 18v and 'cniht ic drink' on 42v ('In the word *drink* the *d* is upright and the *r* has a crooked second limb'). Two references, to Lowe's 1929 facsimile and Ker's 1941 note, conclude the information offered. By contrast, the two-volume collection of homilies, which are also among the Worcester books removed by Lord Hatton in the early 1640s and which ended up as Oxford, Bodleian Library, MSS. Hatton 113 and 114, gets eight and a half pages of detailed description and analysis.

This contrast represents, admittedly, extremes in scantiness or fullness of treatment, but may help to underline the fact that *CMCAS* tends to be useful in proportion to the amount of Old English contained in a given MS; and that therefore it is the 'big' vernacular codices for which it contains the largest amount of information. Even for these, it is necessary to pay close attention, for what is being described is always the Old English component. So the heading for Byrhtferth's Handbook (Oxford, Bodleian Library, MS. Ashmole 328) is perfectly straightforward in its date 's. xi med.', but that for Oxford, Bodleian Library, MS. Auct. D.2.16, a tenth-century gospel book from Landévennec in Brittany, poses a hazard in reading 's. xi^2'. This is because the vernacular aspects of the latter are the precious lists of books given to the church at Exeter by Bishop Leofric and of relics given by King Æthelstan, both preserved in texts of the second half of the eleventh century.

It has seemed necessary to emphasize these cautions precisely because the book is heavily used as a first work of reference about manuscripts; and indeed students are well advised to remember that it may be worth dipping into right away if one is looking for basic information about, say, a Cotton or Harleian MS or one from any collection which suffers from a similarly inadequate or antiquated catalogue. But the work is both much more complex in conception and much more exact in execution, and to use it to maximum advantage takes some effort. Nor is the user assisted at once by the Preface, which seems to start *in medias res*: 'Since 1833, when Kemble's *Beowulf* and Thorpe's *Caedmon* were published, English, German, and American scholars have edited or re-edited nearly the whole body of surviving Old English literature, apart from a not inconsiderable

number of homilies' (p. vii). Ker's point in noting this was to
acknowledge that 'the cataloguer's task has been greatly eased'; but
how that cataloguer has conceived his distinctive task is laid out only
on pp. xiv-xxiii of the Introduction—and after a few preliminary
paragraphs headed, significantly, 'Humfrey Wanley'. Herein lies the
point of meaningful entry to *CMCAS*: to be in effect a new version of
the magnificently titled *Antiquae Literaturae Septentrionalis liber alter,
seu Humphredi Wanleii Librorum Veterum Septentrionalium, qui in
Angliae Bibliothecis extant, nec non multorum Veterum Codicum
Septentrionalium alibi extantium Catalogus Historico-Criticus, cum
totius Thesauri Linguarum Septentrionalium sex Indicibus.*[25]

Humfrey Wanley (1672-1726) earns enduring distinction as the first
great modern student of English (and especially Anglo-Saxon)
manuscripts for two lasting accomplishments: that he was largely
responsible for putting together the Harleian collection of manuscripts
now in the British Library, and that he produced the notable catalogue
of Anglo-Saxon manuscripts just referred to.[26] In the course of the
latter work Wanley had described all but about a dozen of the
manuscripts known now to contain a considerable amount of Old
English; Ker notes the few exceptions, and emphasizes that Wanley
worked before the fire which destroyed or mutilated so many of the
Cottonian manuscripts in 1731. What he does not make plain, except
indirectly, is that a notable departure of *CMCAS* from Wanley's work

---

[25] Published in Oxford, 1705, as the second volume of George
Hickes's *Linguarum Veterum Septentrionalium Thesaurus
Grammatico-Criticus et Archaeologicus*.

[26] Two enjoyable accounts are a 1935 Oxford lecture by Kenneth
Sisam (to whom *CMCAS* is dedicated), published in his *Studies in Old
English Literature* (Oxford, 1953), 259-77, and ch. v of David C.
Douglas, *English Scholars 1660-1730*, 2nd ed. (London, 1951), 98-118.
It is rather surprising that Ker does not refer to the latter, as the first
edition had appeared in 1939. See now also P.L. Heyworth, ed., *The
Letters of Humfrey Wanley* (Oxford, 1989), and C.E. and Ruth C.
Wright, ed., *The Diary of Humfrey Wanley*, 2 vols (London, 1966).
Wanley also played a considerable, if not entirely clear, part in the
compilation of the great *Catalogi Manuscriptorum Angliae (CMA)* of
1697, about which more will be said presently.

is the inclusion of information about manuscripts in which there is only a small amount of Old English. This becomes vivid if one looks at the list on pp. xv-xix of 'the 189 manuscripts which are described in more or less detail' (itself usefully divided into twenty-nine written before 1000, one hundred thirty-three about 1000 and in the eleventh century, and twenty-seven about 1100 and later), for which the comparison with Wanley had been overt, and then notes that there are 412 entries in *CMCAS*—to be sure, sometimes more than one for a given manuscript.

Ker's fifty-page introduction is magisterial, including as it does the 'Notes on the Palaeography and History of the principal manuscripts' (pp. xxiii-lvi) which could make a highly useful separate publication. Subdivided into thirteen discrete sections on such matters as Letter-forms, Decoration, Ownership before 1540, and Sir Robert Cotton, it provides an extraordinarily condensed conspectus of information on many matters concerning the study of Anglo-Saxon manuscripts—but above all on their subsequent history, the aspect which perhaps lay closest to Ker's heart.

Consider for example pages liii-liv, a listing of some 'ninety of the principal OE manuscripts [which] became known to scholars or were in well-known private collections in the years between the Dissolution and the death of Joscelyn [Matthew Parker's Latin secretary, d. 1603]. I have listed them here according to the first known date in their post-Dissolution history'. Here one can see, among many points of interest, that two books are first known as belonging to Cranmer (from references always keyed to the Catalogue numbers) and one to William Cecil, that one was sent to Parker by John Jewel, and so on—a kind of micro-history of the preservation of the Anglo-Saxon past through its manuscripts from 1542 to 1603. Or again, in the section on Scribes and Scriptoria, there is a list (p. lvii) identifying among otherwise anonymous scribes—i.e., not those who have been distinctively identified, often by Ker himself[27]—twenty-one individual hands, or at

---

[27] E.g., 'Aldred the Scribe', *Essays and Studies* 28 (1942-3), 7-12; 'Old English Notes Signed "Coleman"', *Medium Ævum* 18 (1949), 29-31; and (but not until long after *CMCAS*), 'The Handwriting of Archbishop Wulfstan', in *England before the Conquest: Studies in Primary Sources Presented to Dorothy Whitelock*, ed. P. Clemoes and K. Hughes (Cambridge, 1971), 315-31.

least tightly distinctive types of writing, ranging from a hand 'written under the direction of King Alfred' to the thirteenth-century Worcester glossator of the well-named 'tremulous hand'.[28] Of course a great deal has been done along these lines since 1957: mostly by, it is safe to generalize, scholars whose copies of *CMCAS* are all dog-eared with wear.[29]

Among all of Ker's major works, the *CMCAS* is the one most exclusively devoted to matters Anglo-Saxon; but a full appreciation of it, and indeed of his approach as a whole, can be gained only by getting some familiarity with a project which was carried on concurrently: the 1952-3 Lyell Lectures in Bibliography, published by the Clarendon Press in 1960 as *English Manuscripts in the Century after the Norman Conquest* (hereafter *EMCNC*). The James P.R. Lyell Readership in Bibliography had been established only in 1951, and Ker was the first holder of it; the duties of the position were simply to deliver a course of not less than six lectures on subjects in some way related to collections of manuscripts in Oxford.[30] The initial lecture was concerned with the manuscripts which Lyell, a London solicitor who died in 1949, had left to the Bodleian; this was not included in the printed version, but rather appeared at the beginning of the introduction to the splendid catalogue of that collection which appeared in 1971.[31]

Of course the approach of a book which began as a course of lectures is very different from that of *CMCAS*, which is unambiguously a work of reference, to be defined entirely within its own terms. This

---

[28] On which see Ker's note, 'The Date of the "Tremulous" Worcester Hand', *Leeds Studies in English* 6 (1937), 28-9.

[29] Notable examples include T.A.M. Bishop, *English Caroline Minuscule* (Oxford, 1971) and recent articles by, *inter alios*, David Dumville, Michael Lapidge, and Teresa Webber.

[30] I am greatly indebted to Malcolm Parkes for particulars of these lectures and of how they related to the later printed version.

[31] A.C. de la Mare, *Catalogue of the Collection of Medieval Manuscripts Bequeathed to the Bodleian Library, Oxford, by James P.R. Lyell* (Oxford, 1971), xv-xxi. Lyell's bequest provided that the Library authorities could choose one hundred out of the more than 250 MSS he had collected; beyond that hundred, eleven were subsequently bought (the 'Lyell empt.' MSS).

said, it is astonishing to think that such a mass of detailed information as is contained in *EMCNC* could have been offered in a lecture format. There is no prefatory indication as to what, if anything, has been changed or added from the spoken version to the printed; but it is difficult to believe that even Ker, for whom oratorical spellbinding had little appeal,[32] would have concluded his lectures with the final words as printed, 'Thus the same "A1" readings are in the margins of three copies of Augustine on St. John, Hereford Cathedral,[MS.] P.IX.5, [Oxford,] Balliol College, [MS.] 6, and [Oxford,] Bodleian [Library, MS.] Auct. D.1.10'.

The opening words of the printed version lay out both a goal— 'In these lectures my principal aim is to describe the changes during the century after the Norman Conquest in the script of manuscripts written in England'—and a context: 'It is no exaggeration to say that a well-written English twelfth-century manuscript is something we have a good chance of being able to see in many of our towns, from Aberdeen to Exeter and from Aberystwyth to Colchester' (p. 1). This comprehensive sense of trying to see as a whole the relevant contents of all the libraries in Britain will underlie Ker's greatest, though unfinished, achievement, the *Medieval Manuscripts in British Libraries*, to be considered presently; it is therefore instructive to note its existence as early as 1952.

Central to Ker's exposition of the changes in script during the century after the Norman Conquest is his view of what happened at Christ Church, Canterbury which, as the primatial cathedral priory, was the crucial locus of cultural and political interaction between English and Normans in the decades after 1070 (when Lanfranc became archbishop). So in chapter V, Script, he lays out the characteristics of the Christ Church script with a precision which had often been lacking since M.R. James first gave the term wide currency.[33] Though some of these characteristics are found in contemporary Norman scriptoria,

---

[32] He has been described by Parkes as the only lecturer known to him who 'could give his lecture with his back to the audience without noticing it'.

[33] Most notably in his catalogue of the MSS of Trinity College, Cambridge, and in *Ancient Libraries of Canterbury and Dover* (Cambridge, 1903).

Ker asserted that 'There is no real equivalent of the Christ Church type of script on the Continent. It is the deliberate creation of the Christ Church scriptorium at the end of the eleventh century' (p. 28), and goes on to wonder 'Who at Canterbury made a pattern script out of the Norman script, and when'. Unlike that written by some Christ Church hands of the 1140s and later, this script gains rare words of complete approval as having 'just the right weight and proportions'. At St Augustine's, by contrast, the Norman influence is found to be less marked, with an English script of pre-Conquest type co-existing with examples of both the Christ Church script and a mixed script. A similar assessment is offered for Rochester, though there the influence of the Christ Church script was both more marked and more enduring.[34]

The keenness of Ker's eye is apparent in the consideration of certain scribal practices which form the matter of chapter VI. These include 'The Preliminaries to Writing' (especially pricking and ruling); 'Spacing of the Lines'—that is, 'the relation between the lines of writing and the blank spaces between the lines' (p. 44); 'Punctuation', where he maintains that English scribes were ahead of the Normans;[35] a brief paragraph on 'Signatures and Catchwords'; and 'Corrections and Alterations', illustrated largely by reference to the two mid-twelfth century Winchester Bibles, the Oxford, Bodley 'Auct.' Bible (MS. E. inf. 2) and that at Winchester Cathedral (MS. 17).[36]

These headings may indicate why the anonymous author of Ker's obituary notice in *The Times* referred to *English Manuscripts in the Century after the Norman Conquest* as the 'distilled essence of his more purely palaeographical learning'.[37] But of course it has had a much wider importance than merely palaeographical. For example, proof of the important and perhaps surprising fact that scribe A of Greater

---

[34] See Mary P. Richards, *Texts and Their Traditions in the Medieval Library of Rochester Cathedral Priory*, Transactions of the American Philosophical Society 78.3 (Philadelphia, 1988), p. x.

[35] This subject is further considered in appendix II, Punctuation in Carthusian and Cistercian Manuscripts of the Fifteenth Century (pp. 58-9).

[36] Walter Oakeshott, *The Two Winchester Bibles* (Oxford, 1981).

[37] *The Times,* 25 August 1982, p. 10.

Domesday either was English or had long lived in England is based on three characteristics of his hand, two of which were identified in *EMCNC* (and the third in *CMCAS*).[38] Indeed, the overall impact of this 'distilled essence of palaeographical learning' extends to many aspects of what is now generally called the history of the book.

After Ker's appointment as a Companion of the British Empire, 'for services to palaeography', was announced in the New Year's Honours List for 1979, he replied to a letter of congratulation, 'These things must seem rather queer to those who live across the Atlantic or the Channel. But it is an agreeable oddity for recipients—and honourable. I follow Francis Wormald in this, and with about as much claim to have given services to palaeography—he to art history and liturgical studies, I to the history of medieval books, if anything'.[39] Of course he was being overly modest in this self-estimate, but it does show where his own sense of the primary weight of his work lay. The clearest demonstration of this is the enterprise to which he devoted most of the last two decades of his life.

The first volume of *Medieval Manuscripts in British Libraries* was published in 1969, and covered collections in London which fell under the definition stated in the Preface, those 'hitherto uncatalogued or barely catalogued in print'. The statement there that he was asked to undertake this project by 'the sub-committee of SCONUL [Standing Committee on National and University Libraries] concerned with manuscripts' must be balanced against other indications in Ker's work up until then; it is hard to believe that such an ambition would not have formed itself even without committee initiative.

The preface begins with an enumeration of the fifty-one institutions in Great Britain with collections of fifty or more medieval books in manuscript—most of which are said to be 'well or adequately described in printed catalogues' ranging in date from those of the Harleian Collection (largely by Humfrey Wanley) and of Durham Cathedral (by Thomas Rud who died in 1732, though the book was not printed until 1825) to that of the Balliol College MSS by Roger Mynors (1963). By

---

[38] A.R. Rumble, 'The Domesday Manuscripts: Scribes and Scriptoria', in *Domesday Studies*, ed. J.R. Holt (Woodbridge, 1987), 79-99 at 84 n. 28.

[39] In a letter to the present author, 11 March 1979.

contrast the smaller collections, those of fewer than fifty manuscripts, are said to be 'widely dispersed and their cataloguing has progressed very little since M.R. James died'. The coupling of Wanley's and James's names on the same page is highly suggestive. As has been noticed, Wanley is known to have had a hand in the compilation of the *Catalogi Manuscriptorum Angliae* which appeared under the name of Edward Bernard in 1697.[40] This venerable attempt at a kind of union list of all the medieval manuscripts known in British libraries at that time had long offered a model tantalizingly complete in conception and (understandably) inadequate in execution. From the late nineteenth century on, attempts more or less systematic were made to provide 'modern' catalogues, or at least consistent coverage, for the major collections in Cambridge, Oxford, and the British Museum, as well as a few other places.[41] James, who took as a principle not to devote his energies to cataloguing manuscripts for which there existed a published description of any adequacy at all, had made a start at treating some smaller collections by describing those at Wisbech and Ipswich, as well as St. George's Chapel, Windsor.[42] But the contents of the great majority of the smaller collections of medieval manuscripts were known only by hearsay and happenstance.

The resulting gap is the one Ker's enterprise was intended to fill. As his preface further states, 'My aim has been to proceed alphabetically by libraries from Aberdeen (where not everything was catalogued by James) to York. It is an aim which can be independent

---

[40] This is the way the commonly used abbreviation is normally expanded. In fact the title is *Catalogi librorum manuscriptorum Angliae et Hiberniae in unum collecti cum indice alphabetico* (Oxford, 1697).

[41] The *Summary Catalogue of Western Manuscripts in the Bodleian Library at Oxford* began to appear in 1895, the same year as the first of James's catalogues of collections in the Cambridge colleges. 'Modern' catalogues of collections in the British Museum (now Library), i.e. of the Additional MSS, were appearing from 1843 on, but were fairly exiguous until roughly the turn of the century; the great catalogue of a BM Collection, that of the Royal MSS, by G.F. Warner and J.P. Gilson, was published in 1921.

[42] Pfaff (note 2), pp. 287-8.

of my own capacity to achieve it from end to end. In beginning, in fact, with London I have not abandoned the alphabet, but have done what lies nearest to hand. I hope that "Aberdeen-Liverpool" and "Maidstone-York" will fit into volumes of about the same size as the present volume'. This was the conception; for all libraries with the major, and obvious, exclusions of the British Library, the National Libraries of Scotland and Wales, the Bodleian, and the University Library at Cambridge, *MMBL* 'is intended to provide information about manuscripts, other than muniments and binding fragments, written before about 1500, in Latin or a western European language, either by reference to an existing catalogue or by my own description'. In practice this meant that in many collections only a few manuscripts were catalogued by Ker, and that in consequence one finds oneself hoping that a particular manuscript has not been previously described or described only cursorily so that he would have had a go at it.

Such is the case with, for example, London, Gray's Inn MS. 3, which was listed in *CMA* and was at that Inn of Court since probably the early seventeenth century. Like sixteen of its fellow books, MS. 3 was annotated some time between 1509 and, most likely, 1540, by a writer whom, Ker says, 'it is probably best to consider ... as a Chester, or at least a Cheshire man, perhaps a displaced monk, who collected books from the neighbouring religious houses immediately after the Dissolution' (p. 51). This hypothesis is strengthened by the pressmark in MS. 3, which is that of the Benedictines of Chester; and this in turn provides a context for consideration of the contents of the codex, lives of seventy-odd saints whose days fall between 9 February and 29 June. Furthermore, the sixteenth-century annotator has included a table of contents for three further volumes, apparently not extant, which gives us an overall sense of the saints' lives available to the monks of St. Werburg's at least by the fourteenth century (the date of the pressmark) and probably by the early twelfth, when the manuscript was written. In turn, this enables us to have a new point of comparison for study of the famous Fell and Cotton-Corpus cycles of saints' lives of the eleventh and twelfth centuries.[43]

---

[43] Respectively, Salisbury Cathedral MS. 222 (*olim* Bodl. Fell MSS 1 and 4) and London, British Library, MS. Cotton Nero E.i plus Cambridge, Corpus Christi College, MS. 9.

Pages vii-xiii of the preface to this volume contain Ker's most detailed statement of his mature formula (what he called 'points of method') for manuscript cataloguing. The most important part is the discussion of the nomenclature of later medieval hands, which has had a lasting impact for students of that period; indeed, it is their needs which are primarily addressed by most of this preface, but these few pages should be read by anyone who sets out to study a medieval manuscript.[44]

When volume II of *MMBL* appeared in 1977, it covered only as far as Keele rather than the Liverpool destination originally proposed—just one letter of the alphabet, but since II as it is runs to xliii + 999 pages and the Lampeter through Liverpool section of volume III to 316, the alteration in plan was unavoidable. Partly this is because of the one hundred seventy pages devoted to what is in effect a new catalogue of the MSS of Eton College, alluded to above; partly, it may be suspected, because Ker had hit his fullest stride and in the challenge of the variegated collections he encountered in this itinerary allowed himself a bit more amplitude than earlier in his career.

For those interested in things Anglo-Saxon, volume II is important chiefly for the description, at once succinct and highly detailed, of the Exon Domesday (Exeter Cathedral MS. 3500). This was made necessary by the disarray into which the 520-odd leaves had fallen before they were put into some order by the Chapter Clerk, Ralph Barnes, so that the work could be printed by the Record Commissioners in 1816. Barnes's account of his labors had been purchased for the Chapter Library in 1974; on the basis of this Ker was able to construct a table showing Barnes's letter-marks followed by the subjects, make-up, and new and old leaf numbers for each section. He also established a broader context for the suggestion he had made the previous year in his contribution to the Festschrift for Richard Hunt, that two of the quires of the Exon Domesday are in a hand very like

---

[44] There is some useful amplification of the 'points of method' on pp. vii-viii of the preface to vol. II (1977).

that of a professional scribe who wrote many of the early books of Salisbury Cathedral.[45]

Ker's fatal accident—he fell while bilberrying in the Highlands of his native Scotland—happened in August of 1982 just as he had read the proofs of roughly a sixth of volume III of *MMBL*, published in 1983. As Andrew Watson, his literary executor, notes in the preface (of which he wrote everything except the first paragraph), all the descriptions save one are Ker's, and the work follows exactly the pattern of its predecessors—though instead of getting to York as originally planned, it stops at Oxford.[46]   Again, the size of the collections not, or cursorily, catalogued in places beginning L through O (of which Liverpool and Manchester have by far the largest number) made it necessary that the volume end with MSS many of which Ker had known for a long time: those owned by the colleges at Oxford but for one reason or another not included in H.O. Coxe's *Catalogus Codicum Manuscriptorum . . . in collegiis aulisque Oxoniensibus* (1852) or in later enterprises like the 1963 Mynors catalogue of Balliol MSS already mentioned or the magnificent treatment by Malcolm Parkes of the Keble College manuscripts.[47]

As it happens, few pre-twelfth-century manuscripts are described in this volume. An important exception is the early eleventh-century Gospels in the celebrated Kederminster library at Langley Marish parish church (now London, British Library, MS. Loans 11). Here

---

[45] 'The Beginnings of Salisbury Cathedral Library', in *Medieval Learning and Literature* (see n. 9 above), 23-49 at 34-5, and pl. IIIa. For the overall Domesday context, see Pierre Chaplais, 'William of Saint-Calais and the Domesday Survey', in *Domesday Studies* (see n. 37), 65-77 at 66-7 and 75; that of late eleventh-century books is treated by Dr. Teresa Webber in her forthcoming monograph on the early Salisbury scriptorium.

[46] Fortunately the work is near completion. In 1992 Volume IV, covering Paisley to York, was published, under the names of Ker (who had drafted many of the descriptions) and A.J. Piper (who both edited these and described many of the MSS *ab initio*). A final volume, of addenda and indexes, is envisaged.

[47] M.B. Parkes, *The Medieval Manuscripts of Keble College, Oxford* (London, 1979).

Ker's description shows his often astonishing capacity for awareness of what other scholars were doing and for including them in his own network of inquiry: in this case both correcting a very minor point in one of T.A.M. Bishop's fine investigations of eleventh-century manuscripts, where a fragmentary leaf of a Gospel book in private hands had been mentioned as being at Winchester (whereas it was at Salisbury),[48] and including notice of a new fragment in Oslo which Lilli Gjerløw had told him about.

On the whole, there could be said of volume III of *MMBL* what Christopher Hohler wrote in a review of the second volume:

> This is the second volume of a stupendous monument of scholarship, which is certain to keep its author's memory in benediction and reflect lasting distinction on the Scottish nation. It is hard to find adequate words of praise for a work which is new, which will never lose its value, and which is so well done that it will not have to be done again. It is not only that this priceless book constantly tells one that a manuscript of some importance of whose existence one was unaware is or until recently was . . . in some collection of which one has never heard: . . . it gives its contents in such detail that one can nearly always judge precisely how far it would be worth one's while to look at it oneself.[49]

In view of the range of Ker's achievements, as laid out in very brief compass in the preceding pages,[50] multiplication of such tributes is scarcely necessary. It should be sufficient to cite the comment made by Francis Wormald (introducing a lecture by him) as long ago as the late 1950s—that is, after *CMCAS* but before the second edition of

---

[48] 'The Copenhagen Gospel Book', *Nordisk Tidskrift för Bok- och Biblioteksväsen* 54 (1967), 33-41, at 40.

[49] *Journal of the British Archaeological Association* 131 (1978), 143.

[50] Of course, by no means all have been even mentioned—not even all that have special interest to Anglo-Saxonists. An overview of all such writings of his can be obtained by a careful look at Ker's bibliography (n. 1 above).

MLGB or any of *MMBL* had appeared—that 'in the history of manuscript studies in this country three men were outstanding, Humfrey Wanley, M.R. James, and Neil Ker, and that to mention one in connection with the others was to give an indication of his stature'.[51] Those who knew Neil Ker can imagine the look of embarrassment mingled with amusement which would have crossed his face at that moment; but it is a judgment which it is not possible to dispute.[52]

---

[51] Quoted by Andrew Watson in *oratio obliqua* in the preface to Ker's collected essays, *Books, Collectors and Libraries* (n.1 above), p. x.

[52] The network of affection and shared reminiscence which binds Ker's many friends, themselves of a variety of ages and nationalities, is palpable to anyone who has tried to look at his work as a whole. For help with the present essay I am grateful to Malcolm Parkes, Alan Piper, William Stoneman, and Andrew Watson; numerous other friends have over the years enriched both my memories of and my feeling of indebtedness to the subject of these pages.

Further Addenda and Corrigenda to N.R. Ker's *Catalogue*

Mary Blockley

'A Supplement to "Catalogue of Manuscripts Containing Anglo-Saxon"'[1] by N.R. Ker adds fifteen new or recovered items to his *Catalogue of Manuscripts Containing Anglo-Saxon*, describes additional leaves found belonging to six manuscripts previously listed, and notes twelve changes in location and pressmark. The past decade has added at least sixteen items to the twelve addenda and corrigenda in the original version of this supplement to Ker's own 1976 supplement to his 1957 *Catalogue*. It is likely that some published items have unfortunately been overlooked and that other newly-recovered items will come to light. The present supplement to his supplement calls attention to six manuscripts containing Old English that have been identified or uncovered since his article was published, corrects an error in the identification of the text described in item 414, supplies an omission in item 249, and calls attention to nine verse-texts included in the *Catalogue* or 'Supplement', but not identified as such. My comments follow or supplement the format of his *Catalogue* and 'Supplement'.[2]

Corrigenda

12. Over 100 dry-point glosses to Aldhelm in Beinecke MS. 401, a Phillipps manuscript purchased by Yale in 1969, have been

---

[1] *ASE* 5 (1976), 121-31. The supplement is reviewed by T.F. Hoad (*Review of English Studies* 29 [1978], 71-73), H.R. Loyn (*Journal of Ecclesiastical History* 29 [1978], 215-16), and J.E. Cross (*Notes and Queries* 222 [1977], 166-70).

[2] I would like to thank Fred C. Robinson and Carl T. Berkhout for reading a draft of this supplement and for advice on several points.

edited by Philip G. Rusche at Yale University, as announced in *Old English Newsletter* 24 (1991), 34.

34., 40., 52. Scratched glosses unrecorded by Ker or Meritt in these manuscripts are edited by R.I. Page in 'More Old English Scratched Glosses', *Anglia* 97 (1979), 27-45.

38. Add the text appearing on p. 142, described by William P. Stoneman in 'Another Old English Note signed "Coleman"', *Medium Ævum* 56 (1987), 78-82, ill.

91. On f. 252v, to the left of the gloss to Psalm 142.8 appears a parallel to *Paris Psalter* 142, 9, 1-4; identified as being from a common ancestor of that text by Patrick P. O'Neill in 'Another Fragment of the Metrical Psalms in the Eadwine Psalter', *Notes and Queries* 233 (1988), 434-36.

107. (A3) The translation of the proverb *Amicus tam propre longe bonus est* alliterates, though it does not scan, as verse:

> freond deah feor ge neor;
> bið near nyttre.

112. This fragment, reported as missing in Ker's 'Supplement', remains in the Bodleian Library as MS. Broxbourne 90.28. The binding is classified separately as Broxbourne 9.12.

116. 'Unnoticed Punctuation in the Exeter Book', D.S. McGovern, *Medium Ævum* 52 (1983), 90-99.

131. (d) One of the scribbles scans, though it does not properly alliterate:

> Eglaf *comes* and his broðer Vlf.[3]

---

[3] The text cannot be excluded from the canon because of the Latin word *comes*; *rex* appears twice in *Elene* (610, 1041) and *Aldhelm* contains Greek as well as Latin words. The alliteration is faulty, but there are examples of off-verses alliterating in the final stressed syllable in *Maldon* 75b and 288b, both, like this verse, involving names. The

165. Identified as metrical by Fred C. Robinson in 'Old English Literature In Its Most Immediate Context', *Old English Literature in Context: Ten Essays*, ed. John Niles (London, 1980), 24, is the line written in the margin of fol. 255:

ðvs beda ðe broema boecere cueð.

181. The colophon *wulfwi me wrat* is, if regarded as verse, a Sievers type E half-line.[4]

229. Identified as metrical by Robinson in Madeleine M. Bergman's 'Supplement to *A Concordance to The Anglo-Saxon Poetic Records*', *Mediaevalia* 8 (1985) [for 1982], 9-52 at 14, and there printed:

Hwæt! Ic eallfeala ealde sæge.

Ker had noted the similarity of the line to *Beowulf* 869.

---

runic inscriptions Thornhill I and II have double alliteration in the off-verse, and Great Urswick i alliterates only on the final stress; the three runic inscriptions all involve proper names. Is it possible that 'the Scandinavian element' Ker notes in the Thorney *Liber Vitæ* may account for the alliterative faults in some of these pieces? [Norse examples are *Þrymskviða* lines 1 and 91, *Eriksmál* 19, *Vǫlospá* stanza 19, line 1, stanza 64, line 2 and elsewhere.] The construction of the Thorney line suggests a metrical intention: compare *Brunanburh* 2b: *and his broðor eac* [3a: *Eadmund æþeling*] with the prose summary found in the Canterbury Epitome *and Eadmund his broðer*, added to the account in London, British Library, MS. Cotton Domitian A. viii (MS F in *Two of the Saxon Chronicles Parallel*, ed. Charles Plummer and John Earle (Oxford, 1892), 107, entry for 937). Elsewhere in the prose portion of the *Chronicle* the proper name precedes the terms of relationship.

[4] The participation of the syllable with secondary stress in the alliteration is paralleled by *Beowulf* 1584a: *lāðlicu lāc*. See the colophon below (item 292). Ordinarily, isolated half-lines are not credited as being verse, but see A. J. Bliss, 'Some Unnoticed Lines of Old English Verse', *Notes and Queries* 216 (1971), 404.

249. Kenneth and Celia Sisam, *The Salisbury Psalter* (EETS os 242 [1959], 52-53, n. 3) note a metrical translation of a marginal Latin gloss to 17[51]. *Omnis rex in antiquis diebus aput Iudeos nominabatur Christus* is rendered:

Wæs mid Iudeum on geardagum
ealra cyninga gehwelc Cristus nemned.

Also, see Patrick O'Neill's 'A Lost Old-English Charter Rubric: The Evidence for the Regius Psalter', *Notes and Queries* 231 (1986), 292-94.

256. For fol. 107r, note three additional partial items in Phillip Pulsiano's 'A New Anglo-Saxon Gloss in the *Liber Scintillarum*', *Notes and Queries* 229 (1984), 152-53.

292. The second colophon, appearing at the end of John, was identified as 'a poetical distich' by Albert S. Cook, *Biblical Quotations in Old English Prose Writers* (London, 1898), lv:

Hæfe nu boc awritne, bruca mid willa,
symle mið soðum gileafa; sibb is eghwæm leofost.

331. Joyce Hill identifies the marginalia on f. 86 of Hatton 114 as a note by Coleman in 'Ælfric's "silent days"', *Leeds Studies in English* 16 (1985), p. 121.

369. Stephen Morrison increases Ker's count of 'about 50' to 109 glosses in 'On Some Noticed and Unnoticed Old English Scratched Glosses', *English Studies* 68 (1987), 209-13.

373B. A boundary survey on ff. 140v-41v has a debased but unmistakable 'verse intention' according to Peter Kitson, 'Some Unrecognized Old English and Anglo-Latin Verse', *Notes and Queries* 232 (1987), 147-51.

394. Not noted by Ker is a *writ þus* at the foot of fol. 63v, described by L.G. Whitbread in 'A Scribal Jotting from Medieval English', *Notes and Queries* 228 (1983), 198-99.

414. *For* LORD'S PRAYER *read* CREED; for MLN 4 *read* 5. The text appears on p. 138, not 137.[5]

415. Ker identifies these lines as a 'maxim'; like *Maxims I* and *II*, the lines are verse:

A scæl gelæred smið swa he gelicost mæg
be bisne wyrcan, butan he bet cunne.

417. The edition of the fragment described in Ker's 'Supplement' has appeared: Bella Schauman and Angus Cameron, 'A Newly-Found Leaf of Old English from Louvain', *Anglia* 95 (1977), pp. 283-312, ill. The location of the Omont leaf is now Louvain-la-Neuve, Université Catholique de Louvain, Centre Général de Documentation, Fragmenta H. Omont 3; see Audrey L. Meaney, 'Variant Versions of Old English Medical Remedies and the Compilation of Bald's *Leechbook*', *ASE* 13 (1984), p. 243.

Addenda

442. Oxford, Bodleian Library, MS. Hatton 42. A gloss *þus niw* to *in nouo [testamento]* on folio 49r of *Collectio Canonum Hibernensis*, s. xi, printed by P.J. Lucas in 'MS. Hatton 42: Another Manuscript Containing Old English', *Notes and Queries* 224 (1979), 8.

---

[5] Napier prints the text from a transcript sent him by W. M. Lindsay and describes its position in the manuscript as falling between a 'calendar of Saint's Days' and a prayer to Æthelthryth. Ker describes the first of these as 'directions for Lenten processions and litanies for each day of the week'; otherwise, his report is substantially the same as Napier's. The text is a unique version of the shorter confession that he terms the Apostles' Creed and which the Anglo-Saxons called *se læssa creda*. The other prose translations are Ælfrician and the verse translation *The Creed* follows the form of this confession. The longer Nicene Creed, or *mæssecreda*, is also translated by Ælfric and by the 'tremulous hand' of Worcester. Ker notes 7 items in his *Catalogue* (Index I, *Creeds*. p. 522 gives 6; the cross-reference to *Glosses* adds one more to these).

[423.] University of Glasgow, Hunter MS. U.3.2., fol. 210v. Inscription (s. xiii) in margin of Psalter (s. xii) providing directions for the preparation and use of an amulet. The charm to be inscribed 'seems to be a corrupted form of OE': *usy+begete+agala+lentotan +domnes+cibu+glaes*. The editors print plausible normalized Old English forms for all words but *cibu*, which they derive from Latin *cibus*. Printed by Jane Hetherington Brown and Linda Ehrsam Voigts, *Old English Newsletter*, vol. 14, no. 1 (Fall, 1980), pp. 12-13.

[424.] The manuscript discovery announced in 1982 is now published with facsimiles as *Fifty-Six Ælfric Fragments: The Newly-Found Copenhagen Fragments of Ælfric's Catholic Homilies* (Publications of the English Institute, 14 (1986)), edited by Else Fausbøll.

[425.] Glosses unmentioned in Ker or his 'Supplement' in a 'poetic miscellany of the mid-eleventh century' are edited and discussed by Michael Lapidge in 'Some Old English Sedulius Glosses from BN Lat. 8092', *Anglia* 100 (1982), 1-17; see additionally Patrick O'Neill, 'Further Old English Glosses on Sedulius in BN Lat. 8092', *Anglia* 107 (1989), 415.

[426.] A binding fragment in a copy of Thomas Elyot's *The Castel of Helthe* (STC 7649) is described and illustrated by Richard W. Clement in 'An Anglo-Saxon Fragment at the Folger Shakespeare Library', *Old English Newsletter* 22 (1989), 56-57.

[427.] Though Ker explicitly excluded complete descriptions of cartularies containing Old English from his *Catalogue* (p. xiv), he briefly mentions several. He knew, but did not single out for attention, the text in the Canterbury Cathedral archives recently edited as 'The Fonthill Letter' by Simon Keynes in *Words, Texts and Manuscripts: Studies in Anglo-Saxon Culture Presented to Helmut Gneuss*, ed. Michael Korhammer *et al.* (Woodbridge and Rochester, NY, 1992), pp. 53-97, ill. The shelfmark of the Fonthill Letter is Canterbury, Dean and Chapter, Chart. Ant. C. 1282 (Red Book, no. 12).

[428.] The bibliography for 1991 appearing in the *Old English Newsletter* 23 (1992), 21, lists an Aldhelm fragment sold as lot 33 at

Sotheby's on December 6, 1988. Henry Woudhuysen (p. 311) offers the following description:

> *33 ST ALDHELM OF MALMESBURY, *De laude Virginitatis*: bifolium from an ill. MS. on vellum in Latin and Old English, perhaps Worcester, late eighth or early ninth century. Text includes seventeen Kentish glosses, tenth century. £55,000 to Quaritch, now in the Schøyen Collection, London/Oslo, MS 197.

Surviving Booklists from Anglo-Saxon England

Michael Lapidge

In our attempts to understand the mental world of the Anglo-Saxons, and to interpret the literature which they have bequeathed to us, there is one tool of interpretation which allows perhaps a surer estimation than any other, and that is knowledge of the books which the Anglo-Saxons themselves knew and studied. But the attempt to acquire an overall understanding of what books were known to the Anglo-Saxons is no easy matter,[1] for it requires the judicious assessment of information gleaned from a variety of sources, none of them easily controlled. It must begin, obviously, with comprehensive knowledge of the contents of the surviving manuscripts known to have been written or owned in Anglo-Saxon England.[2] This knowledge must then be augmented in various ways, but principally by the identification of sources used by Anglo-Saxon authors writing either in Latin or in English. Such identification may be relatively straightforward in the case of Latin authors such as Aldhelm and Bede who frequently name their sources, but it can be a lengthy and painstaking business in the case of a widely read English author such as the (so-called) Old English

---

[1] There is a preliminary essay by J.D.A. Ogilvy, *Books known to the English, 597-1066* (Cambridge, Mass., 1967). This work, however, is slovenly and unreliable (particularly where the author refers to manuscript evidence), and cannot be consulted with confidence on any point; cf. the review by H. Gneuss, *Anglia* 89 (1971), 129-34.

[2] An excellent (and indispensable) beginning in this direction is H. Gneuss, 'A Preliminary List of Manuscripts written or owned in England up to 1100', *ASE* 9 (1981), 1-60. It is much to be hoped that Gneuss's preliminary list will serve as the basis for an eventual catalogue of the contents of all surviving Anglo-Saxon manuscripts.

Martyrologist,[3] who seldom specifies his sources. Until the sources used by Anglo-Saxon authors have all been identified, and the surviving Anglo-Saxon manuscripts catalogued, it is not possible to form a complete or accurate notion of what books were known and studied in Anglo-Saxon England; but it is welcome news that a number of scholars in different countries have begun to collaborate in the effort to achieve this distant but important goal.[4]

In the meantime there is one source—hitherto insufficiently explored—which can provide a valuable index of what books were available in Anglo-Saxon England: namely the various booklists and inventories which record the contents of Anglo-Saxon libraries or the gifts of donors to these libraries. Although these booklists—some thirteen in number—have all previously been printed, they have never been collected and have not been studied systematically in the attempt to identify their contents. I have re-edited these various booklists below, and have provided each booklist with detailed commentary, establishing where possible the identity of each item; in a separate Appendix I provide an alphabetical list of those identifications which may be regarded as certain. This list will provide some indication of what books and authors were known in Anglo-Saxon England, but I should stress that its evidence must always be used in combination with information derived from the contents of surviving Anglo-Saxon manuscripts and from identifiable sources of Anglo-Latin and Old English texts.

The booklists edited here are of various kinds: some are wills, some are lists of donations. Some, however, are inventories of libraries. Study of the contents of early medieval libraries necessitates some awareness of their physical arrangement and furniture. The

---

[3] See J.E. Cross, 'On the Library of the Old English Martyrologist', *Learning and Literature in Anglo-Saxon England*, ed. Michael Lapidge and Helmut Gneuss (Cambridge, 1985), pp. 227-49.

[4] See the reports in *OEN* 16.2 (1983), 58-69, and 17.1 (1983), 20-2. At a conference held at the University of Leeds on 24 March 1984 a committee (under the chairmanship of J.E. Cross) was formed to co-ordinate work on the sources used by Anglo-Saxon authors and to supervise the collection and eventual publication of such material. See also my *Postscript 1993* at the end of the article.

library as we know it today—a spacious room with bookstacks or standing presses, readers' tables and lecterns—simply did not exist in the early Middle Ages.[5] Books were normally housed in a book-chest or book-cupboard (*armarium*[6] or *arca libraria*[7]). Books could have been kept in *armaria* whether they were owned privately by (say) kings,[8] wealthy aristocrats[9] or secular clerics, or corporately, as by a

---

[5] See J.W. Clark, *The Care of Books*, 2nd ed. (Cambridge, 1902), pp. 51-94, and E. Lehmann, *Die Bibliotheksräume der deutschen Klöster im Mittelalter* (Berlin, 1957), pp. 2-7.

[6] *Ibid.* pp. 72-7.

[7] As evidence for the early Anglo-Saxon period, note Aldhelm's *enigma* on the *arca libraria* (no. lxxxix): *Aldhelmi Opera*, ed. R. Ehwald, MGH, Auct. antiq. 15 (Berlin, 1919), 138.

[8] There is little evidence for libraries owned by Anglo-Saxon kings. King Aldfrith of Northumbria (685-705) had a distinguished reputation for learning, was the dedicatee of Aldhelm's massive *Epistola ad Acircium*, and on one occasion sold eight hides of land in return for a magnificent manuscript of cosmographical writings (*cosmographiorum codice*) which Benedict Biscop had acquired in Rome (see below, n. 39); but we know nothing of Aldfrith's personal library. In the latter part of his reign King Alfred (871-99) was actively engaged in translating various Latin works into English, and must presumably have assembled a royal library of some size; but as to its contents we have no certain information (see S. Keynes and M. Lapidge, *Alfred the Great* [Harmondsworth, 1983], p. 214, n. 26). King Athelstan is well known as a donor of books to various churches (see S. Keynes, 'King Athelstan's Books', *Learning and Literature in Anglo-Saxon England*, ed. M. Lapidge and H. Gneuss [Cambridge, 1985], pp. 143-201), but, again, there is no evidence for a royal library in Athelstan's reign. A twelfth-century writer, Adelard of Bath, refers at one point to a book on hunting owned by Harold Godwinson (see C.H. Haskins, 'King Harold's Books', *EHR* 37 [1922], 398-400), but the book cannot be identified, and a single book does not in any case make a library. By contrast, there is abundant evidence for the royal libraries of Charlemagne, his son Louis the Pious, and his grandson Louis the German: evidence brought to light by Bernhard Bischoff, *Mittelalterliche Studien*, 3 vols. (Stuttgart, 1966-81) III, 149-69 ('Die

monastery.[10]   In the case of a monastery, however, books were needed for various purposes: school-books for the monastic classroom, service-books for the liturgical performance of mass and Office, legendaries for reading aloud in the refectory,[11] monastic rules and

---

Hofbibliothek Karls des Grossen'), 170-86 ('Die Hofbibliothek unter Ludwig dem Frommen') and 187-212 ('Bücher am Hofe Ludwigs des Deutschen und die Privatbibliothek des Kanzlers Grimalt'); see also R. McKitterick, 'Charles the Bald (823-877) and his Library: the Patronage of Learning', *EHR* 95 (1980), 28-47.

[9] I know of no evidence for libraries owned by Anglo-Saxon noblemen, although some, such as Ælfric's patron the ealdorman Æthelweard, must surely have possessed some number of books. By contrast, there is abundant evidence for libraries of continental, Carolingian noblemen; see P. Riché, 'Les Bibliothèques de trois aristocrates laïcs carolingiens', *Le moyen âge* 69 (1963), 87-104.

[10] In the case of Benedictine monks all property (including books) was owned corporately; no monk was permitted to own so much as a book or pen: 'Ne quis praesumat aliquid dare aut accipere sine iussione abbatis neque aliquid habere proprium: nullam omnino rem, neque codicem, neque tabulas, neque graphium, sed nihil omnino' (*Regula S. Benedicti*, ch. 33). Bear in mind, however, that this stipulation would not pertain to colleges of secular canons and the like; cf. my remarks concerning Ælberht and Alcuin, below, p. 106.

[11] Some idea of what books were read at mealtimes in the refectory may be gleaned from a twelfth-century list from Durham: 'Hii sunt libri qui leguntur ad collationem: Vitae patrum; Diadema monachorum; Effrem cum vitis Egiptiorum; Paradisus; Speculum; Dialogus; Pastoralis eximius liber; Ysidorus de summo bono; Prosper de contemplatiua uita; liber Odonis; Iohannes Cassianus decem Collationes' (*Catalogi Bibliothecarum Antiqui*, ed. G. Becker (Bonn, 1885), p. 245). When we encounter some of these titles in pre-Conquest booklists—especially the *Vitas patrum*, Gregory the Great's *Dialogi* and *Regula pastoralis*, Julianus Pomerius's *De uita contemplatiua*, Isidore's *Sententiae* and Cassian's *Collationes*—there is some presumption that they may have been used for refectory reading.

martyrologies for reading at chapter,[12] and reading-books for the private meditation and study of the monks.[13] There may often have been a separate *armarium* at each of these locations;[14] and the total contents of all *armaria* could be thought to constitute a monastic library's holdings. An inventory or booklist, therefore, might be an account of a monastery's entire holdings; on the other hand, it might simply be a record of the contents of one particular *armarium*. Thus, of the booklists edited below it is clear that nos. VI and VII are simple lists of service-books; nos. IV and IX lists of books used in the classroom; and no. XII an inventory of an *armarium commune* containing books for the monks' private study and meditation.

As long as libraries were relatively small, it was possible merely to list the contents of the separately located *armaria*, if indeed any record were needed; in such cases the record need only have been a simple list or inventory. Such inventories as survive are sometimes organized (in the sequence bibles, Church Fathers, theology, classical authors, and so on); more often the books are listed randomly, as they came to hand. From the late eleventh century onwards, however, libraries grew considerably in size, so that the common store of books was typically numbered in the hundreds and housed in many *armaria*.

---

[12] See the remarks of H. Gneuss, 'Liturgical Books in Anglo-Saxon England and their Old English Terminology,' *Learning and Literature in Anglo-Saxon England*, ed. M. Lapidge and H. Gneuss (Cambridge, 1985), pp. 128-31.

[13] The *Regula S. Benedicti* (ch. 48) required each monk to read one book of the bible during Lent. Carolingian commentators reinterpreted this provision to mean that each monk was required to read one entire book (not merely a book of the bible) during the course of each year; see K. Christ, 'In caput quadragesimae', *Zentralblatt für Bibliothekswesen* 60 (1944), 33-59, and A. Mundó, '"Bibliotheca": Bible et lecture du Carême d'après Saint Benoît', *RB* 60 (1950), 65-92. A large part of any monastic library's holdings will have been earmarked for private reading of this sort.

[14] For examples from a later period, see Clark, *The Care of Books*, pp. 98-100; see, further, the discussion by F. Wormald: *The English Library before 1700*, ed. F. Wormald and C.E. Wright (London, 1958), pp. 15-20.

At this point it became necessary to develop a system of recording the contents of the various *armaria* so that books could be located and retrieved. Thus developed the true 'library catalogue' with its corresponding system of shelf-marks; henceforth each entry in a booklist or catalogue was provided with a shelf-mark which directed the enquirer to a particular *armarium* (and, in the case of more sophisticated systems, to a particular shelf of the *armarium*); the shelf-mark was entered in the book as well so that it could be relocated.[15] And in order further to facilitate the search for individual books, lengthy catalogues were often provided with what we would call an 'index'—an alphabetical list of authors and works (such catalogues are referred to as 'double lists').[16] But the complex methods of catalography which were evolved to record the contents of large monastic libraries pertain to the later Middle Ages. In the Anglo-Saxon period, booklists were no more than simple inventories.

Although the inventories of the earlier period are never as extensive or complex as the later medieval catalogues, they are none the less the principal source of information about the nature and contents of early medieval libraries.[17] Numerous inventories or

---

[15] On the development of techniques of catalography, see the general remarks of D.M. Norris, *A History of Cataloguing and Cataloguing Methods 1100-1850* (London, 1939), esp. pp. 7-25, and the excellent discussion by A. Derolez, *Les Catalogues des bibliothèques*, Typologie des sources du moyen âge occidental 31 (Turnhout, 1979).

[16] See Derolez, *Les Catalogues*, pp. 40-2. A good example of a double list from Dover is ptd M.R. James, *Ancient Libraries of Canterbury and Dover* (Cambridge, 1903), pp. 407-95.

[17] On medieval libraries in general, see discussion by K. Christ in *Handbuch der Bibliothekswissenschaft*, ed. F. Milkau, 2nd ed., rev. G. Leyh, 3 vols. in 5 (Wiesbaden, 1952-65) III, 243-498; see also K. Christ, 'Bibliotheksgeschichte des Mittelalters. Zur Methode und zur neuesten Literatur', *Zentralblatt für Bibliothekswesen* 61 (1947), 38-56, 149-66 and 233-52, as well as J.W. Thompson, *The Medieval Library* (New York, 1939), repr. with suppl. by B. Boyer (1957), a book impressive in scope but unreliable in detail. There is also a brief introduction to the subject by K.W. Humphries, 'The Early Medieval

booklists of various origin and date survive from early medieval Europe, and many of these have been listed by Theodor Gottlieb.[18] Gottlieb's catalogue covers the entire medieval period up to the fifteenth century, and is arranged according to the various countries of Europe. Not all the booklists catalogued by Gottlieb have been printed, but for the early period (up to the twelfth century) there is a serviceable

Library', *Paläographie 1981*, ed. G. Silagi (Munich, 1982), pp. 59-70. These general accounts must be supplemented by individual studies. On the relationship of library to scriptorium there is an excellent study by B. Bischoff, 'Die Bibliothek im Dienste der Schule', *Mittelalterliche Studien* III, 213-33. On monastic libraries in general, see D. Leistle, 'Über Klosterbibliotheken des Mittelalters', *Studien und Mitteilungen zur Geschichte des Benediktiner-Ordens und seiner Zweige* 36 (1915), 197-228 and 357-77; for monastic libraries of the Lotharingian and Cluniac reform movements (a topic which has some relevance to Anglo-Saxon England), see R. Kottje, 'Klosterbibliotheken und monastische Kultur in der zweiten Hälfte des 11. Jahrhunderts', *Zeitschrift für Kirchengeschichte* 80 (1969), 145-62. Finally, there are some particular studies of monastic libraries in various countries. For Germany, see K. Löffler, *Deutsche Klosterbibliotheken*, 2nd ed. (Bonn and Leipzig, 1922); B. Bischoff, *Die südostdeutschen Schreibschulen und Bibliotheken in der Karolingerzeit*, 2 vols. (Wiesbaden, 1960-80); and L. Buzas, *Deutsche Bibliotheksgeschichte des Mittelalters* (Wiesbaden, 1975). For France, see E. Lesne, *Les Livres, scriptoria et bibliothèques du commencement du VIIIe à la fin du XIe siècle*, Histoire de la propriété ecclésiastique en France, 6 vols. (Lille and Paris, 1910-43) IV (1938). For Spain, see M.C. Díaz y Díaz, *Libros y librerías en la Rioja altomedieval* (Logroño, 1979). For England, see below, n. 26.

[18] *Über mittelalterliche Bibliotheken* (Leipzig, 1890). Gottlieb's catalogue is indispensable, but is now much in need of revision; see P.G. Meier, 'Nachträge zu Gottlieb, ueber mittelalterliche Bibliotheken', *Zentralblatt für Bibliothekswesen* 20 (1903), 16-32, and J.S. Beddie ('The Ancient Classics in Mediaeval Libraries', *Speculum* 5 [1930], 3-20), who adds seventy-one catalogues to Gottlieb's list.

edition of some 136 lists by Gustav Becker.[19] However, because of
the incompleteness and the limited chronological scope of Becker's
book, the full scholarly edition of surviving booklists and catalogues
has long been a desideratum of students of medieval books and
libraries. As a result of large-scale projects mounted in several
European countries earlier this century, we now have reliable and
scholarly editions of booklists and catalogues from Austria[20] and from
most of Germany and Switzerland;[21] an edition of catalogues from
Belgium is in progress,[22] and work has begun on the edition of
catalogues from France.[23] Unfortunately, for the British Isles, and for
England in particular, we are less well served: no complete list of
surviving booklists and catalogues of English medieval libraries has

---

[19] G. Becker, *Catalogi Bibliothecarum Antiqui* (Bonn, 1885). This
work has been superseded in many respects: by more recent editions of
catalogues, by more accurate attribution of manuscripts containing
booklists. It contains no commentary, and no attempt is made to
identify any of the items in the lists; the index is virtually useless.
Nevertheless, for the early medieval period the book is (as yet)
indispensable.

[20] *Mittelalterliche Bibliothekskataloge Österreichs*, 5 vols. and
suppl. (Vienna, 1915-71).

[21] *Mittelalterliche Bibliothekskataloge Deutschlands und der
Schweiz*, 4 vols. in 6 (Munich, 1918-79) (hereafter *MBKDS*).

[22] *Corpus Catalogorum Belgii I*, ed. A. Derolez (Brussels, 1966);
see also *Contributions à l' histoire des bibliothèques et de la lecture aux
Pays-Bas avant 1600* (Brussels, 1974).

[23] The *Index systematique des bibliothèques anciennes (ISBA)* is in
preparation, under the direction of André Vernet, at the Institut de
recherche et d'histoire des textes in Paris; see 'Pour un traitement
automatique des inventaires anciens de manuscrits', *Revue d'histoire
des textes* 3 (1973), 313-14, and 4 (1974), 436-7. In the meantime,
editions of a large number of medieval French library catalogues are
to be found in L. Delisle, *Le Cabinet des manuscrits de la Bibliothèque
impériale*, 3 vols. (Paris, 1868-81).

ever been published,[24] and the booklists themselves have yet to be collected and edited[25] with the result that we are poorly placed to form an accurate impression of the extent and holdings of medieval English libraries.[26] The British Academy has recently appointed a committee to plan and oversee the publication of Medieval English booklists and catalogues, and the first volumes have begun to appear (see below, p. 166). However, the committee's principal concern is with catalogues of individual houses from the period after 1100. The present edition of surviving booklists from Anglo-Saxon England is complementary to

---

[24] See Gottlieb, *Über mittelalterliche Bibliotheken*, nos. 435-512. There is a useful (but incomplete) list in E.A. Savage, *Old English Libraries* (London, 1911), pp. 263-85; see also L. Gougaud, 'Inventaires de manuscrits provenants d'anciennes bibliothèques monastiques de Grande Bretagne', *RHE* 33 (1937), 789-91 (a brief list of some thirty catalogues). The indispensable tool for the study of medieval English libraries and their catalogues is N.R. Ker, *Medieval Libraries of Great Britain*, 2nd ed. (London, 1964) together with the separately-printed *Supplement to the Second Edition* by A.G. Watson (London, 1987); surviving booklists and catalogues are listed where relevant under individual houses.

[25] See H. Omont, 'Anciens Catalogues de bibliothèques anglaises (XIIIe-XIVe siècle)', *Zentralblatt für Bibliothekswesen* 9 (1892), 201-22 (prints four catalogues), as well as the important studies by M.R. James: *On the Abbey of St Edmund at Bury* (Cambridge, 1895), *Ancient Libraries of Canterbury and Dover* (Cambridge, 1903), and *Lists of Manuscripts formerly in Peterborough Abbey* (Oxford, 1926).

[26] Surviving books from medieval English libraries are listed by Ker, *Medieval Libraries*; but this information needs always to be collated with the evidence of booklists and catalogues. There is a useful (but outdated) survey by Savage, *Old English Libraries*, and valuable introductions to the subject in *The English Library before 1700*, ed. Wormald and Wright, and especially in H. Gneuss, 'Englands Bibliotheken im Mittelalter und ihr Untergang', *Festschrift für Walter Hübner*, ed. D. Riesner and H. Gneuss (Berlin, 1964), pp. 91-121.

that larger project, therefore, and may be seen as a prolegomenon to the history of Anglo-Saxon libraries.[27]

In determining which Anglo-Saxon booklists to print I have been guided by several criteria. I have excluded, for example, statements by churchmen concerning what liturgical books priests were expected to own. Such statements occur in the penitential attributed to Archbishop Egbert of York (732-66),[28] and on several occasions in the pastoral writings of Ælfric;[29] but these lists are desiderata, not actual records of existing books. Also, I have assumed that a 'list' must include at least two specific items. I therefore omit the various references to books (specified and unspecified) which often occur in Anglo-Saxon wills.[30] By the same token I omit the reference to two gospel-books and a lavishly decorated collectary which, according to William of Malmesbury, were bequeathed to Glastonbury by Brihtwold,

---

[27] The history of Anglo-Saxon libraries cannot be written in the present state of knowledge. Various essays on the subject are in print, but none are satisfactory: R.B. Hepple, 'Early Northumbrian Libraries', *AAe* 3rd ser. 14 (1917), 92-106; R. Bressie, 'Libraries of the British Isles in the Anglo-Saxon Period', *The Medieval Library*, ed. Thompson, pp. 102-25; and R. Irwin, 'In Saxon England: Studies in the History of Libraries', *Lib. Assoc. Record* 57 (1955), 290-6. See instead the judicious remarks by Gneuss, 'Englands Bibliotheken', pp. 94-9, and by David Dumville, 'English Libraries before 1066: Use and Abuse of the Manuscript Evidence', printed elsewhere in the present volume.

[28] A.W. Haddan and W. Stubbs, *Councils and Ecclesiastical Documents relating to Great Britain and Ireland*, 3 vols. (Oxford, 1869) III, 417.

[29] *Die Hirtenbriefe Ælfrics in altenglischer und lateinischer Fassung*, ed. B. Fehr, Bibliothek der angelsächsischen Prosa 9 (Hamburg, 1914), repr. with suppl. by P. Clemoes (Darmstadt, 1966), 13, 51 and 126-7.

[30] See D. Whitelock, *Anglo-Saxon Wills* (Cambridge, 1930), pp. 2 and 4 (sacramentaries), 14 and 52 (unspecified books) and 54 (a psalter).

bishop of Ramsbury, on his death in 1045.[31] I also omit reference to Gunhild (sister of Harold Godwinson) who on her death in 1087 bequeathed to Saint-Donatien in Bruges a psalter which, since it contained glosses in Old English, must have been of English origin (see below, n. 93). Similarly, at a later period, Judith of Flanders, sometime wife of Earl Tostig of Northumbria (*ob.* 1066), was well known as a collector of manuscripts, particularly of lavishly decorated gospel-books.[32] After Tostig's death she married a Bavarian duke, and on her death in 1094 she bequeathed her collection of manuscripts to the abbey of Weingarten (in Württemberg).[33] Two at least of these books (both of them gospel-books) were written in Anglo-Saxon England.[34] Another important source of evidence for books and libraries is the various collections of correspondence which have survived from the Anglo-Saxon period. Books are frequently mentioned in the letters of Boniface and his circle of English correspondents,[35] in the letters of Alcuin,[36] in a famous letter of

---

[31] William of Malmesbury, *De Antiquitate Glastonie Ecclesie*, ed. J. Scott (Ipswich, 1981), p. 138: 'Hic misit ... textus euangeliorum .ii. ... Dedit eciam collectaneum auro illuminatum'.

[32] On Judith as book-collector, see M. Harrsen, 'The Countess Judith of Flanders and the Library of Weingarten Abbey', *Papers of the Bibliographical Soc. of America* 24 (1930), 1-13.

[33] The record of her donation is preserved as an addition to Fulda, Landesbibliothek, Aa 21 (Saint-Omer, s. xi^med), 89v: '... tria plenaria cum uno textu euangelii'; see Gottlieb, *Über mittelalterliche Bibliotheken*, no. 938, and *MBKDS* I, 399.

[34] They survive as New York, Pierpont Morgan Library, 708 and 709.

[35] *S. Bonifatii et Lullii Epistolae*, ed. M. Tangl, MGH, Epist. select. I (Berlin, 1916), 27 ('passiones martyrum'; 'congregationes aliquas sanctarum scripturarum'), 54 ('sanctorum librorum munera'), 57 ('interrogationes Augustini pontificis ... et responsiones sancti Gregorii pape'), 59 ('tractatus super apostolum Paulum ... super duas epistolas tractatus, id est ad Romanos et ad Corintheos primam'), 60 ('epistolae ... sancti Petri apostoli'), 131 ('liber [sex] prophetarum'), 144 ('Aldhelmi ... aliqua opuscula'), 158 ('de opusculis Bedan lectoris aliquos tractatus' and 'exemplaria epistolarum sancti Gregorii'), 159

Lupus of Ferrières addressed to Abbot Ealdsige of York[37] and in the

---

('de opusculis ... Bedan'), 207 ('Beda ... super lectionarium anniuersarium et prouerbia Salomonis'), 245 ('librum pyrpyri metri' [=Optatianus Porphyrius, *Carmina?*]), 247 ('saecularis scientiae libros ... de medicinalibus'), 251 ('libellos de uiro Dei Cudbercto metro et prosa conpositos'), 261 ('libros cosmografiorum'), 263 ('Beda ... in primam partem Samuelis usque ad mortem Saulis libros quattuor, siue in Esdram et Nehemiam libros tres, uel in euangelium Marci libros quattuor'), 264 ('Beda ... de edificatione templi, uel in cantica canticorum, siue epigrammatum heroico metro siue elegiaco conpositorum') and 265 ('Baeda de aedificio templi').

[36] In his correspondence Alcuin seldom mentions books (as physical objects, that is, rather than as sources of quotations). Only in letters to very intimate friends are books a subject of discussion: thus, for example, in letters to Hrabanus Maurus (*Ep.* cxlii), Ricbod (*Ep.* cxci) and Arno (*Ep.* cxcii) (MGH, Epist. 4, ed. E. Dümmler *et al.* [Berlin, 1895], 223-4, 318 and 319-21 respectively). By the same token, books are seldom mentioned in his letters to colleagues in England. An interesting exception is a letter of 801 addressed to Archbishop Eanbald II of York (*Ep.* ccxxvi): 'De ordinatione et dispositione missalis libelli nescio cur demandasti. Numquid non habes Romano more ordinatos libellos sacramentarios abundanter? Habes quoque et ueteris consuetudinis sufficienter sacramentaria maiora' (MGH, Epist. 4, 370).

[37] MGH, Epist. 6 (Berlin, 1925), 62: 'Atque ut, quod polliceor, uos exequamini priores, obnixe flagito, ut quaestiones beati Ieronimi, quas, teste Cassiodoro, in uetus et nouum testamentum elaborauit, Bedae quoque uestri similiter quaestiones in utrumque testamentum itemque memorati Ieronimi libros explanationum in Hieremiam, praeter sex primos, qui apud nos reperiuntur, ceteros qui secuntur; preterea Quintiliani Institutionum oratoriarum libros XII per certissimos nuntios mihi ad cellam sancti Iudoci, quae tandem aliquando nobis reddita est, dirigatis tradendos Lantrammo, qui bene uobis notus est, ibique describendos uobisque, quam poterit fieri celerius, remittendos'. The letter is datable to 852, and has been translated by D. Whitelock, *EHD*, pp. 877-8. Nothing further is known of this Abbot Ealdsige (or *Altsig*, as his name is given in Lupus's letter), and I must confess to some suspicions about his role as 'abbot' at York in the mid-ninth century,

various letters of the later Anglo-Saxon period which have been preserved as a collection in London, British Library, MS. Cotton Tiberius A.xv.[38] Such isolated references deserve to be collected and studied in their own right, but they can scarcely qualify as booklists. The same is true of incidental references to books in various historical and hagiographical writings of the period; these too deserve to be collected.[39]

---

since, as far as we can tell from other sources, York was a house of secular clerics.

[38] *Memorials of St. Dunstan*, ed. W. Stubbs, Rolls Ser. (London, 1874), pp. 354-404. Books are mentioned on pp. 362 ('quendam nostri coenobii librum scilicet euangeliorum'), 376 ('commentum Flori ... et alios libellos qui habentur Wintonie') and 388 ('Ealdelmi ... de parthenali laude libellum').

[39] For example, the well-known references in Bede's *Historia abbatum* to the books collected by Benedict Biscop (*Venerabilis Baedae Opera Historica*, ed. C. Plummer, 2 vols. [Oxford, 1896] I, 369: 'innumerabilem librorum omnis generis copiam adportauit') and by Ceolfrith (*ibid.* pp. 379-80: 'bibliothecam utriusque monasterii, quam Benedictus abbas magna caepit instantia, ipse non minori geminauit industria; ita ut tres pandectes nouae translationis, ad unum uetustae translationis quem de Roma adtulerat, ipse super adiungeret; quorum unum senex Romam rediens secum inter alia pro munere sumpsit, duos utrique monasterio reliquit; dato quoque Cosmographiorum codice mirandi operis, quem Romae Benedictus emerat, terram octo familiarum iuxta fluuium Fresca ab Aldfrido rege in scripturis doctissimo in possessionem monasterii beati Pauli apostoli comparuit'); or the lavish gospel-books commissioned by Wilfrid and described in the *Vita S. Wilfridi* (*The Life of Bishop Wilfrid by Eddius Stephanus*, ed. B. Colgrave [Cambridge, 1927], p. 36: 'Nam quattuor euangelia de auro purissimo in membranis depurpuratis, coloratis, pro animae suae remedio scribere iussit'). From the later period we learn of a collection of religious and grammatical books taken from London to Evesham by Bishop Ælfweard (*Chronicon Abbatiae de Evesham*, ed. W.D. Macray, Rolls Ser. [London, 1863], p. 83: 'Libros etiam plurimos tam diuinos quam grammaticos de Londonia transmisit'). And shortly after the Conquest Abbot Frederick of St Albans, being obliged to flee to Ely, took a number of books with him (Thomas Walsingham,

Indirect light may also be thrown on the nature and contents of Anglo-Saxon libraries in the early period by consideration of the monastic libraries in monasteries founded by Anglo-Saxon missionaries,[40] for it is a reasonable assumption that these would in the first instance have been stocked with books sent over from England.[41] It is not possible to trace the early holdings of all the Anglo-Saxon foundations on the continent, but it is especially interesting that early booklists survive from two of these foundations—Fulda (founded 744) and Würzburg (Burghard appointed bishop by Boniface 742)—and that these two booklists are among the earliest such documents to survive. First, the Fulda list. In a copy of Isidore's *De natura rerum* now in Basel (Universitätsbibliothek, MS. F.III.15a),[42] a scribe writing Anglo-Saxon minuscule (datable on palaeographical grounds to the late eighth century) copied on 17v-18r a list of some twenty books. Paul Lehmann, who first recognized the importance of this list, demonstrated that it (like the manuscript) originated at Fulda and was thus the earliest record of the Fulda library.[43] Secondly, the Würzburg list. On a page originally blank (260r) of a copy of Augustine's *De trinitate* now in Oxford (Bodleian Library, MS. Laud Misc. 126)[44] a scribe writing Anglo-Saxon minuscule datable to s. viii[ex] copied a list of some thirty-six books. E. A. Lowe, who first identified the list, argued that it was a record of the

---

Gesta Abbatum Monasterii S. Albani, ed. H. T. Riley, 3 vols., Rolls Ser. [London, 1867-9] I, 51:'assumptis secum quibusdam libris'). Many similar references no doubt await detection and collection.

[40] In general see W. Levison, *England and the Continent in the Eighth Century* (Oxford, 1946), pp. 139-48.

[41] This assumption is confirmed by the repeated requests for books which are found in the letters of Boniface and his colleagues; see above, n. 35.

[42] See E.A. Lowe, *Codices Latini Antiquiores* I-XI and Suppl. (Oxford, 1934-71), and II, 2nd ed. (1972) (hereafter abbreviated *CLA*), VII, no. 842.

[43] P. Lehmann, *Fuldaer Studien*, Sitzungsberichte der bayerischen Akademie der Wissenschaften 1925 (Munich, 1925), pp. 4-6; the list is ed. *ibid*. pp. 48-50.

[44] *CLA* II, no. 252.

episcopal library of Würzburg,[45] and his conclusions have been followed by subsequent scholars.[46] Each of these booklists, therefore, was copied in Anglo-Saxon minuscule at an important Anglo-Saxon foundation within a half-century of that foundation's establishment, and hence has direct relevance to the question of what books were thought essential to the Anglo-Saxon mission. But they have only indirect relevance to the question of library-holdings in England itself, and have therefore been omitted here.

In determining which booklists to include I have adopted a date of *c*. 1100 as an outer chronological limit; but I have included a list from the period *c*. 1070 x *c*. 1100 only when there is evidence that it pertains to a house which was in existence in the pre-Conquest period and that the books in question were the products of Anglo-Saxon rather than Norman scriptoria. I have therefore omitted lists of donations made by Norman churchmen to English libraries. Thus I omit the substantial list of some fifty books donated by William of Saint-Carilef (*ob*. 1096) to Durham,[47] since there is no means of establishing that any of the books in question was in the possession of an English library before 1066; indeed, of those books in William's list which survive and can be identified, nearly all are of Norman, not Anglo-Saxon, manufacture.[48] By the same token, I omit the substantial list of books

---

[45] E.A. Lowe, 'An Eighth-Century List of Books in a Bodleian Manuscript from Würzburg and its Probable Relationship to the Laudian Acts', *Speculum* 3 (1928), 3-15, repr. in his *Palaeographical Papers 1907-1965*, ed. L. Bieler, 2 vols. (Oxford, 1972) II, 239-50.

[46] See B. Bischoff and J.B. Hofmann, *Libri Sancti Kyliani* (Würzburg, 1952), pp. 142-8 (which includes an edition and full commentary on the booklist), and *MBKDS* IV.2, 977-9 (no. 126).

[47] C.H. Turner, 'The Earliest List of Durham Manuscripts', *JTS* 19 (1918), 121-32.

[48] See R.A.B. Mynors, *Durham Cathedral Manuscripts to the End of the Twelfth Century* (Oxford, 1939), pp. 32-45 and pls. 16-31. Of the manuscripts listed by Mynors only one is written in a hand which (in my opinion) is more characteristic of Anglo-Saxon than Norman scribal practice (Mynors described it as being in a hand 'unlike any other Durham book', p. 36). This is a copy of Augustine, *Tractatus in Euangelium Ioannis*, now Durham, Cathedral Library, MS. B.II.16,

which were donated by Paul of Caen, abbot of St Albans (1077-93), to
the abbey of St Albans.[49] The question of the Norman contribution
to English book-production and libraries is a fundamental one, but it is
too vast to be broached here.[50]

In treating booklists and inventories as evidence for early medieval
libraries, the principal problem is that of identifying the items listed.
Although numerous booklists have been printed, they have only rarely
been supplied with a sufficient amount of commentary to permit
reasonable inferences to be drawn about what books were in
question.[51] It is to be hoped that future editors of early medieval
booklists will turn their attention to the need for commentary and
identification of items listed. In some cases identification is simple and
straightforward; in others, it can be extremely problematic. In the case
of classical authors, for example, identification is usually

---

which is written in the characteristic spindly late Anglo-Caroline script
seen in the work of Eadui Basan (T.A.M. Bishop, *English Caroline
Minuscule* [Oxford, 1971], pp. xxiii and 22-4); see Mynors, *ibid.* p.
24. But it is not certain that Durham B.II.16 was one of William's
books, and it may have reached Durham by a different route.

[49] *Gesta Abbatum Monasterii S. Albani* I, 58: 'Dedit igitur huic
ecclesie uiginti octo uolumina notabilia, et octo psalteria, collectarium,
epistolarium, et librum in quo continentur euangelia legenda per
annum; duos textus, auro et argento et gemmis ornatos, sine
ordinalibus, consuetudinariis, missalibus, tropariis, collectariis et aliis
libris qui in armariolis habentur'.

[50] In general see D. Knowles, *The Monastic Order in England*, 2nd
ed. (Cambridge, 1963), pp. 522-7, and N.R. Ker, *English Manuscripts
in the Century after the Norman Conquest* (Oxford, 1960), pp. 7-8. On
the holdings of twelfth-century libraries in general, see J. S. Beddie,
'Libraries in the Twelfth Century: their Catalogues and Contents',
*Anniversary Essays in Mediaeval History by Students of Charles Homer
Haskins*, ed. C.H. Taylor (Boston and New York, 1929), pp. 1-23; on
the holdings of Norman libraries in Normandy, see G. Nortier-
Marchand, *Les Bibliothèques médiévales des abbayes bénédictines de
Normandie*, 2nd ed. (Paris, 1971).

[51] For example, there is no commentary whatsoever in Becker,
Catalogi, and only occasional annotation in *MBKDS*.

unproblematic:[52] as tools of research we have Manitius's detailed study of entries pertaining to classical authors in medieval library catalogues,[53] as well as Munk Olsen's recent and comprehensive catalogue of pre-twelfth-century manuscripts of classical authors.[54] For Latin patristic authors there is the indispensable *Clavis Patrum Latinorum*,[55] which provides convenient bibliographical guidance to the manuscript transmission of patristic texts. There are problems here, however, in that a single patristic work may have travelled under many different titles, and that many pseudonymous works travelled undetected under the name(s) of the great Latin Fathers. Furthermore, references to patristic texts in medieval booklists and catalogues have not been systematically collected or studied in the way that Manitius, for example, has treated references to classical texts. Identification of patristic texts, therefore, is often a matter of guesswork. For works composed later than *c*. 800, when the *Clavis* ceases to be a guide, we have Manitius's compendious *Geschichte der lateinischen Literatur des*

---

[52] The classical holdings of medieval libraries have been a perennial subject of interest; in general see Beddie, 'The Ancient Classics', pp. 3-17, and D. Knowles, 'The Preservation of the Classics', *The English Library before 1700*, ed. Wormald and Wright, pp. 136-47.

[53] M. Manitius, *Handschriften antiker Autoren in mittelalterlichen Bibliothekskatalogen*, ed. K. Manitius (Leipzig, 1935). This work (published posthumously) is a revised and much-amplified version of Manitius's earlier *Philologisches aus alten Bibliothekskatalogen (bis 1300)*, Rheinisches Museum 47, Ergänzungsheft (Frankfurt a.M., 1892).

[54] B. Munk Olsen, *L'Étude des auteurs classiques latins aux XIe et XIIe siècles: Catalogue des manuscrits classiques latins copiés du IXe au XIIe siècle*, 3 vols. in 4 (Paris, 1982-9). An excellent handbook, which presents a brief sketch of the manuscript transmission of each classical Latin author, is *Texts and Transmission: a Survey of the Latin Classics*, ed. L.D. Reynolds (Oxford, 1983).

[55] E. Dekkers and A. Gaar, *Clavis Patrum Latinorum*, 2nd ed. (Steenbrugge, 1961) a work which is now in some need of revision.

Mittelalters,[56] but even this great work has now been superseded in some respects.[57] For the transmission and circulation in the Latin west of Greek patristic authors in Latin translation there is reliable guidance available.[58] But many problematical areas remain.[59] In proposing identifications of items in the following booklists, I have always attempted to indicate where an identification is reasonably certain, and where it is no more than a guess. It is to be hoped that, as work proceeds on cataloguing manuscripts of Anglo-Saxon origin or provenance, and on the literary sources used by Anglo-Saxon authors, hesitant identifications may be tested more thoroughly.

In the Commentary which accompanies each booklist, I use the following abbreviations:

---

[56] M. Manitius, *Geschichte der lateinischen Literatur des Mittelalters*, 3 vols. (Munich, 1911-31). As a matter of course Manitius discusses (with reference to each author) the manuscript transmission and references in medieval catalogues; inevitably, in a work of such enormous scope, the references are not always complete.

[57] For example, Haimo of Auxerre is now recognized as an important and influential biblical commentator and homiliarist (see *Deutschlands Geschichtsquellen im Mittelalter* V, ed. H. Löwe [Weimar, 1973], 564-5), but he is barely mentioned by Manitius (*Geschichte* I, 516-17).

[58] See A. Siegmund (*Die Überlieferung der griechischen christlichen Literatur* [Munich and Pasing 1949]), who provides a convenient conspectus of pre-twelfth-century manuscripts of Latin translations of Greek patristic texts, arranged by author (pp. 49-138); see also the valuable introduction by W. Berschin, *Griechisch-lateinisches Mittelalter* (Bern and Munich, 1980).

[59] Liturgical books, for example. As far as I am aware there exists no comprehensive treatment of the Latin terminology for liturgical books of the early medieval period; cf. the remarks of Helmut Gneuss, 'Liturgical Books in Anglo-Saxon England and their Old English Terminology', in *Learning and Literature in Anglo-Saxon England,* ed. M. Lapidge and H. Gneuss (Cambridge, 1985), pp. 91-141, at 95.

Becker, *Catalogi*	G. Becker, *Catalogi Bibliothecarum Antiqui* (Bonn, 1885)
CLA	E.A. Lowe, *Codices Latini Antiquiores* I-XI and Suppl. (Oxford, 1934-71) and II, 2nd ed. (1972)
Clavis	E. Dekkers and A. Gaar, *Clavis Patrum Latinorum*, 2nd ed. (Steenbrugge, 1961)
Gneuss, 'Liturgical Books'	H. Gneuss, 'Liturgical Books in Anglo-Saxon England and their Old English Terminology', *Learning and Literature in Anglo-Saxon England*, ed. M. Lapidge and H. Gneuss (Cambridge, 1985), pp. 91-141.
Gottlieb	T. Gottlieb, *Über mittelalterliche Bibliotheken* (Leipzig, 1890)
GL	H. Keil, *Grammatici Latini*, ed. H. Keil, 8 vols. (Leipzig, 1857-80)
ICL	D. Schaller and E. Könsgen, *Initia Carminum Latinorum saeculo undecimo Antiquiorum* (Göttingen, 1977)
Manitius, *Geschichte*	M. Manitius, *Geschichte der lateinischen Literatur des Mittelalters*, 3 vols. (Munich, 1911-31)
Manitius, *Handschriften*	M. Manitius, *Handschriften antiker Autoren in mittelalterlichen Bibliothekskatalogen*, ed. K. Manitius (Leipzig, 1935)

Note, finally, that in the booklists edited below the numbers in the left-hand margin refer to individual items, not to line-numbers of text (accordingly material in the texts other than references to books does not figure in the numbering).

I. Books owned by Ælberht, archbishop of York, and bequeathed to Alcuin (c. 778)

In 778 Ælberht, archbishop of York, determined to relinquish his worldly and ecclesiastical authority, and to spend the remainder of his life in seclusion. Before retiring from the world he distributed his earthly possesssions to his two closest followers. To Eanbald, who succeeded him as archbishop, he bequeathed his treasures, estates and money; to Alcuin he bequeathed his books. Our principal source for this distribution of Ælberht's wealth is Alcuin's long poem on the saints of York, called by its editors *Versus de patribus, regibus et sanctis Euboricensis ecclesiae.*[60] Alcuin had been deeply devoted to Ælberht, and he was concerned in his poem to stress the munificence of Ælberht's legacy to him. Hence Alcuin included an extensive account of the library which Ælberht had amassed, and this account has customarily been regarded as one of the earliest surviving medieval booklists.[61]

It is important to stress that Ælberht's books were *bequeathed* to Alcuin, and that he henceforth took ownership of them. Although the books were housed at York, they were not the property of the York *familia*; Ælberht and Alcuin were secular clerics, not monks, and their books accordingly were private property, not owned corporately by the cathedral *familia*. The books mentioned in Alcuin's poem are often referred to as 'the York Cathedral library' (or whatever); but such designations are misleading. When Alcuin left York for the continent in 782 to take up duties as master of Charlemagne's palace school, he left his collection of books behind in York, no doubt as a matter of convenience. However, he did not forget about them. Thus he wrote to Eanbald II on his election to the archbishopric of York in 796 to remind Eanbald that he (Alcuin) had inherited—and hence was owner of—the books that were housed at York: '... et praesse [*sc.* Eanbald II] thesauris sapientiae, in quibus me magister meus dilectus Aelberhtus archiepiscopus *heredem reliquit*' (my italics).[62] Shortly thereafter Alcuin was appointed abbot of Tours; and he then wrote to Charlemagne stating that he greatly missed his 'exquisitiores ... libelli' and reporting to the king that he was making arrangements to have the library transported from York (to Tours, presumably), so that the

---

[60] Ed. E. Dümmler, MGH, PLAC 1 (Berlin, 1881), 169-206; P. Godman, *Alcuin: The Bishops, Kings, and Saints of York* (Oxford, 1982).

[61] Alcuin's description is ptd Becker, *Catalogi*, no. 3. In reprinting Alcuin's list I have renumbered the lines (which are lines 1540-56 in Dümmler's edition and 1541-57 in Godman's).

[62] *Ep.* cxiv (MGH, Epist. 4, 167).

'flowers of Britain' might be brought to France: 'Sed ex parte desunt mihi, seruulo uestro, exquisitiores eruditionis scolasticae libelli ... Ideo haec uestrae excellentiae dico ... ut aliquos ex pueris nostris remittam, qui excipiant inde nobis necessaria quaeque et reuehant in Franciam flores Brittaniae'.[63] Unfortunately we do not know whether the students were indeed dispatched to collect the books, and whether Alcuin was ever united with his library in the last years of his life; but we should be cautious in assuming (without evidence) that any of the books remained in England.[64]

Alcuin's booklist has been discussed on many occasions.[65] But because Alcuin did not give specific titles it is impossible in most cases to be certain of what books were in question. In the commentary which accompanies the text I rely frequently on the detailed discussion of this list by Peter Godman.[66]

> quod pater Hieronymus, quod sensit Hilarius atque
> Ambrosius praesul, simul Augustinus et ipse
> sanctus Athanasius, quod Orosius edit acutus,
> quicquid Gregorius summus docet et Leo papa,
> [5] Basilius quicquid Fulgentius atque coruscant;
> Cassiodorus item, Chrysostomus atque Iohannes;

---

[63] *Ep.* cxxi (*ibid.* p. 177).

[64] Cf. P. Hunter Blair ('From Bede to Alcuin', *Famulus Christi*, ed. G. Bonner [London, 1976], pp. 239-60), who suggests (p. 252) that copies of Vergil and Statius that were available at Worcester in the second half of the tenth century may have come directly from York via Wulfstan (*ob.* 1023), who held the sees of Worcester and York in plurality. This is to assume that Alcuin's books remained in York despite his efforts to retrieve them, and that they survived the (presumed) Viking depredations of the York library in the 860s.

[65] See *inter alia* R.F. West, *Alcuin and the Rise of the Christian Schools* (New York, 1892), pp. 33-7; A.F. Leach, *The Schools of Medieval England* (London, 1915), pp. 60-3; Hepple, 'Early Northumbrian Libraries'; V.R. Stallbaumer, 'The York Cathedral School', *ABR* 22 (1971), 286-97; and C.B.L. Barr, 'The Minster Library', *A History of York Minster*, ed. G.E. Aylmer and R. Cant (Oxford, 1977), pp. 487-538.

[66] Godman, *Alcuin*, pp. 122-7.

quicquid et Althelmus docuit, quid Beda magister;
qua Victorinus scripsere Boethius atque;
historici ueteres, Pompeius, Plinius ipse,
[10]   acer Aristoteles, rhetor quoque Tullius ingens;
quid quoque Sedulius uel quid canit ipse Iuuencus,
Alcimus et Clemens, Prosper, Paulinus, Arator,
quid Fortunatus uel quid Lactantius edunt,
quae Maro Virgilius, Statius, Lucanus et auctor,
[15]   artis grammaticae uel quid scripsere magistri
quid Probus atque Focas, Donatus Priscianusue,
Seruius, Euticius, Pompeius, Cominianus.

COMMENTARY 1 *Hieronymus*: *Clavis*, nos. 580-642. 1 *Hilarius*: *Clavis*, nos. 427-72. 2 *Ambrosius*: *Clavis*, nos. 123-68. 2 *Augustinus*: *Clavis*, nos. 250-386. 3 *Athanasius*: presumably Evagrius's Latin translation of Athanasius's Greek *Vita S. Antonii* (BHL, no. 609). 3 *Orosius*: presumably the *Historiae aduersum paganos* (*Clavis*, no. 571). 4 *Gregorius*: *Clavis*, nos. 1708-14. 4 *Leo papa*: a reference either to the collection of Leo's *Epistolae* (*Clavis*, no. 1656), or, perhaps more likely, his *Sermones* (*Clavis*, no. 1657). 5 *Basilius*: possibly Rufinus's Latin translation of St Basil's monastic Rules (see J. Gribomont, *Histoire du texte des ascétiques de Saint Basile* [Louvain, 1953], pp. 95-107), a work apparently known to Aldhelm, or possibly Basil's nine Homilies on the Hexameron, a work translated into Latin by the obscure Eusthathius and used by Bede in several of his writings (notably the commentary *In Genesim*). 5 *Fulgentius*: presumably a reference to the writings of Fulgentius of Ruspe (*ob*. 533), an eloquent defender of Augustine's doctrine of grace, some of whose writings—notably the three-book treatise *Ad Thrasamundum* (*Clavis*, no. 816) and the *De fide ad Petrum* (*Clavis*, no. 826)—were known to Bede and Alcuin; but certainty is not possible, for in the early Middle Ages the writings of Fulgentius 'the Mythographer', author of the *Mitologiae* and the *Sermones antiqui*, were in wide circulation (see M.L.W. Laistner, 'Fulgentius in the Carolingian Age', *The Intellectual Heritage of the Early Middle Ages*, ed. C.G. Starr [Ithaca, NY, 1957], pp. 202-15). 6 *Cassiodorus*: an important and voluminous author, many of whose works (*Clavis*, nos. 896-908) might here be in question; it is interesting to note, nevertheless, that an abbreviated version of Cassiodorus's *Expositio psalmorum* was used by Alcuin and is preserved in an early manuscript possibly from York (see D.A. Bullough, 'Alcuin and the Kingdom of Heaven: Liturgy, Theology and the Carolingian Age', (*Carolingian Essays*, ed. U.-R. Blumenthal [Washington, D.C., 1983], pp. 1-69, at 18-19, and n. 39). **6** *Iohannes Chrysostomus*: Greek Father (patriarch of Constantinople, 397-407) whose twenty-five Homilies on Matthew and seven Homilies on St. Paul were translated into Latin by one Anianus (cf. *Clavis*, nos. 771-2, and C. Baur, 'L'Entrée de Saint Chrysostome dans le monde littéraire', *RHE* 8 [1906], 249-65), as were various other homilies such as the *De compunctione* and *De reparatione lapsi* (fragments of a mid-eighth-century Northumbrian manuscript of the last two items survive: see *CLA* VIII, no. 1187); see also below, no. XIII, line 18. **7** *Althelmus*: Aldhelm (*Clavis*, nos. 1331-5). **7** *Beda*: *Clavis*, nos. 1343-82. **8** *Victorinus*: possibly a reference to Marius Victorinus's theological writings (*Clavis*, nos. 95-8); the coupling with Boethius suggests, however, that the work here in question was the *De definitionibus* (*Clavis*, no. 94), which was frequently transmitted with the logical writings of Boethius (see H. Chadwick, *Boethius* [Oxford, 1981], pp.115-18). **8** *Boethius*: as Godman observes (*Alcuin*, p. 124), it has yet to be demonstrated that the *De consolatione Philosophiae* was known in England before the late ninth century; the works in question here are probably Boethius's logical writings (see Chadwick, *Boethius*, pp. 108-73). **9** *Pompeius*: the work in question is Justinus's *Epitome* of the *Historiae Philippicae* of Pompeius Trogus; a single leaf of this *Epitome* of Northumbrian origin and mid-eighth-century date survived till recent times (see *CLA* IX, no. 1370, and *Texts and Transmission*, ed. Reynolds, pp. 197-9), and another leaf has recently been found: J. Crick, 'An Anglo-Saxon Fragment of Justinus's *Epitome*', *ASE* 16 (1987), 181-96. **9** *Plinius*: the Elder Pliny, a natural historian rather than a historian proper, parts at least of whose *Historia naturalis* were known to Aldhelm and Bede; an important early-eighth-century Northumbrian manuscript of bks II-VI of this text survives (CLA X, no. 1578; see *Texts and Transmission*, ed. Reynolds, p. 309). **10** *Aristoteles*: presumably the Latin translations by Boethius of two logical treatises, the Categories and the *Peri hermeneias* (=*De interpretatione*), both of which were widely known in the early Middle Ages. **10** *Tullius*: Cicero (M. Tullius Cicero), two of whose works—the *De inuentione* and *De oratore*—were known to Alcuin; see Godman, *Alcuin*, p. 125. **11-13**: The Christian-Latin poets listed here formed the staple of the medieval school curriculum (see G. Glauche, *Schullektüre im Mittelalter. Entstehung und Wandlungen des Lektürekanons bis 1200* [Munich, 1970], esp. pp. 10-11); for the study of these authors in Anglo-Saxon England, see M. Lapidge, 'The Study of Latin Texts in Late Anglo-Saxon England: I. The Evidence of Latin Glosses', *Latin and the Vernacular Languages in Early Medieval Britain*, ed. N. Brooks (Leicester, 1982), pp. 99-140. **11** *Sedulius*: the *Carmen Paschale* of Caelius Sedulius (*Clavis*, no. 1447). **11** *Iuuencus*: the hexametrical *Euangelia quattuor* of the Spanish priest Juvencus (*Clavis*, no. 1385). **12** *Alcimus*: Alcimus Avitus, *De spiritalis historiae gestis* (*Clavis*, no. 995). **12** *Clemens*: Aurelius Prudentius Clemens (best known as Prudentius), whose various poems—*Cathemerinon, Apotheosis, Hamartigenia, Psychomachia, Contra Symmachum, Peristephanon and Dittochaeon* (*Clavis*, nos. 1438-44)—were widely studied in the early Middle Ages; for an example of the study of the *Psychomachia* at late Anglo-Saxon Canterbury, see G.R. Wieland, *The Latin Glosses on Arator and Prudentius in Cambridge University Library MS Gg. 5. 35* (Toronto, 1983). **12** *Prosper*: Prosper of Aquitaine, whose *Epigrammata* (*Clavis*, no. 518), metrical versions of various apophthegms by Augustine, were also widely studied in early medieval schools. **12** *Paulinus*: Paulinus of Nola, whose *Carmina* (*Clavis*, no. 203), for the most part concerning the local patron saint of Nola, St Felix, were known early in Northumbria and are preserved in two early-eighth-century Northumbrian manuscripts (*CLA* I, no. 87, and I, no. 1622); see T.W. Mackay, 'Bede's Hagiographical Method: his Knowledge and Use of Paulinus of Nola', *Famulus Christi*, ed. Bonner, pp. 77-92. **12** *Arator*: Arator, *De actibus apostolorum* (*Clavis*, no. 1504); on the study of Arator at late Anglo-Saxon Canterbury, see Wieland, *The Latin Glosses on Arator and Prudentius* (note, however, that Wieland's statements [p. 4] on the dating and origin of Arator manuscripts need correction). **13** *Fortunatus*: Venantius Fortunatus, whose *Carmina* (*Clavis*, no. 1033) were well known in early Anglo-Saxon England (see my remarks in *ASE* 8 [1979], 287-95). **13** *Lactantius*: since Lactantius is here listed among the Christian-Latin poets, Alcuin's reference is presumably to the poem *De aue phoenice* (*Clavis*, no. 90) which is possibly but not certainly by Lactantius. **14** *Maro Virgilius*: see Manitius, *Handschriften*, pp. 47-55, and *Texts and Transmission*, ed. Reynolds, pp. 433-6. **14** *Statius*: see Manitius, *Handschriften*, pp. 125-9, and *Texts and Transmission*, ed. Reynolds, pp. 394-9. **14** *Lucanus*: see Manitius, *Handschriften*, pp. 115-20, and *Texts and Transmission*, ed. Reynolds, pp. 215-18. **15-17**: on the knowledge of these various grammatical texts in Anglo-Saxon England, see V. Law, *The Insular Latin Grammarians* (Ipswich, 1982), pp. 11-29, and 'The Study of Latin Grammar in Eighth-Century Southumbria', *ASE* 12 (1983), 43-71. **16** *Probus*: Law (*The Insular Latin Grammarians*, pp. 26-7) argues convincingly that the grammatical writings of Probus did not cross the Alps until the end of the eighth century, and that Insular authors of the seventh and eighth centuries knew them only at second hand from other grammarians; one must wonder how many other authors mentioned by Alcuin were known to him only at second hand (see the note on Cominianus, below). **16** *Focas*: Phocas, *Ars de nomine et uerbo*; see C. Jeudy, 'L'*Ars de nomine et uerbo* de Phocas: Manuscrits et commentaires médiévaux', *Viator* 5 (1974), 61-156. **16** *Donatus*: the *Ars maior* and *Ars minor* of Donatus were the introductory grammars *par excellence* of the early Middle Ages; see L. Holtz, *Donat et la tradition de l'enseignement grammatical* (Paris, 1981). **16** *Priscianus*: either the lengthy *Institutiones grammaticae* (see J.R. O'Donnell, 'Alcuin's Priscian', *Latin Script and Letters A.D. 400-900*, ed. J.J. O'Meara and B. Naumann [Leiden, 1976], pp. 222-35, together with M. Gibson, 'Priscian, *Institutiones Grammaticae*: a Handlist of Manuscripts', *Scriptorium* 26 [1972], 105-24), or the shorter *Institutio de nomine et pronomine et uerbo* (see C. Jeudy, 'L'*Institutio de nomine, pronomine et uerbo* de Priscien: Manuscrits et commentaires médiévaux', *Revue d'histoire des textes* 2 [1972], 73-144, as well as the recent edition by M. Passalacqua, *Prisciani Caesariensis Institutio de nomine et pronomine et verbo* [Urbino, 1992])—or both. **17** *Seruius*: possibly either the commentaries on Vergil or the *De finalibus* (a metrical treatise) of Seruius, or, more likely perhaps, the *De littera* of Sergius (a commentary on Donatus, *Ars maior*), a work which frequently travelled under the name of Servius (see Law, *The Insular Latin Grammarians*, p. 17). **17** *Euticius*: Eutyches, *Ars de uerbo* (see Jeudy, 'Les Manuscrits de l'*Ars de uerbo* d'Eutychès et le commentaire de Remi d'Auxerre', *Études de civilisation médiévale (IXe-XIIe s.): Mélanges offerts à E.-R. Labande* [Poitiers, 1974], pp. 421-36). **17** *Pompeius*: the author of a commentary on the *Ars maior* of Donatus; see L. Holtz, 'Tradition et diffusion de l'oeuvre grammaticale de Pompée, commentateur de Donat', *Revue de philologie* 45 (1971), 48-

83. **17** *Cominianus*: a Late Latin grammarian whose writings are not extant and do not appear to have been transmitted intact to the Middle Ages, but are known only through the grammatical compilation of Charisius (see Law, *The Insular Latin Grammarians*, pp. 19 and 75, n. 108); it is most unlikely, therefore, that Alcuin knew the work at first hand.

II. Books donated by King Athelstan (924-39) to the congregation of St Cuthbert at Chester-le-Street

The *Historia de S. Cuthberto*[67] is a text, probably composed in the eleventh century,[68] which purports to record the early history of the congregation or *familia* of St Cuthbert, housed at Lindisfarne and later at Chester-le-Street, from its foundation to 945. It records various grants and bequests to the congregation, and among these is the record of a grant by King Athelstan of various lands, liturgical books and ecclesiastical furnishings.[69] The *Historia* is best preserved in Cambridge, University Library, MS. Ff.1.27 (Sawley, s. xiii[in]),[70] pp. 195-202; the text printed below is found on pp. 201-2. Athelstan's donation has been discussed on several occasions.[71]

---

[67] *Symeonis Monachi Opera Omnia*, ed. T. Arnold, 2 vols., Rolls Ser. (London, 1882-5) I, 196-214.

[68] See H.E. Craster, 'The Patrimony of St. Cuthbert', *EHR* 69 (1954), 177-99.

[69] *Symeonis Monachi Opera Omnia*, ed. Arnold, I, 211; it is also ptd J.M. Kemble, *Codex Diplomaticus Aevi Saxonici*, 6 vols. (London, 1839-48), no. 1125, and W. de G. Birch, *Cartularium Saxonicum*, 3 vols. and index (London, 1885-99), no. 685.

[70] On the manuscript, see D.N. Dumville, 'The Sixteenth-Century History of Two Cambridge Books from Sawley', *Trans. of the Cambridge Bibliographical Soc.* 7 (1977-80), 427-44.

[71] See J.A. Robinson, *The Times of St Dunstan* (Oxford, 1923), p. 53, and discussion by Battiscombe in *The Relics of St Cuthbert,* ed. C.F. Battiscombe (Oxford, 1956), pp. 7 n. 2, and 31-3, as well as discussion by Simon Keynes, 'King Athelstan's Books', *Literature and Learning in Anglo-Saxon England*, ed. M. Lapidge and H. Gneuss (Cambridge, 1985), pp. 177-8.

In nomine Domini nostri Iesu Christi. Ego Æþelstanus rex do sancto Cuthberto

        hunc textum euuangeliorum ...
        et .i. missalem
        et .ii. euangeliorum textus, auro et argento ornatos
[4]   et .i. sancti Cuthberti uitam, metrice et prosaice scriptam.

COMMENTARY 1 *hunc textum euuangeliorum*: these words imply that the list of Athelstan's donations was once copied in a gospel-book, but, as Simon Keynes suggests ('King Athelstan's Books', p. 177), it was more likely concocted by the author of the *Historia de S. Cuthberto* from information contained in a note entered in London, British Library, MS. Cotton Otho B.ix, which would accordingly be the gospel-book in question here. 2 *missalem*: at this date the book in question was presumably a sacramentary, not a plenary missal (see Gneuss, 'Liturgical Books', p. 99). 3 *.ii. euangeliorum textus*: it is not possible to identify these two gospel-books; see Keynes, 'King Athelstan's Books', p. 178. 4 *.i. sancti Cuthberti uitam*: apparently a book containing both Bede's verse and his prose *Vitae S. Cuthberti* (*BHL*, nos. 2020-1), which almost certainly survives as Cambridge, Corpus Christi College, MS. 183 (see Keynes, 'King Athelstan's Books', p. 182); Mynors (*Durham Cathedral Manuscripts*, p. 26) noted in discussing the Athelstan donation that 'the volume does not appear in the medieval catalogues, and was no doubt kept among the treasures of the Cathedral church'; but note the entry in a twelfth-century Durham catalogue: 'duae uitae sancti Cuthberti' (Becker, *Catalogi*, no. 117).

III. Books owned by a grammarian named Athelstan (s. x^2)

To an English copy of Isidore's *De natura rerum*, now London, British Library, MS. Cotton Domitian i (written in Anglo-Caroline minuscule of mid-tenth-century date) was added on 55v a list of books belonging to one Athelstan in a late form of Anglo-Saxon square minuscule, datable perhaps to the second half of the tenth century.[72] The manuscript is from St Augustine's, Canterbury, and was apparently written there.[73] The booklist has been variously attributed to King Athelstan[74] and to Ealdorman Athelstan the 'Half-King',[75] but the date of the script rules out the king, and the subject-matter of the list rules out the ealdorman, and indicates rather that an otherwise unknown schoolmaster or grammarian was the owner of the books.[76] The booklist has been printed and discussed several times.[77]

> Þis syndon ða bec þe Æþestanes wæran:
> De natura rerum
> Persius

---

[72] Cf. N.R. Ker (*Catalogue of Manuscripts Containing Anglo-Saxon* [Oxford, 1957], pp. 185-6 [no. 146]), who dates the entry s. x/xi. The square minuscule script has several Caroline features which suggest a date late in the career of square minuscule script; but the chronology of that career is as yet improperly understood. For the early phases of the career, see now D.N. Dumville, 'English Square Minuscule Script: the Background and Earliest Phases', *ASE* 16 (1987), 147-79.

[73] T.A.M. Bishop, 'Notes on Cambridge Manuscripts, Part IV: MSS. connected with St Augustine's, Canterbury', *Trans. of the Cambridge Bibliographical Soc.* 2 (1954-8), 323-36, at 334-5; a plate showing the booklist is included by Bishop as pl. XIV (b). Bishop avoids assigning a date to the square minuscule additions on 55v. See also P. Lendinara, 'The Abbo Glossary in London, British Library, Cotton Domitian i', *ASE* 19 (1990), 133-49.

[74] Gottlieb, no. 436.

[75] F.J. Haverfield, 'The Library of Æthelstan, the Half-King', *The Academy* 26 (1884), 32.

[76] It is interesting to note that the names of Æthelstan and Ælfwold mentioned in this list recur in the document recording Bishop Æthelwold's donations to Peterborough (Birch, *Cartularium Saxonicum*, no. 1128), part of which is ptd below as no. IV; but the combination of names (which are not rare) may be merely coincidental.

[77] M.R. James, *Ancient Libraries of Canterbury and Dover*, p. lxix; R.M. Wilson, 'More Lost Literature II', *Leeds Stud. in Eng.* 6 (1937), 30-49, at 49; and A.J. Robertson, *Anglo-Saxon Charters* (Cambridge, 1939), p. 250.

    De arte metrica
    Donatum minorem
[5]   Excerptiones de metrica arte
    Apocalipsin
    Donatum maiorem
    Alchuinum
    Glossam super Catonem
[10] Libellum de grammatica arte que sic incipit
      'Terra que pars'
    Sedulium[78]
    7.i. gerim wæs Alfwoldes preostes
    Glossa super Donatum
    Dialogorum

COMMENTARY **1** *De natura rerum*: Isidore, *De natura rerum* (*Clavis*, no. 1188), the work which constitutes the major part of the manuscript to which this booklist is appended; on the work itself and its transmission, see J. Fontaine, *Isidore de Séville, Traité de la nature* (Bordeaux, 1960). **2** *Persius*: see Manitius, *Handschriften*, pp. 112-15, and *Texts and Transmission*, ed. Reynolds, pp. 293-5. **3** *De arte metrica*: possibly Bede's treatise of that name (*Clavis*, no. 1565), but without further specification certainty is impossible. **4** *Donatum minorem*: Donatus, *Ars minor*; on the manuscript tradition of Donatus, see Holtz, *Donat et la tradition de l'enseignement grammatical*, pp. 445-97. **5** *Excerptiones de metrica arte*: without further specification it is impossible to guess what this might be. **6** *Apocalipsin*: presumably the biblical Apocalypse (Revelations), but why such a biblical text should be included amongst a grammarian's books is not clear. **7** *Donatum maiorem*: Donatus, *Ars maior*; on the manuscript tradition of Donatus, see Holtz, *Donat et la tradition de l'enseignement grammatical*, pp. 445-97. **8** *Alchuinum*: given the context, the work in question was presumably either Alcuin's *De orthographia* (PL 101, cols. 901-20) or his *De grammatica* (PL 101, cols. 849-902)—or both. **9** *Glossam super Catonem*: a commentary on the *Disticha Catonis* (a favourite school-text in the early Middle Ages), presumably that of Remigius of Auxerre; a fragmentary copy of Remigius's commentary

---

[78] There is an erasure of one entry here in the manuscript.

that was later owned by St Augustine's survives as Cambridge, Gonville and Caius College, MS. 144/194, and may be the book in question here (see Lapidge, 'The Study of Latin Texts', p. 104 and n. 36). **10** *Libellum* ... *'Terra que pars'*: apparently a copy of what may be called a 'parsing grammar', a type of grammar which appears from the mid-ninth century onwards, and which is characterized by an opening question—'what part of speech is X?'—with examples varying from text to text and including *anima, codex, columna, iustus, terra* etc.; a copy of such a work beginning 'Terra quae pars' is found in Bern, Burgerbibliothek, MS. A.92 (34) (s. xi/xii), 7r-8v but no copy of the work from Anglo-Saxon England has yet come to light (I am extremely grateful to Vivien Law for this information); the only copy of a 'parsing' grammar yet known from Anglo-Saxon England, as Helmut Gneuss points out to me, is one beginning 'Iustus quae pars' in London, British Library, MS. Cotton Cleopatra A.vi, 31v-47r. **11** *Sedulium*: Caelius Sedulius, *Carmen Paschale* (*Clavis*, no. 1447). **12** *gerim*: a manuscript of computistical materials; on the OE term *gerim*, see Gneuss, 'Liturgical Books', p. 139. **13** *Glossa super Donatum*: presumably a copy of one of the Late Latin commentaries on Donatus—Pompeius, Consentius, Cledonius or Sergius (see Law, *The Insular Latin Grammarians*, pp. 16-17 and 30). **14** *Dialogorum*: the title may suggest Gregory the Great's *Dialogi* (*Clavis*, no. 1713), but it is not clear what such a text would be doing in the hands of a grammarian; one might suspect, therefore, that the book in question was a manuscript of scholastic colloquies (*dialogi*) such as we know to have been used in Anglo-Saxon England for elementary instruction in Latin (see G.N. Garmonsway, 'The Development of the Colloquy', *The Anglo-Saxons*, ed. P. Clemoes [London, 1959], pp. 248-61).

IV. Books donated by Æthelwold, bishop of Winchester (963-84),
to the monastery at Peterborough

In 963 Æthelwold was consecrated bishop of Winchester. Shortly thereafter, according to a lengthy entry in the E- (or Peterborough-) version of the Anglo-Saxon Chronicle, Æthelwold determined to restore all the minsters in Edgar's kingdom which had fallen into desuetude through Viking attacks; among these was the minster at *Medeshamstede* or Peterborough which, according to the E-version, then consisted of nothing more than 'old walls and wild woods'.[79] Æthelwold's biographer, Wulfstan of Winchester, reports in his *Vita S. Æthelwoldi* that the bishop subsequently consecrated to St Peter 'the church adorned with appropriate structures of buildings and abundantly enriched with adjacent lands'.[80] A record of Æthelwold's endowment of Peterborough survives in the Peterborough *Liber niger*, a mid-twelfth-century cartulary now preserved as London, Society of Antiquaries, MS. 60; the charter in question is on 39v-40v.[81] Part of Æthelwold's donation was some twenty-one books, and these have been discussed on various occasions.[82] The donation cannot be dated exactly; the outer limits are the dates of Æthelwold's bishopric (963 x 984); to judge from the account in the E-version of the *Chronicle*, the grant may have occurred within a few years of Æthelwold's elevation to Winchester.

---

[79] *The Anglo-Saxon Chronicle*, ed. B. Thorpe, 2 vols., Rolls Ser. (London, 1861) I, 220: 'Syððon com se biscop Aðelwold to þære mynstre þe wæs gehaten medeshamstede. Þe hwilon wæs fordon fra heðene folce . ne fand þær nan þing buton ealde weallas 7 wilde wuda'.

[80] *Wulfstan of Winchester: the Life of St Æthelwold*, ed. M. Lapidge and M. Winterbottom (Oxford, 1991), p. 40: 'Cuius loci basilicam congruis domorum structuris ornatam et terris adiacentibus copiose ditatam in honore beati Petri principis apostolorum consecrauit'.

[81] The cartulary is listed by G.R.C. Davis, *Medieval Cartularies of Great Britain* (London, 1958), p. 86 (no. 754). The charter is listed by P.H. Sawyer, *Anglo-Saxon Charters: an Annotated List and Bibliography* (London, 1968), no. 1448; it is ed. Birch, *Cartularium Saxonicum*, no. 1128, and Robertson, *Anglo-Saxon Charters*, pp. 72-5.

[82] See A. Way, 'The Gifts of Æthelwold, Bishop of Winchester (A.D. 963-984) to the Monastery of Peterborough', *ArchJ* 20 (1863), 355-66, and M.R. James, *Lists of Manuscripts formerly in Peterborough Abbey Library*, pp. 19-20; see also Robertson, *Anglo-Saxon Charters*, pp. 326-7, and D.A. Bullough, 'The Educational Tradition in England from Alfred to Ælfric: Teaching *utriusque linguae*', *Settimane di studio del Centro italiano di studi sull'alto medioevo* 19 (1972), 453-94, at 481-2.

Þis synd þa madmas þe Adeluuold bisceop sealde into þam mynstre
þe is Medeshamstede gehaten ... þæt is þonne
    an Cristes boc mid sylure berenod ...
And antwentig is þara boca þe Adeluuold biscop gesealde into
Burch . þæt þonne

	Beda in Marcum
	Liber miraculorum
	Expositio Hebreorum nominum
[5]	Prouisio futurarum rerum
	Augustinus de achademicis
	Vita sancti Felicis metrice
	Sinonima Isidori
	Vita Eustachii
[10]	Descidia Parisiacae polis
	Medicinalis
	De duodecim abusiuis
	Sermo super quosdam psalmos
	Commentum cantica canticorum
[15]	De eucharistia
	Commentum Martiani
	Alchimi Auiti
	Liber differentiarum
	Cilicius Ciprianus
[20]	De litteris Grecorum
	Liber bestiarum

COMMENTARY **1** *an Cristes boc*: a gospel-book (on the terminology,
see Gneuss, 'Liturgical Books', p. 107). **2** *Beda in Marcum*: Bede's
Commentary on Mark (*Clavis*, no. 1355). **3** *Liber miraculorum*:
possibly the work of that title by Gregory of Tours (*Clavis*, no. 1024);
but the title could equally well refer to any collection of miracle stories
(see also below, no. XIII, line 64). **4** *Expositio Hebreorum nominum*:
presumably a copy of Jerome, *Liber interpretationis Hebraicorum
nominum* (*Clavis*, no. 581). **5** *Prouisio futurarum rerum*: Julian of
Toledo, *Prognosticum futuri saeculi* (*Clavis*, no. 1258; see also below,
no. XIII, line 40). **6** *Augustinus de achademicis*: Augustine, *Contra
Academicos* (*Clavis*, no. 253). **7** *Vita sancti Felicis metrice*:
presumably the *Carmina* of Paulinus of Nola (*Clavis*, no. 203), the
majority of which concern St Felix, the patron saint of Nola; see also

below, no. XIII, line 38. **8** *Sinonima Isidori*: Isidore's *Synonyma de lamentatione animae peccatricis* (*Clavis*, no. 1203). **9** *Vita Eustachii*: without further specification, it is not possible to determine which of the various *uitae* of St Eustace may be in question; it is probable, however, that this book is identical with that listed below, no. XIII, line 60 (on which see the accompanying Commentary, below). **10** *Descidia Parisiacae polis*: Abbo of Saint-Germain-des-Prés, *Bella Parisiacae urbis* (MGH, PLAC 4, 72-122); on knowledge of this work in Anglo-Saxon England, see my remarks in *ASE* 4 (1975), 75-6, together with excellent discussion by P. Lendinara, 'The Third Book of the *Bella Parisiacae Urbis* by Abbo of Saint-Germain-des-Prés and its Old English Gloss', *ASE* 15 (1986), 73-89. **11** *Medicinalis*: a particular work cannot be recognized in so general a title; for the range of medical writings known in Anglo-Saxon England, see M.L. Cameron, 'The Sources of Medical Knowledge in Anglo-Saxon England', *ASE* 11 (1982), 135-55. **12** *De duodecim abusiuis*: a work which passed during the Middle Ages under the name of St Cyprian, but which is known to have been composed in seventh-century Ireland (*Clavis*, no. 1106). **13** *Sermo super quosdam psalmos*: not identifiable as such; but note that commentaries on a few selected psalms were composed by Ambrose, Origen as translated by Rufinus, and Prosper of Aquitaine (*Clavis* nos. 140, 198f and 524). **14** *Commentum cantica canticorum*: a number of commentaries on the Song of Songs circulated in the early Middle Ages, including those of Aponius (*Clavis*, no. 194) and Gregory the Great's *Homiliae .ii. in Canticum Canticorum* (*Clavis*, no. 1709), but the commentary most likely to be in question is that of Bede (*Clavis*, no. 1353), which survives in a large number of manuscripts (see M.L.W. Laistner and H.H. King, *A Handlist of Bede Manuscripts* [Ithaca, NY, 1943], pp. 66-70); other medieval commentaries on the Song of Songs were compiled by Alcuin (PL 100, cols. 641-64), Angelomus of Luxeuil (PL 115, cols. 551-628) and Haimo of Auxerre (PL 117, cols. 295-358). **15** *De eucharistia*: I have been unable to discover a patristic work—in Latin—with this title; the reference is possibly to a work of Ambrose, either *De sacramentis* (*Clavis*, no. 154) or *De mysteriis* (*Clavis*, no. 155), or to one of Augustine's letters (*Ep*. liv, addressed 'ad inquisitiones Ianuarii ... de sacramentis ... et eucharisti': PL 33, cols. 199-204); or to one of the ninth-century treatises entitled *De corpore et sanguine Domini* by Paschasius Radbertus (PL 120, cols. 1255-1350) or Ratramnus of

Corbie (PL 121, cols. 103-70); or just possibly it refers to one of the various *expositiones missae* which circulated widely in the early Middle Ages (see A. Wilmart, *Dictionnaire d'archéologie chrétienne et de liturgie* 5 [Paris, 1922], 1014-27, s.v. 'Expositio missae'), such as is found in Oxford, Bodleian Library, MS. Hatton 93 (*CLA* II, no. 241). **16** *Commentum Martiani*: presumably the Commentary on Martianus Capella by Remigius of Auxerre; for a recently discovered copy of this work from Anglo-Saxon England, see M.B. Parkes, 'A Fragment of an Early-Tenth-Century Anglo-Saxon Manuscript and its Significance', *ASE* 12 (1983), 129-40. **17** *Alchimi Auiti*: the hexametrical poem by Alcimus Avitus, *De spiritalis historiae gestis* (*Clavis*, no. 995). **18** *Liber differentiarum*: Isidore, *De differentiis uerborum* (*Clavis*, no. 1187). **19** *Cilicius Ciprianus*: if the book in Æthelwold's donation is identical with that in the later Peterborough booklist (below, no. XIII, line 56), it was a copy of the *Epistolae* of Caecilius Cyprianus, or St Cyprian (*Clavis*, no. 50). **20** *De litteris Grecorum*: presumably a Greek-Latin glossary. **21** *Liber bestiarum*: the Latin *Physiologus*, a text which survives in various recensions, all of them dependent (directly or indirectly) on various Greek originals. Some redaction of the *Physiologus* was known in early Anglo-Saxon England, for it was used by Aldhelm and the anonymous author of the *Liber monstrorum*; in the late Anglo-Saxon period a redaction of the *Physiologus* was used by the author of the Old English poems 'Panther', 'Whale' and 'Partridge' in the Exeter Book—possibly the redaction known as 'Redaction B' (*Physiologus Latinus. Editions préliminaires, versio B*, ed. F.J. Carmody [Paris, 1939]); on the transmission of the Latin *Physiologus* in Anglo-Saxon England, see now L. Frank, *Die Physiologus-Literatur des englischen Mittelalters und die Tradition* (Tübingen, 1971), and the concise discussion by G. Orlandi, 'La tradizione del *Physiologus* e la formazione del bestiario latino', *Settimane di studio del Centro italiano di studi sull'alto medioevo* 31 (1985), 1057-1106.

V. Books mentioned in the will of Ælfwold,
bishop of Crediton (c. 997-c. 1016)

Among the collection of Crawford Charters (now Oxford, Bodleian Library, MS. Eng. hist. a.2) is an original copy of a will by Ælfwold, bishop of Crediton, who died 1011 x 1016. Ælfwold's will[83] is no. XIII in the Crawford collection, and has been edited by Napier and Stevenson,[84] and translated and discussed on two occasions by Whitelock.[85] Among the list of possessions bequeathed by Ælfwold were the five books listed below.

> + Þis is Alfwoldes bisceopes cwyde þæt is ðæt he
> geann ... Ordulfe twegra boca
> > Hrabanum
> > 7 martyrlogium ...
> 7 in to Crydian tune þreo þeningbec
> > mæsseboc
> > 7 bletsungboc
> [5]   7 pistelboc

COMMENTARY   **1-2** *Hrabanum 7 martyrlogium*: a copy of an unspecified work by Hrabanus Maurus (see Manitius, *Geschichte* I, 288-302) and a martyrology; conceivably the martyrology in question was that by Hrabanus ('Rabani Mauri Martyrologium', ed. J. McCulloh, CCSL, CM 44 (Turnhout, 1979), 1-134), but there is no possibility of proof. **3-5** the three service-books (*þeningbec*) in question were probably a sacramentary (*mæsseboc*), a pontifical (*bletsungboc*) and an epistolary (*pistelboc*); on these various Old English terms, see Gneuss, 'Liturgical Books', pp. 100, 131 and 110, respectively.

---

[83] Listed by Sawyer, *Anglo-Saxon Charters*, no. 1492.

[84] *The Crawford Collection of Early Charters and Documents now in the Bodleian Library*, ed. A.S. Napier and W.H. Stevenson, Anecdota Oxoniensia (Oxford, 1895), pp. 23-4 (no. 10).

[85] *EHD*, pp. 580-1 (no. 122); *Councils and Synods with other Documents relating to the English Church I: A.D. 871-1204*, ed. D. Whitelock, M. Brett and C.N.L. Brooke, 2 vols. (Oxford, 1981) I, 382-6 (no. 51).

VI. Liturgical books belonging to the church of
Sherburn-in-Elmet (s. xi^{med})

In a lavish Anglo-Saxon gospel-book written in the early eleventh
century (possibly at Christ Church, Canterbury) and known generally
as the 'York Gospels', now York, Minster Library, MS. Add. 1,[86]
there are numerous additions of various date. Among these additions
is a list of service-books and other ecclesiastical furniture (161r)
belonging to the church of Sherburn-in-Elmet;[87] the list is datable on
palaeographical grounds to s. xi^{med}. The books in question are as
follows.

> Þis syndon þa cyrican madmas on Scirburnan . þæt synd
> twa Cristes bec ...
>   7 .i. aspiciens
>   7 .i. adteleuaui
>   7 .ii. pistolbec
>   [5] 7 .i. mæsseboc
>   7 .i. ymener
>   7 .i. salter ...

COMMENTARY **1** *twa Cristes bec*: two gospel-books (on the
terminology, see Gneuss, 'Liturgical Books', p. 107). **2** *aspiciens*: an
antiphonary, so named from the first word of the respond following the
first lesson in the Night Office of the first Sunday in Advent (see
Gneuss, 'Liturgical Books', p. 117). **3** *adteleuaui*: a gradual, so named
from the opening words of the introit for mass on the first Sunday in
Advent; see Gneuss, 'Liturgical Books', p. 103. **4** *pistolbec*:
epistolaries; see Gneuss, 'Liturgical Books', p. 110. **5** *mæsseboc*: a
sacramentary; see Gneuss, 'Liturgical Books', p. 100. **6** *ymener*: a

---

[86] See Ker, *Catalogue*, pp. 468-9 (no. 402), and E. Temple, *Anglo-
Saxon Manuscripts 900-1066* (London, 1976), pp. 79-80 (no. 61). The
book has been published in a lavish facsimile edition by the Roxburghe
Club: *The York Gospels*, ed. N. Barker (London, 1986).

[87] Birch, *Cartularium Saxonicum*, no. 1324; W.H. Stevenson,
'Yorkshire Surveys and other Eleventh-Century Documents in the York
Gospels', *EHR* 27 (1912), 1-25, at 9; and Robertson, *Anglo-Saxon
Charters*, p. 248.

hymnal; see Gneuss, 'Liturgical Books', p. 119. 7 *salter*: a psalter; see Gneuss, 'Liturgical Books', p. 114.

VII. Liturgical books belonging to Bury St Edmunds in the time of Abbot Leofstan (1044-65)

Oxford, Corpus Christi College, MS. 197 is a copy of the *Regula S. Benedicti* in Latin with accompanying Old English translation.[88] The origin of the manuscript is unknown; its script is datable to the second half of the tenth century. At some point the book came to Bury St Edmunds, for into a quire of four added at the end of the manuscript (fols. 106-9) was copied a lengthy account of the possessions and rents of Bury in the time of abbots Leofstan and Baldwin (106v-108r).[89] The handwriting of this addition is of the second half of the eleventh century. The possessions include a number of books (all listed on 107r-v).[90]

> Betæhte nu cincg se goda Eadward 7 se wurðfulla his mæges
> mynstre on Bædericeswyrde Leofstan abbode þæt he bewiste
> þæt þæt þær wære inne 7 ute . 7 he þa þær þus mycel funde
> .x. bec inne ðæra circean
>   .iiii. Cristes bec
>   7 .i. mæsseboc
>   7 .i. pistelboc
>   7 .i. salter
> [5]   7 .i. god spellboc
>   7 .i. capitularia
>   7 sancte Eadmundes uita ...
> Blakere hæfð .i. winter rædingboc
> Brihtric hæfð ... .i. mæsseboc
> [10]   7 winter rædingboc
>   7 sumerboc

---

[88] See Ker, *Catalogue*, pp. 430-2 (no. 353).

[89] See D.C. Douglas, 'Fragments of an Anglo-Saxon Survey from Bury St Edmunds', *EHR* 43 (1928), 376-83, and Robertson, *Anglo-Saxon Charters*, pp. 192-201.

[90] See also M.R. James, *On the Abbey of St Edmund at Bury*, p. 6.

Siuerþ ... mæsseboc
7. Leofstan an handboc
Æperic an mæsseboc
[15]   7 capitularia
Durstan an psalter
Oskytel hæfð ... mæsseboc
      7 an Ad te leuaui ...
Her syndon .xxx. boca ealre on Leofstanes abbodes hafona
buton mynsterbec.

COMMENTARY 1 .iiii. *Cristes bec*: four gospel-books; see Gneuss, 'Liturgical Books', p. 107. 2 *mæsseboc*: a sacramentary or, possibly, at this date, a plenary missal; see Gneuss, 'Liturgical Books', p. 100. 3 *pistelboc*: an epistolary; see Gneuss, 'Liturgical Books', p. 110. 4 *salter*: a psalter; see Gneuss, 'Liturgical Books', p. 114. 5 *god spellboc*: probably a homiliary rather than a gospel-book; see Gneuss, 'Liturgical Books', p. 123. 6 *capitularia*: a collectar; see Gneuss, 'Liturgical Books', p. 113. 7 *sancte Eadmundes uita*: a copy of Abbo of Fleury's *Passio S. Eadmundi* (*BHL*, no. 2392; see also *Three Lives of English Saints*, ed. M. Winterbottom [Toronto, 1972], pp. 67-87); although several English manuscripts of the late eleventh century survive (for example, London, British Library, MS. Cotton Tiberius B. ii, and London, Lambeth Palace, MS. 362, and Copenhagen, Kongelige Bibliotek, MS. G.K.S. 1588 [4°]), none of them appears to have been written by the time of Leofstan's abbacy, and the manuscript mentioned in this list must be presumed lost. 8 *winter rædingboc*: presumably an Office lectionary; see Gneuss, 'Liturgical Books', p. 121. 9 *mæsseboc*: see above, line 2. 10 *winter rædingboc*: an Office lectionary, as above, line 8. 11 *summerboc*: also an Office lectionary, as above, line 8. 12 *mæsseboc*: see above, line 2. 13 *handboc*: presumably a ritual or manual, a book containing occasional offices which a priest might have to perform; see Gneuss, 'Liturgical Books', p. 134. 14 *mæsseboc*: see above, line 2. 15 *capitularia*: a collectar, as above, line 6. 16 *psalter*: see Gneuss, 'Liturgical Books', p. 114. 17 *mæsseboc*: see above, line 2. 18 *Ad te leuaui*: a gradual, so named from the opening words of the introit for mass on the first Sunday in Advent; see Gneuss, 'Liturgical Books', p. 103.

VIII. *Books donated by Sæwold, sometime abbot of Bath, to the church of Saint-Vaast in Arras (c. 1070)*

At the time of the Norman Conquest, the abbot of the monastery of St Peter, Bath, was one Sæwold, about whom very little is known.[91] In the aftermath of the Conquest, the family of Harold Godwinson first took refuge in Exeter and later were forced to flee to Flanders, probably in 1068 or 1069.[92] Among the refugees was Gunhild, Harold's sister (and the daughter of King Cnut), and it is interesting to note that she took at least one book with her, for on her death in 1087 she bequeathed to the church of Saint-Donatien in Bruges a psalter which was glossed in Old English.[93] It would appear that Abbot Sæwold fled to Flanders at the same time, for he is next recorded as having made a donation of thirty-three books to the church of Saint-Vaast in Arras where, presumably, he had taken refuge. In an eleventh-century copy of Augustine, *Tractatus in euangelium Ioannis*, now Arras, Bibliothèque Municipale, MS. 849 (539), the main scribe has entered on 159r a list of the books donated by Sæwold to Saint-Vaast.[94] Because a number of Sæwold's books which survive were evidently written in England (see below), there is some presumption that Sæwold, like Harold's sister Gunhild, took his books with him when he left England and subsequently bequeathed them to the house which gave him refuge. Although it is preserved in a continental manuscript, therefore, the Sæwold booklist may be taken as evidence

---

[91] Sæwold attests a charter of Edward the Confessor in favour of Wells, dated 4 May 1065 (Sawyer, *Anglo-Saxon Charters*, no. 1042), and one undated manumission from Bath (Kemble, *Codex Diplomaticus*, no. 1351).

[92] See E.A. Freeman, *The Norman Conquest*, 6 vols. (Oxford, 1867-79) IV, 138-60.

[93] Ker, *Catalogue*, p. 469 (no. 403). Ker gives the date of Gunhild's death erroneously as 1043; the psalter in question, known as 'Gunhild's Psalter', was still at Bruges in the sixteenth century, but is now presumably lost.

[94] *Catalogue général des manuscrits des bibliothèques publiques des départements* [quarto ser.] IV (Paris, 1872), 215-16.

of the personal[95] library of an English ecclesiastic at the time of the Conquest. The booklist has been printed by Becker,[96] and reprinted and furnished with excellent commentary by Philip Grierson.[97] In what follows I am heavily indebted to Grierson, particularly for the identification of surviving books.

Abbas deuotus probus ac uita Seiwoldus
Contulit hos libros Christo dominoque Vedasto.

> Textum argenteum
> Missalem
> Librum heptaticum Moysi
> Librum moralium Gregorii .xx.

[5] Librum Haimonis usque in Pascha
> Librum Claudii super Matheum
> Librum regule sancti Benedicti et Diadema monachorum
> Librum dialogorum Gregorii
> Librum uitarum patrum

[10] Librum expositionis Ambrosii de psalmo CXVIII
> Librum item (Ambrosii) De initiandis (liber I) eiusdem
> De mysteriis (libri VI), Commonitorium Palladii de
> Bragmanis (liber I), Ysidori De officiis (libri II) in
> uno uolumine
> Librum pronosticon
> Librum enkiridion
> Librum exameron Ambrosii

[15] Librum Prosperi ad Iulianum et Ambrosii De officiis
> Librum Bede super VII epistolas canonicas
> Librum epistolarum Bacharii, Augustini, Eubodii, Macedonii
> Librum uite sancti Richarii

---

[95] It is possible, of course, that some of the books donated by Sæwold had been the property of the monks of Bath, and that Sæwold in flight had absconded with them (the book listed above, line 7, for example, would appear to have been a book used for reading at chapter).

[96] *Catalogi*, no. 58.

[97] 'Les Livres de l'Abbé Seiwold de Bath', *RB* 52 (1940), 96-116.

Librum uitae sanctorum confessorum Cutberti, Gutlaci,
Aichadri, Filiberti, Dunstani
[20] Librum De assumptione sancte Mariae
Librum canonum
Librum hystoriae aecclesiastice gentis Anglie
Librum uite sancti Walerici, Mauri, passionum sanctorum
martirum Luciani, Maxiani atque Iuliani, in uno
uolumine
Librum medicinalis
[25] Librum Cassiodori De ortographia
Librum uersuum et tractuum totius anni
Librum parabolarum Salomonis
Librum De laude uirginitatis
Librum De professione coniugatorum
[30] Librum Prudentii
Iuuencus, Sedulius in uno uolumine
Librum Rabbani super Iudith et Hester
Librum tripartite historie ecclesiastice

COMMENTARY 1 *Textum argenteum*: a gospel-book, decorated with silver. **2** *Missalem*: a sacramentary or plenary missal; see Gneuss, 'Liturgical Books', p. 101. **3** *heptaticum Moysi*: the Old Testament Heptateuch (Genesis, Exodus, Leviticus, Numbers, Deuteronomy, Joshua and Judges), thought in the Middle Ages to have been composed by Moses. **4** *moralium Gregorii .xx.*: Gregory's *Moralia in Iob* (*Clavis*, no. 1708), a work which in fact consists of thirty-five books. **5** *Haimonis usque in Pascha*: the first part of the Homiliary of Haimo of Auxerre, containing homilies from Advent to Easter; see H. Barré, *Les Homéliaires carolingiens de l'école d' Auxerre*, Studi e testi 225 (Rome, 1962), 49-70. **6** *Claudii super Matheum*: the commentary—in fact it is a *catena* of earlier authorities—on Matthew by Claudius of Turin (*ob.* 827), which is as yet unprinted (see PL 104, cols. 833-8, and Manitius, *Geschichte* I, 394). **7** *regule ... monachorum*: the *Regula* of St Benedict (*Clavis*, no. 1852), together with the *Diadema monachorum* of Smaragdus of Saint-Mihiel (PL 102, 593-690); the collocation of texts is found in other Anglo-Saxon manuscripts (for example, Cambridge, Corpus Christi College, MS. 57) and suggests a book intended for reading at chapter. **8** *dialogorum Gregorii*: Gregory the Great, *Dialogi* (*Clavis*, no. 1713). **9** *uitarum patrum*: the so-called *Vitas patrum*, an early title used to describe a massive but heterogeneous collection of lives and sayings principally of the early Egyptian Desert Fathers (see *BHL*, nos. 6524-47); the manuscript in question survives as Brussels, Bibliothèque Royale, MS. 9850-2 (Soissons, s. vii/viii: see *CLA* X, no. 1547a). **10** *expositionis Ambrosii*: Ambrose, *Expositio de psalmo CXVIII* (*Clavis*, no. 141); the manuscript survives as Arras, Bibliothèque Municipale, MS. 899 (590) (s. ix). **11** *Ambrosii De initiandis (liber I)*: Ambrose, *De mysteriis* (*Clavis*, no. 155). **11** *eiusdem De mysteriis (libri VI)*: Ambrose, *De sacramentis* (*Clavis*, no. 154). **11** *Palladii de Bragmanis*: Palladius, *De moribus Brachmanorum* (PL 17, cols. 1131-46); see A. Wilmart, 'Les Textes latins de la lettre de Palladius sur les moeurs des Brahmanes', *RB* 45 (1933), 29-42. **11** *Ysidori De officiis*: Isidore, *De ecclesiasticis officiis* (*Clavis*, no. 1207); the manuscript containing the four items listed in line 11 survives as Arras, Bibliothèque Municipale, 1068 (276) (s.x). **12** *pronosticon*: Julian of Toledo, *Prognosticum futuri saeculi* (*Clavis*, no. 1258). **13** *enkiridion*: Augustine, *Enchiridion ad Laurentium* (*Clavis*, no. 295). **14** *exameron Ambrosii*: Ambrose, *Exameron* (*Clavis*, no. 123); the manuscript survives as Arras, Bibliothèque Municipale, MS. 346 (867) (s. x^{ex} and xi^{med}) and is listed by Gneuss, 'A Preliminary List', no. 778. **15** *Prosperi ad Iulianum*: Julianus Pomerius, *De uita contemplatiua* (*Clavis*, no. 998); on the manuscript tradition of this work, see M.L.W. Laistner, 'The Influence during the Middle Ages of the Treatise *De vita contemplativa* and its Surviving Manuscripts', in his *The Intellectual Heritage of the Early Middle Ages*, ed. C.G. Starr (Ithaca, NY, 1957), pp. 40-56; the manuscript in question survives as Arras, Bibliothèque Municipale, MS. 435 (326), fols. 65-122 (s. xi). **15** *Ambrosii De officiis*: Ambrose, *De officiis ministrorum* (*Clavis*, no. 144); note that the copy of Ambrose, which was once cognate with (or bound with) the copy of Julianus Pomerius in Arras 435 (326) is no longer extant. **16** *Bede*: Bede, *Super epistolas catholicas expositio* (*Clavis*, no. 1362). **17** *epistolarum Bacharii*: for the various letters transmitted under the name of Bachiarius, see *Clavis*, nos. 568-70. **17** *Augustini, Eubodii, Macedonii*: apparently a collection of *epistolae* of Augustine (*Clavis*, no. 262) to Evodius (*Epp.* clviii, clx, clxi, clxiii and clxxvii) and Macedonius (*Epp.* clii and cliv). **18** *uite sancti Richarii*: probably Alcuin's *Vita S. Richarii* (*BHL*, nos. 7223-7, ptd PL 101, cols. 681-90), on which see now I Deug-Su, *L'opera agiografica di Alcuino*

(Spoleto, 1983), pp. 115-65; on the possible identity of the manuscript in question, see Grierson, 'Les Livres', p. 109, n. 18. **19** *uitae sanctorum* ... *Dunstani*:   a manuscript now preserved as Arras, Bibliothèque Municipale, MS. 1029 (812) (? Bath, s. x^(ex)), which contains the anonymous *Vita S. Cuthberti* (*BHL*, no. 2019), Felix's *Vita S. Guthlaci* (*BHL*, no. 3723), the *Vita S. Aichardi* (*BHL*, no. 181), the *Vita S. Filiberti* (*BHL*, no. 6806), and the anonymous *Vita S. Dunstani* by the English cleric .B. (*BHL*, no. 2342). **20** *De assumptione*: the manuscript in question survives as Arras, Bibliothèque Municipale, MS. 732 (684) (s. xi), and contains Jerome's *Epistola ad Paulam et Eustochium de assumptione beate Virginis* (*Ep*. xlvi; see *Clavis*, no. 620), as well as Cassiodorus, *De anima* (*Clavis*, no. 897) and *Institutiones* (*Clavis*, no. 906). **21** *Librum canonum*: the manuscript survives as Arras, Bibliothèque Municipale, MS. 644 (572) (s. viii/ix); its principal content is the collection of canons known as the *Collectio Quesnelliana* (*Clavis*, no. 1770). **22** *Librum hystoriae* ... *Anglie*: Bede, *Historia ecclesiastica gentis Anglorum* (*Clavis*, no. 1375); see further the discussion by Grierson ('Les Livres', p. 110, n. 22), who suggests that a fragment of the manuscript in question was preserved as a Phillipps manuscript; the fragment is now New York, Pierpont Morgan Library, MS. M.826 (Northumbria, s. viii^(ex): *CLA* XI, no. 1662). **23** *Librum uite sancti Walerici* ... *uno uolumine*:   the manuscript does not appear to survive; for the *uitae* in question, see *BHL*, nos. 8762 (Walaricus), 5783 (Maurus), 5015 (Lucianus and Marcianus) and 4544-5 (Iulianus). **24** *Librum medicinalis*:   not identifiable without further specification; but see Grierson's note ('Les Livres', p. 110, n. 24). **25** *Librum Cassiodori*: Cassiodorus, *De orthographia* (*Clavis*, no. 907). **26** *Librum uersuum et tractuum totius anni*:   a gradual or responsorial which contained the verses and responds as well as the tracts (that is, the chants which replaced the Alleluia during penitential periods and which were sung without response) for the entire liturgical year; the scribe has added the word *tonos* after *anni*, which may suggest that the manuscript was notated. **27** *Librum parabolarum Salomonis*: the manuscript survives as Arras, Bibliothèque Municipale, MS. 1079 (235), fols. 28-80 (s.ix/x); it contains three apparently unedited commentaries on Proverbs, Ecclesiastes and the Song of Songs, as well as Bede's *In Esdram et Nehemiam prophetas allegorica expositio* (*Clavis*, no. 1329); on the manuscript, see further Grierson, 'Les Livres', pp. 114-16. **28** *De* *laude uirginitatis*: a copy either of Aldhelm's prose *De uirginitate* (*Clavis*, no. 1332) or his *Carmen de uirginitate* (*Clavis*, no. 1333), both of which bore the rubric *De laude uirginitatis* on occasion, and which, to judge from surviving manuscripts, do not seem ever to have been combined in one codex. **29** *De professione coniugatorum*: Grierson ('Les Livres', p. 111, n. 29) confessed himself unable to identify this item, and I agree that it is unidentifiable without further specification, although possibly Augustine's *De bono coniugali* (*Clavis*, no. 299) is in question. **30** *Librum Prudentii*: a copy of all or some of Prudentius's *Carmina* (*Clavis*, nos. 1437-45). **31** *Iuuencus, Sedulius*: Juvencus, *Evangelia quattuor* (*Clavis*, no. 1385) together with Caelius Sedulius, *Carmen Paschale* (*Clavis*, no. 1447). **32** *Librum Rabbani ... Hester*: Hrabanus Maurus, *Expositio in librum Iudith* (PL 109, cols. 539-92) and *Expositio in librum Esther* (PL 109, cols. 635-70); the manuscript survives as Arras, Bibliothèque Municipale, MS. 764 (739), fols. 1-93 (s. x), and is listed by Gneuss, 'A Preliminary List', no. 779. **33** *Tripartite historie ecclesiastice*: Cassiodorus, *Tripartita historia ecclesiastica* (PL 69, cols. 879-1214); on the medieval transmission of this work, see M.L.W. Laistner, 'The Value and Influence of Cassiodorus's Ecclesiastical History', *The Intellectual Heritage of the Early Middle Ages*, ed. Starr, pp. 22-39.

IX. *Books belonging to Worcester (c. 1050)*

Cambridge, Corpus Christi College, MS. 367 is a composite manuscript, consisting of two parts each separately foliated and each composite in turn. Into a single and separate quire (Part ii, fols. 45-52) containing the conclusion of a *Vita S. Kenelmi*, a scribe has copied a list of books in handwriting datable to the mid-eleventh century (48v).[98] Because some of the books listed can be identified with surviving books from Worcester, and because a Worcester document was later copied into the quire, there are good grounds for thinking that

---

[98] Ker, *Catalogue*, p. 110 (no. 64).

the booklist itself is from Worcester. It has been printed and discussed on several occasions.[99]

        Ðeo englissce passionale

        7 .ii. englissce dialogas

        7 Oddan boc

        7 Þe englisca martirlogium

[5]   7 .ii. englisce salteras

        7 .ii. pastorales englisce

        7 Þe englisca regol

        7 Barontus

COMMENTARY **1** *Ðeo englissce passionale*: a legendary in Old English (see Gneuss, 'Liturgical Books', p. 126), possibly a copy of Ælfric's *Lives of Saints*. **2** *.ii. englissce dialogas*: two copies of Werferth's Old English translation of Gregory's *Dialogi* (*Bischof Waerferths von Worcester Übersetzung der Dialoge Gregors des Grossen*, ed. H. Hecht, 2 vols. [Hamburg, 1900-7]); the two manuscripts in question are probably London, British Library, MS. Cotton Otho C.i, vol. 2 (Worcester, s. xi[in] and xi[med]) and Oxford, Bodleian Library, MS. Hatton 76 (Worcester, s. xi[1]). **3** *Oddan boc*: presumably a book belonging to one *Odda* or *Oda* (hence the genitive) rather than a book *by* Oda; it is interesting to note that a charter of Edward the Confessor dated 1044 x 1051 (listed Sawyer, *Anglo-Saxon Charters*, no. 1058 and ptd Kemble, *Codex Diplomaticus*, no. 797) leasing land at Lench, Worcestershire, to Lyfing, bishop of Worcester, is witnessed by a monk of Worcester named Odda: 'Ego Odda monachus consensi'; this Odda was arguably the owner of the book in question. **4** *Þe englisca martirlogium*: apparently a copy of the so-called Old English Martyrology (*Das altenglische Martyrologium*, ed. G. Kotzor, 2 vols., Bayerische Akademie der Wissenschaften, Phil.-hist. Klasse, Abhandlungen n.s. 88 [Munich, 1981]; see Gneuss, 'Liturgical Books', p. 128); but it does not seem possible to identify the entry in this booklist with any surviving manuscript of the work. **5** *.ii. englisce salteras*: two psalters, either in Old English translation

---

[99] Robertson, *Anglo-Saxon Charters*, pp. 250 and 498-9, and R.M. Wilson, *The Lost Literature of Medieval England*, 2nd ed. (London, 1970), pp. 81-2.

or, more likely perhaps, with extensive interlinear glossing in Old English (see Gneuss, 'Liturgical Books', p. 128). **6** .*ii. pastorales englisce*: two copies of King Alfred's English translation of Gregory's *Regula pastoralis* (*King Alfred's West Saxon Version of Gregory's Pastoral Care*, ed. H. Sweet, EETS o.s. 45 and 50 (London, 1871)); the two manuscripts in question are probably Cambridge, Corpus Christi College, MS. 12 (Worcester, s. x^2) and Oxford, Bodleian Library, MS. Hatton 20 (Worcester, s. ix^{ex}). **7** *Þe englisca regol*: probably a copy of Æthelwold's English translation of the *Regula* of St Benedict (*Die angelsächsischen Prosabearbeitungen der Benediktinerregel*, ed. A. Schröer, rev. H. Gneuss [Darmstadt, 1964]); the manuscript in question is probably Cambridge, Corpus Christi College, MS. 178, pp. 287-457 (Worcester, s. xi^1). **8** *Barontus*: the *Visio S. Baronti monachi* (*Clavis*, no. 1313; *BHL*, no. 997); the occurrence of the work in the present list may suggest that an Old English translation of the *Visio Baronti* is in question, but no such translation has come down to us (the only Latin version known to me in an Anglo-Saxon manuscript is some fragments in London, British Library, MS. Cotton Otho A.xiii); on the work itself, see M.P. Ciccarese, 'La *Visio Baronti* nella tradizione letteraria delle *uisiones* dell'aldilà', *Romanobarbarica* 6 (1981-2), 25-52; see also below, no. XIII, line 51.

X. *Inventory of books procured by Bishop Leofric for the church of Exeter (1069 x 1072)*

When Leofric moved his see from Crediton to Exeter in 1050 he found at Exeter no more than a handful of worn-out service-books. During the years of his episcopacy he evidently took great pains to acquire or have copied a full complement not only of necessary service-books, but also of other books, so that on his death in 1072 he was able to bequeath some sixty-six books to his church. Leofric's bequest (of estates and ecclesiastical furnishings as well as of books) is recorded in a document copied in the third quarter of the eleventh century into a preliminary quire (now fols. iv, 1-6) that was prefixed to a gospel-book which Leofric had acquired, now Oxford, Bodleian Library, MS. Auct.

D.2.16 (Landévennec, Brittany, s. x);[100] the list is found on 1r-2v.
It is this copy which serves as the basis for the edition printed below.
A second contemporary copy is found in a quire now prefixed to the
Exeter Book (Exeter, Cathedral Library, MS. 3501, fols. 0, 1-7; the
list is on 1r-2v); this quire was originally part of a copy of the West
Saxon gospels, now Cambridge, University Library, MS. Ii.2.11.[101]
The few minor variants which occur in the Exeter Book-version have
also been recorded below. Leofric's booklist has been printed and
discussed on many occasions,[102] most thoroughly by Max Förster in
his introduction to the facsimile of the Exeter Book.[103] It is possible
to identify a number of items in Leofric's list because Leofric took care
to have *ex libris* inscriptions copied into the books which he
donated;[104] I note below those cases where an identification can be

---

[100] See Ker, *Catalogue*, pp. 351-2 (no. 291).

[101] *Ibid*. pp. 28-31 (no. 20).

[102] H. Wanley, *Librorum Veterum Septentrionalium . . . Catalogus*
(Oxford, 1705), p. 80 (interesting annotation); T. Wright, 'On Bishop
Leofric's Library', *JBAA* 18 (1862), 220-4; F.E. Warren, *The Leofric
Missal* (Oxford, 1883), pp. xxii-xxiv; C. Edmonds, 'The Formation
and Fortunes of Exeter Cathedral Library', *Report and Trans. of the
Devonshire Assoc.* 31 (1899), 25-50; Robertson, *Anglo-Saxon
Charters*, pp. 226-30 and 473-80; L.J. Lloyd, 'Leofric as Bibliophile',
Leofric of Exeter, ed. F. Barlow *et al.* (Exeter, 1972), pp. 32-42; M.
McC. Gatch, *Preaching and Theology in Anglo-Saxon England: Ælfric
and Wulfstan* (Toronto, 1977), pp. 42-4; E.M. Drage, 'Bishop Leofric
and Exeter Cathedral Chapter (1050-1072): A Reassessment of the
Manuscript Evidence' (unpubl. D. Phil. dissertation, Oxford Univ.,
1978), *passim*.

[103] *The Exeter Book of Old English Poetry*, ed. R.W. Chambers, M.
Förster and R. Flower (London, 1933), pp. 10-32, esp. 25-30.

[104] A convenient list of manuscripts with Leofric's inscriptions is
found in R. Frank and A. Cameron, *A Plan for the Dictionary of Old
English* (Toronto, 1973), p. 193. Note that one manuscript which has
a Leofric *ex libris* inscription (Cambridge, Corpus Christi College, MS.
41) does not apparently figure in the list of Leofric's donation, unless
it is one of the sacramentaries listed in line 2 (though it could hardly
be described as a *fulle mæsseboc*; on its liturgical contents, see R.J.S.

confirmed by such evidence.

Her swutelað on þissere Cristes[105] bec hwæt Leofric bisceop hæfð gedon inn to sancte Petres minstre on Exanceastre þær his bisceopstol is ...

.ii. mycele Cristes bec gebonede ...

7 .ii. fulle mæssebec

7 .i. collectaneum

7 .ii. pistelbec

[5]   7 .ii. fulle sangbec

7 .i. nihtsang

7 .i. adteleuaui

7 .i. tropere

7 .ii. salteras

[10]   7 se þriddan saltere[106] swa man singð on Rome

7 .ii. ymneras

7 .i. deorwyrðe bletsingboc

7 .iii. oðre

7 .i. englisc Cristes boc[107]

[15]   7 .ii. summerrædingbec

7 .i. winterrædingboc

7 regula canonicorum

7 martyrlogium

7 .i. canon on leden

[20]   7 .i. scriftboc on englisc

7 .i. full spelboc wintres 7 sumeres

7 Boeties boc on englisc

7 .i. mycel englisc boc be gehwilcum þingum on leoðwisan geworht

---

Grant, *Cambridge, Corpus Christi College 41; the Loricas and the Missal* [Amsterdam, 1979]).

[105] The Exeter Book omits the word *Cristes*.

[106] The Exeter Book omits the word *saltere*.

[107] In lieu of this entry the Exeter Book has 'Þeos englisce Cristes boc' (but recall that the quire containing this document was originally prefixed not to the Exeter Book—which is in no way a *Cristes boc*—but to Cambridge, University Library, MS. Ii.2.11).

7 he ne funde on þam mynstre þa he tofeng boca na ma
buton ane capitularie
[25]   7 .i. forealdodne nihtsang
7 .i. pistelboc
7 .ii. forealdode rædingbec swiðe wake ...
7 þus fela leden boca he beget inn to þam mynstre.
liber pastoralis
7 liber dialogorum
[30]   7 libri .iiii. prophetarum
7 liber Boetii De Consolatione[108]
7 Isagoge Porphirii[109]
7 .i. passionalis
7 liber Prosperi
[35]   7 liber Prudentii psicomachie
7 liber Prudentii ymnorum
7 liber Prudentii de martyribus[110]
7 liber Ezechielis prophete
7 Cantica canticorum
[40]   7 liber Isaie prophete on sundron
7 liber Isidori Ethimolagiarum
7 Passiones apostolorum
7 Expositio Bede super euuangelium Luce
7 Expositio Bede super apocalipsin
[45]   7 Expositio Bede super .vii. epistolas canonicas
7 liber Isidori De nouo et ueteri testamento
7 liber Isidori De miraculis Christi
7 liber Oserii
7 liber Machabeorum
[50]   7 liber Persii
7 Sedulies boc
7 liber Aratoris

---

[108] In the Exeter Book this entry is followed by *Liber officialis Amalarii*; see below, line 55.

[109] Following this item there is an erasure of one item in Auct. D.2.16.

[110] After *martyribus* the Exeter Book adds 'on anre bec'.

          7 Diadema monachorum [111]
          7 Glose Statii
[55]   7 liber officialis Amalarii

COMMENTARY **1** *.ii. mycele Cristes bec gebonede*: two large
gospel-books, ornamented. **2** *fulle mæssebec*: sacramentaries or
missals (see Gneuss, 'Liturgical Books', p. 100); it is not precisely
clear what *fulle* means in this context, and it is possible that the scribe
was attempting to distinguish the plenary missal from the sacramentary;
one of the books in question is possibly Oxford, Bodleian Library, MS.
Bodley 579 (the 'Leofric Missal'), which bears a Leofric *ex libris*
inscription. **3** *collectaneum*: a collectary (see Gneuss, 'Liturgical
Books', p. 113); the book probably survives as London, British
Library, MS. Harley 2961 (Exeter, s. xi^{med}) (*The Leofric Collectar*, ed.
E.S. Dewick and W.H. Frere, 2 vols., HBS 45-6 [London, 1914-21]);
Harley 2961 once bore a Leofric *ex libris* which is no longer preserved
(see Ker, *Catalogue*, p. 308). **4** *pistelbec*: epistolaries for the mass;
see Gneuss, 'Liturgical Books', p. 110. **5** *fulle sangbec*: possibly
books for the Office, but the precise meaning of *sangbec* (and the
qualifying adjective *fulle* in this context) is not clear; see Gneuss,
'Liturgical Books', p. 103. **6** *nihtsang*: an antiphonary for the
nocturnal hours (*antiphonarium nocturnale*); see Gneuss, 'Liturgical
Books', p. 117. **7** *adteleuaui*: a gradual; see Gneuss, 'Liturgical
Books', p. 103. **8** *tropere*: a troper for the mass; see Gneuss,
'Liturgical Books', p. 104. **9** *salteras*: two psalters, presumably of
the Gallican type, since a Roman psalter in the following line is
distinguished from them; one of these Gallican psalters may survive as
London, British Library, MS. Harley 863 (Exeter, s. xi^2). **10** *se
þriddan ... on Rome*: a psalter of 'Roman' type (*psalterium
Romanum*). **11** *ymneras*: hymnals for the Office; see Gneuss,
'Liturgical Books', p. 119. **12** *deorwyrðe bletsingboc*: a valuable
pontifical or benedictional—or both combined (see Gneuss, 'Liturgical
Books', p. 131); the manuscript in question is possibly London, British
Library, MS. Add. 28188 (Exeter, s. xi^2). **13** *.iii. oðre*: three other
(less valuable) pontificals or benedictionals—or both combined. **14**

---

[111] The Exeter Book omits this entry; in its stead a later hand has
written 'liber de sanctis patribus'.

englisc Cristes boc: the West Saxon version of the gospels, now Cambridge, University Library, MS. Ii.2.11 (Exeter, s. xi²), a manuscript which bears a Leofric *ex libris* inscription. **15-16** *.ii. sumerrædingbec 7 .i. winterrædingboc*: as Gneuss points out ('Liturgical Books', p. 121), the division of the lectionary (*rædingboc*) into winter and summer volumes suggests an Office book rather than a mass lectionary. **17** *regula canonicorum*: a copy of Chrodegang of Metz's *Regula canonicorum* (*Clavis*, no. 1876); Leofric is known to have introduced Chrodegang's *Regula* to his secular clergy at Exeter, and it is possible that the book in question survives as Cambridge, Corpus Christi College, MS. 191 (Exeter, s. xi²). **18** *martyrlogium*: presumably a copy of the Old English Martyrology, and possibly that which survives as Cambridge, Corpus Christi College, MS. 196 (Exeter, s. xi²). **19** *canon on leden*: a collection of ecclesiastical canons which (without further specification) cannot be identified. **20** *scriftboc on englisc*: a manuscript containing penitential texts in Old English (see A.J. Frantzen, *The Literature of Penance in Anglo-Saxon England* [New Brunswick, NJ, 1983], pp. 133-41); it is probable that the *scriftboc* in question survives as Cambridge, Corpus Christi College, MS. 190 (Exeter, s. xi¹ and xi^{med}). **21** *full spelboc*: a homiliary in two volumes, for summer and winter; see Gneuss, 'Liturgical Books', p. 123. **22** *Boeties boc*: apparently a copy of King Alfred's English translation of Boethius, *De consolatione Philosophiae*; the manuscript in question does not survive. **23** *mycel englisc boc*: 'a large book in English on various subjects composed in verse', presumably the Exeter Book itself, now Exeter, Cathedral Library, MS. 3501 (s. x²). **24** *ane capitularie*: a collectar, presumably; see Gneuss, 'Liturgical Books', p. 113. **25** *forealdodne nihtsang*: a worn-out antiphonary; see Gneuss, 'Liturgical Books', p. 117. **26** *pistelboc*: an epistolary; see Gneuss, 'Liturgical Books', p. 110. **27** *.ii. forealdode rædingbec swiðe wake*: 'two worn-out (Office) lectionaries in very bad condition'; see Gneuss, 'Liturgical Books', p. 121. **28** *liber pastoralis*: Gregory's *Regula pastoralis* (*Clavis*, no. 1712); the book in question survives as Oxford, Bodleian Library, MS. Bodley 708 (Christ Church, Canterbury, s. x^{ex}; provenance Exeter), which has a Leofric *ex libris* inscription. **29** *liber dialogorum*: Gregory the Great, *Dialogi* (*Clavis*, no. 1713). **30** *libri .iiii. prophetarum*: a copy of the four 'great' biblical prophets (Isaiah, Jeremiah, Ezekiel and Daniel). **31** *Boetii De consolatione*: Boethius,

De consolatione Philosophiae (*Clavis*, no. 878); the book survives as Oxford, Bodleian Library, MS. Auct. F.1.15 (St Augustine's, Canterbury, s. x^2; provenance Exeter), and has a Leofric *ex libris* inscription. **32** *Isagoge Porphirii*:   Porphyry's *Isagoge* or 'Introduction' to Aristotle's *Categories* was, in the Latin translation of Boethius, the standard account of logic in the early Middle Ages; Boethius also wrote a commentary (*Clavis*, no. 881) on Porphyry's *Isagoge*, which is also conceivably in question here. **33** *passionalis*: a passional or legendary (see Gneuss, 'Liturgical Books', p. 126); its position here in the list may suggest that it was intended for meditational rather than liturgical reading. **34** *liber Prosperi*:   in medieval booklists references to Prosper almost invariably refer to his *Epigrammata* (*Clavis*, no. 518), which were a standard school-text in the early Middle Ages; see Manitius, *Handschriften*, p. 247. **35-7**: three works of Prudentius—the *Psychomachia* (*Clavis*, no. 1441), the *Cathemerinon* (*Clavis*, no. 1438) and *Peristephanon* (*Clavis*, no. 1443); in the Exeter Book-version of this list the three works of Prudentius are said to be *on anre bec*; and indeed all three survive as Oxford, Bodleian Library, MS. Auct. F.3.6 (Exeter, s. xi^1), which also has a Leofric *ex libris* inscription. **38** *liber Ezechielis*: another copy of the prophet Ezekiel; see above, line 30. **39** *Cantica canticorum*: the biblical Song of Songs. **40** *liber Isaie*: another copy of the prophet Isaiah, said to be *on sundron* because distinct from that listed above (line 30). **41** *liber Isidori Ethimolagiarum*: Isidore, *Etymologiae* (*Clavis*, no. 1186). **42** *Passiones apostolorum*: any one of a number of works might be in question here: pseudo-Abdias, *Historiae apostolicae*; the anonymous *Breuiarium apostolorum* (*BHL*, no. 652); Isidore, *De ortu et obitu patrum* (*Clavis*, no. 1191); a Hiberno-Latin treatise of the same name (unptd, but cf. PL 83, cols. 1275-94); or a collection of *passiones apostolorum* such as that in Würzburg, Universitätsbibliothek, MS. M.p.th.f.78 (see *CLA* IX, no. 1425). **43** *Expositio Bede ... Luce*: Bede, *In Lucae euangelium expositio* (*Clavis*, no. 1356). **44** *Expositio Bede ... apocalipsin*: Bede, *Explanatio Apocalypsis* (*Clavis*, no. 1363); the book possibly survives as London, Lambeth Palace Library, MS. 149 (s. x^2). **45** *Expositio Bede ... canonicas*: Bede, *Super epistolas catholicas expositio* (*Clavis*, no. 1362); the manuscript possibly survives as Oxford, Bodleian Library, MS. Bodley 849 (Loire region, s. ix^1; provenance Exeter). **46** *Liber Isidori ... testamento*: it is not clear whether the work in question here is Isidore's *Prooemia* to the books of the Old and New Testaments (*Clavis*, no. 1192; see below, no. XI, line 33), or the pseudo-Isidorian *Quaestiones de ueteri et nouo testamento*, a work of Hiberno-Latin origin (*Clavis*, no. 1194; see R. E. McNally, 'The pseudo-Isidorian *De ueteri et nouo Testamento Quaestiones*', *Traditio* 19 [1963], 37-50). **47** *Isidori De miraculis Christi*: Isidore, *De fide catholica contra Iudaeos* (*Clavis*, no. 1198); the book in question is possibly Oxford, Bodleian Library, MS. Bodley 394 (s. xi; provenance Exeter). **48** *liber Oserii*: a much-discussed entry which has been thought to be a garbled reference either to Asser's Life of King Alfred (*liber Asserii*) or to Orosius's *Historiae aduersum paganos* (*liber Orosii*), or possibly to a work of Isidore (see full discussion by Förster, *The Exeter Book*, p. 29). **49** *liber Machabeorum*: the biblical books of Maccabees. **50** *liber Persii*: see Manitius, *Handschriften*, pp. 112-15, and *Texts and Transmission*, ed. Reynolds, pp. 293-5; the book in question is possibly Oxford, Bodleian Library, MS. Auct. F.1.15, fols. 78-93 (St Augustine's, Canterbury, s.x^2; provenance Exeter). **51** *Sedulies boc*: Caelius Sedulius, *Carmen Paschale* (*Clavis*, no. 1447). **52** *liber Aratoris*: Arator, *De actibus apostolorum* (*Clavis*, no. 1504). **53** *Diadema monachorum*: Smaragdus of Saint-Mihiel, *Diadema monachorum* (PL 102, cols. 593-690). **54** *Glose Statii*: presumably a glossed copy of Statius, *Thebaid*, such as that in Worcester, Cathedral Library, MS. Q.8, part II + Add. 7 (English, s. x/xi) (see T.A.M. Bishop, *English Caroline Minuscule* [Oxford, 1971], p. 18); for Statius, see Manitius, *Handschriften*, pp. 125-9, and *Texts and Transmission*, ed. Reynolds, pp. 394-7. **55** *liber ... Amalarii*: Amalarius of Metz, *De ecclesiasticis officiis* (PL 105, cols. 985-1242, and *Amalarii episcopi Opera Liturgica Omnia*, ed. J. M. Hanssens, 3 vols., Studi e testi 138-40 [Rome, 1948-50] II, 13-543); the manuscript survives as Cambridge, Trinity College, MS. B.2.2 (St Augustine's, Canterbury, s. x^2; provenance Exeter), which has a Leofric *ex libris* inscription.

XI. *Booklist from an unidentified centre,*
possibly Worcester (s. xi^{ex})

Oxford, Bodleian Library, MS. Tanner 3 (S.C. 9823) is an early-eleventh-century copy of Gregory's *Dialogi* written at an unidentified English centre. At some later time, probably in the late eleventh century, a list of books and ecclesiastical vestments was added on blank folios at the end of the manuscript (189v-190r). The manuscript was at Worcester by the second half of the twelfth century, when a letter from Pope Alexander III to Bishop Roger of Worcester (1164-79) was copied onto the front flyleaf; but it is an open question whether the manuscript was at Worcester when the booklist was copied, and therefore whether it can be used as evidence for the library at Worcester in the late eleventh century. In a recent study of Worcester manuscripts it is stressed that the handwriting of the booklist 'does not resemble that of any known Worcester books of a similar date';[112] on the other hand, the later Worcester provenance of the manuscript combined with the fact that Worcester librarians had a pronounced interest in acquiring texts of Gregory the Great,[113] indicates that a Worcester origin for the booklist cannot be ruled out in the present state of our knowledge. The booklist has previously been printed and discussed by Bannister.[114] It is principally a list of books intended for use in a schoolroom (note the multiple copies of some school-texts), with the subsequent addition of a few liturgical books (lines 57-60).

	Daniel propheta
	Orosius
	Sedulius
	Dialogus
[5]	Glosarius
	Martianus
	Persius
	Prosper
	Terrentium
[10]	Sedulius
	Sychomagia

---

[112] E.A. McIntyre, 'Early Twelfth-Century Worcester Cathedral Priory with special Reference to the Manuscripts copied there' (unpubl. D. Phil. dissertation, Oxford Univ., 1978), p. 87.

[113] *Ibid.* pp. 94-8.

[114] H.M. Bannister, 'Bishop Roger of Worcester and the Church of Keynsham, with a List of Vestments and Books possibly belonging to Worcester', *EHR* 32 (1917), 387-93.

Boetius
Lucanus
Commentum Remigii super Sedulium
[15] Isidorus De natura rerum
Arator
Glosarius
Priscianus maior
Tractatus grammatice artis
[20] Commentum super Iuuenalem
Bucholica et Georgica Virgilii
Persius
Hystoria anglorum
Vita Kyerrani
[25] Liber pronosticorum Iuliani
.XL. omelia
Arator
Psalterium Hieronimi
Commentum Boetii super Categorias
[30] Liber Luciferi
Epigrammata Prosperi
Beda De temporibus
Liber proemiorum ueteris et noui[115]
Liber dialogorum
[35] Prosper
Seruius De uoce et littera
Apollonius
Ars Sedulii
Boetius Super Perhiermenias
[40] Ordo Romanus
Liber Albini
Psalterium
Historia anglorum
Glosarius per alfabetum
[45] Textus euangeliorum
Expositio psalterii
Kategorie Aristotili

---

[115] The word *testamenti* has been omitted by the scribe.

Aeclesiastica istoria
Liber soliloquiorum
[50]   Vita S. Willfridi episcopi
Haimo
Textum .i.
Omelia .i.
Liber magnus de grammatica arte
[55]   Troparium .i.
Hymnarium .i. ...[116]
Missalem .i.[117]
Epistolarem .i.
Ad te leuaui
[60]   et Aspiciens

COMMENTARY 1 *Daniel propheta*: the biblical book of Daniel. 2
Orosius: presumably the *Historiae aduersum paganos* (*Clavis*, no.
571). 3 *Sedulius*: Caelius Sedulius, *Carmen Paschale* (*Clavis*, no.
1447). 4 *Dialogus*: one thinks inevitably of Gregory's *Dialogi*
(*Clavis*, no. 1713), but the context and the nominative singular form of
the title may rather suggest that the book in question was a volume of
scholastic colloquies (see above, no. III, line 14, and below, line 34).
5 *Glosarius*: an unidentifiable glossary. 6 *Martianus*: Martinus
Capella, *De nuptiis Philologiae et Mercurii*; see Manitius,
Handschriften, pp. 237-42, and *Texts and Transmission*, ed. Reynolds,
pp. 245-6. 7 *Persius*: see Manitius, *Handschriften*, pp. 112-15, and
Texts and Transmission, ed. Reynolds, pp. 293-5. 8 *Prosper*: Prosper
of Aquitaine, *Epigrammata* (*Clavis*, no. 518). 9 *Terrentium*:
presumably a play (or plays) by Terence; see Manitius, *Handschriften*,
pp. 12-16, and *Texts and Transmission*, ed. Reynolds, pp. 412-20. 10
Sedulius: another copy of the *Carmen Paschale*; see above, line 3. 11
Sychomagia: Prudentius, *Psychomachia* (*Clavis*, no. 1441). 12
Boetius: presumably (but not necessarily) the *De consolatione
Philosophiae* (*Clavis*, no. 878). 13 *Lucanus*: Lucan, *Pharsalia*; see
Manitius, *Handschriften*, pp. 115-20, and *Texts and Transmission*, ed.

---

[116] I omit here the list of ecclesiastical vestments.

[117] Lines 57-60 were added by the same scribe, but on the
following leaf (190r) and after a break.

Reynolds, pp. 215-18. **14** *Commentum Remigii super Sedulium*: Remigius of Auxerre's unptd commentary on the *Carmen Paschale* of Caelius Sedulius (excerpts are ptd J. Huemer, CSEL 10 [Vienna, 1885], 319-59; cf. also Huemer's discussion, *Über ein Glossenwerk zum Dichter Sedulius*, Sitzungsberichte der kaiserlichen Akademie der Wissenschaften zu Wien, phil.-hist. Klasse, 96 [Vienna, 1880], 505-51); two manuscripts of Anglo-Saxon origin or provenance survive in Cambridge, Gonville and Caius College, MS. 144/194 (s. x; provenance St Augustine's, Canterbury) and Salisbury, Cathedral Library, MS. 134 (English, s. x/xi); the latter manuscript has the rubric *Commentum Remegii super Sedulium* (1r) and may possibly be the book in question here. **15** *Isidorus De natura rerum*: *Clavis*, no. 1188. **16** *Arator*: Arator, *De actibus apostolorum* (*Clavis*, no. 1504). **17** *Glosarius*: another glossary; see above, line 5. **18** *Priscianus maior*: in manuscripts of Priscian the term *maior* usually refers to his *Institutiones grammaticae*, bks I-XVI (GL II, 1-597, and III, 1-377). **19** *Tractatus grammatice artis*: unidentifiable as such. **20** *Commentum super Iuuenalem*: possibly the commentary on Juvenal by Remigius of Auxerre, which is not extant but is known from medieval library catalogues; see Manitius, *Geschichte* I, 512-13, and E.M. Sanford, 'Juvenal', *Catalogus Translationum et Commentariorum: Medieval and Renaissance Latin Translations and Commentaries*, ed. P.O. Kristeller *et al.*, 4 vols. so far (Washington, DC, 1960-80) I, 175-238, at 176. **21** *Bucholica ... Virgilii*: the Eclogues and Georgics of Vergil; see Manitius, *Handschriften*, pp. 47-55, and *Texts and Transmission*, ed. Reynolds, pp. 433-6. **22** *Persius*: another copy; see above, line 7. **23** *Hystoria anglorum*: presumably Bede, *Historia ecclesiastica gentis Anglorum* (*Clavis*, no. 1375). **24** *Vita Kyerrani*: a *uita* of an Irish St Ciaran, either the saint of Clonmacnois (*BHL*, nos. 4654-5; see R.A.S. Macalister, *The Latin and Irish Lives of Ciaran* (London, 1921)) or of Saigir (*BHL*, nos. 4657-8; see P. Grosjean, 'Vita S. Ciarani episcopi de Saighir', *AB* 59 [1941], 217-71). **25** *Liber pronosticorum Iuliani*: Julian of Toledo, *Prognosticum futuri saeculi* (*Clavis*, no. 1258). **26** *.XL. omelia*: the specific number of homilies—forty—suggests that the work in question is Gregory's *Homiliae .xl. in euangelia* (*Clavis*, no. 1711). **27** *Arator*: another copy; see above, line 16. **28** *Psalterium Hieronimi*: the specification of Jerome's authorship probably indicates that a copy of the version *iuxta Hebraeos* is in question here; see below, no. XIII, line 62:

'psalterium Hieronimi secundum Hebreos'. **29** *Commentum Boetii*:
Boethius's Commentary on Aristotle's Categories (*Clavis*, no. 882).
30 *Liber Luciferi*: apparently one of the works of Lucifer of Cagliari
(*Clavis*, nos. 112-18). **31** *Epigrammata Prosperi*: another copy; see
above, line 8. **32** *Beda De temporibus*: *Clavis*, no. 2318. **33** *Liber
proemiorum*: Isidore, *In libros ueteris ac noui testamenti prooemia*
(*Clavis*, no. 1192). **34** *Liber dialogorum*: presumably Gregory,
Dialogi (*Clavis*, no. 1713), but see above, line 4; note that the book
containing the present booklist is a copy of Gregory's *Dialogi*. **35**
Prosper: another copy; see above, line 8. **36** *Seruius De uoce et
littera*: the title suggests that the work in question was not by Seruius
but by Sergius, whose commentary on Donatus's *Ars maior* (bk I) was
entitled *De littera* (GL IV, 475-85); the names Servius and Sergius
were inevitably confused in medieval manuscripts (see Law, *The
Insular Latin Grammarians*, p. 17). **37** *Apollonius*: a copy of the
Latin romance entitled *Historia Apollonii regis Tyri* (ed. A. Riese
[Leipzig, 1893]), a work which was evidently known in Anglo-Saxon
England, given that an Old English translation of the work is found in
Cambridge, Corpus Christi College, MS. 201 (*The Old English
Apollonius of Tyre*, ed. P. Goolden [Oxford, 1958]); the Latin original
on which this translation was based does not appear to survive (see J.
Zupitza, 'Welcher Text liegt der altenglischen Bearbeitung der
Erzählung von Apollonius von Tyrus zu Grunde?', *Romanische
Forschungen* 3 [1886], 269-79), nor, apparently, does the book listed
here. **38** *Ars Sedulii*: one of the grammatical commentaries by
Sedulius Scottus (see Manitius, *Geschichte* I, 318-19), who wrote
commentaries on Donatus (*Ars maior* and *Ars minor*), Priscian and
Eutyches (all of which are ed. B. Löfstedt, CCSL, CM 40B-C
[Turnhout, 1977]). **39** *Boetius Super Perhiermenias*: Boethius's
commentary on Aristotle's *Peri Hermeneias*, also called *De
interpretatione* (*Clavis*, no. 883). **40** *Ordo Romanus*: a copy of one
of the many *ordines Romani* (books, that is, which give directions for
the performance of liturgical ceremonies), of which Michel Andrieu
identified and edited fifty in his monumental *Les Ordines Romani du
haut moyen âge*, 5 vols. (Louvain, 1931-61). **41** *Liber Albini*: a work
(unspecified) by Alcuin. **42** *Psalterium*: as above, line 28. **43**
Historia anglorum: as above, line 23. **44** *Glosarius per alfabetum*:
a glossary arranged in alphabetical order. **45** *Textus euangeliorum*:
a gospel-book. **46** *Expositio psalterii*: to judge from the title, the

work in question was Cassiodorus, *Expositio psalmorum* (*Clavis*, no. 900); but a number of commentaries on the psalter were in circulation, in particular those by Augustine (*Clavis*, no. 283), Hilary (*Clavis*, no. 428) and Jerome (*Clavis*, no. 582), as well as various anonymous compilations, any one of which could be in question here. **47** *Kategorie Aristotili*: presumably Boethius's Latin translation of Aristotle's Categories (rather than the *Categoriae decem*, which in the Middle Ages passed under the name of Augustine). **48** *Aeclesiastica istoria*: possibly Bede's *Historia ecclesiastica* (see above, lines 23 and 43), but more likely the *Historia ecclesiastica* of Eusebius in the Latin translation of Rufinus (ed. T. Mommsen, 3 vols., Griechisch-christliche Schriftsteller 9 [Leipzig, 1903-9]); see below, no. XIII, line 7. **49** *Liber soliloquiorum*: Augustine, *Soliloquia* (*Clavis*, no. 252). **50** *Vita S. Willfridi episcopi*: presumably the *Vita S. Wilfridi* attributed to 'Eddius' Stephanus (*BHL*, no. 8889; *The Life of Bishop Wilfrid by Eddius Stephanus*, ed. B. Colgrave [Cambridge, 1927]; see also below, no. XIII, line 41). **51** *Haimo*: one of the works of Haimo of Auxerre (on whom see *Deutschlands Geschichtsquellen im Mittelalter*, ed. H. Löwe, V, 564-5), either one of his many biblical commentaries (see below, no. XIII, lines 32-3) or else his Homiliary (see above, no. VIII, line 5). **52** *Textum*: a gospel-book; see above, line 45. **53** *Omelia*: probably a homiliary; see Gneuss, 'Liturgical Books', p. 122. **54** *Liber magnus ... arte*: unidentifiable, unfortunately. **55** *Troparium*: a troper; see Gneuss, 'Liturgical Books', p. 104. **56** *Hymnarium*: a hymnal; see Gneuss, 'Liturgical Books', p. 118. **57** *Missalem*: a sacramentary or missal; see Gneuss, 'Liturgical Books', p. 99. **58** *Epistolarem*: an epistolary; see Gneuss, 'Liturgical Books', p. 110. **59** *Ad te leuaui*: a gradual; see Gneuss, 'Liturgical Books', p. 102. **60** *Aspiciens*: an antiphonary; see Gneuss, 'Liturgical Books', p. 116. Although the last two items in the list are linked by *et*, it is perhaps unlikely that the chants for mass and Office would have been bound in one book (certainly no such combination is found in a surviving Anglo-Saxon manuscript), and hence I have listed them separately; note, however, that the combination occurs—but rarely—in continental manuscripts.

XII. *Various books in the possession of monks of
Bury St Edmunds (s. xi^{ex})*

Oxford, Bodleian Library, MS. Auct. D.2.14 (S.C. 2698) is an
uncial gospel-book written probably in Italy (s. vi/vii).[118] The book
was in England by the end of the eighth century, when some marginalia
were added by Anglo-Saxon scribes. On a flyleaf which was not part
of the original volume two scribes have copied a list of some fifteen
books (173r); their handwriting is excessively crude and is datable to
the late eleventh century. Following the list are several names (copied
by yet another scribe) including 'Bealdwine abb.'; if this is Baldwin,
abbot of Bury St Edmunds (1065-98), then the booklist was probably
copied at Bury. The scribe(s) apparently did a certain amount of
tinkering with the list: three items have been erased, leaving only
fifteen; but since one scribe wrote *.xv. bocas* at the end of the list, it
was clearly he who made the erasures. It is possible that the list is a
librarian's record of what books from the monastery's *armarium
commune* were on loan to whom—note the wording 'þas bocas haueð
Salomon preost'—and that the erasures indicate that books had been
returned (and hence the record of the loan was deleted); but the large
number of service-books in the list may cast some doubt on this
hypothesis. The booklist has been printed and discussed by
Robertson.[119]

> Þas bocas haueð Salomon preost
> þæt is þe codspel traht
> 7 þe martyrliua
> 7 þe[120]
> 7 þe æglisce saltere
> 7 þe cranc
> [5]   7 ðe tropere
> 7 Wulfmer cild
> þe atteleuaui

---

[118] *CLA* II, no. 230.

[119] *Anglo-Saxon Charters*, pp. 250 and 501; see also Ker,
Catalogue, p. 350 (no. 290).

[120] Following *þe* is an erasure of some seven letters, now illegible.

              7 pistelari
              7 þe[121]
              7 ðe imnere
              7 ðe captelari[122]
     [10]   7 þe spel boc
          7 Sigar preost
              þe lece boc
              7 blake had boc
          7 Æilmer
              ðe grete sater
              7 ðe litle tropere forbeande
     [15]   7 ðe donatum
          .xv. bocas

COMMENTARY **1** *codspel traht*: a homiliary; see Gneuss, 'Liturgical Books', p. 122. **2** *martyrliua*: a martyrology; see Gneuss, 'Liturgical Books', p. 128. **3** *æglisce saltere*: either a psalter in Old English or (more probably) a Latin psalter with continuous Old English interlinear gloss (no manuscript of a prose translation of the psalter has come down to us, whereas some thirteen psalters with continuous Old English gloss survive, of which none, I think, is certainly from Bury St Edmunds). **4** *cranc*: OE *cranc* or *cranic* is a loan-word from *chronicon*, and could refer to a historical work in general, or possibly to a particular text entitled *Chronicon* or *Chronica*, such as those by Sulpicius Severus (*Clavis*, no. 474), Prosper (*Clavis*, no. 2257; cf. below, no. XIII, line 49), Isidore (*Clavis*, no. 1205) or Bede (*Clavis*, no. 2273); but certainty is impossible. **5** *tropere*: a troper; see Gneuss, 'Liturgical Books', p. 105. **6** *atteleuaui*: a gradual; see Gneuss, 'Liturgical Books', p. 103. **7** *pistelari*: an epistolary; see Gneuss, 'Liturgical Books', p. 110. **8** *imnere*: a hymnal; see Gneuss, 'Liturgical Books', p. 118. **9** *captelari*: a collectar; see Gneuss, 'Liturgical Books', p. 113. **10** *spel boc*: a homiliary; see Gneuss, 'Liturgical Books', p. 123. **11** *lece boc*: a book containing medical

---

[121] Following *þe* is an erasure of four letters; I read the erased letters as *lece* (with ultraviolet light), not *litle*, as Ker suggested (*Catalogue*, p. 350).

[122] Following *captelari* is an erasure of six letters, now illegible.

recipes in Old English; the best known of such books is Bald's *Leechbook* (London, British Library, MS. Royal 12. D. xvii), but a number of other 'leechbooks' survive from Anglo-Saxon England; see A.L. Meaney, 'Variant Versions of Old English Medical Recipes', *ASE* 13 (1984), 235-68. **12** *blake had boc*: Robertson suggests (*Anglo-Saxon Charters*, p. 501) that the reference is to a copy of the *Regula S. Benedicti*, for the reason that 'Benedictines were called "black monks" from the colour of their dress'. However, this solution is not entirely satisfactory: it is unlikely that 'Black Monks' would have been so designated before there was a need to distinguish them from other orders, in particular from the Cistercians, who wore a white habit and consequently were referred to as 'White Monks'. The first Cistercian houses established in England were Waverley (1128-9) and Rievaulx (*c.* 1131), and I can discover no reference in English sources to 'Nigri Monachi' earlier than the second half of the twelfth century (cf. *OED*, s.v. 'black'). The entry is in need of some other explanation, therefore, and several possibilities may be raised. First, it is just conceivable that *Blake* is a proper name (see W.G. Searle, *Onomasticon Anglo-Saxonicum* [Cambridge, 1897], p. 108; M. Redin, *Studies on Uncompounded Personal Names in Old English* (Uppsala, 1919), pp. 11 and 179; O. von Feilitzen, *The Pre-Conquest Personal Names of Domesday Book* (Uppsala, 1937), p. 203; G. Tengvik, *Old English Bynames* (Uppsala, 1938), pp. 292-3); in this case Blake, like Wulfmer, Sigar, etc., will have had a *had boc* in his possession (though one might accordingly expect a definite article before *had boc*). What the *had boc* was is not clear either: possibly a *handboc* (with a suspension-mark omitted) or (less likely) a *hadboc*, that is, a book on the various ecclesiastical grades, such as Isidore, *De ecclesiasticis officiis* (*Clavis*, no. 1207). Alternatively, *blake* could be acc. sg. fem. of *blæc*, and so refer to the colour of the binding. Finally, given that the other book in Sigar's possession was a *leceboc*, it is worth asking if *blakehad* is a *hapax legomenon* formed from *blæco* (n.), 'pallor', 'leprosy', + -*had*, hence meaning 'the condition of leprosy': in other words, the *blakehad boc* could have been a collection of remedies for leprosy, such as that found in Bald's *Leechbook* I.xxxii ('Læcedomas wiþ blæce') (*Leechdoms, Wortcunning and Starcraft of Early England*, ed. O. Cockayne, 3 vols., Rolls Ser. [London, 1864-6] II, 76-80); but this solution is an improbable one. (I am very grateful to Helmut Gneuss for advice on this problem, which remains insoluble at present.)

13 *grete sater*: a psalter in large format, presumably. **14** *litle tropere forbeand*: a troper in small format. What *forbeande* means is not clear; I suggest a misspelling of *forbearnde* (p.p. of *forbærnan*: one would normally expect *forbærnde*, but the spelling in this booklist is chaotic), and that the book in question was badly damaged by fire. **15** *donatum*: a copy of Donatus, either the *Ars maior* or *Ars minor*, or perhaps simply a miscellaneous grammar-book.

XIII. *Booklist from Peterborough (?) (s. xi/xii)*

Oxford, Bodleian Library, MS. Bodley 163 (S.C. 2016), is a composite manuscript made up of three separate parts. Of these the first (fols. 1-227) contains Bede's *Historia ecclesiastica gentis Anglorum* and Æthelwulf's so-called *De abbatibus*, in Anglo-Caroline minuscule (s. xi^in). The second part (fols. 228-49) is a copy of the Gildasian recension of the *Historia Brittonum*, datable to s. xii^in. The third part, which contains *inter alia* the booklist, is a single bifolium (fols. 250-1). The three parts have been together since the late Middle Ages, for the binding is medieval, probably of fourteenth-century date. A scribble in the third part (250v) records the obit of a monk of Peterborough in 1359.[123] The booklist itself is found on 251r and is datable on palaeographical grounds to *c.* 1100 (s. xi/xii). There may be reason to think that the booklist was written at Peterborough, not only because of the later Peterborough provenance of fols. 250-1, but because several items in the list appear to be identical both with books donated to Peterborough by Æthelwold (see above, no. IV) and with books listed in the abbey's fifteenth-century *Matricularium*.[124] On the other hand, it is worth recalling that Peterborough Abbey was utterly destroyed by fire in 1116 (ASC 1116 E). Few books are likely to have escaped such a conflagration, and this must make one cautious in accepting any book written before 1116 as the erstwhile property of the abbey's library. In any case several items in the list are said to be written in English, and the list can therefore be accepted as the record

---

[123] See Ker, *Catalogue*, p. 358 (no. 304).

[124] See M.R. James, *Lists of Manuscripts formerly in Peterborough Abbey*, pp. 30-81.

of a monastic library—arguably Peterborough's—of the late Anglo-Saxon period, in spite of its post-Conquest date. The list has been printed on several occasions.[125]

	Augustinus De ciuitate Dei
	Augustinus De uerbo Domini
	Augustinus De bono coniugii et uirginitatis
	Augustinus Super Iohannem
[5]	Augustinus Retractionum
	Augustinus De uidendo Deum et uera religione
	Ecclesiastica historia Eusebii Cesaris
	Historia anglorum
	Tripartita historia
[10]	Hieronimus Super Iosue
	Hieronimus Contra Iouinianum
	Hieronimus Super Isaiam
	Hieronimus Super prophetas
	Hieronimus Super Ezechielem (libri duo)
[15]	Hieronimus Super Danihelem
	Ambrosius De Sacramentis et Vita sanctorum Nicolai, Botulfi, Guðlaci
	Origenis De singularitate clericorum
	Dialogus Basilii et Iohannis
	Augustinus De penitentia
[20]	Genadius ecclesiasticorum dogmatum
	Collatio Nesterotis abbatis de spirituali scientia, Abraham de mortificatione, Cremonis de perfectione
	Ambrosius De uirginitate
	Hisidorus Super Genesim
	Amalarius De diuinis officiis
[25]	Fredulfus historiographus
	Iosephus Antiquitatum
	Isidorus In Hebreis numeris
	Gregorius Pastoralis cure

---

[125] It is listed in Gottlieb, no. 515; it has been ptd Becker, *Catalogi*, no. 96; R. Pauli, 'Aus Oxforder Handschriften', *Neues Archiv* 2 (1886), 432-4, at 433; James, *Lists of Manuscripts*, pp. 27-8.

Gregorii Moralia in Iob
[30]   Epistole Pauli
Vite patrum
Haimo Super epistolas Pauli
Haimo In euangeliis
Epistolares Hieronimi .iii. (unus maior, duo minores)
[35]   Liber notarum
Questiones in Genesi et diffinitio philosophie et liber
    differentiarum
Item liber differentiarum
Vita sancti Felicis uersifice
Vita sancti Aðeluuodi
[40]   Pronosticon futuri secli
Vita sancti Wilfridi
Vita sancti Giseleni
Diadema monachorum
Lectionarius
[45]   Paradisus
Glosa in Genesim
Super Psalterium
Isidorus De summo bono
Cronica Prosperi
[50]   Augustinus De diuersis rebus
Vita sancti Fursei et Baronti uisio
Gregorii Nazanzeni apologiticus
Historia Romanorum et Africanorum
Vite sanctorum anglice
[55]   Expositio super .i. psalmos
Epistolaris Cipriani
Vita beati Gregorii pape
Exameron Ambrosii
Canones
[60]   Passio Eustachii Placide uersifice
Historia Clementis et Vita beati Martini
Psalterium Hieronimi secundum Hebreos
Rabanus De institutione clericorum
Liber miraculorum
[65]   Elfredi regis liber anglicus

COMMENTARY 1 *Augustinus De ciuitate Dei*: *Clavis*, no. 313. 2 *Augustinus De uerbo Domini*: Augustine wrote no work with this title (but cf. Becker, *Catalogi*, nos. 36, line 75, and 51, line 34); the work in question is probably the two-book treatise *De sermone Domini in monte* (*Clavis*, no. 274). 3 *Augustinus ... uirginitatis*: two works are in question here, the *De bono coniugali* (*Clavis*, no. 299) and the *De sancta uirginitate* (*Clavis*, no. 300). 4 *Augustinus Super Iohannem*: the *Tractatus in euangelium Ioannis* (*Clavis*, no. 278). 5 *Augustinus Retractionum*: the *Retractiones* (*Clavis*, no. 250). 6 *Augustinus ... religione*: the first of these items is in fact one of Augustine's *epistolae* (*Ep.* cxlvii), although it often circulated separately (see Becker, *Catalogi*, no. 11, line 45); the other is his treatise *De uera religione* (*Clavis*, no. 264). 7 *Ecclesiastica ... Cesaris*: the *Historia ecclesiastica* of Eusebius, in the Latin translation of Rufinus (see above, no. XI, line 48); for *Cesaris* understand *Cesariensis* (Eusebius was from Caesarea in Palestine). 8 *Historia anglorum*: presumably Bede, *Historia ecclesiastica gentis Anglorum* (*Clavis*, no. 1375); the book in question is possibly Bodley 163 itself, assuming that the part containing Bede (fols. 1-227) was at Peterborough when the booklist was written. 9 *Tripartita historia*: Cassiodorus, *Tripartita historia ecclesiastica* (PL 69, cols. 879-1214; see above, no. VIII, line 33). 10 *Hieronimus Super Iosue*: Jerome did not write a commentary on Joshua; conceivably the work in question is Rufinus's Latin translation of Origen's twenty-six homilies on Joshua, which frequently passed during the Middle Ages under the name of Jerome (see M. Schanz, *Geschichte der römischen Literatur* IV.1 [Munich, 1914], 419); other commentaries on Joshua were composed by Claudius of Turin (unptd) and Hrabanus Maurus (PL 108, cols. 999-1108). 11 *Hieronimus Contra Iouinianum*: Jerome, *Aduersus Iouinianum* (*Clavis*, no. 610). 12 *Hieronimus Super Isaiam*: Jerome, *Commentarii in Isaiam* (*Clavis*, no. 584). 13 *Hieronimus Super prophetas*: presumably Jerome's *Commentarii in prophetas minores* (*Clavis*, no. 589). 14 *Hieronimus Super Ezechielem*: Jerome, *Commentarii in Ezechielem* (*Clavis*, no. 587). 15 *Hieronimus Super Danihelem*: Jerome, *Commentarii in Danielem* (*Clavis*, no. 588). 16 *Ambrosius De sacramentis*: *Clavis*, no. 154. 16 *Vita ... Guðlaci*: the *uitae* in question are probably Otloh of St Emmeram's *Vita S. Nicholai* (*BHL*, no. 6126), Folcard of Saint-Bertin's *Vita S. Botulfi* (*BHL*, no. 1428), and Felix's *Vita S. Guthlaci* (*BHL*, no. 3723); if so, the manuscript in question survives as

London, British Library, MS. Harley 3097 (note that in addition to the three *uitae* listed here the manuscript also contains Ambrose *De sacramentis*). **17** *Origenis ... clericorum*: the work of this title (*Clavis*, no. 62) is not by Origen; it was frequently transmitted during the Middle Ages under the name of Cyprian (see P. Schepens, 'L'Épître *De singularitate clericorum* du ps.-Cyprien', *Recherches de science religieuse* 13 [1922], 178-210 and 297-327, and 14 [1923], 47-65; cf. also Becker, *Catalogi*, no. 115, line 161). **18-21**: according to the fifteenth-century Peterborough *Matricularium*, the items listed in lines 18-21 were all one book; see James, *Lists of Manuscripts*, p. 30. **18** *Dialogus Basilii et Iohannis*: the work in question is the Latin translation of John Chrysostom's *De sacerdotio*, a dialogue in six books between John and one Basil; the identity of the Latin translator is unknown, though some have suggested Anianus of Celeda, who translated other of John's works; the translation was available from at least the early ninth century, for it is quoted by Hilduin of Saint-Denis; the Latin translation has not apparently been printed, though it survives in some eight manuscripts (see A. Siegmund, *Die Überlieferung der griechischen christlichen Literatur* [Munich and Pasing, 1949], p. 97). **19** *Augustinus De penitentia*: presumably a copy of Augustine's two *sermones* (nos. cccli-ccclii) which together form a treatise *De utilitate agendae poenitentiae* which often circulated separately; but note also that two of Augustine's *epistolae* (nos. xci and cliii) are concerned with penitence and may be in question here. **20** *Genadius ... dogmatum*: Gennadius, *Liber siue diffinitio ecclesiasticorum dogmatum* (*Clavis*, no. 958). **21** *Collatio ... de perfectione*: the three works listed separately here are from Cassian's *Conlationes* (*Clavis*, no. 512), nos. xiv (*de spirituali scientia*), xxiv (*de mortificatione*) and xi (*de perfectione*) respectively. **22** *Ambrosius De uirginitate*: *Clavis*, no. 147. **23** *Hisidorus Super Genesim*: although Isidore did not devote a separate commentary to Genesis, the work in question is probably his *Mysticorum expositiones sacramentorum seu quaestiones in uetus testamentum* (*Clavis*, no. 1195), an extensive work of exegesis which begins with a long section on Genesis (PL 83, cols. 207-88). **24** *Amalarius ... officiis*: Amalarius of Metz, *De ecclesiasticis officiis*, see above, no. X, line 55. **25** *Fredulfus historiographus*: presumably Freculf of Lisieux, a ninth-century historian (see Manitius, *Geschichte* I, 663-8), whose *Historia* (PL 106, cols. 917-1258) enjoyed fairly wide circulation during the Middle Ages; several manuscripts of the Anglo-

Saxon period survive (see Gneuss, 'Preliminary List', nos. 74, 724 and 725). **26** *Iosephus Antiquitatum*: Cassiodorus's Latin translation of Josephus, *Antiquitates*; see Manitius, *Geschichte* I, 51-2. **27** *Isidorus In Hebreis numeris*: Isidore wrote no work of this title; the work in question is probably the pseudo-Isidorian *Liber de numeris*, a Hiberno-Latin compilation of the eighth century (incomplete ed. in PL 83, cols. 1293-1302; see R. E. McNally, *Der irische Liber de Numeris* [Munich, 1957]); that the work was known in late Anglo-Saxon England is clear from the fact that the names of Noah's wife—Percova—and of his three sons' wives—Olla, Olliva and Ollivana—were interpolated into the Old English poem *Genesis* (lines 1547-8), apparently from this source (see McNally, *Der irische Liber de Numeris*, pp. 127-8). **28** *Gregorius Pastoralis cure*: Gregory, *Regula pastoralis* (*Clavis*, no. 1712). **29** *Gregorii ... Iob*: Gregory, *Moralia siue expositio in Iob* (*Clavis*, no. 1708). **30** *Epistole Pauli*: the Pauline Epistles, presumably. **31** *Vite patrum*: the so-called *Vitas patrum*, an early title used to describe a massive but heterogeneous collection of lives and sayings principally of the early Egyptian Desert Fathers (*BHL*, nos. 6524-47; see above, no. VIII, line 9). **32** *Haimo ... Pauli*: Haimo of Auxerre's Commentary on the Pauline Epistles (PL 117, cols. 359-820). **33** *Haimo In euangeliis*: Haimo of Auxerre is not known to have composed a commentary on the gospels; the work in question, therefore, is probably the commentary on the gospels by Haimo of Halberstadt (PL 118, cols. 11-804). **34** *Epistolares Hieronimi*: three volumes of Jerome's *epistolae* (*Clavis*, no. 620). **35** *Liber notarum*: the scribe apparently misread *Liber rotarum* (which may suggest that the title before him was in some grade of Insular minuscule script), a title which was frequently applied to Isidore's *De natura rerum* (*Clavis*, no. 1188), because it contained a large number of diagrams. **36** *Questiones ... differentiarum*: assuming that the third of these titles refers to Isidore's treatise *De differentiis uerborum* (*Clavis*, no. 1187), it is possible that the first was a copy of Isidore's *Quaestiones in uetus testamentum* (*Clavis*, no. 1195; cf. above, line 23); on the other hand, the *liber differentiarum* could conceivably be Boethius, *De differentiis topicis* (*Clavis*, no. 889), in which case the *diffinitio philosophie* might be the treatise *De definitionibus* (*Clavis*, no. 85), a work now known to be by Marius Victorinus but which passed under Boethius's name during the Middle Ages; it was intended as an introduction to Cicero's *Topica* and would have combined well with Boethius's *De differentiis* *topicis*. And if Isidore was not the author of the *liber differentiarum*, there is perhaps no reason to link his name with the *Questiones in Genesim*; recall that Jerome composed a treatise *Quaestiones Hebraicae in Genesim* (*Clavis*, no. 580) and that Alcuin compiled a set of *Questiones in Genesim* (PL 100, cols. 515-66). **37** *Item*: another copy of the (unidentifiable) work mentioned in line 36. **38** *Vita ... uersifice*: presumably Paulinus of Nola's *Carmina* (*Clavis*, no. 203) on Felix, the patron saint of Nola. **39** *Vita sancti Aðeluuodi*: the *uita* of St Æthelwold of Winchester (*ob.* 984) by Wulfstan of Winchester (*BHL*, no. 2647); on knowledge of this work at Peterborough, see *Wulfstan of Winchester: the Life of St Æthelwold*, ed. M. Lapidge and M. Winterbottom (Oxford, 1991), pp. clxi-clxii. **40** *Pronosticon*: Julian of Toledo, *Prognosticum futuri saeculi* (*Clavis*, no. 1258). **41** *Vita sancti Wilfridi*: presumably the *uita* of Wilfrid attributed to 'Eddius' Stephanus (*BHL*, no. 8889; see above, no. XI, line 50). **42** *Vita sancti Giseleni*: one of the several *uitae* of this Flemish saint (*BHL*, nos. 3552-61); it is interesting to note the *uita* of a Flemish saint at Peterborough at this time. **43** *Diadema monachorum*: Smaragdus of Saint-Mihiel, *Diadema monachorum*; see above, nos. VIII, line 7, and X, line 53. **44** *Lectionarius*: a lectionary, but whether intended for mass or Office is not clear without further specification (see Gneuss, 'Liturgical Books', p. 105). **45** *Paradisus*: presumably the text referred to as *Paradisus Heraclidis* (*BHL*, no. 6532; PL 74, cols. 243-342), which is a Latin translation of part of the *Historia Lausiaca* of Palladius, which in turn circulated as part of the massive collection of *Vitas patrum* (see above, line 31); at least two manuscripts of the *Paradisus Heraclidis* survive from late Anglo-Saxon England (see Gneuss, 'Preliminary List', nos. 10 and 267). **46** *Glosa in Genesim*: unidentifiable as such. **47** *Super Psalterium*: unidentifiable as such; see above, no. XI, line 46. **48** *Isidorus De summo bono*: Isidore, *Sententiae* (*Clavis*, no. 1199); the title *De summo bono* derives from the first sentence of the treatise ('Summum bonum Deus est ...'). **49** *Cronica Prosperi*: Prosper of Aquitaine, *Epitoma chronicorum* (*Clavis*, no. 2257). **50** *Augustinus De diuersis rebus*: possibly a copy of Augustine's *De diuersis quaestionibus .lxxxiii.* (*Clavis*, no. 289), or perhaps simply a miscellaneous collection of his writings. **51** *Vita sancti Fursei*: presumably the Merovingian *uita* of Fursa (*BHL*, no. 3209). **51** *Baronti uisio*: *Clavis*, no. 1313; see above, no. IX, line 8. **52** *Gregorii ... apologiticus*: Gregory of Nazianzus, *Oratio II (Liber* *apologeticus de fuga*) in the Latin translation of Rufinus (*Tyranii Rufini Orationum Gregorii Nazianzeni nouem Interpretatio*, ed. A. Engelbrecht, CSEL 46 [Vienna, 1910], 7-84; see also M.M. Wagner, *Rufinus the Translator: a Study of his Theory and Practice as Illustrated in his Version of the Apologetica of St Gregory Nazianzen* [Washington, DC, 1945], and A.C. Way, in *Catalogus Translationum et Commentariorum* II, 127-34); the work is preserved in at least one manuscript of the Anglo-Saxon period (Oxford, Trinity College, MS. 4 [St Augustine's, Canterbury, s. xi], 112r-142v). **53** *Historia Romanorum et Africanorum*: probably Victor of Vita, *Historia persecutionis Africanae prouinciae* (*Clavis*, no. 798); on the probable identity, see Manitius, *Handschriften*, p. 261. **54** *Vite sanctorum anglice*: a collection of saints' lives in English, possibly that of Ælfric. **55** *Expositio super .l. psalmos*: either an incomplete copy of a full commentary on the psalms (see above, no. XI, line 46), or possibly the commentary attributed to Prosper of Aquitaine (*Clavis*, no. 524) on Psalms C-CL. **56** *Epistolaris Cipriani*: Cyprian, *Epistolae* (*Clavis*, no. 50); see above, no. IV, line 19. **57** *Vita beati Gregorii pape*: probably not the Anglo-Latin *Vita S. Gregorii* composed at Whitby in the late seventh century (*BHL*, no. 3637), but more likely the later continental *uita* by John the Deacon (*BHL*, no. 3641), which survives in at least one manuscript of the Anglo-Saxon period (Oxford, Bodleian Library, MS. Bodley 381 [s. x; provenance St Augustine's, Canterbury]). **58** *Exameron Ambrosii*: Ambrose, *Exameron* (*Clavis*, no. 123). **59** *Canones*: an unidentifiable collection of ecclesiastical legislation. **60** *Passio Eustachii Placide uersifice*: a number of metrical versions of the *Vita S. Eustachii* existed in the Middle Ages, but three are perhaps early enough to be in question here: a rhythmical poem preserved in a late-ninth-century manuscript from Verona (*ICL*, no. 12031), a poem in elegiacs preserved only in a late-fourteenth-century manuscript (*ICL*, no. 2175), and a poem in hexameters preserved in an eleventh-century German manuscript (*ICL*, no. 14237). Several factors help us to identify the poem in question: a *Vita Eustachii* was given by Æthelwold to Peterborough (see above, no. IV, line 9); the same book was still at Peterborough *c*. 1100, to judge from the present entry; and the book apparently remained at Peterborough until the Dissolution, for it was seen by John Leland and described by him as *Vita S. Eustachii carmine heroico* (*Collectanea*, ed. T. Hearne, 2nd ed., 6 vols. [London, 1770] IV, 31). Leland's observation that the poem was in hexameters (*carmine heroico*) rules out the poems in rhythmical verse and elegiacs, and indicates that the hexameter poem must be in question here (it is ed. H. Varnhagen, 'Zwei lateinische metrische Versionen der Legende von Placidus-Eustachius II. Eine Version in Hexametern', *ZDA* 25 [1881], 1-25); on the evidence of the Æthelwold donation, the poem must have been in existence by the late tenth century, and there is good reason to think that it was composed in England under Æthelwold's patronage: see M. Lapidge, 'Æthelwold and the *Vita S. Eustachii*', in *Scire litteras. Forschungen zum mittelaltherlichern Geistesleben*, ed. S. Krämer and M. Bernhard, Bayerische Akademie der Wissenschaften: Abhandlungen 99 (Munich, 1988), 255-65. **61** *Historia Clementis*: the pseudo-Clementine *Recognitiones* in the Latin translation of Rufinus; see B. Rehm, *Die Pseudoklementinen II. Rekognitionen in Rufins Übersetzung*, ed. F. Paschke (Berlin, 1965). **61** *Vita beati Martini*: Sulpicius Severus, *Vita Martini Turonensis* (*Clavis*, no. 475; *BHL*, no. 5610). **62** *Psalterium ... Hebreos*: Jerome's Latin translation of the psalter *iuxta Hebraeos*. **63** *Rabanus ... clericorum*: Hrabanus Maurus of Fulda, *De institutione clericorum* (PL 107, cols. 293-420; cf. Manitius, *Geschichte* I, 296-8). **64** *Liber miraculorum*: one of the books earlier given by Æthelwold to Peterborough, possibly the work of this title by Gregory of Tours; see above, no. IV, line 3. **65** *Elfredi ... anglicus*: a copy of one of the Old English translations by King Alfred—Gregory's *Regula pastoralis*, Boethius's *De consolatione Philosophiae*, Augustine's *Soliloquia*, or possibly the first fifty psalms of the psalter; see Keynes and Lapidge, *Alfred the Great*, pp. 28-34.[126]

---

[126] I am extremely grateful to David Dumville and Helmut Gneuss for commenting on an earlier draft of this article and saving me from a number of errors, and to Vivien Law for advice on the various grammatical entries in the booklists.

APPENDIX

Books and authors known in Anglo-Saxon England
from surviving booklists

Abbo of Fleury
  Passio S. Eadmundi: VII.7
Abbo of Saint-Germain-des-Prés
  Bella Parisiacae urbis: IV.10
Ælfric of Eynsham
  Lives of Saints: XIII.54(?)
Alcimus Avitus: I.12, IV.17
Alcuin: III.8, XI.41
  Vita S. Richarii: VIII.18
Aldhelm: I.7
  De laude uirginitatis: VIII.28
Alfred, King: XIII.65
Amalarius of Metz
  De ecclesiasticis officiis: X.55, XIII.24
Ambrose: I.2
  De psalmo CXVIII: VIII.10
  De mysteriis: VIII.11
  De sacramentis: VIII.11, XIII.16
  Hexameron: VIII.14, XIII.58
  De officiis ministrorum: VIII.15
  De uirginitate: XIII.22
Arator: I.12, X.52, XI.16, XI.27
Aristotle: I.10
  Categories: XI.47
Athanasius: I.3
Augustine: I.2
  Contra Academicos: IV.6
  Enchiridion: VIII.13
  Epistolae: VIII.17, XIII.6 (*Ep.* cxlvii)
  Soliloquia: XI.49
  De ciuitate Dei: XIII.1
  De sermone Domini in monte: XIII.2(?)
  De bono coniugali: XIII.3
  De sancta uirginitate: XIII.3

Tractatus in euangelium Ioannis: XIII.4
Retractiones: XIII.5
De uera religione: XIII.6
Sermones (cccli-ccclii): XIII.19(?)
De diuersis quaestionibus *.lxxxiii.*: XIII.50(?)

Bachiarius
    Epistola: VIII.17
Basil: I.5
Bede: I.7
    Vitae S. Cuthberti: II.4
    In Marci euangelium expositio: IV.2
    Super epistolas catholicas expositio: VIII.16, X.45
    Historia ecclesiastica gentis Anglorum: VIII.22, XI.23,
        XI.43, XIII.8
    In Lucae euangelium expositio: X.43
    Explanatio Apocalypsis: X.44
    De temporibus: XI.32
Benedict of Nursia
    Regula: VIII.7, IX.7 (OE), XII.12 (OE)
Bible
    Gospels: II.1, II.3, IV.1, VI.1, VII.1, VIII.1, X.1,
        X.14 (OE), XI.45, XI.52
    Apocalypse: III.6
    Psalms: VI.7, VII.4, VII.6, IX.5 (OE), X.9, X.10, XI.28,
        XI.42, XII.3 (OE), XII.13, XIII.62 (*iuxta Hebraeos*)
    Heptateuch: VIII.3
    Four 'great' prophets: X.30
    Ezekiel: X.38
    Cantica canticorum: X.39
    Isaiah: X.40
    Maccabees: X.49
    Daniel: XI.1
    Epistles of Paul: XIII.30
Boethius: I.8, XI.12
    De consolatione Philosophiae: X.22 (OE), X.31
    In categorias Aristotelis: XI.29
    In librum Aristotelis de interpretatione: XI.39
    De differentiis topicis: XIII.36(?)

Caelius Sedulius: I.11, III.11, VIII.31, X.51, XI.3, XI.10
Cassian
   Collationes: XIII.21
Cassiodorus: I.6
   De orthographia: VIII.25
   Historia ecclesiastica tripartita: VIII.33, XIII.9
   Expositio psalmorum: XI.46(?)
   translation of Josephus, *Antiquitates*: XIII.26
Charisius: I.17
Chrodegang of Metz
   Regula canonicorum: X.17
Cicero: I.10
Claudius of Turin
   Commentum super Mattheum: VIII.6
colloquies (anonymous): III.14(?), XI.4(?)
Cominianus: *see* Charisius
commentaries, biblical (anonymous)
   Sermo super quosdam psalmos: IV.13
   Commentum Cantica canticorum: IV.14
   Liber parabolarum Salomonis: VIII.27
   Expositio psalterii: XI.46 (*see also* Cassiodorus)
   Glossa in Genesim: XIII.46
   Super psalterium: XIII.47
   Expositio super .l. psalmos: XIII.55
commentaries on school-texts (anonymous)
   Glossa super Catonem (Remigius?): III.9
   Commentum Martiani (Remigius?): IV.16
   Glose Statii: X.54
   Commentum super Iuuenalem (Remigius?): XI.20
computistical writings (anonymous): III.12
Cyprian: IV.19
   De singularitate clericorum (pseudo-Cyprian; pseudo-Origen):
      XIII.17
   Epistolae: XIII.56

Donatus: I.16, XII.15
   Ars minor: III.4
   Ars maior: III.7

Eusebius of Caesarea
   Historia ecclesiastica (trans. Rufinus): XI.48(?), XIII.7
Eutyches: I.17

Felix
   Vita S. Guthlaci: VIII.19, XIII.16
Folcard of Saint-Bertin
   Vita S. Botulfi: XIII.16
Fortunatus: *see* Venantius Fortunatus
Freculf of Lisieux: XIII.25
Fulgentius: I.5

Gennadius
   Liber siue diffinitio ecclesiasticorum dogmatum: XIII.20
glossaries: IV.20 (Greek-Latin)(?), XI.5, XI.17, XI.44
grammatical texts (anonymous)
   De arte metrica: III.3
   Excerptiones de metrica arte: III.5
   'Terra que pars': III.10
   Glossa super Donatum: III.13
   Tractatus grammatice artis: XI.19
   Liber magnus de grammatica arte: XI.54
Gregory the Great: I.4
   Dialogi: III.14(?), VIII.8, IX.2 (OE), X.29, XI.34
   Moralia in Iob: VIII.4, XIII.29
   Regula pastoralis: IX.6(OE), X.28, XIII.28
   Homiliae .xl. in euangelia: XI.26
Gregory of Nazianzus
   Oratio II (*Liber apologeticus de fuga*) (trans. Rufinus): XIII.52
Gregory of Tours
   Liber miraculorum: IV.3(?), XIII.64(?)

Haimo of Auxerre: XI.51
   Homiliarium VIII.5
   Super epistolas Pauli: XIII.32
Haimo of Halberstadt
   In euangeliis: XIII.33
Hiberno-Latin writings (anonymous)
   De duodecim abusiuis saeculi: IV.12

Liber de numeris: XIII.27
Quaestiones de ueteri et nouo testamento: X.46(?)
Hilary: I.1
Historia Apollonii regis Tyri: XI.37
Hrabanus Maurus: V.1
    Super Iudith et Hester: VIII.32
    De institutione clericorum: XIII.63

Iohannes Diaconus
    Vita beati Gregorii pape: XIII.57(?)
Isidore
    De natura rerum: III.1, XI.15, XIII.35
    Synonyma IV.8
    De differentiis uerborum: IV.18, XIII.36(?), XIII.37(?)
    De ecclesiasticis officiis: VIII.11
    Etymologiae: X.41
    De fide catholica contra Iudaeos: X.47
    In libros ueteris ac noui Testamenti prooemia: X.46(?), XI.33
    Quaestiones in uetus Testamentum: XIII.23(?), XIII.36(?)
    Sententiae: XIII.48

Jerome: I.1
    Liber interpretationis Hebraicorum nominum: IV.4
    Epistolae: VIII.20 (*Ep.* xxii), XIII.34
    Aduersus Iouinianum: XIII.11
    Commentarii in Isaiam: XIII.12
    Commentarii in Prophetas minores: XIII.13
    Commentarii in Ezechielem: XIII.14
    Commentarii in Danielem: XIII.15
John Chrysostom: I.6
    De sacerdotio: XIII.18
Josephus
    Antiquitates (trans. Cassiodorus): XIII.26
Julian of Toledo
    Prognosticum futuri saeculi: IV.5, VIII.12, XI.25, XIII.40
Julianus Pomerius
    De uita contemplatiua: VIII.15
Justinus: I.9
Juvencus: I.11, VIII.31

Lactantius: I.13
legislative texts (anonymous): X.19
    Liber canonum (*Collectio Quesnelliana*): VIII.21
    Canones: XIII.59
Leo, Pope: I.4
liturgical books
    sacramentary (missal): II.2, V.3, VI.5, VII.2, VII.9, VII.12,
        VII.14, VII.17, VIII.2, X.2, XI.57
    martyrology: V.2, IX.4 (OE), X.18 (OE?), XII.2
    pontifical: V.4, X.12, X.13
    epistolary: V.5, VI.4, VII.3, X.4, X.26, XI.58, XII.7
    antiphonary: VI.2, X.6, X.25, XI.60
    gradual: VI.3, VII.18, VIII.26, X.5, X.7, XI.59, XII.6
    'hadboc': XII.12
    hymnal: VI.6, X.11, XI.56, XII.8
    homiliary: VII.5, X.21, XI.53, XII.1, XII.10
    collectar: VII.6, VII.15, X.3, X.24, XII.9
    lectionary (Office): VII.8, VII.10, VII.11, X.15, X.16, X.27,
        XIII.44
    ritual (manual): VII.13
    passional (legendary): IX.1 (OE), X.33, XIII.53 (OE)
    troper: X.8, XI.55, XII.5, XII.14
    ordo romanus: XI.40
Lucan: I.14, XI.13
Lucifer of Cagliari: XI.30(?)

Martianus Capella: XI.6
medical writings: IV.11, VIII.24, XII.11 (OE)

Origen
    Homiliae super Iosue (trans. Rufinus): XIII.10(?)
Orosius: I.3, XI.2
Otloh of St Emmeram
    Vita S. Nicholai: XIII.16

Palladius (*see also Paradisus Heraclidis*)
    De moribus Brachmanorum: VIII.11
Paradisus Heraclidis (Palladius, *Historia Lausiaca*): XIII.45
Paulinus of Nola: I.12, IV.7, XIII.38

Terence: XI.9

uitae (anonymous)
   Vita S. Eustachii (hexametrical): IV.9, XIII.60
   Vita S. Aichardi: VIII.19
   Vita S. Cuthberti: VIII.19
   Vita S. Dunstani: VIII.19
   Vita S. Filiberti: VIII.19
   Passio S. Iuliani: VIII.23
   Passio SS. Luciani et Marciani: VIII.23
   Vita S. Mauri: VIII.23
   Vita S. Walerici: VIII.23
   Passiones apostolorum: X.42
   Vita S. Ciarani: XI.24
   Vita S. Wilfridi: XI.50, XIII.41
   Vita S. Giseleni: XIII.42
   Vita S. Fursei: XIII.51

Venantius Fortunatus: I.13
Vergil: I.14
   Bucolica: XI.21
   Georgica: XI.21
Victor of Vita
   Historia persecutionis Africanae prouinciae: XIII.53
Victorinus: I.8
   De definitionibus: XIII.36(?)
Visio Baronti: IX.8 (OE?), XIII.51
Vitas patrum: VIII.9, XIII.31 (*see also Paradisus Heraclidis*)

Wulfstan of Winchester
   Vita S. Æthelwoldi: XIII.39

MISCELLANEOUS
   Odda's book: IX.3
   The Exeter Book: X.23

UNIDENTIFIED
De eucharistia: IV.15
De professione coniugatorum: VIII.29

Liber Oserii: X.48
Chronicon (OE *cranc*): XII.4
blake had boc: XII.12

POSTSCRIPT (1993)

Although the present article is essentially a reprint of that published
in 1985, I have taken the opportunity to correct a few errors and to
supply references to new editions and discussions where relevant.
Several recent developments in the study of Anglo-Saxon books and
libraries deserve special mention, however. The collaborative work on
the sources of Anglo-Saxon authors mentioned above (n. 4) has now
become the international project known as *Fontes Anglo-Saxonici*.
Under the chairmanship of Peter Clemoes, *Fontes Anglo-Saxonici* is a
collaborative project designed to identify and record comprehensively
the literary sources quoted or used by Anglo-Saxon authors, whether
writing in Latin or Old English; to date a substantial number of Old
English texts have been sourced and work is beginning in earnest on
Anglo-Latin texts as well.   Texts which have been sourced and
recorded in the *Fontes* data-base at the University of Manchester are
registered annually in *ASE* (and have been so registered since vol. 18
[1989]). Further information on *Fontes Anglo-Saxonici* (including the
question of access to its ever-expanding data-base) is available from Dr.
D.G. Scragg, Centre for Anglo-Saxon Studies, University of
Manchester, Manchester, England M13 9PL. A related and complementary international project is the 'Sources of Anglo-Saxon Literary
Culture' (SASLC) under the direction of Professor P.E. Szarmach; the
intention of this project is to produce a complete (alphabetically
ordered) list of the authors which were known or studied in Anglo-
Saxon England. The eventual publication of this important material
(which will replace the work of Ogilvy mentioned in n. 1) has been
heralded by the appearance of *Sources of Anglo-Saxon Literary Culture:
a Trial Version*, ed. F.M. Biggs, T.D. Hill and P.E. Szarmach
(Binghamton, NY, 1990). The joint British Academy-British Library
project (referred to above, p. 95) entitled 'Corpus of British Medieval
Library Catalogues', has, under the energetic editorship of Dr. Richard
Sharpe, begun to produce volumes at an impressive rate: three of a
projected sixteen volumes have now been published and more are in

press. Finally, it may be worth noting that the Cambridge University Press has in hand a large, multi-volume work entitled *A History of the Book in Britain*, edited by D.F. McKenzie, D. McKitterick and I.R. Willison. The first volume of this series (edited by myself) will cover *The Anglo-Saxon Period, c. 600-1100*; it will include a revised version of Helmut Gneuss's indispensable list of manuscripts written or owned in Anglo-Saxon England (see above, n. 2) as well as full discussion, by a team of distinguished scholars, of the origin, growth and contents of Anglo-Saxon libraries.

English Libraries Before 1066:
Use and Abuse of the Manuscript Evidence

David N. Dumville

For an approach to the subject of the library, its function, and its holdings in Anglo-Saxon England we must rely on assemblages of data which can then be manipulated, classified, and analysed in response to specific needs. Unfortunately, however, these basic collections of materials are, for the most part, not available. Research has, as always, proceeded in a disorderly fashion. We have Neil Ker's invaluable *Medieval Libraries of Great Britain* and *Catalogue of Manuscripts Containing Anglo-Saxon* (now with its supplement),[1] Alan Bishop's *English Caroline Minuscule* and the fundamental series of papers which preceded it,[2] the first two volumes (by Jonathan Alexander and Elżbieta Temple, respectively) of Alexander's 'Survey of Illuminated Manuscripts in the British Isles',[3] and—in a quite different class—Ogilvy's *Books Known to the English 597-1066* (which

---

[1] N.R. Ker, *Medieval Libraries of Great Britain. A List of Surviving Books* (2nd ed, London, 1964), first published in 1941, and N.R. Ker and A.G. Watson, *Supplement to the Second Edition* (London, 1987); *Catalogue of Manuscripts Containing Anglo-Saxon* (Oxford, 1957), and supplement in *Anglo-Saxon England* 5 (1976), 121-31 (reprinted together, Oxford, 1990).

[2] T.A.M. Bishop, *English Caroline Minuscule* (Oxford, 1971); for his other essays, see nn. 34 and 71 below.

[3] J.J.G. Alexander, *Insular Manuscripts, 6th to the 9th Century* (London, 1978); E. Temple, *Anglo-Saxon Manuscripts 900-1066* (London, 1976).

is more concerned with texts than with manuscripts).[4] We possess, in addition, a series of more detailed and pointed studies.

I have, of course, ignored thus far one monumental work. But I offer this brief listing in order to make the point that the major reference-works which have appeared are works of analysis or, at least, of classification. In other words, splendid as these books are when taken on their own terms, they in fact invite us to run before we can walk. They give us classified or analytic lists when we do not have assembled the raw materials from which they have been created. Each of these works has been a boon to every scholar in the field and on innumerable occasions; without them we should undoubtedly have made many (perhaps I should say, many more) foolish mistakes. In the cases of *Medieval Libraries of Great Britain* and *English Caroline Minuscule*, the works invite a host of further questions of the most basic nature. The *Catalogue*, on the other hand, gives a conspectus—if that is the right word for a volume of such a size—of a whole literature, and no doubt a much more accurate and representative one (giving full weight in particular to the extensive and popular prose literature) than many a recent history of Old English literature. Yet one may legitimately doubt, I think, the wisdom and value of focussing attention on a vernacular literature in a way which divorces it from its essential Latin literary context; for if we study English literature in the vernacular without thoroughly integrating it with its native and external Latin context, we make a travesty of English culture—and, as with the literature, so *a fortiori* of the libraries which housed that literature and of the scriptoria which disseminated it.

Desiderata in this field of study are, therefore, many and fundamental. I wish to discuss here some of the more general problems with which the subject is concerned, problems which may seem, at first glance, to be made more difficult of solution by the state of publication discussed above. I propose to consider also some of the

---

    [4] J.D.A. Ogilvy, *Books Known to the English 597-1066* (Cambridge, Mass., 1967), first published as *Books Known to Anglo-Latin Writers from Aldhelm to Alcuin (670-804)* (Cambridge, Mass., 1936). For a development of Ogilvy's work see now *Sources of Anglo-Saxon Literary Culture: a Trial Version*, ed. Frederick M. Biggs *et al.* (Binghamton, N.Y., 1990).

problems, of both method and interpretation, which are suggested by recent research and publication and by recent scholarly trends.

Surveys of the Manuscript Materials

What, then, are the desiderata of our field of enquiry? It seems to me that everything depends on the collection and publication of the raw manuscript evidence. Until such material is readily available, our efforts, in whichever direction, must of necessity be amateurish. When all the evidence is eventually assembled, we shall be in possession of only a fraction (an incalculable fraction, given so many variables) of what once existed; to accept an even smaller fraction, dictated merely by our own inertia, is a recipe for grievous error.

Do we then have a model to follow? The work which I have so far avoided mentioning is, of course, E.A. Lowe's monumental *Codices Latini Antiquiores* (and I should put alongside it, as an essential complement, the companion *Chartae*).[5] Here, of course, is *the* comprehensive collection of manuscript materials for a whole era of book-production. From it could be launched, I think it is fair to say, a major work of reinterpretation like Julian Brown's examination of Insular script in his magnificent series of Lyell Lectures, 'The Insular System of Scripts, *ca* 600—*ca* 850', whose eventual appearance in print will give us many new and valuable insights.

For my purpose of looking at the library-holdings of Anglo-Saxon England, one has only to undertake the straightforward task of making an abstract from *Codices Latini Antiquiores* of the directly relevant matter before beginning more detailed work; and that from which one is making the abstract is itself an assemblage of the total context, both codicological and literary. In *Codices Latini Antiquiores*, as complemented by the essential *Chartae*, one lacks for only one thing: thorough indexing, telling one—above all—the texts which the

---

[5] E.A. Lowe, *Codices Latini Antiquiores. A Palaeographical Guide to Latin Manuscripts prior to the Ninth Century* (11 vols and supplement, Oxford, 1934-71; with revised edition of vol. 2, Oxford, 1972); see also B. Bischoff and V. Brown, 'Addenda to *Codices latini antiquiores*', *Mediaeval Studies* 47 (1985), 317-66. Albert Bruckner and R. Marichal, *Chartae Latinae Antiquiores* (Olten, 1954-, in progress).

manuscripts contain. Even here, however, our wants are being supplied by the extraordinarily comprehensive indices undertaken by Professor James John, of Cornell University; one hopes that such an invaluable resource will soon be available.

For the period up to A.D. 800, then, we are remarkably well served. We have only to extract the material and ask the right questions. If we remain ignorant, it is because we have asked the wrong questions or because we do not have sufficient surviving information to enable us to give an answer.

For the years from 800 to 1066 we are in a wholly different position. We have to go back almost to a pre-Lowe type of situation. Yet the surviving manuscript materials for the cultural history of these two and a half centuries in England are enormously greater in quantity than for the preceding period. Where, then, do we begin? What I should like to suggest at the outset is that an English equivalent of *Codices Latini Antiquiores* for this period should not be our model, but at best our long-term aim. If the approach which we adopt towards this material is too grandiose, too comprehensive, and in every way too demanding, much time will be spent waiting for someone to finish a task which he or she almost certainly will not complete. The very success of Lowe, starting such a major project after a lifetime's experience with manuscripts, having a succession of the most formidably able and learned collaborators, and completing it (against all odds) just before he died at a ripe old age forty years later, should in fact be a warning to us of the scale of such a comprehensive project and of the near impossibility of achieving it.[6]

Various more limited projects have, in fact, been put in motion over the years. In 1962, in his inaugural lecture, Professor Julian Brown announced a project to list all manuscripts of pre-Conquest English provenance, and ultimately to catalogue them.[7] In 1978, I received generous funding from the University of Pennsylvania, intended to enable me to complete an annotated handlist of these

---

[6] Cf. Lowe, *Codices, Supplement*, p. xi, and J.J. John's account of Lowe's work, *American Council of Learned Societies Newsletter* 20/5 (October 1969).

[7] T.J. Brown, 'Latin Palaeography since Traube', *Transactions of the Cambridge Bibliographical Society* 3 (1959-63), 361-81 (at p. 372).

manuscripts, which could then be circulated as a working guide to the manuscript sources for the period. Happily, these efforts, and many others tending in the same direction or on a more limited scale by other scholars, have now effectively been superseded by or incorporated in the project which Professor Helmut Gneuss has announced. The first result is the appearance of 'A preliminary list of manuscripts written or owned in England up to 1100'.[8] The eventual intention is the publication of 'a bibliographical hand-list of Anglo-Saxon manuscripts': such a reference-work, carried through under the auspices of a remarkable university-department, would be an aid of immense value to Anglo-Saxonists.

The Types of Evidence Provided by Manuscripts

We can hope, therefore, to have the bulk of the raw materials available for us before too long. Our approach to the libraries, and to the manuscript production, of Anglo-Saxon England will be revolutionised. In the meantime, I can write only with the information and experience accumulated in a one-man effort, but aided at the final stage of preparation by a preview (which Professor Gneuss generously allowed me) of the 'Preliminary list'.

We need to think carefully about what kind of evidence we can expect and hope to obtain from such a collection of basic sources. We shall still not be able to rush at a cultural history of later Anglo-Saxon England, for the mass of information to be retrieved from this corpus will be enormous, and the interpenetrating issues are potentially so complex.

I think that the material offered divides itself, for my purposes here, into three principal groups, although no doubt opinions will differ on this: (1) the evidence provided by the physical existence of the

---

[8] *ASE* 9 (1981), 1-60. Two studies by Gneuss should also be mentioned here: 'Englands Bibliotheken im Mittelalter und ihr Untergang', in *Festschrift für Walter Hübner*, ed. D. Riesner and H. Gneuss (Berlin, 1964), pp. 91-121; 'Anglo-Saxon Libraries from the Conversion to the Benedictine Reform', *Settimane di studio del Centro italiano di studi sull'alto medioevo* 32 (1984), 643-99; see also his paper cited in n. 65, below.

manuscripts; (2) the evidence offered by the texts purveyed by these manuscripts; and (3) the evidence for lost (or unidentified) manuscripts and their contents.

The 'physical' evidence gives us, above all, a sense of the size of manuscript output, though in a purely relative way since we possess no formula which will enable us to relate the quantity of surviving manuscripts to the quantity originally produced. We can gain a sense of how output and standards compare with other periods or places; but even the route to this modest type of comparison is fraught with difficulties arising from our many areas of ignorance. Observation also of the layout and make-up of manuscripts and of the juxtaposition of texts can tell us something about attitudes to types of texts, to competing or complementary languages, and so on.

We are offered also, of course, evidence for the existence of a certain body of texts in English libraries in the period in question. Naturally, we cannot guarantee from their presence, especially in foreign immigrant manuscripts, that because a copy of a text existed it was read. But we are at least made aware of the possibility of physical evidence able to support an argument which may have been made on textual grounds; or we may be offered a new range of possible literary influences, hitherto unsuspected or unproved, on English authors of the period. This is not, of course, to assert that because a manuscript of a given work existed at Worcester it could have been used by a Canterbury author, for example: one must be on one's guard against that kind of supporting argument.

We learn, too, not merely which authors and texts were available and might have been read, but what kind of literature was being produced and copied at that time. The work of Michael Lapidge has indicated what riches there are for those who wish to work on Anglo-Latin and who can cope with the rigours of the hermeneutic style.[9]

---

[9] See his survey, 'The Hermeneutic Style in Tenth-Century Anglo-Latin Literature', *ASE* 4 (1975), 67-111; on tenth-century poetry see also 'Three Latin Poems from Æthelwold's School at Winchester', *ibid.*, 1 (1972), 85-137, and 'Some Latin Poems as Evidence for the Reign of Athelstan', *ibid.*, 9 (1981), 61-98. See now also 'Schools, Learning and Literature in Tenth-Century England', *Settimane di studio del Centro italiano di studi sull'alto medioevo* 38 (1990), 951-1005.

The recognition and examination of consistent patterns of gloss or comment in a manuscript or, better, a group of manuscripts can introduce us in a revealing way to the cultural milieu of a literary or quasi-literary personality. The obvious example from recent scholarship is the group of manuscripts associated—whether rightly or not—with Archbishop Wulfstan. That was the growth-industry of the last generation.[10] That of the present generation of scholarship seemed to be about to be St Dunstan,[11] a figure who—like Wulfstan—transcends simple institutional boundaries; but Byrhtferth of

----

[10] The work of Karl Jost, Dorothy Bethurum, and Dorothy Whitelock, who brought Wulfstan to full scholarly attention, was summarised and discussed by D. Bethurum, 'Wulfstan', in *Continuations and Beginnings. Studies in Old English Literature*, ed. E.G. Stanley (London, 1966), pp. 210-46. For a close study of one of the manuscripts see H.R. Loyn, *A Wulfstan Manuscript Containing Institutes, Laws and Homilies, British Museum Cotton Nero A.i* (Copenhagen, 1971), a facsimile reproduction. The palaeographical arguments were developed by N.R. Ker, 'The handwriting of Archbishop Wulfstan', in *England before the Conquest. Studies in Primary Sources Presented to Dorothy Whitelock*, ed. Peter Clemoes and K. Hughes (Cambridge, 1971), pp. 315-31, reprinted in Ker's *Books, Collectors and Libraries. Studies in the Medieval Heritage* (London, [1985]), pp. 9-30. That their work created something of a scholarly fiction has been suggested by C.E. Hohler, 'Some Service-Books of the Later Saxon Church', in *Tenth-Century Studies*, ed. David Parsons (Chichester, 1975), pp. 60-83 and 217-27.

[11] See R.W. Hunt, *Saint Dunstan's Classbook from Glastonbury* (Amsterdam, 1961), a facsimile edition of Oxford, Bodleian Library, MS. Auct. F.4.32 (*S.C.* 2176); T.A.M. Bishop, 'An Early Example of Insular-Caroline', *Transactions of the Cambridge Bibliographical Society* 4 (1964-8), 396-400; H. Gneuss, 'Dunstan und Hrabanus Maurus: zur Hs. Bodleian Auctarium F.4.32', *Anglia* 96 (1978), 136-48; M. Lapidge, 'St Dunstan's Latin Poetry', *Anglia* 98 (1980), 101-6. See also n. 17 below.

Ramsey has suddenly seized the stage.[12]   No doubt other figures—some of whom will (one hopes) be anonymous and perhaps, therefore, able to be viewed more dispassionately—will emerge from the new corpus of materials.

The literary borrowings by datable or localisable Anglo-Latin authors will also be of considerable interest when considered in the light of the manuscript evidence. Various points may emerge. With the aid of an indexed handlist, it may indeed be possible, by collation, to identify the precise copy of a source used by an author.[13] This would lead to various possible conclusions. Such an identification would help to give the manuscript a provenance and perhaps, through consequent links with other scribes or manuscripts, would give it a point of origin. Annotations in the manuscript might then be able to be associated with the English author in question, and more could be learned about him as a literary personality.

Alternatively, study of the English manuscript tradition of a work might indicate a lack of evidence for the circulation of a given branch of the tradition in England. An authorial borrowing from that branch might then be questioned, and a context for an alternative indirect borrowing sought.

There are various ways, with the aid of the handlist under discussion, in which the former existence of now lost manuscripts can be demonstrated. The greatest difficulty will arise in the situation

---

[12] See in particular C. Hart, 'The Ramsey *Computus*', *EHR* 85 (1970), 29-44, and 'Byrhtferth and his Manual', *Medium Ævum* 41 (1972), 95-109; M. Lapidge, 'Byrhtferth and the *Vita S. Ecgwini*', *Mediaeval Studies* 41 (1979), 331-53, and 'Byrhtferth of Ramsey and the Early Sections of the *Historia Regum* Attributed to Symeon of Durham', *Anglo-Saxon England* 10 (1982), 97-122; P.S. Baker, 'The Old English Canon of Byrhtferth of Ramsey', *Speculum* 55 (1980), 22-37.

[13] This possibility seems to have been realised in the case of Saint-Omer, Bibliothèque municipale, MS. 202, written in northeastern France in the ninth century, whose copy of the *Euangelium Nicodemi* was apparently the immediate source of the Old English translation now surviving in Cambridge, University Library, MS. Ii.2.11. Professor J.E. Cross has publication of his discovery in hand.

where such a manuscript (whose existence in, say, the tenth century can be demonstrated) was a Continental book. That Continental manuscript may still survive but bear no physical indication that it has ever been in England; if it remains in an English library it cannot escape forever, but if it returned to the Continent its English history might escape detection almost indefinitely.

However, such caveats aside (for it is no use postponing a handlist on such considerations), lost manuscripts can be documented. A non-authorial copy of a text must have an exemplar; if the manuscript is English, and the exemplar cannot be identified as extant in the textual history, then we have clear evidence for another copy of that text in England (whether it was itself English or foreign is another matter) at the period of copying. The English tradition of a work may presuppose any number of lost copies of the work, to complete the stemma; and stemmatics can only ever give a minimal number of lost copies. Borrowings by Anglo-Latin authors may indicate an exemplar of Insular or Continental origin which cannot otherwise be identified. Text-historical or palaeographical criteria, or both together, may establish dependence of a copy on two different (and perhaps incomplete) exemplars. It may be possible to show, once glossing traditions are better understood,[14] that text and gloss (or different layers of gloss) depend on different exemplars. Collations may be identified, pointing to that constant mediaeval inferiority-complex about the state of one's own copy of a text and incidentally indicating the former existence of another copy. A lost copy of a text can never be posited without a great deal of hard work, but over a period we should be able to build up a rather less skeletal picture of English library-resources in the Anglo-Saxon period, and particularly in its latter half.

We might refer to one final source of indications of now lost manuscripts, and these at particular centres, namely, deliberate statements about library-holdings. The best known are, of course, Alcuin's account of the library at York and the twelfth-century copy of

---

[14] Cf. two papers by M. Lapidge and R.I. Page, 'The Study of Latin Texts in Late Anglo-Saxon England', in *Latin and the Vernacular Languages in Early Medieval Britain*, ed. Nicholas Brooks (Leicester, 1982), pp. 99-140, 141-65. See now René Derolez, ed., *Anglo-Saxon Glossography* (Brussels, 1992).

the list of Bishop Æthelwold's donation of books to Peterborough.[15]
All the surviving library-catalogues (which also belong to this type of
statement) are of post-Conquest date, but it is sometimes possible to
extract some pre-Conquest information from them.[16]

The Actual Manuscripts: Analysis of the Materials

It is still very difficult to say with any certainty how many
manuscripts survive which were in English libraries before 1066. Two
major difficulties are the scatter of English manuscripts in Continental
libraries (and, for the early period, doubts as to whether or not they
were products of expatriate—or Celtic—institutions) and the problem of
identifying Continental manuscripts once in England but since returned,
under whatever circumstances, to the Continent. A case in point is the
tangled history of the recently fashionable Vaticanus latinus MS. 3363,
a ninth-century French Boethius, annotated in an Insular hand of *ca* 900
or later (Asser has been both suggested and doubted) and in the hand
currently identified as Dunstan's; it now lies in a Continental
repository.[17] Less exotic, perhaps, is a history like that of the Utrecht

---

[15] Alcuin, *Versus de Sanctis Euboricensis Ecclesiae*, lines 1541-
1557: ed. and transl. Peter Godman, *Alcuin: The Bishops, Kings, and
Saints of York* (Oxford, 1982), pp. 122-7. On this and other library-
lists from the period before A.D. 1100, see now M. Lapidge,
'Surviving Booklists from Anglo-Saxon England', in *Learning and
Literature in Anglo-Saxon England. Studies presented to Peter
Clemoes*, ed. Michael Lapidge and H. Gneuss (Cambridge, 1985),
reprinted pp. 87-167 of this volume; for Æthelwold's donation, see pp.
116-20.

[16] See M.R. James, *The Ancient Libraries of Canterbury and Dover*
(Cambridge, 1903), pp. xxxii-xxxiii, for an approach to the
fragmentary twelfth-century catalogue from Christ Church, Canterbury,
in Cambridge, University Library, MS. Ii.3.12; cf. Ker, *Medieval
Libraries*, p. 29. The British Academy has initiated a project to publish
all English mediaeval library-catalogues.

[17] Pierre Courcelle, *La 'Consolation de Philosophie' dans la
tradition littéraire* (Paris, 1967), pp. 267-70; Fabio Troncarelli, 'Per
una ricerca sui commenti altomedievali al *De Consolatione* di Boezio',

Psalter which spawned a pre-Conquest Canterbury progeny and remained in England, but returned to the Continent in modern times.[18] Here are famous manuscripts; but many more humble ones undoubtedly lie unnoticed on the Continent. They are likely to be found, in any numbers, only by someone looking for tell-tale traces,[19] however few, of an English history. Anglo-Caroline manuscripts themselves, however, are similarly scattered: the extraordinary Vergil in the Vatican's Reginensis collection (discovered a generation ago for English scholars, and assigned by Mr Bishop to Worcester)[20] and a

---

in *Miscellanea in memoria di Giorgio Cencetti* (Torino, 1973), pp. 363-80, and *Tradizioni perdute. La "Consolatio Philosophiae" nell'alto medioevo* (Padova, 1981); D.K. Bolton, 'Remigian Commentaries on the "Consolation of Philosophy" and their Sources', *Traditio* 33 (1977), 381-94. I owe to Professor Julian Brown my knowledge of the identification of the hand of 'Dunstan' in the glosses to this manuscript and am grateful to him for giving me a copy of his typescript description of the book. See further M.B. Parkes, 'A note on MS. Vatican, Bibl. Apost., lat. 3363', in *Boethius: his Life, Thought and Influence*, ed. Margaret Gibson (Oxford, 1981), pp. 425-7; D.N. Dumville, 'English Square Minuscule Script: the Background and Earliest Phases', *ASE* 16 (1987), 147-79 (at pp. 173-8).

[18] Francis Wormald, *The Utrecht Psalter* (Utrecht, 1953); D. Tselos, 'English Manuscript Illustration and the Utrecht Psalter', *Art Bulletin* 41 (1959), 137-49; Suzy Dufrenne, 'Les copies anglaises du Psautier d'Utrecht', *Scriptorium* 18 (1964), 185-97, and *Les Illustrations du Psautier d'Utrecht: sources et apport carolingien* (Paris, 1978).

[19] The productive, deliberate search for Breton manuscripts by Léon Fleuriot—see his publications, 'La découverte de nouvelles gloses en Vieux-Breton', *Comptes rendus de l'Académie des inscriptions et belles-lettres* (1959), 186-95, and *Dictionnaire des gloses en Vieux Breton* (Paris, 1964), introduction—is an example of the procedure which would have to be followed.

[20] Bishop, *English Caroline Minuscule*, p. 17. At least three other copies of Vergil have been attributed to Anglo-Saxon England (Gneuss, nos 477, 503, and 648); nos 477 and 503 share a Bury St Edmunds provenance *ca* 1300, when the former (which seems Continental to me,

liturgical manuscript found in Poland by Dr Temple[21] are merely two examples of what will continue to disturb any comfortable but hasty assumptions that we have identified all the important surviving manuscripts.

Something of the order of four hundred Insular manuscripts of the seventh and eighth centuries have been extracted from *Codices Latini Antiquiores*; of these about one hundred should be deleted as doubtfully relevant to England. For the ninth century, on the other hand, we have, as far as I know, no count, although the number of surviving books is assuredly very small indeed.[22] Again, as far as I know, no public attempt has been made to count the Latin books in that characteristically tenth-century English script, the Anglo-Saxon Square minuscule; in fact, there would seem to be about eighty. Of the Anglo-Caroline minuscule whose use spans the last century, or century and a quarter, of the English state—from the mid-tenth-century copy of Smaragdus on the Rule of St Benedict (Cambridge, University Library, MS. Ee.2.4) to the 'Cambridge Songs' manuscript (Gg.5.35) or the Worcester Passional (Cambridge, Corpus Christi College, MS. 9), if I may stay with Cambridge manuscripts!—there survive, according to Mr Bishop's count, some six hundred books and fragments,[23] although I must confess that I have not yet identified anything like that number. And of course we know from Dr Ker's *Catalogue* of some four hundred vernacular items, of which perhaps 150 were written wholly

---

not English) was used as pastedowns, while the latter, in Insular script perhaps of the tenth century, was palimpsested; both were glossed copies of the *Aeneid*.

[21] Temple, *Anglo-Saxon Manuscripts*, pp. 7, 107-8 (Gneuss, no. 942).

[22] Excluding books dated '*saec.* viii/ix' (nine volumes: Gneuss, nos 45, 432, 443, 456, 635, 646, 780, 885, 911) and 'saec. ix/x' (three books: Gneuss, nos 52, 298, 462), I count fifteen in Gneuss's list (nos 28, 88, 125-7, 282, 327, 375, 385, 448, 576, 611, 626, 857, 898).

[23] *English Caroline Minuscule*, pp. xiv, xv, xvi.

or principally in Old English; of these, approximately five sixths belong to the tenth and eleventh centuries.[24]

Some divisions, on grounds of script, between manuscripts (or annotating hands) originating in different areas can also be made, both for the pre-viking period and for the tenth century, between either major political units or geographical regions or spheres of ecclesiastical influence. In any event, we have a substantial amount of material, and various preliminary ways—primarily palaeographical—of classifying it. This brings me to the question of the evidence on which manuscripts have been assigned to specific centres.

The Attribution of Manuscripts to Centres

There are innumerable items of evidence which allow us to assign manuscripts a location, whether a simple provenance or even a point of origin. In this matter, I propose to focus here on two questions: first, on what the sum-total of that evidence appears to tell us; and secondly, on the disturbing implications of new work, on Anglo-Saxon royal diplomas of the period 924-1016, for the attribution of manuscripts of that period to a given centre on the evidence of script or scribe.

The second edition of Neil Ker's *Medieval Libraries of Great Britain*, published in 1964 (and now accompanied by the supplement published in 1987), is the reference-base for an attempt to obtain an overview of library-holdings in this period. But it is not, of course, one of the aims of that book to answer straightforward questions about library-holdings *before 1066*, and we must proceed with caution. By my count, some 340 manuscripts of pre-Conquest date, and about a hundred others written in the second half of the eleventh century and *ca* 1100, were noted in 1964 by Ker as having been in the possession

---

[24] See his list, *Catalogue*, pp. xiv-xix. For facsimiles of Old English scribal hands from books and fragments catalogued by Ker, see David N. Dumville, *Specimina Codicum Palaeoanglicorum* (Copenhagen, forthcoming). But only twenty date from the tenth century, and the last quarter of the eleventh century is (interestingly) almost bare; we therefore have more than a hundred vernacular manuscripts of the Anglo-Saxon eleventh century.

of an identifiable institution at any time before 1540.[25] It is in the
nature of his book that it cannot tell us in detail when the manuscript
was at a given place or what the evidence is that it was indeed there.[26]
A code simply indicates the class of evidence used. In general, where
an attribution depends on script alone, that was regarded as an
insufficient basis for inclusion.[27] Contents and external features are,
therefore, the crucial classes of evidence. Criteria of inclusion and
exclusion were deliberately not applied with rigorous consistency,
however.[28]

Among those 448 notices there are some duplications of entry:
some manuscripts, which have travelled, naturally show evidence for
their presence at more than one centre.[29] Ker's listing does not tell

---

[25] See the Appendix for details. There are 448 notices, referring
to some 428 manuscripts (on duplications see n. 29), distributed among
sixty-four institutions.

[26] The supplement published in 1987 (see n. 1 above) has some
details of this sort, a welcome development.

[27] *Medieval Libraries*, pp. xx-xxi.

[28] *Ibid.*, prefaces, passim.

[29] Twenty manuscripts are recorded as having belonged to two
identifiable institutions.   They are Gneuss's nos 40 (St Aug.,
Canterbury, & Ely), 46 (Winchester O.M. & Worcester), 52-3 (one
entry: Christ Church, Canterbury, & Winchester O.M.), 186 (St Aug.,
Canterbury & Hyde), 291 (Canterbury: Christ Church & St Aug., both
queried), 293 (Jarrow & Worcester), 301 (Hyde & Winchester O.M.,
both queried), 343 (Durham & Lindisfarne), 357 (Southwick &
Winchester O.M.), 373 (Battle & Winchester O.M.), 376 (Salisbury &
Sherborne), 407 (Hyde & Winchester O.M.), 454-6 (one entry: Hyde
& Worcester), 545 (Canterbury: Christ Church & St Aug.), 558
(Windsor & Worcester), 617 (Crowland & Lewes, both queried), 627
(Malvern & Worcester), 628 (Glastonbury & Worcester), 658 (Durham
& Finchale), 659 (St Aug., Canterbury, & Malmesbury).   All this
means that the number of manuscripts under consideration is (on Ker's
terms, at any rate) 428. There are other inconsistencies of numbering:
Ker sometimes divided a codex into parts, where Gneuss has not, or
into more or fewer parts than Gneuss has, or Gneuss has divided where
Ker did not. Companion-volumes are treated now as single entities,

us which manuscripts are English and which are not,[30] or, therefore, when the foreign books came to England, if indeed that is known.

There are many difficulties for us, then, in using these data. How are we to refine the information to our purpose? The first point to be borne in mind is that, given the criteria for inclusion, the number cited is a maximum. I have rarely, if ever, seen those citing Ker's book notice his indications of doubt. In fact, almost twenty per cent of his notices carry a question-mark to warn the user that the evidence for the manuscript's location is not wholly satisfactory.[31] Of the pre-

---

now as two or more separate books. All these factors make precise numbers difficult to achieve and even more problematic to interpret.

[30] Sixty-eight of the manuscripts listed by Ker may be considered as non-English: Gneuss, nos 61, 77, 81, 83, 87, 120, 128, 133-7, 140, 148, 185, 196, 263, 266 (probably English), 269 (probably English), 279, 283, 295, 311, 316, 325, 334, 354, 361-2, 376 (two entries), 409, 417-18, 423, 444, 459, 485, 489-90, 513, 515-16, 521-2, 530, 538, 565, 570, 575, 581, 583, 585, 607, 629, 651, 659 (two entries), 661, 688, 715-16, 734, 744, 752, 754, 761, 794, 939. To them must be added Oxford, Bodleian Library, MS. e Museo 113 (*S.C.* 3584), '*saec.* x-xii', not listed by Gneuss. These sixty-eight are distributed between twenty-three provenances. Cf. n. 74 below for a list of the manuscripts designated as foreign by Gneuss in his list.

[31] There are eighty-five notices concerning a total of eighty-two manuscripts. These are Gneuss's nos 14, 21, 23, 26, 40, 47, 77, 100, 102, 106, 108-9, 111, 118, 160, 180, 190, 191-2 (counted together as one manuscript), 198, 206-7, 251, 290, 291 (queried in two entries), 293, 300, 301 (queried twice), 304, 313, 322, 333, 342, 358, 373, 375-6, 386, 397, 402-3, 407, 411, 417, 422, 426, 430, 447, 449-51, 455, 466, 479, 496, 514, 520, 535, 611, 617 (queried twice), 627, 640, 651, 667-8, 688, 693, 721, 733, 764, 767, 775-6, 794, 806, 880, 895, 922, 923, 927. There are also three manuscripts noticed and queried by Ker but not included in Gneuss's list: Cambridge, University Library, MS. Gg.4.15 (Eynsham); Copenhagen, Royal Library, MS. G.K.S. 1653.4° (Oxford, Carmelites); Oxford, Bodleian Library, MS. Bodley 796 (Windsor). The categories of evidence which Ker found ambiguous or barely adequate were distributed as follows: binding materials (4); contents (24); *ex-libris* inscriptions (3);

Conquest books, some eighteen manuscripts are assigned to institutions which did not exist before the Norman conquest.[32] Indeed, there are many manuscripts—and perhaps especially those of foreign origin—which are unlikely to have been, before 1066, at the place of their later known provenance. This is perhaps the most difficult area: it is where the palaeographer's working rule (most frequently enunciated by Mr Bishop)[33]—that, barring specific indications to the contrary, a manuscript may be presumed to have originated at the place of its mediaeval provenance—is most likely to be a false guide.

In other words, Ker's listing can, for our purpose, be only the very beginning of an enquiry. I shall have more to say later about other difficulties in store for us as users of this material. However, I wish now to try to assess the usefulness to us of work done since 1964, in particular the researches embodied in T.A.M. Bishop's *English Caroline Minuscule* (1971) and in his series of preliminary papers, published principally in the *Transactions of the Cambridge Bibliographical Society*.[34] It is a tragedy that when this enormous

---

inscriptions of personal ownership (2); liturgical (17), marginalia (3), script (10), shelfmarks (3), identifications with entries in mediaeval catalogues (4), identifications with entries in Patrick Young's catalogues (3), identifications with books seen by John Leland (2). In seven instances (Gneuss's nos 21, 108, 293, 342, 375, 403, 651) Ker offered a footnote indicating his reasons in more detail or giving a reference to a discussion; in five further instances (Gneuss's nos 106, 180, 301 [Winchester Cathedral], MS. 733; and Oxford, Bodleian Library, MS. Bodley 796) Ker gave no reason for the query. In two cases (Gneuss's nos 333, 611) Ker cited both contents and liturgical evidence.

[32] Battle (2), Buildwas (1), Hatfield Peverel/Regis (1), Hexham (1), Lanthony (3), Lewes (1), London (Cripplegate Hospital) (1), Oxford (Carmelites) (1), Shrewsbury (1), Snape (1), Southwick (2), Windsor (3).

[33] For example, *English Caroline Minuscule*, pp. xiv-xv.

[34] 'Notes on Cambridge Manuscripts', *Transactions of the Cambridge Bibliographical Society* 1 (1949-53), 432-41; 2 (1954-8), 185-99, 323-36; 3 (1959-63), 93-5, 412-23; 4 (1964-8), 70-7; 'An Early Example of Insular-Caroline', *ibid.*, 4 (1964-8), 396-400; 'The Copenhagen Gospel Book', *Nordisk Tidskrift för Bok- och*

work, of well over a decade's intensive researches, came to be summarised, it had to be within the exceedingly brief compass of an Oxford Palaeographical Handbook. We have been deprived thereby of an enormous amount of information, insight, and considered judgment. Mr Bishop has since taken up another major subject and we are unlikely to see further fruits of his Anglo-Caroline labours. Starting from the evidence of ownership, of the sort which I referred to earlier, following the working rule about the *stabilitas* of the average manuscript book, and then concentrating above all on identifying individual scribes and their work and the relations of these with one another, Bishop has assigned between three hundred and four hundred specimens an origin at one of a small number of important centres—hardly more than thirteen in number.[35] And he makes the point that 'no more than seven scriptoria [St Augustine's, Canterbury; Christ Church, Canterbury; Abingdon; Winchester, Old Minster; Winchester, New Minster; Worcester; and Exeter] supplied about half the items [about three hundred, therefore] recognised as examples of English Caroline.'[36]

It is plain that the tenth and eleventh centuries constituted a period of considerable manuscript production in England, and principally in the south. If Mr Bishop's assignments of manuscripts to given centres are accurate, and if some means could be found by which all his detailed judgments could be made available to the interested public, we should have at our disposal an incomparable resource for the history of the period.

However, there is one recent major development which casts some considerable doubt, in principle at least, on the potential accuracy of these attributions of origin to groups of Anglo-Caroline manuscripts. Bishop's principal method was to proceed by linking in chains manuscripts sharing collaborating scribes. Occasionally, a generic likeness would be invoked to make a connexion between an attributed

---

Biblioteksväsen 54 (1967), 33-41; 'Lincoln Cathedral MS 182', *Lincolnshire History and Archaeology* 2 (1967), 73-6; *Aethici Istrici Cosmographia: Codex Leidensis Scaligeranus* (Amsterdam, 1966), introduction.

[35] *English Caroline Minuscule*, pp. xv, xiv.
[36] *Ibid.*, p. xv.

and an unattributed group,[37] a procedure which has its dangers but where the opinion of an acknowledged expert must be treated with considerable respect. Another caveat which would be entered by someone like myself—a historian interested in manuscripts rather than a professional palaeographer—would be that these long chains, depending on the identification of the work of individual scribes, contain what appears to be a worryingly high degree of subjectivity of judgment. A more tangible and substantial difficulty has been presented by new work on the Latin diplomas of English kings from Æthelstan to Æthelred, A.D. 924-1016.

It has been the generally received doctrine (if the details have nonetheless been the subject of uncertainty and dispute) that the substantial series of Latin royal diplomas issued at this period was produced by ecclesiastical institutions acting as, or on behalf of, the recipient of the benefit conveyed by the charter.[38] However, Dr Simon Keynes has now systematically demolished this view, demonstrating the existence in this period of what must certainly be called a royal-chancery staff.[39] Recognition of the centralised production of royal diplomas, based on a professional group of royal scribes, brings in its train a series of acute problems for our study of book-production in these years.

Under the old view of their production, original single-sheet diplomas—once they were recognised as such—offered specimens of script which were not merely precisely dated but localised too. A royal diploma for Abingdon could automatically be assigned to the Abingdon scriptorium, for example.[40] (It was partly for this reason that the new British Academy series of editions of Anglo-Saxon charters was designed to be published by archive, rather than by reign or other period. It now seems plain that when the current series has been

---

[37] *Ibid.*, p. 13, for example; more fully in his 'Lincoln Cathedral MS 182' (n. 34 above).

[38] See, for example, the contributions of Pierre Chaplais in *Prisca Munimenta. Studies in Archival and Administrative History presented to Dr A.E.J. Hollaender*, ed. Felicity Ranger (London, 1973), pp. 28-107.

[39] *The Diplomas of King Aethelred 'the Unready' 978-1016. A Study in their Use as Historical Evidence* (Cambridge, 1980).

[40] For example, *English Caroline Minuscule*, pp. xix, 9.

completed, we shall have to have another, and much more heavily edited, series arranged chronologically to complement it.) Charter-evidence could, on this view of charter-production, be used as crucial testimony to the location of scribes or script-varieties. The same scribe, identified in a diploma and in a book, would locate that book beyond reasonable doubt. This argument must now be stood on its head, or worse. At best, the identification would show either that the book in question was itself the product of a royal writing office (and, in the present state of our knowledge, that would probably be a rather rash conclusion) or that the scribe of the charter was also, at some point in his career, a member of the scriptorium in which the book had been produced. In other words, we must now use the evidence of books to help us to identify the scriptoria whose members also saw service in the royal writing office, rather than relying on charters to locate manuscript books.[41] Plainly we have lost a good deal of apparent evidence, and our task of localising tenth- and eleventh-century manuscripts has become noticeably more troublesome.

It is difficult, as yet, to assess the full impact of this development on Bishop's attributions. Examination of his detailed papers does indicate reliance on such charter-evidence at significant points in

---

[41] It is not clear whether there was a normal paradigm of the life of a royal-chancery scribe at this period. Would he be a trained scribe from an episcopal or monastic scriptorium when he entered the king's service? If so, we could use his appearance in localised specimens to learn of the centres which contributed personnel to the staff of the royal secretariat. Would he continue to function, at least sporadically, as a member of the scriptorium of an ecclesiastical institution during his period of service with the king? Or would his term of royal service, if it did not lead to promotion, come to an end with the result that he then joined an ecclesiastical scriptorium? If so, his appearance in localised specimens would be less useful to us (unless we should suppose that he would return to the place where he entered religion). At present, we can answer none of these questions. Nor can we say whether the royal chancery trained its own new scribes, whether service there might be for life, or whether the chancery had a shifting population of trained scribes seconded from ecclesiastical scriptoria. Progress in dispelling ignorance depends on identifying the work of many charter-scribes in books.

various arguments. There is, of course, no question at all of his conclusions being uniformly vitiated. His researches always begin with the solid external and contextual evidence of provenance and origin. However, all that work will have to be reconsidered in detail. Here, surely, is a classic case of developments in a related field overturning assumptions and constructs in ours.

The principal casualty will be apparent identifications of the scribes and scripts of the less important centres, from which books are not yet directly identifiable: a good example is St Albans, for which an Æthelredian charter of the year 1007 has been taken by Bishop as a representative script-specimen.[42] There are also wider implications: the type of Anglo-Caroline script thought to be characteristic of houses of the Æthelwold-connexion has been supposed, on the evidence of its royal diplomas of the early years of the reform-period, to be particularly associated with, and perhaps even to have been created at, Abingdon.[43] In fact, the removal of this charter-evidence creates great doubts about the productivity of the Abingdon scriptorium before *ca* 1000 and destroys the argument for early association of Anglo-Caroline Style I with Abingdon.[44]

The Library and the Use of Books

I wish to turn now to a very rapid consideration of just what we mean when we speak of a 'library' at this period. We can attack this rather important question both from the manuscripts themselves and

---

[42] *English Caroline Minuscule*, p. 15.

[43] *Ibid.*, pp. xix, xxi-xxii, xxiv.

[44] The only arguably Abingdon product of *saec.* x^2 would then be London, British Library, MS. Cotton Tiberius A.vi (Gneuss, no. 364), of A.D. 977/8, a vernacular manuscript written in Square minuscule. Its contents have been edited by Simon Taylor in *The Anglo-Saxon Chronicle. A Collaborative Edition*, gen. ed. David Dumville and S. Keynes (23 vols, Cambridge, 1983-), IV. For a possible scribal relative see Ker, *Catalogue*, pp. 428-9, no. 351—Oxford, Bodleian Library, MS. Tanner 10 (*S.C.* 9830), fols 105-114. I hope to discuss the pre-Conquest history of the Abingdon scriptorium and library in another paper.

from external evidence. Many scholars have written on the general problems of understanding the history of the early mediaeval library, but probably the most convenient general introduction for students of English culture is Francis Wormald's paper on 'The Monastic Library'.[45]

In this period we are perhaps talking primarily, though not exclusively, about the monastic library. But, before following up the more complex implications of that point, I should like to mention some of the specific functions of books in the monastic context. A high proportion of our surviving manuscript volumes comprises gospel-books, miscellaneous books of the bible, legendaries and passionals, and more strictly liturgical books. We cannot guarantee that any of these would have served as what we should recognise nowadays as a library-book. Some of the biblical matter and all of the *liturgica* would belong in church.[46] The legendary and the passional would probably find their principal employment in the refectory, in the provision of pious reading during meals.[47] In short, the bulk of the largest group of our surviving manuscripts can hardly be referred to a library-context. In later English library-catalogues such volumes are often not listed, but turn up in inventories of movable property, including relics, the church-plate, and other church-furnishings. Wormald, in fact, conjectured that some saints' *uitae* and some *liturgica* were kept with the local saints' relics, or at any rate in close proximity to the shrine of a local saint.[48]

One of our major problems, especially in dealing with the earlier period, is to understand the general attitude to books and reading prevalent in any given minster or federation of minsters. A plethora of rules, particularly in Ireland, enunciated conflicting positions concerning almost every facet of monastic life.[49] We know—or think

---

[45] In the *English Library before 1700. Studies in its History*, ed. Francis Wormald and C.E. Wright (London, 1958), pp. 15-31.

[46] *Ibid.*, p. 16.

[47] *Ibid.*

[48] *Ibid.*, pp. 16-17.

[49] For the Irish rules, the standard, if rather outdated, resource is by L. Gougaud, 'Inventaire des règles monastiques irlandaises', *Revue Bénédictine* 25 (1908), 167-84, 321-33; and 28 (1911), 86-9. There is

we know—what St Benedict had to say on the subject. But a major desideratum is the study of all the other surviving rules to determine their attitudes. In Benedictine monasteries—and for England this is not a serious trend until the tenth-century reform[50]—there are certain normal features. There was a corporate book-collection, an institutional library. The monks spent a certain amount of time reading the bible, and on a regular basis. St Benedict's prescriptions are found in §48 of his *Regula*, and those for reading aloud in the refectory are in §38. As far as we can tell, on very poor evidence, the books were kept in cupboards or closets (*almarium* or *almariolum* is the usual word).[51]

There are many accounts of the ceremony at which, on the first Monday in Lent, there was a solemn distribution of books in the chapter-house.[52] This would serve as reading for a specified period, sometimes for an entire year. Dom Anscari Mundó, in a now classic article,[53] showed how, by a fundamental misunderstanding of the word *bibliotheca* from the carolingian period onwards, library-reading rather

•

---

a catalogue, still of use, by Benedictus van Haeften, *Disquisitiones Monasticae* (Antwerp, 1644), t. 1, tract. V, disq. XVI, p. 58, of pre-Benedictine Western *regulae*. See also Bruno Albers, *Untersuchungen zu den ältesten Mönchsgewohnheiten* (München, 1905), and the series of edited *Consuetudines Monasticae* which he initiated; Adalbert de Vogüé, *Les Règles monastiques anciennes (400-700)* (Turnhout, 1985).

[50] I do not dissent from the conclusions of Henry Mayr-Harting, *The Venerable Bede, the Rule of St. Benedict, and Social Class*, Jarrow Lecture 1976 (Jarrow, [1977]), but wish to see its important findings within the broadest context. Of the thoroughgoing Benedictinism of the tenth-century reform-period the manuscript evidence leaves no doubt: we know already of twelve late Anglo-Saxon copies of the Rule (Gneuss, nos 29, 41, 55, 101, 189, 248, 262, 379, 440, 672, 758, and 926), and an eighth-century copy which remained at Worcester (Gneuss, no. 631), as well as various copies of Smaragdus's relevant works.

[51] Wormald, 'The Monastic Library', p. 17.

[52] *Ibid.*, p. 21.

[53] '"Bibliotheca." Bible et lecture du Carême d'après saint Benoît', *Revue Bénédictine* 60 (1950), 65-92.

than strictly bible-reading came to be specified. As a result, suitable matter needed to be chosen, especially for Lent. One charming list of acceptable reading was referred to by Mundó: specified for Lent was that most bizarre text of Insular associations, the *Cosmographia* of Ethicus Ister![54]

The institutional library therefore needed a point of supply for its reading matter. But it would probably be a mistake to assume that the house-scriptorium necessarily provided most of these needs. There was likely to have been an unending, if very occasional, supply of books from outside, obtained by gift, by purchase at home or abroad, or by exchange. It would be interesting to study the proportion of liturgical to non-liturgical books among those manuscripts whose writing could be assigned to the scriptorium of the house which (later) owned them; we might find that the smaller scriptoria in particular devoted all or most of their efforts to liturgical books, and obtained other types of books by various different means.

In the late Anglo-Saxon period, the example of Leofric, though famous, may nonetheless have been fairly typical. Leofric, bishop of Crediton, arranged to move his diocesan seat to St Peter's Minster, Exeter, in 1050. But he found it necessary to endow his canons with a library, for when he got to Exeter he found no general library, but one capitulary, one epistle-book, one old private breviary, and one old lectionary in a poor condition. Many monastic houses were founded or re-founded in the reform-period, and would have needed books. It is interesting to ask, for I shall do no more, how the founders—whether lay or ecclesiastical—got hold of books for this purpose. Leofric's impressive library—the list of the donation survives—includes

---

[54] *Ibid.*, p. 67, n. 1, referring to M. Van Assche, '"Divinae vacare lectioni." De "ratio studiorum" van Sint Benedictus', *Sacris Erudiri* 1 (1948), 13-34 (at p. 25, n. 1). On this whole subject see further two important articles by K. Christ: 'In Caput Quadragesimae', *Zentralblatt für Bibliothekswesen* 60 (1943/4), 33-59, and 'Mittelalterliche Bibliotheksordnungen für Frauenklöster', *ibid.*, 59 (1942), 1-29.

manuscripts written at the two Canterbury houses and some interesting foreign volumes.[55]

The current appearance of manuscripts may give some indication of how books were used, but we should beware of too facile generalisations. Glossing does not necessarily mean that the particular copy of a book was read, much less used in class—the whole concept of the 'classbook' seems to be in severe need of a re-evaluation.[56] Judging by consistent (if undatable) marking which one does find in pre-Conquest books, they were indeed used as research-resources,[57] whether by authors or by someone doing a little research, perhaps for the purposes of legal (or even theological) controversy.

We need to look also at the institutional evidence for libraries. We find a few books which seem to be candidates for recognition as volumes tied to an office, handed down from one incumbent to the next: one might mention the Parker Chronicle and, in Ireland, the Book of Armagh.[58] But libraries *seem* to be found in at least one

---

[55] Wormald, 'The Monastic Library', p. 27; Bishop, *English Caroline Minuscule*, p. xvi; Ker, *Medieval Libraries*, pp. 81-5, and *Catalogue*, pp. xlii-xliii, xlvi. Leofric's texts have been re-edited and his place in Exeter's cultural history re-evaluated by Patrick W. Conner, *Anglo-Saxon Exeter* (Woodbridge, 1993), who has suggested that it is unwise to take Leofric's own statements on this matter at face-value.

[56] The extensive glossing in the extraordinarily large group of manuscripts of Boethius, *De consolatione Philosophiae*, found in late Anglo-Saxon England has recently been made the subject of a preliminary study by D.K. Bolton, 'The study of the Consolation of Philosophy in Anglo-Saxon England', *Archives d'histoire doctrinale et littéraire du moyen âge* 44 (1977), 33-78. The manuscripts are Gneuss's nos 12, 23, 68, 193, 347 (OE), 408, 533, 643 (OE), 671, 678, 776, 823, 829, 886?, 887, 899, 901, 908. For an extension of Bolton's enquiry, see J.S. Wittig, 'King Alfred's *Boethius* and its Latin Sources: a Reconsideration', *ASE* 11 (1983), 157-98.

[57] Ker, *Catalogue*, p. xlviii.

[58] On the Parker Chronicle, see M.B. Parkes 'The Palaeography of the Parker Manuscript of the *Chronicle*, Laws and Sedulius, and Historiography at Winchester in the Late Ninth and Tenth Centuries',

other context, the royal. Whether Anglo-Saxon kings ever had court-libraries or palace-schools is uncertain: a case could perhaps be made for Alfred of Wessex. A case has been made, if not conclusively, for the importance of the New Minster, Winchester, as a point of dissemination of manuscripts in the tenth and eleventh centuries,[59] and one is bound to wonder if this alleged process owed anything to royal patronage. We know that Alfred, through necessity, farmed out his works far and wide to scriptoria;[60] Æthelstan commissioned a book to give to Chester-le-Street in the 930s.[61] But Æthelstan was also the owner of a whole series of foreign volumes, often of luxurious quality—impressively studied by J. Armitage Robinson and more recently by Simon Keynes[62]—which he mostly donated to religious houses. We see relatively few kings taking a direct interest in books. In the earlier period Aldfrith of Northumbria and, a generation or so later, Ceolwulf—who vetted or (to put it more unkindly) censored Bede's *Historia ecclesiastica gentis Anglorum*—are those who are known to have had literary interests.[63] Whether kings ever

---

ASE 5 (1976), 149-71; on the Book of Armagh, see R. Sharpe, 'Palaeographical Considerations in the Study of the Patrician Documents in the Book of Armagh', *Scriptorium* 36 (1982), 3-28.

[59] Bishop, *English Caroline Minuscule*, p. xv and n. 1.

[60] Preface to his translation of St Gregory's *Regula pastoralis*. See the study by N.R. Ker, *The Pastoral Care* . . . (Copenhagen, 1956), a facsimile edition of the earliest manuscripts.

[61] Cambridge, Corpus Christi College, MS. 183. I reject the ascription to Winchester, reaffirmed by Temple, *Anglo-Saxon Manuscripts*, pp. 37-8. See D.N. Dumville, 'The Anglian Collection of Royal Genealogies and Regnal Lists', *ASE* 5 (1976), 23-50, and Keynes, 'King Athelstan's Books' (as n. 62 below), pp. 180-5.

[62] J.A. Robinson, *The Times of Saint Dunstan* (Oxford, 1923), pp. 25-80 (esp. 51-71); S. Keynes, 'King Athelstan's Books', in *Learning and Literature in Anglo-Saxon England. Studies presented to Peter Clemoes*, ed. Michael Lapidge and H. Gneuss (Cambridge, 1985), pp. 143-201.

[63] *Historia ecclesiastica*, V.15, and *Praefatio*. For Aldfrith, see also Bede, *Historia Abbatum*, §15. On the broader question of commissions, see M. Lapidge, 'Artistic and Literary Patronage in

commissioned copies of books for themselves we do not know; if they did so in the tenth or the eleventh century we equally do not know whether or not the royal writing office could have coped. In short, we know nothing of any possible relationship of chancery, court-library, and palace-school.

Learning and External Contacts

Naturally, one of the important results which we can obtain from a study of manuscripts of the whole period is a sense of the shifting patterns of cultural development or stagnation or decline, the effects of external influences, and so on. I am not going to try to survey all these developments here, but I should like to draw attention to areas where—it seems to me—particularly promising developments can be expected to take place. A census of manuscripts will obviously produce its most valuable results in the period after 800, for which we have so far had no compendious work. There are perhaps four areas where (I think) we may hope for some enlightenment.

The ninth is, of course, the dark century when visible manifestations of the literary culture of the Anglo-Saxon golden age vanish, to be replaced by the evidence for barbarity of the sort which Michael Lapidge has described.[64] I should not wish to stress that collapse to the same extreme degree as Nicholas Brooks and he have done nor, I think, should I wish to take King Alfred's words absolutely at face-value.[65] I remind myself that from the last third of the ninth

---

Anglo-Saxon England', *Settimane di studio del Centro italiano di studi sull'alto medioevo* 39 (1991), pp. 137-98.

[64] 'The Present State of Anglo-Latin Studies', in *Insular Latin Studies. Papers on Latin Texts and Manuscripts of the British Isles: 550-1066*, ed. Michael W. Herren (Toronto, 1981), pp. 45-82 (at 54-5).

[65] 'England in the Ninth Century: the Crucible of Defeat', *Transactions of the Royal Historical Society*, 5th series, 29 (1979), 1-20. King Alfred, in the preface to his 'Pastoral Care', on the state of learning in England when he ascended the throne in 871: on this see further H. Gneuss, 'King Alfred and the History of Anglo-Saxon Libraries', in *Modes of Interpretation in Old English Literature. Essays*

century, for example, we have a perfectly respectable, if provincial, piece of work in Oxford, Bodleian Library, MS. Digby 63, a collection of computistical matter; this comes from the very period when Northumbria, its area of origin, is supposed to have lain most heavily under the Danish yoke.[66] In short, I hope that a census of manuscripts will produce material which will give us a more rounded view of ninth-century Anglo-Latin culture than we have at present, and which will, perhaps, dispel somewhat of the gloom in the background to my next area of desired enlightenment.

We need to know a great deal more about the development of script, of scriptoria, and of Latin learning in the last decade of the ninth century and in the first quarter of the tenth. There has been recent, important work on the subject by Dr Robert Deshman of the University of Toronto[67] and there are general signs of a quickening of interest among scholars.[68] However, work in this field has proceeded from non-palaeographical assumptions, and again I should like to stress the dangers, as with charters, of relying for first principles on work or assumptions from other fields of study, which, when challenged, may wreak havoc in one's own. It is a commonplace among scholars studying the period that there survives a group of five manuscripts, from a single scriptorium (which has been argued to be the Old Minister at Winchester) in the last decade of the ninth century and the earlier part of the tenth: the first section of the Parker Chronicle

---

in Honour of Stanley B. Greenfield, ed. Phyllis Rugg Brown *et al.* (Toronto, 1986), pp. 29-49, and Dumville, *Wessex and England* (as n. 73 below), *passim*.

[66] Ker, *Catalogue*, p. 381, no. 319; Gneuss, no. 611. For further discussion of this book and its context, see my paper, 'Motes and Beams: Two Insular Computistical Manuscripts', *Peritia: Journal of the Medieval Academy of Ireland* 2 (1983), 248-56.

[67] 'Anglo-Saxon Art after Alfred', *Art Bulletin* 56 (1974), 176-200; 'The Leofric Missal and Tenth-Century English Art', *ASE* 6 (1977), 145-73.

[68] See especially Parkes, 'The Palaeography of the Parker Manuscript' (n. 58 above). See also Dumville, 'English Square Minuscule Script: the Background and Earliest Phases', and references given there.

(Cambridge, Corpus Christi College, MS. 173), at least in part; the Tollemache Old English Orosius (London, British Library, MS. Add. 47967); the Bedan part of BL MS. Cotton Otho B.xi; BL MS. Royal 12.D.xvii (Bald's Leechbook); and Oxford, Bodleian Library, MS. Junius 27 (the Junius Psalter). This is stated bluntly, for example, in *Medieval Libraries of Great Britain*,[69] and has been elaborated by many writers. It is on this group of manuscripts that, as Alistair Campbell put it, our knowledge of Early West Saxon is grounded.[70] And here is the English evidence for the beginnings of that Square type of Anglo-Saxon minuscule which is so characteristic a script of the tenth century. It is imperative that we understand the origins of this script-type,[71] for it is an index of the revival of English scriptorial standards during or, as I should now prefer, in the wake of the Alfredian revival. I have searched high and low for independent evidence which would confirm the dating assigned to these examples of incipient and early Square minuscule. But the received dating seems to depend entirely on arguments arising from perceptions of the early history of the Anglo-Saxon Chronicle. In the course of work towards a new collaborative edition of the Chronicle and its related records, I have been re-examining its textual history. The first scribe's portion of the A-text (CCCC 173) stops in the middle of the annal for 891; from this it has generally been concluded that the manuscript was first written at that date.[72] Yet, for want of comparable but independently dated specimens of script, I do not think that that judgment could be even approximately confirmed on palaeographical evidence. For a

---

[69] Ker, *Medieval Libraries*, p. 200.

[70] In *The Tollemache Orosius (British Museum Additional Manuscript 47967)* (Copenhagen, 1953), p. 13, referring specifically to this, to CCCC 173, and to Oxford, Bodleian Library, MS. Hatton 20.

[71] An important study is that by T.A.M. Bishop, 'An Early Example of the Square Minuscule', *Transactions of the Cambridge Bibliographical Society* 4 (1964-8), 246-52; cf. 'The Corpus Martianus Capella', *ibid.*, pp. 257-75. I have tried to take this further in 'English Square Minuscule Script: the Background and Earliest Phases'.

[72] This view was expressed cautiously by Charles Plummer, *Two of the Saxon Chronicles Parallel* (2 vols, Oxford, 1892-9), II.xxvii, but has been stated much more precisely by subsequent writers.

series of reasons which seem to me to be compelling, I do not think that that dating can be correct; I should conclude instead that a case can be made for a view that the text up to the annal for 920, ending on fol 25v, was written by collaborating scribes in the 910s and 920s.[73] Such a redating would necessarily affect the chronology of the development of the script. In short, the unfortunate circumstance recurs that reconsideration of a textual question causes great difficulties for settled palaeographical doctrine. Our subject is still at the stage of development where too much certainty can arise from an insufficient assemblage of evidence.

A census of manuscripts owned in Anglo-Saxon England necessarily throws into relief immigrants from the Celtic-speaking countries of the British Isles and from the Continent. Approximately one hundred such manuscripts are at present known from the whole period.[74] Among these, one notable group has recently been the subject of investigation, books of Breton origin.[75] Brittany, as a Continental country of Celtic speech and institutions but politically and in its ecclesiastical culture heavily influenced by the Frankish empire, almost falls between the two general areas which I have distinguished here. During the century beginning with the arrival of Asser at King Alfred's court, the Celtic-speaking countries provided a great source of intellectual stimulus for the reviving ecclesiastical learning of Anglo-

---

[73] The views summarised here are documented in my book, *Wessex and England from Alfred to Edgar* (Woodbridge, 1992), chapter 3.

[74] Gneuss has designated the following manuscripts as foreign: nos 7, 19, 48, 61, 70, 77, 81, 83, 87, 96, 105, 112, 119-20, 128, 133-7, 140, 148, 179, 211, 245, 263, 266, 279, 281, 283-4, 295, 297, 299, 311-12, 316-17, 334, 354, 362, 376, 384, 392, 409, 417-19, 423, 444, 459, 485-6, 489-90, 492, 512-13, 515-16, 521, 529-32, 538, 541, 557, 564-5, 570, 575, 581, 583, 585, 607, 629, 651, 654, 659, 661, 681, 688, 715-16, 734, 744, 752, 754, 779, 794-5, 801, 804, 809, 834, 889, 908, 939, 944-5. There has been a first study of this evidence by F.A. Rella, 'Continental Manuscripts Acquired for English Centers in the Tenth and Early Eleventh Centuries: a Preliminary Checklist', *Anglia* 98 (1980), 107-16.

[75] I have given a preliminary list of early mediaeval Breton manuscripts as an appendix to my book cited in the next note.

Saxon England.[76] Brittany was an early and major influence on the ecclesiastical revival in southern England at the beginning of the tenth century, a development which would have been perceived very dimly but for the cumulative effect of manuscript evidence. The Welsh and Cornish contribution could hardly have been appreciated without such testimony. Detailed work on tenth-century manuscripts of English origin is also revealing evidence for the use of exemplars of Celtic origin, and has even suggested the presence of Celtic scribes in Anglo-Saxon scriptoria.[77] Further work will assuredly produce more insights of this sort. But it was not only the Celtic-speaking countries which contributed to the revivification of English religion and learning in the tenth century. As work proceeds on the history of tenth-century Anglo-Latin literature, more points of contact are found with Continental centres, scholars, and literary fashions.[78] The manuscript evidence, while very varied, is nonetheless fairly consistently pointing to Rheims,[79] northeastern France,[80] the Liège region,[81] and Flanders[82] as principal sources of imported manuscripts. What further work must seek to promote is a greater comprehension of the particular contexts in which the known imported books arrived in England; very useful results can be expected in this area, which may lead to further modification of traditional views on the sources of English tenth-century reform-culture.

---

[76] This whole movement is discussed in my O'Donnell lectures, *England and the Celtic World in the Ninth and Tenth Centuries* (publication forthcoming).

[77] See especially the papers by T.A.M. Bishop cited in n. 71 above. For a Welsh teacher at Winchester in Æthelwold's episcopacy, see M. Lapidge, 'Three Latin Poems' (as n. 9 above).

[78] In addition to the articles by M. Lapidge cited in nn. 9, 11, 12, and 14 above, see his paper, 'L'influence stylistique de la poésie de Jean Scot', in *Jean Scot Érigène et l'histoire de la philosophie*, ed. René Roques (Colloques du CNRS, 561) (Paris, 1977), pp. 441-52.

[79] Gneuss, nos 77, 140, 263, 490, 492, 939.

[80] Gneuss, nos 311, 585, 661.

[81] Gneuss, nos 334, 362. Nos 423 and 809 are probably Lotharingian.

[82] Gneuss, nos 70, 804. Nos 112 and 516 are from Saint-Amand.

Finally, there are, I think, grounds for the supposition that our view may change of the Anglo-Saxon eleventh century in respect of book-production and ecclesiastical learning. It has long been held that the steam went out of the reforming monastic movement by the early eleventh century, leading to an increased secularism and a decline in learning in the late Anglo-Saxon Church. Professor Frank Barlow has provided an effective, if only partial, defence of the English Church from *ca* 1000 to 1066,[83] but powerful confirmation of the old-established view was suggested upon the publication of *English Caroline Minuscule*. Mr Bishop wrote that the 'intellectual movement which the Caroline accompanied seems to have been poorly sustained' and noted that in the eleventh century 'the script seems to be in decline', a decline parallelled 'in intellectual interests and commerce';[84] his harshest comments were reserved for the period from the middle years of the century where he saw 'intellectual curiosity and Anglo-Latin letters alive but hardly flourishing'.[85] It might be supposed from all this that English book-production went into a sharp decline during the first quarter of the eleventh century, a trend which was not reversed until the massive Anglo-Norman multiplication of texts at the end of the century.[86] The statistics which may now be

---

[83] *The English Church 1000-1066. A History of the Later Anglo-Saxon Church* (2nd edn, London, 1979), first published in 1963.

[84] *English Caroline Minuscule*, pp. xi, xxiii.

[85] *Ibid.*, p. xviii.

[86] This period of English book-production was discussed by N.R. Ker, *English Manuscripts in the Century after the Norman Conquest* (Oxford, 1960); cf. 'The Beginnings of Salisbury Cathedral Library', in *Medieval Learning and Literature. Essays presented to Richard William Hunt*, ed. J.J.G. Alexander and M.T. Gibson (Oxford, 1976), pp. 23-49 (reprinted in Ker's *Books, Collectors and Libraries*, pp. 143-73). For a bracing account of late Anglo-Saxon literary culture, see R.M. Thomson, 'The Norman Conquest and English Libraries', in *The Role of the Book in Medieval Culture*, ed. P. Ganz (2 vols, Turnhout, 1986), II.27-40. According to Ker, *Medieval Libraries*, there are fifty-four provenanced books dated '*saec.* xi²' and a further forty-three dated '*saec.* xi/xii'. Manuscripts attributed to *saec.* xi *ex.* and *saec.* xi/xii by Gneuss are his nos 1, 5-6, 10, 16-17,

collected from Gneuss's list suggest nothing of the sort, however. From the middle years of the tenth century to the beginning of the eleventh, we have some two hundred surviving books and fragments.[87] In the roughly comparable period from then until the Norman conquest we have approximately the same number, perhaps a few more.[88]

20, 24, (26), 32, 43, (46), 57, 71, 74, 79-80, 84-6, 89, 94-5, 102, 107, 113, 118, 144-5, 149, 156, 158, 160-2, 164-7, 169-71, 182-3, 187, 192, 197-200, 203-5, 217, 222, 225-32, 234-6, 238-43, 247, (248), 251-2, 254, 256, 265, 270, 272-3, (279), (295), 303, 305, 318, 328, 335, (345), (366), 371, (376), 388, 398, 405, (411), 420, 424, 426, 439, 452, 460-1, 481, 483, 495, 504, 507, 527, 543-4, 547-8, 550, 552-3, 556, 560-3, 566, 571, 573-4, 578-80, 582, 586-9, 591, 593-4, 596, 598-603, 605-6, 609-10, 614, 618-20, 623-5, 634, 645, 650, 653, 658, 662, (664), 666, 669, 676, 685, 691, 694, 697-9, 701-6, 708-13, 717-21, 723-33, 736-9, 741, (742), 745-50, 753, 760, 789, 813, 826, 865, 873-4, 920, 934, 943. Note also the books, dated '*saec.* xi[2]', listed at the end of n. 88 below; most of those are likely to be of post-Conquest date.

[87] Gneuss, nos 2-3, 8, 11, 23, 27, 33, 37-8, 41, (48), (52), 56, 67, 69, 72, 90, 93, 97-8, 101, 103, 106, 110, 114, 142, 152-3, 155, 157, 159, 168, 174-5, 178, 180, 185, 188-91, 193, 195-6, 207, 246, 253, 257-9, 261, 274, 277-8, (279), 280, (284), 285, 291, 296, 301-2, 308, 314, 319, 321, 324, 326, (327), (334), 338, 342, 345, 347, 353, 357, 360-1, 364-5, 382, 386, 389, 393-6, 399, 401, 403, 408, 415, 421, 430, 436, 438, 440, 449, 451, 453, 455, 458, 464, 467, 472-5, 478-9, 482, 484, 491, 493, 496-8, 502-3, 506, 509, 511, 522-3, 525, 528, 533-4, (538), 540, 542, 546, 554, 567-8, 572, 584, (585), 590, 592, 613, 615, 628, (629), 640, 643, 648, 652, 660, 663, 672, 678, 680, 682, 684, 692, 707, 722, 735, 740, 751, 762, 765-9, 774, 776, 778, 781-2, 784, 796, 798, 803, 805, 808, 810-12, 815-16, 823, 829, 839, 843, 864, 867, 870, 872, 877, 879-80, 882-4, 886-8, 896, 899, 901, 905, 914, 918-19, 923-4, 926-8, 936, 938, 941-2. Each manuscript cited Gneuss has attributed, as a whole (or in part), to *saec.* x[1], x *med.*, x[2], x *ex.*, x/xi, or x.

[88] Gneuss, nos 4, 12, 18, 26, 31, 34, 36, 39-40, 44, 46, 47, 49-51, 54-5, 58-9, 64-6, 68, 73, 75, 82, 91, 99-100, 108-9, 111, 115-17, 122, 132, 138-9, 141, 146-7, 150-1, 163, 172, 177, 181, 186, 194, 201,

These two corpora will have to be studied in much more detail before one can elaborate on the proposition that book-production did not suffer a serious decline in the Anglo-Saxon eleventh century. When manuscripts can be more closely dated (say, to quarter-centuries), we must discover what changes occur over shortish periods.[89] We must ask which centres were active at which particular times. We shall need to know about evidence for continuing use of tenth-century books. The contents of new books will have to be scrutinised for changes in taste. The relationship between Latin and the vernacular in the book-production of a period when a formal separation of Latin and

---

208-10, 212, 244, 250, (255), 262, 264, 267, 271, (279), 287, 289-90, 294, 306, 309-10, (314), 315, 323, 325, (327), 329, 332-3, 336-7, 339-41, 344, 348-9, 351-2, 355-6, (357), 358-9, (362), 363, 366, 368, 370, 372-3, 378-80, 383, 390-1, 397, 402, (403), 404, 406-7, 412-14, 416, (421), 422, 427-9, 431, 433-5, 437, 441-2, 446-7, (451), 454, 463, 465, (467), 468-70, 476-7, 480, 499-501, 505, 510, 517, 519, (521), 524, 526, 537, (538), 539, (541), 545, (546), 555, 558-9, 569, 577, (583), (585), 595, 597, 608, 612, 617, 621-2, 627, 630, 632-3, 636, 642, 649, 656, 667, 670-1, 673-4, 679, 686-7, 689-90, 693, 695-6, 700, 714, 742, 758-9, 761, 764, (774), 775, 777, (778), (781), 800, 806-7, (808), 814, 817, 827, 830-1, 851-2, 855, 859-61, 869, 871, 876, (879-80), 881, 890-1, 895, 902-3, 906, 912-13, 915-17, (918), 921-2, 925. Each manuscript cited Gneuss has attributed, as a whole (or in part), to *saec.* xi *in.*, xi[1], xi *med.*, or xi. An additional quantity of books has been assigned by Gneuss to the second half of the eleventh century and is probably post-Conquest, but all require further study; they are Gneuss's nos 13-15, 22, 29-30, 35, (44), 60, 62, (64), 76, 92, (100), 104, (109), 123, 129-31, 143, 184, 206, 215-16, 233, 248, (262), 276, 286, 288, 304, 307, 313, 322, 331, (344), 350, (370), (372), 387, 400, 411, 425, 457, 466, 487-8, 494, 508, 514, 518, 520, (530), 535-6, 549, 551, 637-9, 644, 655, 657, 664, 675, 683, 743, 763, (774), 783, 828, 837, 866, 875, 900, 930.

[89] Ker, *Catalogue*, pp. lx-lxi, listed some manuscripts which are closely datable; but, in general, manuscripts in our period still tend to be dated only within a *half*-century.

vernacular scripts took place will bear much study,[90] although it already seems clear that in the eleventh century a greater proportion of English books was written in the vernacular than was the case in the tenth[91] (unless tenth-century vernacular manuscripts were subject to more severe vicissitudes than their Latin counterparts). In brief, we may say that the eleventh century must necessarily come into its own as an area of study, in the same way as the tenth century has held our attention during the past decade.[92]

The cultural history of Anglo-Saxon England still offers many avenues of enquiry and many revelations for its students. To the extent that the period after A.D. 800 has been less comprehensively studied, the greatest gains may be expected there. The publication of Helmut Gneuss's 'Preliminary list' permits a period of substantial advances from a secure base of primary materials.[93] The student now has the raw materials to hand; he has only to start to manipulate them. Studies of manuscripts and of the circulation of texts should flourish, in much the same way as the study of Anglo-Latin letters burgeoned in the 1970s. With the resources now available we may hope to see more use and less abuse of manuscript-evidence in writing early English cultural history.[94]

---

[90] Ker, *Catalogue*, pp. xxv-xxvii and plates II-V; Bishop, *English Caroline Minuscule*, pp. 9, 15, 20, 24.

[91] Cf. n. 24 above.

[92] For the major studies on tenth-century books and texts see the works of Bishop (cited in nn. 2, 34, and 71) and Lapidge (nn. 9, 11, 12, 14, 63, and 78, above).

[93] One caveat must be entered, however. All the information in the fourth column (date, provenance/origin) is to be regarded with some reserve, especially that on location, for no effective distinction was made between provenance and origin (see 'A Preliminary List', p. 4) and no consistent criteria seem to have been applied in determining which suggestions about provenance or origin to report.

[94] This paper first appeared in 1981. For republication it has been thoroughly revised in detail but the substance of my arguments remains the same.

Appendix

Books written by *ca* 1100 and assigned by N.R. Ker (*Medieval Libraries*, 2nd edn) to specific provenances.

Abbreviations

BL	British Library
BM	Bibliothèque Municipale
BN	Bibliothèque Nationale
Bodl.	Bodleian Library
CCCC	Corpus Christi College, Cambridge
CL	Cathedral Library
CUL	Cambridge University Library
NLS	National Library of Scotland
PCC	Pembroke College, Cambridge
TCC	Trinity College, Cambridge
UL	University Library

A prefixed bold asterisk (*) denotes a manuscript not recorded in Gneuss's 'Preliminary list'.
(?) Denotes Dr Ker's uncertainty about the attribution of provenance.

ABINGDON (8)

(?) Antwerp 47 + BL Add. 32246	xi^1
(?) Antwerp 190	x/xi
(?) Brussels, Bibl. Roy., 1520	xi^1
(?) CUL Kk.3.21	x/xi
CCCC 57	x/xi
BL Cott. Tib. B.i	xi
Oxford, Bodl., Digby 39	xi/xii
146	xi^1

BARKING (1)

Oxford, Bodl., Bodley 155	x/xi

BATH (3)

CCCC 111	xi-xiii
CCCC 140 + 111 (pp. 7-8, 55-56)	xi
BL Cott. Claud. B.v	ix

BATTLE (2)
BL Cott. Tib. B.v, vol. 1 (fols 2-73, 77-88)
   + Nero D.ii (fols 238-241)   x/xi-xiii
(?) Oxford, Univ. Coll., 104   xi

BODMIN, ST PETROC'S PRIORY (1)
BL Add. 9381 x^1

BUILDWAS (1)
TCC 27   xi-xiii^1

BURTON-UPON-TRENT (1)
BL Add. 23944   ix

BURY ST EDMUNDS (26)PC
        17   ix/x
        23   xi
        24   xi
        25   xi
        41   xi
        81   ix^1
        83   ix/x-xiii
        88   ix
        91   ix/x
        108   ix
        120   xi-xii
Cambridge, St John's College, 35   xi
BL   Add. 24199   x-xii
        Cott.   Iulius E.vii   'xii^1'(*recte* xi^1)
                Tib. B.ii (fols 2-85)   xi
        Harley 76   xi
London, Coll. of Arms, Arundel 30 x^1-xiv
London, Lambeth Palace,   218 (fols 115-208)   x
(?)   362   xi
Oxford, Bodl., Bodley 130   xi/xii
               e Mus. 6   xi/xii
               e Mus. 7   xi/xii
               e Mus. 8   xi/xii
               Rawl. C.697   'xi'(*recte* ix)

Oxford, Corpus Christi College, 197   x-xi
Rome, B.A.V., Reg. lat. 12 xi^1

CANTERBURY, CHRIST CHURCH (45)

*CUL	Dd.8.15	xi/xii
	Ff.4.43	'ix'(*recte* x/xi)
	Ii.3.33	xi/xii
CCCC	173	viii-xi
	187	xi/xii
	192	x
	260	x
(?)	272	ix^2
	304	viii^1
	326	x/xi
	*341 (inserted leaf)	xi^2
(?)	411	x
	*452	xi
TCC	104	xi
	116	xi/xii
	141	x
	289	x/xi
	405	xi^2
(?)	1135	x^2
Canterbury,	CL, 57/ii	xi^2
(?)	Add. 25	x^2
(?)	Box CCC, no. 19a	xi^2
(?) BL	Add. 37517	x
	Arundel 155	xi^1
	Cott.Tib. A.ii + Claud. A.iii	
	(fols 2-7, 9*)	
	+ Faust. B.vi, vol. 1	
	(fols 95, 98-100)	$ix/xi/xii^1$
	Tib. A.iii (fols 2-173)	xi
	Tib. A.iii (fols 174-177)	
	+ Faust. B.iii (fols 159-198)	xi
(?)	Calig. A.xiv (fols 1-92)	xi-xii
	Calig. A.xv (fols 120-153)	xi^2
(?)	Claud. A.iii (fols 9-18, 87-105)	xi
(?)	Vitell. C.iii	xi

	Dom. A.viii (fols 30-70)	xi/xii
	Egerton 3314	xi-xii
(?)	Royal 1.D.ix	x
(?)	1.E.vii-viii	x^2
	7.C.iv	xi
London, Lambeth Palace, 1370		
	+ BL Cott. Tib. B.iv (fol 87)	ix; xi^1
Oxford, Bodl., Bodley 97		xi
(?)	Junius 11	x/xi
Oxford, St John's College, 89		xi/xii
(?)	194	ix^2
(?) Paris, BN, lat. 987		x/xi
(?)	lat. 10062 (fols 162-163)	xi
Stockholm, Kungl. bibl., A.135		viii
Utrecht, UL, 32 (fols 1-91)		ix

CANTERBURY, ST AUGUSTINE'S ABBEY (63)

CUL Gg.5.35		xi
(?) CCCC	44	xi
	144	viii/ix
	267	xi
	270	xi
	*274	xi
	276	xi-xii
	286	vi
	291	xi/xii
	312	xi/xii
	352	ix/x
	389	x
Cambridge, Gonville & Caius College, 144		ix^2
Cambridge, St John's College, 164		x
TCC	38	xi/xii
	40	x
	939	x
	945	xi
(?)	1155	x/xi-xi/xii
	1179	x
	1241	x
	1242	x

Canterbury, CL, 68		xi/xii
*Elmstone, Rectory, s.n.		xi/xii
Leiden, UL, Scaliger 69		x^2
BL	Add.　33241	xi
(?)	37517	x
	Cott. Tib. A.vi (fols 1-35)	
	+ Tib. A.iii (fol 178)	x
	Calig. A.xv (fols 3-117)	viii
	Claud. B.iv	xi
	Otho E.xiii	x/xi
	Vitell. A.vi	x
	Vitell. C.xii	xi/xii
	Vesp. A.i	viii
	Vesp. D.vi (fols 2-77)	x
	Dom. A.i (fols 2-55)	x-xi
	Cleo. B.xiii (fols 59-90)	xi^1
	Cleo. D.i (fols 1-128)	xi
	Egerton 874	ix
(?)	Harley　603	xi^1
	647	x^1
	652	xi-xii
	5431	x-xiv
	Royal　1.A.xviii	x^1
	1.E.vi + Canterbury,	
	CL, Add. 16	viii^2
	5.B.xv	xi/xii
	13.A.xxii	xi^2
	15.A.xvi	ix-x
London, Lambeth Palace, 414 (fols 1-80)		x
Oxford, Bodl.,		
	Bodley 97	xi
	381	xi
	391	xi/xii
	426 (fols 1-118)	viii/ix
	572	ix-x
	596 (fols 175-214)	xi/xii
	Lat. bib. b.2(P)	viii/ix
	Marshall 19	ix
	Rawl. C.570	x/xi

	*Selden supra 25	xi-xiii
	30	viii
Oxford, Trinity College, 4		xi
Redlynch, Major J.R. Abbey, s.n.		xi
(now: Canterbury, CL, s.n.)		

CERNE (1)
CUL Ll.1.10   ix-xv

CHESTER, ST WERBURH (1)
*London, Gray's Inn, 3   xi/xii

CHICHESTER, CATHEDRAL (1)
TCC 1207   xi

CROWLAND (1)
(?) Oxford, Bodl., Douce 296   xi

DOVER, BENEDICTINE PRIORY (2)
Cambridge, St John's College, 59 x^2
                                    87   xi-xiii

DURHAM, CATHEDRAL (47)
CUL Gg.3.28   x/xi
CCCC 183 x^1
Cambridge, Jesus College, 28 xi^2
Cambridge, Peterhouse, 74 xi^2
Cambridge, Sidney Sussex College, 100/2   xi
TCC 216 + BL Cott. Vitell. C.viii (fols 85-90)   viii
Durham, CL, A.2.4 xi^2
Durham, CL, A.2.16
        + Cambridge, Magdalene College, Pepys 2981,
            no. 18   viii
Durham, CL, A.2.17
        + Cambridge, Magdalene College, Pepys 2981,
            no. 19   vii/viii
Durham, CL, A.3.29   xi
                    A.4.19 x^1
                    B.2.2 xi^2

B.2.6	xi^2
B.2.9	xi^2
B.2.10	xi^2
B.2.11	xi^2
B.2.13	xi^2
B.2.14	xi^2
B.2.16	xi med.
B.2.17	xi^2
B.2.21	xi^2
B.2.22	xi^2
B.2.30	viii
B.2.35	xi^2-xv
B.3.1	xi^2
B.3.9	xi^2
B.3.10	xi^2
B.3.11	xi^2
B.3.16	xi^2
B.4.9	x
B.4.13	xi^2
B.4.24	xi^2-xii
C.3.18	xi^2
C.3.20 (binding leaves)	
+ A.2.10 (binding leaves)	
+ C.3.13 (binding leaves)	vii/viii
(?) Durham, UL, V.v.6	xi/xii
BL Cott. Iulius A.vi	xi^1
Nero D.iv	viii^1
Otho B.ix	ix
Dom. A.vii	ix-xvi
*Royal 6.A.v	xi med.
London, Lambeth Palace, 325	x^1
Oxford, Bodl., Bodley 819	viii
Digby 81 (fols 133-140)	xi^1
(?) Lat. liturg. f.5	xi
Laud misc. 546	xi^2
Oxford, St John's College, 154	xi^1
Stonyhurst, College, s.n.	vii

ELY (4)
CUL Kk.1.24   + BL Cott. Tib. B.v, vol. 1 (fols 74,76)
(?)   + BL Sloane 1044 (fol 2)   viii
CCCC 44   xi
PCC 308   ix
London, Lambeth Palace, 204   x/xi

ETON (1)
*Eton, College, 106   xi/xii

EXETER, CATHEDRAL (36)
(?) CUL   Ii.2.4   xi
             Ii.2.11 + Exeter 3501 (fols 0-7)   xi
CCCC   41   xi
             190   xi
             {191   xi
             {196   xi
             {201 (pp. 179-272)   xi
(?)   {419   xi
(?)   {421   xi
TCC 241   x
Exeter, CL, 3501 (fols 8-130) x^2
             3507 x^2
BL Add. 28188 xi^2
      Cott. Tib. B.v, vol. 1 (fol 75)   viii-x
(?)Cleo. B.xiii (fols 1-58)   xi
   Harley   863   xi
             2961   xi med.
(?)Royal 6.B.vii   xi/xii-xii
London, Lambeth Palace, 149 (fols 1-138)   x
(?)   489   xi
Oxford, Bodl., Auct. D.2.16   x
             D.inf.2.9   x-xi
             F.1.15   xi
             F.3.6   xi
             Bodley 229   xi
                    311   x
                    319   x
                    394   xi-xii

579	x-xi
707	xi
708	xi
718	x
783	xi/xii
815	xi^2
849	an. 818
865 (fols 89-115)	xi

EYNSHAM (1)
(?) *CUL Gg.4.15   xi/xii

FINCHALE (1)
Oxford, Bodl., Laud misc. 546 xi^2

GLASTONBURY (3)
(?) CUL Kk.5.32 xi^1-xii^1
Oxford, Bodl., Auct. F.4.32   ix-xi
        Hatton 30   x

GLOUCESTER, ST PETER'S ABBEY (2)
(?) TCC 75   xi/xii
BL Royal 13.C.v xi^2

GREAT BEDWYN, PARISH CHURCH (1)
(?) Bern, Burgerbibliothek, 671   viii/ix

HATFIELD PEVEREL/REGIS (1)
*Berlin, Staatsbibl., Th. lat. oct. 167   xi-xii

HEREFORD, CATHEDRAL (4)
PCC 302   xi
Hereford, CL, 0.3.ii   ix
        0.8.viii   xi/xii
        P.1.ii viii^2

 HEREFORD, BENEDICTINE PRIORY (2)
*Hereford, CL, O.6.xi   xi
Oxford, Jesus College, 37   xi

HEXHAM (1)
(?) CCCC 149   xi

HORTON (1)
El Escorial, E.ii.1   xi¹

HYDE ABBEY (= WINCHESTER, NEW MINSTER) (12)
TCC   215   xi¹
       945 (pp. 13-36)   xi¹
(?) BL Add.   34890   xi¹
(?)   49598   x
(?) Arundel 60   xi²
(?) Cott. Vitell. E.xviii   xi med.
       Vesp. A.viii   x
       Titus D.xxvi-xxvii   xi¹
(?) {Royal 2.B.v   x
(?) {   4.A.xiv   x
Stowe 944   xi¹-xvi¹
(?) Rouen, BM, 369   x²

JARROW & MONKWEARMOUTH (1)
BL Add. 37777 + Add. 45025   vii/viii

LANTHONY SECUNDA (3)
London, Lambeth Palace,   377   x
                          427   x/xi
                          431 (fols 146-160)   xi

LEWES (1)
(?) Oxford, Bodl., Douce 296   xi

LICHFIELD, CATHEDRAL (1)
Lichfield, CL, s.n.   viii¹

LINCOLN, CATHEDRAL (5)
{TCC 148   xi²
{Lincoln, CL, 1   xi²
               13   xi

*67	xi/xii
182	x/xi

LINCOLN, FRANCISCAN CONVENT (1)
*London, Westminster Abbey, 17   xi/xii

LINDISFARNE (1)
BL Cott. Nero D.iv   viii[1]

LONDON, CATHEDRAL (1)
(?) CCCC 383   xi/xii

LONDON, HOSPITAL OF BVM NEAR CRIPPLEGATE (1)
*Oxford, Bodl., e Mus. 113   x-xii

MALMESBURY (5)
CCCC	23 (fols 1-104)	x/xi
	361	xi
(?) BL Cott. Otho C.i, vol. 1, + Otho B.x (fol 51)		xi
*Oxford, Bodl., Bodley 852		xi
	Marshall 19	ix

MALVERN (1)
(?) Oxford, Bodl., Hatton 23   xi/xii

NORWICH, CATHEDRAL (2)
| CUL | Ii.2.19 | xi^2-xii^1 |
| | Kk.4.13 | xi-xii |

OXFORD, CARMELITE CONVENT (1)
(?) *Copenhagen, Royal Lib., G.K.S. 1653.4°   xi

PETERBOROUGH (2)
| CCCC 160 | xi |
| Oxford, Bodl., Bodley 163 | xi |

RAMSEY (2)
| (?) BL | Cott. Vitell. A.vii (fols 1-112) | xi |
| (?) | Harley 2904 | x |

ROCHESTER (8)
BL Royal   1.D.iii   xi
         2.C.iii xi^2
     15.C.x x^2
*Manchester, UL, lat. 109   xi/xii
{Oxford, Bodl.,   Bodley 340 xi^1
{   342 xi^1
*   Wood B.3   xi
San Marino (USA), Huntington Lib., HM 62 (2 vols)   xi

ST ALBANS (2)
CCCC 290   xi/xii
(?) BL Harley 865   xi/xii

ST GERMANS (1)
(?) Rouen, BM, 368 x^2

SALISBURY, CATHEDRAL (35)
Aberdeen, UL, 216   xi/xii
(?) TCC 717 (fols 72-158)   x/xi
Dublin, Trinity College, 174 (B.4.3) xi^2
BL Cott. Tib. C.i (fols 43-203)   xi
     Royal   5.E.xvi xi^2
              5.E.xix   xi/xii
            15.B.xix (fols 200-205)
(?)   + Salisbury, CL, 115 $xi/xii-xii^1$
Oxford, Bodl., Bodley 392 xi^2
                   516   x
                   756   xi^2
          Fell   1 xi^2
           (now: Salisbury, CL, 222)
                4   xi^2
           (now: Salisbury, CL, 221)

          Lat. bib. c.8(P) + Salisbury, CL,
           117 (flyleaves) + Tokyo,
           Takamiya, 21   viii/ix
          Rawl. C.723   xi/xii

Salisbury, CL,	37	xi/xii
	38	xi^1
	78	xi^2
	88	xi^2
	89	xi
	96	x
	101	x
	112	xi^2
	114 (flyleaves) + 128 (flyleaves)	xi^2
	117	x
(?)	132	xi^2
	133	ix
	134	x/xi
	150	x^2
	157	xi
	158	ix-xi
	172	x^2
	173	x^2
	179	xi^2-xii^1
	180	x
	*197 + BL Royal App. i	xi^2-xii

SHERBORNE (Dorset) (4)

(?) CCCC 422	xi
(?) BL Cott. Tib. C.i (fols 43-203)	xi
(?) Oxford, Bodl., Auct. F.2.14	xi^2
Paris, BN, lat. 943	x^2

SHREWSBURY, BENEDICTINE ABBEY (1)
(?) London, Prof. F. Wormald, s.n.
(now: Cambridge, Fitzwilliam Museum,
   88-1972 [218])   xi-xii

SNAPE (1)
(?) TCC 1369   xi

SOUTHWICK (2)

BL Cott. Otho B.xi	+ Otho B.x (fols 55, 58, 62)	
	+ Add. 34652 (fol 2)	x-xi^1

Oxford, St John's College, 185   xi

TAVISTOCK (2)
CUL Ii.4.6   xi
(?) BL Cott. Vitell. C.v xi^1

THORNEY (5)
Edinburgh, NLS, Adv. 18.6.12   xi/xii
                    18.7.7 x^2
                    18.7.8   xi/xii

BL Add. 40000   x-xv
(?) Oxford, Bodl., Tanner 10   x

WALTHAM CROSS (1)
London, Lambeth Palace, 200 (fols 66-113)   x

WESTMINSTER, ST PETER'S ABBEY (1)
TCC 1365   xi/xii-xiii

WINCHCOMB (1)
Orléans, BM, 127 x^2

WINCHESTER, CATHEDRAL (= OLD MINSTER) (27)
CCCC   146 (pp. 63-318)   x/xi
           163   xi
           173   viii-x
           328                                      $xi-xii^1$
           473   xi
Le Havre, BM, 330 xi^2
(?) BL   Add.   47967   x
(?)   49598   x
           Cott. Galba A.xviii + Oxford, Bodl., Rawl.
           B.484 (fol 85)   ix/x
(?)   Tib. B.v, vol. 1 (fols 2-73, 77-88)   x/xi
(?)   Tib. B.xi + Kassel, Landesbibl., Anhang 19 ix^2
           Tib. D.iv, vol. 2 (fols 158-166)
           + Winchester, CL, 1 xi^1

	Otho B.xi + Otho B.x (fols 55, 58, 62)		
	+ Add. 34652 (fol 2)		x-xi
	Vitell. E.xviii		xi^1
	Harley 213		x
(?)	Royal 12.D.xvii		x
(?)	15.C.vii		xi^1
London, Soc. of Antiquaries, 154*			x
Oxford, Bodl., Bodley	49		x
	535		xi^2
	775		xi^1-xii^1
(?)	Digby	63	ix
	Douce	125	x^2
	Junius	27	x^1
Oxford, Trinity College, 28			xi
(?) Rouen, BM, 1385 (fols 28-<85>)			xi^1
(?) Worcester, CL, F.173			xi^1

WINCHESTER, NUNNAMINSTER (3)

(?) BL	Cott. Nero A.ii (fols 3-13)	xi^1
(?)	Galba A.xiv	xi^1
	Harley 2965	viii

WINDSOR (4)

BL Loans 11		xi
Oxford, Bodl., Bodley	223	xi^2
(?)	*796	xi
	*866	xi

WORCESTER, CATHEDRAL (45)

CUL Kk.3.18		xi^2
Cambridge, Clare College, 30		xi
CCCC 9	+ BL Cott. Nero E.i, vol. 1,	
	+ Nero E.i, vol. 2 (fols 1-180, 187-188)	xi
CCCC	12	x
	146	x/xi-xi^2
	178 + 162 (pp. 139-160)	xi
	198	xi
	265	xi-xii
	279	ix/x

(?)	367, pt 2 (fols 45-52)	xi
	391	xi
	557 + Lawrence, Univ. of Kansas, Y.103	xi
Glasgow, UL, 431 (V.5.1)		x/xi-xii^1
(?) BL	Add. 37777 + Add. 45025	vii/viii
	Cott. Tib. B.iv (fols 3-9, 19-86)	xi
	Otho B.x (fols 29-30)	xi
	Otho C.i, vol. 2	xi
(?)	Vesp. B.x (fols 31-124)	x/xi
	Harley 55 (fols 1-4)	xi
(?)	Royal 2.A.xx	viii
	4.A.xiv	x
	5.E.xiii	ix^2
	5.F.iii	ix
	6.A.vii	xi^1
	15.A.xxxiii	x^1
Oxford, Bodl.,	Barlow 4	xi
	Bodley 223	xi^2
	Hatton 20	ix^2
	23	xi^2
	30	x
	30 (flyleaves) + 93 (flyleaves)	xi^1
	42	ix-x
	48	viii
	76	xi-xii
	93	viii/ix
	113-114	xi
	115 + Lawrence, Univ. of Kansas, Y.104	xi
	Junius 121	xi
	Laud misc. 482	xi
(?)	Tanner 3	xi^1
Worcester, CL	F.48	xi
	F.91	xi^1
	Q.5	x^2
(?)	Q.21	x
	Q.28	x

YORK, CATHEDRAL (2)
(?) BL Harley 208   ix/x
York, Minster, s.n.   x/xi

YORK,' CONVENT OF AUSTIN FRIARS (1)
Oxford, St John's College, 150   xi-xiv

Orality and the Developing Text of Caedmon's *Hymn*

Katherine O'Brien O'Keeffe

The modern editorial practice of printing Old English poetry one verse to a line with a distinct separation between half-lines distracts attention from a well-known and important fact, that Old English poetry is copied without exception in long lines across the writing space.[1] Normal scribal practice does not distinguish verses, reserving capitals and points for major divisions of a work.[2] In manuscripts of Latin

---

[1] The Metrical Epilogue to the *Pastoral Care* in Oxford, Bodleian Library, MS. Hatton 20, beginning at the top of fol 98v, is laid out in an inverted triangle. The commendatory verses, 'Thureth', in London, British Library, MS. Cotton Claudius A.iii, fol. 31v, are similarly formatted, but in each case the arrangement of the words actually works against the sense of the verse.

[2] See N. R. Ker, *Catalogue of Manuscripts Containing Anglo-Saxon* (Oxford, 1957), pp. xxxiii-xxxvi. The use of points and capitals in the greater part of the corpus of Old English poetry is infrequent and irregular. For an exemplary discussion of pointing practice in the Exeter Book see Craig Williamson, ed., *The Old English Riddles of the Exeter Book* (Chapel Hill, 1977), pp. 12-19 and 35-48, esp. p. 16. A notable exception to common practice is Oxford, Bodleian Library, MS. Junius 11, whose half-lines are generally, if not systematically, pointed. See Ker, *Catalogue*, no. 334, p. 408. Other manuscripts containing more or less regularly pointed verse are: London, British Library, MS. Cotton Tiberius B.i, fols. 112-15v (Ker, no. 191, s. xi med.); Oxford, Bodleian Library, MS. Junius 121, fols. 43v-52r, 53v (Ker, no. 338, s. xi [3rd quarter]); Cambridge, Corpus Christi College, MS. 201, pp. 161-67 (Ker, no. 49, s. xi in.) and pp. 167-69 (Ker, s. xi med.); and London, British Library, MS. Cotton Julius A.ii, fols. 136-44 (Ker, no. 159, s. xii med.). The verse which occurs in these

poetry, however, quite another practice holds. Latin verses copied in England after the eighth century are regularly transmitted in a format familiar to modern readers: verses are set out one to a line of writing, capitals begin each line, and often some sort of pointing marks the end of each verse. The regularity of this distinction in copying practice and the difference in the nature and level of the graphic conventions used for verse in the two languages imply that such scribal practice was deliberate and was useful and significant for contemporary readers.

Caedmon's *Hymn* is the earliest documented oral poem in Old English. Although the manuscripts of the *Hymn* have been examined to analyze Old English dialects, to describe oral formulae, and to establish a text of the poem, almost no attention has been paid to the variety of ways in which the text is set out.[3] This variety of formatting and the poem's origin as an oral composition make Caedmon's *Hymn* an especially rewarding work to study. Because the poem is found in fourteen manuscripts copied in England from the eighth through the twelfth centuries, representing two manuscript environments and two dialects, it provides much evidence about the transformation of a work as it passes from an oral to a literate medium,

---

late manuscripts is largely translation from biblical or liturgical sources.

[3] See especially Donald K. Fry, 'The Memory of Caedmon', in *Oral Traditional Literature: A Festschrift for Albert Bates Lord*, ed. John Miles Foley (Columbus, 1981), pp. 282-93, and 'Caedmon as Formulaic Poet', in *Oral Literature: Seven Essays*, ed. Joseph J. Duggan (Edinburgh, 1975), pp. 41-61. Jeff Opland, *Anglo-Saxon Poetry: A Study of the Tradition* (New Haven, 1980), examines Bede's account and understanding of the 'miracle' (pp. 112-29). Dobbie's careful study (*The Manuscripts of Caedmon's **Hymn** and Bede's **Death Song*** [New York, 1937]) provides some 'diplomatic' transcriptions of versions of Caedmon's *Hymn*. These are broken into half-lines and are printed with modern spacing of words. I note errors in his record of manuscript punctuation below. M.B. Parkes, in *The Scriptorium of Wearmouth-Jarrow*, Jarrow Lecture (n.p., 1982), examines some implications of the writing of Caedmon's *Hymn* in Leningrad, Public Library, MS. Q.v.I.18, and in Cambridge, University Library, MS. Kk.5.16.

about the consequent development of a text in Old English, and about the presuppositions underlying the way a text was to be read.[4]

My study of Caedmon's *Hymn* approaches the issue of orality and literacy in Old English verse from the viewpoint of the reception rather than the composition of a work. While arguments about the composition of Old English poetry have provided much valuable information on orality in Anglo-Saxon England, they have not been conclusive, since the presence of formulae in verse (a critical element in defining oral character) is ambiguous evidence at best.[5] It may thus

---

[4] I omit from consideration the versions of the *Hymn* in Dijon, Bibliothèque Municipale, MS. 574 (12th c.); Paris, Bibliothèque Nationale, MS. lat. 5237 (15th c.); and Cambridge, Trinity College, MS. R.5.22 (14th c.). The first two are products of Continental scribes; the last is English, but too late to be useful to this study.

In terms of numbers of manuscripts, Bede's *Death Song* is the most attested Old English poetic text, surviving in Northumbrian dialect in twelve Continental manuscripts (9th through 16th c.) and in thirty-three Insular manuscripts transmitting the West-Saxon version (12th c. and later). However, for evidence of the native reading and copying of an Old English poetic text, Bede's *Death Song* is unsatisfactory on several grounds. Of the twelve copies of the Northumbrian version, two are early (9th and 11th c.), but all are copied by foreign scribes whose careful but mechanical copying tells us little about reading practice in Old English. The West-Saxon copies of Bede's *Death Song* descend from the same original copy (Dobbie, *Manuscripts*, p. 115), and the unanimity of these records is a tribute to the accurate copying of scribes whose familiarity with Old English is, nevertheless, questionable (Dobbie, p. 115). While the Insular copies of Bede's *Death Song* offer some parallel for my contentions about transmission of the *Z group of Caedmon's *Hymn* (see below, p. 14), the manuscripts of Bede's *Death Song* do not provide the rich evidence offered by Caedmon's *Hymn* for native English copying and reading in the eighth, tenth, and eleventh centuries.

[5] On the evidence of formulae for oral composition see Francis P. Magoun, Jr., 'The Oral-Formulaic Character of Anglo-Saxon Narrative Poetry', *Speculum* 28 (1953), 446-67. Larry D. Benson's much-cited reply, 'The Literary Character of Anglo-Saxon Formulaic Poetry',

be useful to examine the survival of orality from the opposite quarter—the contemporary reception of poetic works. If the voices are silent, perhaps the manuscripts may be made to speak.

Three assumptions underlie the argument I will make about the manuscript evidence of Caedmon's *Hymn*. The first is that orality and literacy are 'pure' states only in theory. In fact, cultures and individuals find themselves on a continuum between the theoretical end points of orality and literacy.[6] My second assumption is that the appearance of a work in manuscript provides no assurance that the work was conceived of as a 'text' in the modern sense or even originally written (as opposed to composed orally). My third, and perhaps most important, assumption is that the movement from orality to literacy involves the gradual shift from aural to visual reception and that such a shift is reflected in the increasing spatialization of a written text.[7]

This third point requires some further explanation. In an oral situation, communication takes place within a discrete time. That the listener must be present when the speaker performs is only one aspect of the intense temporality of the speech act. Emphasis, clarity, surprise, and suspense all depend on the speaker's modulation of his speech in time. When a work is written, however, its tempo no longer

---

PMLA 81 (1966), 334-41, at p. 334, n. 4, argued that Old English poetry was composed within a 'lettered tradition'. The assumptions of 'orality' and 'literacy' behind both arguments are called into question by the verse of Aldhelm, a superbly literate author whose Latin verse is, nonetheless, formulaic. See Michael Lapidge, 'Aldhelm's Latin Poetry and Old English Verse', *Comparative Literature* 31 (1979), 209-31.

[6] See Franz H. Bäuml, 'Varieties and Consequences of Medieval Literacy and Illiteracy', *Speculum* 55 (1980), 237-65, at p. 239 on the inadequacies of the definition of medieval literacy as the ability to read and write Latin. On documents as an index of the early growth of literacy in England see M.T. Clanchy, *From Memory to Written Record: England, 1066-1307* (London, 1979), p. 97 and p. 183.

[7] Walter J. Ong, *Orality and Literacy: The Technologizing of the Word* (London, 1982), pp. 117-23.

depends on the speaker or writer.[8] In fact, tempo virtually disappears. Surprise and emphasis, and most especially clarity, now depend on the transformation of temporal modulations into space. Irregular pauses in the stream of speech become conventionalized by more or less regular spaces between 'words'.[9] Dots and marks indicate special status for portions of text; scripts and capitals indicate a hierarchy of material and meaning.[10] Literacy thus becomes a process of spatializing the once exclusively temporal, and the thought-shaping technology of writing is an index of the development of this process. The higher the degree of conventional spatialization in the manuscripts, the less oral and more literate the community.

The manuscript records of Caedmon's *Hymn* have much to tell us about the reception of the poem throughout the Old English period. In the West-Saxon translation of the *Historia ecclesiastica*, Caedmon's *Hymn* is part of the main text; in the Latin text it is a gloss to the paraphrase of the *Hymn*. It survives in two dialects of Old English and

---

[8] Of writing, Isidore of Seville observes, 'Litterae autem sunt indices rerum, signa verborum, quibus tanta vis est, ut nobis dicta absentium sine voce loquantur. [Verba enim per oculos non per aures introducunt.] Vsus litterarum repertus propter memoriam rerum. Nam ne oblivione fugiant, litteris alligantur. In tanta enim rerum varietate nec disci audiendo poterant omnia, nec memoria contineri. Litterae autem dictae quasi legiterae, quod iter legentibus praestent, vel quod in legendo iterentur'. W.M. Lindsay, ed., *Isidori Hispalensis episcopi Etymologiarum siue originum libri XX* (Oxford, 1911), 1.3.1-3.

[9] On the functional difference between the spoken and written word see Bäuml, 'Varieties', pp. 247-48. See also Jacques Derrida, *Of Grammatology*, trans. Gayatri Chakravorty Spivak (Baltimore, 1976), pp. 30-73, esp. p. 39.

[10] Until M.B. Parkes's book on medieval punctuation appears, see Edward Maunde Thompson, *An Introduction to Greek and Latin Palaeography* (Oxford, 1912), pp. 55-64, for an overview of arrangement of text, punctuation, and accents. For early conventions of punctuation to mark the colon, comma, and periodus, see Isidore, *Etymologiae* 1.20.1-6. Patrick McGurk, 'Citation Marks in Early Latin Manuscripts', *Scriptorium* 15 (1961), 3-13, discusses scribal practices for distinguishing quoted material.

in several centuries of manuscripts. In short, the *Hymn* offers a range of evidence sufficient for the study of formatting practices in Old English and Latin poetry over a considerable period of time. The extralinguistic markers to examine are location of text on the page, lineation, word division, capitalization, and punctuation. The differing use of these visual cues between Latin and Old English will point to differences in expectations about reading Latin, an almost purely textual language, and Old English, a living language only newly being committed to writing.[11]

1

From the eighth century on, Latin poetry in England was copied in lines of verse.[12] Because this technique is so commonplace to the

---

[11] On the significance of layout and punctuation in prose and poetic texts see M.B. Parkes, 'Punctuation, or Pause and Effect', in *Medieval Eloquence: Studies in the Theory and Practice of Medieval Rhetoric*, ed. James J. Murphy (Berkeley, 1978), pp. 127-42, esp. p. 130, n. 14. In 'The Influence of the Concepts of *Ordinatio* and *Compilatio* on the Development of the Book', in *Medieval Learning and Literature: Essays Presented to Richard William Hunt*, ed. J.J.G. Alexander and M.T. Gibson (Oxford, 1976), pp. 115-41, Parkes examines the integral connection of 'the structure of reasoning' and the physical appearance of books (at p. 121). Chirographic control of learned Latin is discussed in Ong, *Orality and Literacy*, pp. 112-14.

[12] Helmut Gneuss, 'A Preliminary List of Manuscripts Written or Owned in England up to 1100', *ASE* 9 (1981), 1-60, lists ten eighth-century manuscripts written in England which contain verse. In addition to the manuscripts of the *Historia ecclesiastica* discussed below, manuscripts containing verse are: Cambridge, Corpus Christi College, MS. 173 (*CLA* 2, no. 123, Sedulius); Vatican City, Biblioteca Apostolica Vaticana, MS. Pal. lat. 235 (*CLA* 1, no. 87, Paulinus of Nola); Leningrad, Saltykov-Schedrin Public Library, MS. Q.v.XIV.1 (*CLA* 11, no. 1622, Paulinus of Nola); Leningrad, Saltykov-Schedrin Public Library, MS. Q.v.I.15 (*CLA* 11, no. 1618, Aldhelm); Miskolc, Zrinyi Ilona Secondary School, *s.n.* (*CLA* Suppl., no. 1792, Aldhelm). Formatting varies from the old practice in CCCC 173 of separating

reader of modern verse, the significance of such a shift in formatting is easily overlooked. But the developing convention of copying Latin poetry spatially by lines of verse underlies an important step in using spatial and nonverbal cues (especially capitals and punctuation) to assist readers in their tasks. As information in a text shifts from purely linguistic to partially visual, verse becomes increasingly chiro-graphically controlled and its formatting increasingly conventional.

The *Historia ecclesiastica* contains verses in hexameters, elegiac distichs, and epanaleptic distichs, each of which invites different types of spatial organization to distinguish its metrical form from the surrounding prose.[13]   In their treatment of these verses, the manuscripts of the *Historia ecclesiastica* written in England document the incorporation of a complex set of visual cues to present Latin verse in writing. Those of the eighth century show considerable fluidity and experimentation in the formatting of verse, while the eleventh-century manuscripts (none from the ninth or tenth centuries survive) exhibit highly consistent and conservative layouts.

Five manuscripts of the *Historia ecclesiastica* written in England in the eighth century survive: Leningrad, Saltykov-Schedrin Public Library, MS. Q.v.I.18 (*CLA* 11, no. 1621); Cambridge, University Library, MS. Kk.5.16 (*CLA* 2, no. 139); London, British Library, MS. Cotton Tiberius A.xiv (*CLA* Suppl., no. 1703); London, British Library, MS. Cotton Tiberius C.ii (*CLA* 2, no. 191); and Kassel, Landesbibliothek, MS. 4° Theol. 2 (*CLA* 8, no. 1140). Most scholars

---

verses by point to the newer practice in Leningrad Q.v.I.15, which writes Aldhelm's *Enigmata* in lines of verse. By the tenth century, English manuscripts of Latin verse are consistently formatted in lines of verse with redundant initial capitals and points at the ends of lines.

[13] Those in simple distichs are: Prosper's brief epigram against Pelagius (1.10) and the epitaphs on Gregory the Great (2.1), Caedwalla (5.7), and Theodore (5.8). Bede's own hymn on Etheldreda (4.20 [23]) is an epanaleptic alphabetic acrostic, and Wilfrid's epitaph (5.19) is in hexameters. I follow throughout the chapter numbers in B. Colgrave and R.A.B. Mynors, eds., *Bede's Ecclesiastical History of the English People* (Oxford, 1969). G.R. Blakley, Department of Mathematics, Texas A&M University, provided many useful observations on the scansion of these verses.

of the manuscripts have assigned priority to CUL Kk.5.l6, which is usually dated to 737, but recently M.B. Parkes has cogently argued that the Leningrad manuscript is conceivably older and closer to Bede's scriptorium.[14]   In addition to these two early Northumbrian manuscripts are Tiberius A.xiv, a mid-eighth-century copy of Leningrad Q.v.I.18, probably also written at Wearmouth-Jarrow, and Kassel 4° Theol. 2, a fragmentary manuscript written in several small Northumbrian hands of the second half of the century.[15] Tiberius C.ii dates to the second half of the eighth century and is most probably southern.[16]   While the first three manuscripts transmit the M text,

---

[14] Peter Hunter Blair, ed., *The Moore Bede: An Eighth Century Manuscript of the Venerable Bede's 'Historia ecclesiastica gentis Anglorum' in Cambridge University Library (Kk.5.16)*, EEMF 9 (Copenhagen, 1959), p. 28; Peter Hunter Blair, 'The Moore Memoranda on Northumbrian History', in *Early Cultures of North-West Europe*, ed. C. Fox and B. Dickins (Cambridge, Eng., 1950), pp. 245-57. See especially D.H. Wright, review of Blair, *The Moore Bede*, *Anglia* 82 (1964), 110-17. Parkes, *Scriptorium*, pp. 5-6, supports arguments advanced by E.A. Lowe, 'A Key to Bede's Scriptorium', *Scriptorium* 12 (1958), 182-90. Lowe's further argument on the copying of the colophon on fol. 161 ('An Autograph of the Venerable Bede?' [*Revue bénédictine* 68 (1958), 200-202]) is disputed by Paul Meyvaert, 'The Bede "Signature" in the Leningrad Colophon', *Revue bénédictine* 71 (1961), 274-86, and by D.H. Wright, 'The Date of the Leningrad Bede', *Revue bénédictine* 71 (1961), 265-73.

[15] On Cotton Tiberius A.xiv see Colgrave and Mynors, *Ecclesiastical History*, pp. xlvi-xlvii. On Kassel 4° Theol. 2 see T.J.M. Van Els, *The Kassel Manuscript of Bede's 'Historia ecclesiastica gentis Anglorum' and Its Old English Material* (Assen, 1972), pp. 6-18, 26.

[16] Sherman M. Kuhn, 'From Canterbury to Lichfield', *Speculum* 23 (1948), 591-629, at pp. 613-19, and 'Some Early Mercian Manuscripts', *Review of English Studies*, n.s. 8 (1957), 355-74, at pp. 366-68, suggests a Mercian provenance. But see Kenneth Sisam, 'Canterbury, Lichfield, and the Vespasian Psalter', *Review of English Studies*, n.s. 7 (1956), 1-10, 113-31, who questions his criteria. D.H. Wright, review of *The Moore Bede*, p. 116, suggests St. Augustine's.

Tiberius C.ii and Kassel 4° Theol. 2 transmit the C text, the version represented by all later English manuscripts.[17]

In these early manuscripts of the *Historia ecclesiastica*, verse is formatted spatially according to the complexity of verse form. Of the six poems in the *Historia*, Bede's epanaleptic alphabetic acrostic distichs on St. Etheldreda, 'Alma deus trinitas' (4.20 [18]), is the most complex, and for these verses all the manuscripts use capitalization, lineation, and punctuation to highlight alphabet, repetition, and distichs. The Leningrad manuscript's treatment of these verses is instructive: as the manuscript closest to Bede's scriptorium, it illustrates the early development of Insular minuscule and of graphic conventions. For the verses on Etheldreda, Scribe D carefully distinguishes the visual features of the hymn.[18] A capital initial at the margin and a fresh line signal the beginning of each distich. While the two verses of the distich are run on within the column, a comma-shaped sub-distinctio separates hexameter and pentameter lines.[19] The hymn ends with heavy punctuation. In a similar fashion, Tiberius A.xiv, probably a copy of Leningrad Q.v.I.18, uses layout to highlight both verse form and alphabetic acrostic, beginning each distich on a fresh line with a colored initial.

See also Helmut Gneuss, 'Zur Geschichte des MS. Vespasian A.I', *Anglia* 75 (1957), 125-33.

[17] Colgrave and Mynors, *Ecclesiastical History*, follow Plummer's distinction of a C text and a later M text (p. xli on versions of the C text). Charles Plummer, *Venerabilis Baedae historia ecclesiastica gentis Anglorum, historia abbatum, epistola ad Ecgberctum una cum historia abbatum auctore anonymo*, 2 vols. (Oxford, 1896), 1:lxxx-cxxxii.

[18] On the stints of the scribes see O. Arngart, ed., *The Leningrad Bede: An Eighth Century Manuscript of the Venerable Bede's 'Historia ecclesiastica gentis Anglorum' in the Public Library, Leningrad*, EEMF 2 (Copenhagen, 1952), p. 18, and Parkes, *Scriptorium*, pp. 6-11.

[19] I have not been able to see Leningrad Q.v.I.18 and am wary of making any argument about scribal pointing on the basis of the facsimile, especially since some repointing has been done. However, the comma-shaped point is characteristically early.

The hurried and rather careless scribe of CUL Kk.5.16 is exceptionally careful with Bede's hymn. The capital initial of 'Alma' is of the sort reserved for the beginnings of chapters. Each distich begins with a capital initial. The unusual care taken in spacing between the last word of a distich and the following capital initial, as well as the consistent pointing between distichs, suggests that the scribe was mindful of the visual dimension of Bede's demanding hymn. The treatment of the hymn in Tiberius C.ii shows some uncertainty over method but a clear intent to produce a visual display. To highlight the alphabetic acrostic, the scribe placed each large initial in the margin, dotting and coloring many of them. His intention seems to have been to give two column lines to each distich. However, the overrun of the last word of the prose introduction necessitated dropping each epanaleptic clause to the line below, breaking the visual symmetry. With this practice, whenever a distich ends mid-column, the scribe uses two hair strokes to separate the completed distich from the following squeezed-in line end.[20]   While the scribe's effort to highlight the alphabetic acrostic obscures the epanalepsis, his mixed result shows that he conceived of the distich as a visual unit.

In the eighth-century manuscripts, verses in distichs show some ambivalence in the choice of layout. The two epitaphs of book 5, on Caedwalla (5.7) and Theodore (5.8), are useful examples. CUL Kk.5.16 writes the verses in long lines but distinguishes each verse with a capital initial, and remaining scribal punctuation marks verse length, not grammatical divisions. Tiberius C.ii employs a different format for each epitaph. In that on Caedwalla, the scribe highlights verse lines at the expense of the distich by beginning each verse line with a capital in the margin. However, in the following epitaph on Theodore, the scribe emphasized the distich instead, beginning lines 1 and 3 in the margin. For these epitaphs, Scribe D in Leningrad Q.v.I.18 appears to be experimenting with combinations of techniques. The first distich of Caedwalla's epitaph is written across the column, and heavy punctuation separates the two verses. Lines 3-10 each begin at the margin, and lines 11-24 revert to presentation in distich form. In the latter format, each distich begins with a capital initial; in line

---

[20] As a result of considerable repointing in the manuscript, each distich now appears marked by a punctus versus, but the original punctuation is by medial point.

format, each verse begins with a capital. In the two excerpts Bede quotes from Theodore's epitaph there is a similar ambivalence about the technique of lineation. The poem begins with a capital, and lines 1 and 2 each begin at the margin. The following two lines, however, are run on. In the second set of verses, following 'ultimi hi', lines 5 and 6 run on but lines 7 and 8 begin at the margin.[21] Spacing between verses is clear, and each line of verse was apparently pointed by a distinctio.

The epitaph on Wilfrid (5.19), in simple hexameters, shows the least complexity in graphic display. Scribe D writes the first verses in long lines (though separating each verse by a sub-distinctio), but shifts method to begin verses 4 through 20 at the margin with a capital. While both Kassel 4° Theol. 2 and Tiberius A.xiv format this epitaph in lines of verse, Tiberius C.ii distinguishes verses with capital initials only. CUL Kk.5.16 distinguishes the first two lines with capital initials and terminal punctuation, but then discontinues the practice.[22]

The eighth-century manuscripts of the *Historia ecclesiastica* show a clear intent to provide visual cues to aid in reading the verses in the text. At the simplest level, this purpose is served by pointing. At its most complex, graphic interpretation involves capitalization and the fitting of verses into the columnar lines. This practice becomes fixed in the manuscripts of the following centuries. No English manuscripts of the *Historia ecclesiastica* survive from the ninth or tenth centuries, and from the eleventh century, to my knowledge, only six manuscripts remain. In these manuscripts, layout for poetry is highly consistent. The graphic representation of the poetry in the *Historia* in Oxford, Bodleian Library, MS. Bodley 163 (Ker, no. 304, xi in.), is typical of the other surviving eleventh-century manuscripts: Oxford, Bodleian Library, MS. Hatton 43 (Ker, no. 326, xi in.); Cambridge, Trinity College, MS. R.7.5 (early eleventh century); Winchester Cathedral,

---

[21] Bede quotes two sections of the epitaph: the opening and the closing four lines. Kassel, Landesbibliothek, 4° Theol. 2 and BL Cotton Tiberius A.xiv both write these epitaphs in lines of verse.

[22] The formatting for verses in 1.10 and 2.1 raises questions beyond the scope of this paper. For a full account see my 'Graphic Cues for the Presentation of Verse in the Earliest English Manuscripts of the *Historia ecclesiastica*', *Manuscripta* 31 (1987), 139-46.

MS. 1 (Ker, no. 396, xi[1]); London, British Library, MS. Royal 13.C.v
(second half of the eleventh century); and Durham, Dean and Chapter
Library, MS. B.II.35 (late eleventh century). Verses (except for the
hymn in 4.20 [18]) are written across the writing space but are
carefully distinguished by pointing.[23] Prosper's epigram (1.10) begins
with a large red capital, and black capitals begin the next two distichs.
Punctuation reinforces that structure with a low point to separate verses
of the distichs and a high point as terminal punctuation for the
distich.[24]

Each verse of Gregory's epitaph (2.1) begins with a red capital.[25]
The pointing has been considerably altered, though originally the
system must have consisted of high and low points. This practice is
followed as well for the epitaphs of book 5.[26]   The hymn on

---

[23] The practice in the eleventh-century manuscripts of the *Historia
ecclesiastica* of running verses across the writing space and using only
capitals and points to separate verses is a throwback to much earlier
practice, probably owing to pressures of space. In this period,
manuscripts of poetry are always formatted spatially in lines of verse.

[24] Hatton 43 begins each verse with a capital.

[25] Winchester 1 points each verse, but capitalization is inconsistent.
BL Royal 13.C.v writes the epitaph in lines of verse beginning with
line 4. Durham B.II.35 distinguishes hexameters with capital initials
and separates all verses by a point on the line of writing.

[26] For the epitaph in 5.7, Winchester 1 and Royal 13.C.v follow
this practice. Hatton 43 points at the end of each verse but uses
capitals inconsistently. The practice in Trinity R.7.5 is impossible to
ascertain because the original punctuation has been erased. For the
epitaph in 5.8, Royal 13.C.v and Trinity R.7.5 point at the end of each
line of verse. Winchester 1 capitalizes by distich, omitting the capital
for line 1. Hatton 43 has a capital for 'hic' only. For Wilfrid's
epitaph in 5.19, Trinity R.7.5 follows Bodley 163's practice of
separating verses by marking them with high and low points. Royal
13.C.v and Hatton 43 change formats here and write the epitaph in
lines of verse introduced by capital initials. Winchester 1 separates all
lines by punctus versi but is inconsistent with capitals. Durham B.II.35
formats these in lines of verse, beginning each distich with a capital
initial and marking each line with a terminal point.

Etheldreda (4.20 [18]), however, is written in lines of verse with the size of script reduced. Each verse begins with a red rustic capital initial.[27] Present terminal punctuation for each line is a punctus versus, but the tail of the versus is in much lighter ink. The original system probably used a low point to mark the caesura and a high point for terminal punctuation. This system, by highlighting each line of verse, obscures the alphabetic acrostic which begins each distich. The twelfth-century manuscripts examined for this study consistently write the poems in lines of verse.[28]

Although there is room for variation in the use and ornamentation of capitals, the manuscript tradition carefully distinguishes the verses in the *Historia ecclesiastica* from the surrounding prose. Pointing and capitalization mark off lines of verse, not sense or breath pauses. The evidence points to an awareness that Latin required extralinguistic cues to help the reader work through the verse.[29] The methods used to distinguish Latin verse were not adopted in the written record of Old English poetry. An examination of manuscripts containing the surviving records of Caedmon's *Hymn* may suggest some reasons for this difference.

2

Caedmon's *Hymn* travels in two textual environments, as a marginal addition to the account of Caedmon's miraculous composition

---

[27] Hatton 43 follows this practice. Winchester 1 begins each distich with a capital, writes the poem in lines of verse through *M*, and then reverts to long lines. Royal 13.C.v and Trinity R.5.7 begin each distich with a capital and run the verses across the space.

[28] Given the number of twelfth-century English copies, I have limited my discussion to a consideration of those English manuscripts which contain Caedmon's *Hymn*. Examination of most of the other twelfth-century English manuscripts of the *Historia ecclesiastica* revealed that the pattern of verse presentation discussed here holds.

[29] See Parkes, 'Pause and Effect', p. 139, on the scribe's awareness of the needs of his audience.

in the *Historia ecclesiastica* (4.24[22])[30] and as an integral part of the West-Saxon translation of the *History*. Its promotion from margin to text proper is consonant with the other modifications the Old English translator made in the Latin text. His inclusion of Caedmon's *Hymn* necessitated as well some rearrangement of the Latin material, for example the omission of the paraphrase and Bede's apology for the Latin translation. In the context of these changes, the anonymous translator affirmed his faith in the version of Caedmon's *Hymn* which he transmitted by introducing it with the words: 'þara endebyrdnes ðis is'. An examination of the twelve Latin manuscripts in which Caedmon's *Hymn* appears offers evidence on the status of the text, the conventions of copying Old English poetry, and practices of word division and punctuation. From these we may make inferences about practices of reading.

Dobbie divided the textual tradition of Caedmon's *Hymn* into two main lines, the 'aelda'/'ylda' group and the 'eorðu' group, which he then subdivided by dialect.[31] Each of these groups has two Northumbrian witnesses, though the copies of the Northumbrian 'eorðu' version are Continental and too late to be useful to this study. The two Northumbrian records of the 'aelda'/'ylda' group, Leningrad Q.v.I.18

---

[30] The exception is the late manuscript, Cambridge, Trinity College, MS. R.5.22 (14th c.), where Caedmon's *Hymn* has been copied into the main text.

[31] Dobbie, *Manuscripts*, p. 48, prints a stemma. He defines four groups. For the 'aelda'/'ylda' text, the Northumbrian witnesses are CUL Kk.5.16 and Leningrad Q.v.I.18 [M-L]; the West-Saxon members of this group [*Z] are: Oxford, Bodleian Library, MS. Hatton 43 and MS. Bodley 163; Oxford, Lincoln College, MS. lat. 31; Oxford, Magdalen College, MS. lat. 105; Winchester Cathedral, MS. 1; Cambridge, Trinity College, MS. R.5.22. For the 'eorðu' text the West-Saxon members [*AE] are: Oxford, Bodleian Library, MS. Tanner 10; London, British Library, MS. Cotton Otho B.xi; Oxford, Corpus Christi College, MS. 279; Cambridge, University Library, MS. Kk.3.28; Cambridge, Corpus Christi College, MS. 41. The peculiar Oxford, Bodleian Library, MS. Laud Misc. 243, and Hereford Cathedral, MS. P.5.1, are in this group. The two Continental manuscripts form the *Y group.

and CUL Kk.5.16, are, however, the earliest witnesses to the text of Caedmon's *Hymn* and as such are of crucial importance. In many ways, as records of the *Historia ecclesiastica*, CUL Kk.5.16 and Leningrad Q.v.I.18 are very different. The latter is a particularly careful copy of the text. Outside of errors in the sources quoted by Bede (and thus, probably, in the originals), there are only six errors in the text written by Bede, and these errors are minor.[32] Given the length of the *Historia*, the high accuracy of Leningrad Q.v.I.18 argues that its copying was close to the author's draft. Leningrad Q.v.I.18 is also a handsome copy of the text, and the individual work done by four Wearmouth-Jarrow scribes shows a high level of concern for calligraphy in the manuscript as a whole.[33] The stints of the first two scribes, which supply the first eight quires, are clearly later than the work of scribes C and D, and, Parkes argues, were added to make up for loss from the original state of the Leningrad manuscript. The work of scribes C and D may thus well be the oldest witness to the text of the *Historia ecclesiastica* in existence. Early scholars of Leningrad Q.v.I.18 thought that the system of numerals in the margin, a dating device which yields the year 746, provided a terminus a quo for the manuscript.[34] The marks, however, are in the ink of a corrector,[35] making the date of the CD portion earlier than 746. This issue assumes particular significance, since scribe D added Caedmon's *Hymn* at the bottom of fol. 107r.

Scribe D wrote Caedmon's *Hymn* in three long lines across the bottom margin of fol. 107r. Whether he added it at the time of writing

---

[32] Colgrave and Mynors, *Ecclesiastical History*, pp. xxxix-xl, xliv.

[33] Parkes, *Scriptorium*, p. 11.

[34] Olga Dobiache-Rojdestvensky, 'Un manuscrit de Bède à Léningrad', *Speculum* 3 (1928), 314-21, at p. 318, makes this argument. O. Arngart revises his initial agreement with this position (*Leningrad Bede*, pp. 17-18) in 'On the Dating of Early Bede Manuscripts', *Studia neophilologica* 45 (1973), 47-52, where he argues that the calculations are Bede's own and thus useless for dating.

[35] Lowe, 'Key', rejects the significance of '746' on the basis of the difference in ink. While admitting Meyvaert's arguments on the possible forgery of the colophon ('"Signature,"' p. 286), Parkes (*Scriptorium*, p. 26, n. 35) questions the priority of CUL Kk.5.16.

or at some point afterwards is impossible to determine. It is clear that he did not alter his usual arrangement of twenty-seven lines per column to accommodate the *Hymn*. Functionally, the *Hymn* is a gloss to Bede's Latin paraphrase in 4.20 [18]. The hand is Insular minuscule, and though just as precise as that in the Latin columns, much smaller. The *Hymn* begins with a capital *N*, there is no other capital, and the only point occurs after 'all mehtig'.[36] The orthography and spacing of the words in the *Hymn* show characteristic attention to detail. Word division is as scrupulous as in the Latin text. While separation of free morphemes is possible, no words are run on.

In the Latin text of the *Historia ecclesiastica*, where the Leningrad manuscript is deliberate, measured, calligraphic, and accurate, CUL Kk.5.16 is hurried, uncalligraphic, and imprecise. Ornament is lacking; the scribe wrote his Insular minuscule in long lines across the writing space, leaving only very narrow margins. Punctuation is spare, and the spacing, though not cramped, is not kind to a reader. Spacing between words is about the same size as spacing between letters within words, and the Latin text often appears to be a series of undifferentiated letters. There is, however, a considerable difference between the scribe's work on the *Historia* and his execution of Caedmon's *Hymn* on the first three lines of fol. 128v, a sort of addendum to the text of the history.[37] Like Leningrad Q.v.I.18, CUL Kk.5.16 begins with the *Hymn*'s only capital letter. The word division of the *Hymn* is actually better than that of the Latin text. The scribe runs together 'nu scylun', and splits 'hefaen ricaes' and 'middun geard'. Word separations are limited to free morphemes. His orthography is highly consistent as well, although 'dryctin' is consistent by correction, and the scribe varies 'hefaen' with 'heben'. The point

---

[36] Dobbie, *Manuscripts*, p. 17, prints a point after 'astelidae'. This point is visible neither on the fascimile (O. Arngart, *The Leningrad Bede*) nor on the photograph of fol. 107r which M.B. Parkes kindly showed me.

[37] See A.H. Smith, ed., *Three Northumbrian Poems* (London, 1933, rpt New York, 1968), pp. 20-22, who summarizes views of earlier scholars and accepts the view that the scribe of the Latin text also wrote Caedmon's *Hymn*. So too Hunter Blair, *Moore Bede*, p. 29. Ker, *Catalogue*, no. 25, describes it as a 'contemporary addition'.

which occurs after 'scepen' (l. 6) is the only point in the text of Caedmon's *Hymn* in CUL Kk.5.16.

The inclusion of Caedmon's *Hymn* by the original scribes in both CUL Kk.5.16 and Leningrad Q.v.I.18 suggests that from earliest times Caedmon's *Hymn* was considered a worthy companion to the Latin account of Caedmon's miracle. Its appearance in Leningrad Q.v.I.18, a manuscript from Wearmouth-Jarrow very close to the author's copy, and the discipline obvious in its script, spacing, and orthography speak to the care which the Old English poem was thought to merit. Equally, that it is recognized as verse, but not marked off as such by the techniques used by the same scribe for Latin verses, strongly suggests that such graphic marking was perceived to be redundant. Given its scribal origin, the quality of the copy of Caedmon's *Hymn* in CUL Kk.5.16, otherwise a hastily written production, argues a self-consciousness about writing the Old English verses not apparent in the Latin.

The six surviving eleventh-century English copies of the *Historia ecclesiastica*—Oxford, Bodleian Library, MS. Bodley 163; Oxford, Bodleian Library, MS. Hatton 43; Cambridge, Trinity College, MS. R.7.5; Winchester Cathedral, MS. 1 (all manuscripts of the early eleventh century); London, British Library, MS. Royal 13.C.v; and Durham, Dean and Chapter Library, MS. B.II.35 (both late eleventh century)—while grouped as C versions, preserve different strands of the textual tradition.[38] Hatton 43 transmits a very accurate text, quite close to that of the eighth-century southern C version, BL Cotton Tiberius C.ii, though not a copy.[39] According to Plummer, Bodley 163 is a copy of the carelessly executed Winchester 1.[40] These two manuscripts (part of a 'Winchester' group) share alterations in the chronology of 5.24 with the 'Durham' group (headed by Durham B.II.35) but show a northern connection by the presence of

---

[38] Colgrave and Mynors, *Ecclesiastical History*, p. xli.

[39] The other early manuscript, Cambridge, Trinity College, R.7.5, is sufficiently close to BL Cotton Tiberius C.ii to suggest that it is a copy (Colgrave and Mynors, *Ecclesiastical History*, p. li).

[40] Plummer, *Historia ecclesiastica*, 1:cxviii-cxix. Ker, *Catalogue*, no. 396, calls them 'closely related'.

Aethelwulf's poem on the abbots of a northern English monastery.[41]
Royal 13.C.v (Gloucester?) transmits a C text which nonetheless shares
some readings with BL Cotton Tiberius A.xiv, an M text.

All six of these manuscripts were originally copied without
Caedmon's *Hymn*. Only Hatton 43, Winchester 1, and Bodley 163
contain the *Hymn*, and in each case the copying of the *Hymn* into the
Historia ecclesiastica was done at least a quarter-century later than the
writing of the Latin text.[42] This circumstance and the wide selection
of textual strands attested by the surviving eleventh-century copies
suggests that Caedmon's *Hymn* did not travel integrally with the text in
any one textual tradition. The addition of the *Hymn* to Hatton 43,
Bodley 163, and Winchester 1 would seem to have been fortuitous.

Especially interesting is the disparity in date between the copying
of the text of the *Historia ecclesiastica* in Hatton 43 (which Ker dates
to xi in.) and that of the *Hymn* (which Ker dates to xi[2]). The color of
ink for the addition is similar to that used for many corrections. The
placement of the *Hymn* is interesting as well. It is written in four long
lines at the bottom of fol. 129r. The scribe has keyed the *Hymn* to the
Latin paraphrase by a *signe de renvoi* and has drawn a box around the
text. The location of the text here is similar to that in Leningrad
Q.v.I.18. One wonders what kind of exemplar the scribe of the
addition had before him.[43]

In any event, Hatton 43 preserves the most orthographically pure
text of Caedmon's *Hymn* in the *Z version, although it is later than
either Winchester 1 or Bodley 163. On the basis of the textual
relations between Winchester 1 and Bodley 163, Dobbie thought it
probable that Caedmon's *Hymn* in Bodley 163 was copied from the
Winchester manuscript. The independence of Caedmon's *Hymn* from

---

[41] See Colgrave and Mynors, *Ecclesiastical History*, pp. xlix-li.

[42] Ker, *Catalogue*, dates Caedmon's *Hymn* in Hatton 43 to xi[2] (no.
326), in Winchester 1 to xi med. (no. 396), and in Bodley 163 to xi
med. (no. 304).

[43] The only surviving texts transmitting the Northumbrian dialect
(and hence the earlier version) of Caedmon's *Hymn* are M texts. At
what point Caedmon's *Hymn* was added to a C text is impossible to
determine. Dobbie does note that *Z derives directly from a
Northumbrian version of the *Hymn* (*Manuscripts*, p. 47).

the copying of the Latin text makes this circumstance unlikely. Winchester 1 is a peculiar manuscript. Caedmon's *Hymn* is copied in the upper right outer margin of fol. 81r with a *signe de renvoi* to the text. The copying is careless,[44] but apart from some orthographic differences, Winchester differs from *Z only in the substitution of 'word' for 'ord'. Given the copyist's carelessness, it is probable that this variant is unique to Winchester. About the text of the *Hymn* in Bodley 163 we can conclude little, save that this version has 'gehwylc' rather than 'gehwaes'. On this basis it can be placed confidently in the *Z group. The few remaining letters of the *Hymn* in the left margin of fol. 152v survive a considerable attempt made to erase it.[45]

The copies of Caedmon's *Hymn* in the twelfth-century manuscripts show a comparable independence of the *Hymn* from the Latin text. Of the four manuscripts which transmit the *Hymn*,[46] only Oxford, Magdalen College, MS. lat. 105, and Oxford, Bodleian Library, MS. Laud Misc. 243, have the text in the hand of the original scribe. Ker describes the hand of the *Hymn* in Hereford Cathedral, MS. P.v.1 as 'contemporary'. The *Hymn* in Oxford, Lincoln College, MS. lat. 31, was added by one of the correctors.[47]

While Magdalen 105 and Hereford P.v.1 belong to the same textual group, that of the common text in southern England, they transmit different versions of the *Hymn*. The version in Magdalen 105 is the standard *Z text of the 'aelda'/'ylda' group. Hereford is peculiar in transmitting a corrupt 'eorðu' text, which comes either from Laud Misc. 243 or its exemplar. Laud Misc. 243 transmits a 'Gloucester'

---

[44] On the second line, 'heri' is dotted for omission; 'metoddes' has the first *d* dotted; 'heofen' has been corrected by the addition of an *o* over the second *e*.

[45] Could we know when this was done, we might learn something about the eraser's vision of the relationship between text and *Hymn*.

[46] These four twelfth-century manuscripts are only a fraction of the twelfth-century English manuscripts extant. See Colgrave and Mynors, *Ecclesiastical History*, pp. xlvi-lxi.

[47] On the relationship between the text of the *History* ('Burney' group) and the additions and corrections from the 'Digby' group, see Dobbie, *Manuscripts*, pp. 88-89, and Colgrave and Mynors, *Ecclesiastical History*, p. liv.

version of the history but its text of the *Hymn*, thoroughly corrupt, derives from an *AE text (i.e., was copied from the version in the West-Saxon *History*).

The version of the *Hymn* in this manuscript needs further examination. At issue is the nature of the transmission of Caedmon's *Hymn* in Laud Misc. 243. Dobbie favored Frampton's conclusion[48] that Laud Misc. 243 is a transcript from memory, on the basis that the appending of 'halig scyppeod' at the end of the poem could not have been done by a scribe with a correct copy before him. This argument might be persuasive were it not for the presence of other errors of a purely graphic nature, that is, the dittography of 'herian herian', the spelling 'scyppeod',[49] and the impossible syntax caused by the omission of 'or astealde'. Despite Dobbie's assertion to the contrary,[50] it is quite possible that the transposition of 'halig scyppeod' could have been made from a 'correct' copy. This is far more likely than the memorial transmission of so corrupt a text, especially since the corruption violates the alliteration, the main means of aiding correct memorial transmission.

The copyist who added Caedmon's *Hymn* in Hereford Cathedral, P.v.1 reproduced the error with 'scyppeod' and introduced one of his own, 'drihtent'. However, he corrected the syntax caused by the missing 'ord astealde' by omitting the whole phrase 'swa ... drihten' (ll. 3b-4a). Once again, we see Caedmon's *Hymn* included in the Latin text by chance. The text was obviously not in Hereford's exemplar for the *Historia*, and at some point along the line either the scribe of Laud Misc. 243 or the scribe of his exemplar departed from his Latin text to use the *Hymn* from a West-Saxon translation of Bede's history. The final twelfth-century manuscript to be considered, Lincoln College, lat. 31, also adds Caedmon's *Hymn* from another exemplar. The text of the *Historia ecclesiastica* in Lincoln 31 is in the 'Burney' group of

---

[48] M.G. Frampton, 'Caedmon's *Hymn*', *Modern Philology* 22 (1924), 1-15, at p. 4.

[49] Dobbie, *Manuscripts*, p. 41, claims that photostats indicate that the *o* in '*scyppeod*' had been partially erased to make it look like an *n*. Upon examination of the manuscript I could see no evidence of erasure or scraping. The vellum is quite smooth.

[50] Dobbie, *Manuscripts*, p. 43.

manuscripts, but it has been collated with and corrected from the 'Digby' group, from which the corrector added the West-Saxon version of Bede's *Death Song*.[51]

The change of hand in the copying of the *Hymn* in all but Magdalen 105 and the peculiar Laud Misc. 243 suggests that the inclusion of Caedmon's *Hymn* in the eleventh and twelfth centuries is fortuitous. This inference is strengthened by the fact that these copies containing the *Hymn* are largely from different textual groups. No group is identifiable by the presence of the *Hymn*. Caedmon's *Hymn* did not, in fact, normally travel with the *Historia ecclesiastica*. The circumstances of its inclusion indicate that the *Hymn* appears in the *Z version as a gloss with its own discrete textual tradition. Given the various lines of descent represented by its host text, it is surprising that the West-Saxon 'ylda' text is in the good shape it is. That this is so argues that Caedmon's *Hymn* in the *Historia ecclesiastica* became textual fairly early, that is, became a *written* poem in a relatively modern sense. A possible objection to this conclusion might be that the *Z group dates from the eleventh and twelfth centuries, and thus one might expect the text to be fossilized. The best answer to this objection is an examination of the five surviving manuscripts of the West-Saxon translation of the *Historia ecclesiastica*. With the exception of Oxford, Bodleian Library, MS. Tanner 10, these are eleventh-century productions. An examination of the state of their records of the *Hymn* should demonstrate that something other than age is responsible for the fixity of the text in *Z.

There are five witnesses to the text of Caedmon's *Hymn* as it was contained in the West-Saxon translation of the *History*: Oxford, Bodleian Library, MS. Tanner 10 (Ker, no. 351, x¹); Oxford, Corpus Christi College, MS. 279 (Ker, no. 354, xi in.); Cambridge, Corpus Christi College, MS. 41 (Ker, no. 32, xi¹); Cambridge, University Library, MS. Kk.3.18 (Ker, no. 23, xi²); and London, British Library, MS. Cotton Otho B.xi (Ker, no. 180, x med.), now thoroughly burnt, but whose readings survive in the sixteenth-century transcript by Nowell in London, British Library, MS. Add. 43703. The transcript is useless as evidence for orthography, punctuation, spacing, and mise-en-page, since Nowell was hardly xerographic in his reproduction of

---

[51] Dobbie, *Manuscripts*, pp. 37, 88–89.

the text. Certain readings: 'ne' (for 'nu'), 'eorþū' (for 'eorþan'), 'eode' (for 'teode'), 'finū' (for 'firum') are clearly the usual mistakes of a sixteenth-century transcriber. However, one variant, 'weoroda' (l. 3a), is useful to the study of the relationships among the five manuscripts. 'Weoroda' can only have been an original reading, since it is highly improbable that a nonnative speaker would by accident produce a likely and grammatical variant.

Miller's examination of the manuscript tradition of the West-Saxon *History* established that the West-Saxon texts of the *History* as a whole derive from the same original translation.[52] In this light, the extensive variation shown by these copies, apart from orthographic differences, is remarkable and demands consideration. In the nine lines of the *Hymn*, *AE contains seven variations, all of which are grammatically and semantically appropriate. In the variations *nu/nu we; weorc/wera/weoroda; wuldorfaeder/wuldorgodes; wundra/wuldres; gehwaes/fela; or/ord; sceop/gescop* we see a dynamic of transmission where the message is not embellished but where change within the formula is allowed. The variations in the *AE version are that much more startling by contrast with the record of the *Z texts. In the five manuscripts of this West-Saxon version traveling with the *Historia ecclesiastica* there is only one nonorthographic variant, 'word' in Winchester 1. How can this difference be accounted for? The likeliest explanation would be independent translation, but this has been demonstrated not to be the case on other grounds.[53] The *Z and *AE groups each descend from one original. The dating of the copies would not appear to be significant either, since the core of variables in *AE lies in the eleventh-century manuscripts, and the eleventh-century records of *Z are extremely stable. Nor is there compelling evidence that an unusual wave of scribal incompetence is responsible for the variants. There is, however, one circumstance not accounted for—the textual environment. The *Z group travels as a gloss to the Latin paraphrase in the *Historia ecclesiastica*. The *AE version, on the contrary, finds its place in the vernacular redaction of Bede's story of

---

[52] Thomas Miller, ed., *The Old English Version of Bede's Ecclesiastical History*, 2 vols., EETS 95, 96, 110, 111 (London, 1890-98), 1:xxiii-xxiv.

[53] Miller, *Old English Version* 1:xxiv-xxvi.

Caedmon. Since the only variable circumstance in the transmission of *Z and *AE is textual environment, I would suggest that the variability of text in *AE is a consequence of its environment in a purely vernacular text, a vernacular whose character as a living language kept it close to the oral status which until fairly recently was its only state.

When we examine the variations in these five records of the West-Saxon version, we see in the despair of the textual editor palpable evidence of a fluid transmission of the *Hymn* somewhere between the formula-defined process which is an oral poem and the graph-bound object which is a text. We see a reading activity reflected in these scribal variants which is formula-dependent, in that the variants observe metrical and alliterative constraints, and which is context-defined, in that the variants produced arise within a field of possibilities generated within a context of expectations.[54] The reading I am proposing is reading by suggestion, by guess triggered by key words in formulae. It is a method of reading which is the natural and inevitable child of an oral tradition only recently wedded to the possibilities of writing. Variance in an oral tradition is made inevitable by the subjectivity of the speaker (and hearer) but is constrained by impersonal meter and alliteration. The writing of a poem acts as a very powerful constraint on variance, and in the face of such constraint, the presence of variance argues an equally powerful pull from the oral.

The process of copying manuscripts is rarely simply mechanical. Given the normal medieval practice of reading aloud, or at least subvocalizing, the scribe likely 'heard' at least some of his text.[55] And copying done in blocks of text required the commission of several words or phrases to short-term memory.[56] The trigger of memory is responsible for various sorts of contamination,[57] as seen, for example,

---

[54] On the 'grammar' of formulae see Berkley Peabody, *The Winged Word* (Albany, 1975).

[55] Henry John Chaytor, 'The Medieval Reader and Textual Criticism', *Bulletin of the John Rylands Library* 26 (1941-42), 49-56.

[56] Martin L. West, *Textual Criticism and Editorial Technique* (Stuttgart, 1973), pp. 20-21.

[57] On the role of memory in various sorts of textual corruption in Latin classical texts see Louis Havet, *Manuel de critique verbale appliquée aux textes latins* (Paris, 1911, rpt. Rome, 1967), items 1082-

in the importation of Old Latin readings into the copying of the Vulgate Bible. Quite another sort of memory trigger is responsible for 'Freudian' substitutions in a text.[58] Here the substitutes, if syntactically correct, are usually not semantically or contextually appropriate. The presence of variants in Caedmon's *Hymn*, however, differs in an important way from the appearance of memorial variants in biblical or liturgical texts. Both sorts depend to some degree on memory, but the variants in Caedmon's *Hymn* use memory not to import a set phrase but to draw on formulaic possibility. Reception here, conditioned by formulaic conventions, produces variants which are metrically, syntactically, and semantically appropriate. In such a process, reading and copying have actually conflated with composing.[59] The integral presence of such variance in transmitting the *Hymn* in *AE argues for the existence of a transitional state between pure orality and pure literacy whose evidence is a reading process which applies oral techniques for the reception of a message to the decoding of a written text.[60]   Caedmon's *Hymn* shows us neither purely literate nor memorial transmission,[61] but a tertium quid whose nature remains to be explored.

97.

[58] R.M. Ogilvie, 'Monastic Corruption', *Greece and Rome*, 2nd ser., 18 (1971), 32-34; Sebastiano Timpanaro, *The Freudian Slip: Psychoanalysis and Textual Criticism*, trans. Kate Soper (London, 1976).

[59] On the intrusion of oral processes into what he terms 'pre-literate written transmission' of medieval music see Leo Treitler, 'Oral, Written, and Literate Process in the Transmission of Medieval Music', *Speculum* 56 (1981), 471-91, at p. 482.

[60] Bäuml, 'Varieties', p. 246, n. 23, notes that without functional dependence on literacy, the ability to write does not imply recognition of the fixity of a text.

[61] See Alan Jabbour, 'Memorial Transmission in Old English Poetry', *Chaucer Review* 3 (1969), 174-90.   My argument is particularly in conflict with his comments on pp. 181-82.

3

To this point, the argument about the varying degrees of fixity in the text of Caedmon's *Hymn* has focused on evidence offered by textual transmission. The practices of punctuation displayed in the paraphrase of the *Hymn* and in the *Hymn* itself in the manuscripts under consideration offer a different kind of evidence to support the argument about fixity in the text, reading, and visual cues.

In reviewing Table 1, displaying the punctuation of the Latin paraphrase of the *Hymn*, one cannot help but be struck by the regularity of pointing in these records. The pointing in the fullest case separates the *Hymn* into three major clauses (beginning 'nunc ...'; 'quomodo ...'; 'qui ...'), which are in turn subdivided. In the first case points separate the variations on the direct object, in the second and third they distinguish dependent clauses. These points are grammatical markers, and if they function as breath pauses, they do so only secondarily.[62] The table shows unanimity in marking the main clauses, save for CUL Kk.5.16, the hastily executed eighth-century M text. The marking of objects or dependent clauses also shows little variety.

The pointing of the Old English *Hymn* shows no such uniformity. From an examination of Table 2, several observations may be made. The only larger agreement in punctuation is a terminal point which marks off the *Hymn* as a whole. Even here, there is not unanimity, for neither CUL Kk.5.16 nor, more significantly, Bodleian Library Hatton 43 supplies terminal points.[63] Caedmon's *Hymn* divides into three main clauses (beginning 'nu ...'; 'he ...'; 'þa middangeard ...'). The first contains three variations on the direct object (or on the subject in versions without 'we') and the subordinate 'swa' clause. The second is a simple main clause with a variation on the subject. The third is a complex sentence with OSV structure and nested variations on subject and object. Of all the records of the *Hymn* under consideration, only Tanner 10 provides a consistent grammatical pointing terminating each main clause. As might be expected, the *AE group shows great variety. One might note especially the difference in pointing between

---

[62] On the various practices of pointing for verse and prose see Parkes, 'Pause and Effect', p. 130, esp. n. 14.

[63] Dobbie, *Manuscripts*, p. 39, incorrectly prints a terminal point.

Table 1: Pointing in the Latin Paraphrase of Caedmon's *Hymn*

Manuscripts	Placement of Points by Clause*							
	caelestis	creatoris	illius	gloriae	deus	extitit	tecti	creavit
Leningrad Q.v.I.18	X	X	X	X	X	X	X	X
CUL Kk.5.16						X		X
Tiberius C.ii		X				X	X	X
Tiberius A.xiv	X	X		X	X	X	X	X
Cambridge Trinity R.7.5	X		X	X		X	X	X
Winchester 1	X	X		X	X	X	X	X
Hatton 43	X		X	X		X	X	X
Bodley 163	X	X		X	X	X	X	X
Royal 13.C.v	X	X	X	X	X	X	X	X
Laud Misc. 243	X		X	X	X	X	X	X
Magdalen 105	X	X	X	X	X	X	X	X
Lincoln 31	X		X	X	X	X	X	X
Cambridge Trinity R.5.27	X	X		X	X	X	X	X
Hereford P.v.1	X		X	X	X	X	X	X

*The punctuation follows the last word of the clause.

CUL Kk.3.18 and its probable exemplar. The later manuscript clearly added points to separate the variant objects, but pays no attention to the full stop wanting after 'onstealde'. The *Z group shows, predictably, both a higher incidence of punctuation and a higher incidence of agreement within itself. The system of punctuation in Hatton 43, in many ways the best record in the group, is similar to that in the Latin paraphrase of the *Hymn*. Hatton 43 divides the *Hymn* into two statements ('nu ... astealde'; 'he ... aelmihtig'), though the final point is missing. These statements are further divided, the first by object variant and the dependent 'swa' clause. The second separates two variants on the main clause, both depending on 'gesceop'. This scheme is followed by Magdalen College, lat. 105 (with terminal punctuation); Lincoln College, lat. 31, adds points after 'bearnum' and 'scyppend' while omitting the point after 'drihten'. Winchester 1, Laud Misc. 243, and Hereford P.v.1 are predictably idiosyncratic.

There are several issues here, and these are best examined in Dobbie's manuscript groups, beginning with the last, *Z. Just as an examination of mise-en-page and textual descent in *Z established the high degree of fixity in the text, so its frequent use of punctuation as an extralinguistic signal confirms that fixity as a movement from the subjectivity of the speaker to the objectivity of the graph committed to vellum. Yet the Old English records show a high variability in pointing as compared with Latin records of the paraphrase copied in the same time period.

*AE shows an idiosyncrasy in punctuation consonant with the variability it shows in the transmission of the *Hymn*. While pointing in Tanner 10 can be analyzed as 'grammatical', such a pattern is lacking in the other three extant *AE records. Most interesting are the relationships between Oxford, Corpus Christi College 279, and CUL Kk.3.18. Whether Kk.3.18 is a copy of the Oxford manuscript's exemplar or of the manuscript itself, we see an acute case of the spontaneous nature of Old English pointing. In this group one might make a case for pointing as breath markers.

The group comprised of CUL Kk.5.16 and Leningrad Q.v.I.18 stands apart from the West-Saxon versions in several ways. Its antiquity, its closeness to Wearmouth-Jarrow, the exquisite care lavished on its copying (even for the hurried CUL Kk.5.16) make the record it transmits of supreme importance. What we see are systems of pointing in Latin and Old English at variance with one another.

Table 2: Pointing in Caedmon's *Hymn*

Manuscripts[b]	Placement of Points by Clause (Expressed in Half-Lines)[a]																	
	1a	1b	2a	2b	3a	3b	4a	4b	5a	5b	6a	6b	7a	7b	8a	8b	9a	9b
Leningrad Q.v.I.18																		x
CUL. Kk.5.16											x							
Tanner 10								x				x						x
CCCC 41												x		x				x
OxCCC 279																		x
CUL Kk.3.18							x					x						x
Hatton 43		x	x	x	x	x		x			x							
Winchester 1			x						x						x			x
Laud Misc. 243		x		x	x						x							[x][c]
Hereford P.v.1											x							[x][c]
Magdalen 105		x	x	x	x	x		x			x							x
Lincoln 31		x	x	x	x	x		x		x	x							x

[a] In each case where punctuation occurs, a point follows the last word of a half-line.

[b] Bodley 163 is not considered here because it is too badly damaged to discern pointing.

[c] In Laud Misc. 243 and Hereford P.v.1, 6b is placed at the end of the *Hymn*.

Even discounting CUL Kk.5.16 as a careless copy, and hence of little use for argument, we have the testimony of Leningrad Q.v.I.18, where the Latin text and Caedmon's *Hymn* are both written by Scribe D. The copy of Caedmon's *Hymn* in the Leningrad manuscript is a very careful and correct record in the same way as the text of the *Historia ecclesiastica* is careful and correct. Yet the pointing of the Latin paraphrase is copious while the pointing of the Old English poem is limited to a purely formal terminal point. The points, so useful in Latin, are missing precisely because they were redundant in Old English, unnecessary either for scansion or sense. In the early copies of the *Hymn*, the omission of pointing, a visual cue for decoding, is a powerful indication of the still strongly oral component in the *Hymn's* transmission and reception.

The records of Caedmon's *Hymn* show that the status of the *Hymn* as text and the degree of fixity of the text depend on the environment of the *Hymn*, whether Latin or Old English. When the *Hymn* travels as a gloss to the *Historia ecclesiastica*, the text is subject to little variation, while those records of the *Hymn* which are integrated in the West-Saxon translation of the *History* show a high degree of freedom in transmission. Examination of the conventions of lineation and punctuation in Latin and Old English poetic texts within the *History* demonstrates a considerable variation in conventions for each language. Lineation and, certainly, pointing for poetry are necessary extralinguistic cues which assist the reader in decoding the Latin text. These conventions are uniformly applied. The Old English *Hymn*, however, is never displayed graphically by metrical line, nor does punctuation distinguish lines or half-lines or act consistently as a marker of grammatical divisions.

The transmission and reception of Caedmon's *Hymn* have several implications for the larger understanding of literacy in Anglo-Saxon England and for our own reading of Anglo-Saxon poetic works. The differing level and nature of extralinguistic cues in Latin and Old English imply that Caedmon's *Hymn* was read with different expectations, conventions, and techniques than those for the Latin verses with which it traveled. Techniques of reading Old English verse which allowed the incorporation of 'formulaic' guesses into the written text represent an accommodation of literacy, with its resistant text, to the fluidity of the oral process of transmission. The evidence suggests that for Caedmon's *Hymn*, at least, an oral poem did not automatically become a fixed text upon writing and that under certain conditions the 'literate' reception of the text had a considerable admixture of oral processes. This demonstrable accommodation of literate to oral in the manuscript records suggests a starting place for future investigation into the features of a transitional state between pure orality and pure literacy in the reception of a poetic text. An investigation of the formatting conventions, pointing, and variants in Old English verse in multiple copies, especially *Solomon and Saturn*, the poems of the *Anglo-Saxon Chronicle*, and the metrical Preface and Epilogue to Alfred's translation of the *Pastoral Care*, should provide further information about the growth of literacy and the development of a text in Anglo-Saxon England.

The Construction of Oxford, Bodleian Library, Junius 11

Barbara C. Raw

In recent years a number of books and articles has appeared in which new and contradictory claims have been made about the compilation of Oxford, Bodleian Library, Junius 11. In view of these contradictions it is necessary to re-examine the manuscript and to set out what information can be gained from it and what can reasonably be inferred from that information.[1]

Argument has centred on three points: the relationship between the defects in gathering 2 and the interpolation of *Genesis B* into *Genesis A*, whether *Daniel* is complete as preserved, and how and when *Christ and Satan* was added to these three Old Testament poems. In addition there have been disagreements about the number of leaves missing from the manuscript and about the date of the binding, which has been attributed to the second quarter of the eleventh century at one extreme and to the third quarter of the fifteenth at the other.[2] But the major difficulty arises from the last gathering of the manuscript, which contains the end of *Daniel* and the whole of *Christ and Satan*. Robert

---

[1] My thanks are due to the staff of the Bodleian Library, and especially to Dr B.C. Barker-Benfield, for their help while I was preparing this article.

[2] A.R. Doane, *Genesis A: a New Edition* (Madison, Wisc., 1978), p. 6, accepts the fifteenth-century date given by F.H. Stoddard, 'The Caedmon Poems in MS Junius 11', *Anglia* 10 (1887), 157-67, at 158, and followed by I. Gollancz, *The Caedmon Manuscript* (Oxford, 1927), p. xxxv, and B.J. Timmer, *The Later Genesis* (Oxford, 1948), p. 3. P.J. Lucas, *Exodus* (London, 1977), p. 4, claims that the binding dates from 1025 x 50. O. Pächt and J.J.G. Alexander, *Illuminated Manuscripts in the Bodleian Library Oxford* III (Oxford, 1973), 5, date the re-sewing and, presumably, the binding to *c.* 1200.

Farrell has argued that *Daniel* is complete as preserved; Ker, Hall and
Lucas, on the other hand, have considered that its ending has been
lost.[3] Hall believed that *Christ and Satan* formed part of the original
plan for the manuscript; Lucas, however, argued that it was a separate,
folded booklet which had later been inserted into the last gathering of
the manuscript, the end of the poem having been copied on to the final
leaf of the original gathering.[4] The argument about the losses from
gathering 2 relates to the position of the remaining two leaves in the
original gathering and the number and nature of the gaps in the text.[5]
The major conclusions of the present article are that the manuscript has
been re-stitched and that the binding dates from the time of the re-
stitching; that the end of *Daniel* has almost certainly been lost; and that
Christ and Satan was not originally a separate manuscript but was

---

[3] R.T. Farrell, *Daniel and Azarias* (London, 1974), pp. 5-6; N.R.
Ker, *Catalogue of Manuscripts Containing Anglo-Saxon* (Oxford,
1957), p. 407; J.R. Hall, 'The Old English Epic of Redemption: the
Theological Unity of MS Junius 11', *Traditio* 32 (1976), 185-208, at
186; and P.J. Lucas, 'On the Incomplete Ending of *Daniel* and the
Addition of *Christ and Satan* to MS Junius 11', *Anglia* 97 (1979), 46-
59, at 52.

[4] Hall, 'Old English Epic of Redemption', p. 208; Lucas,
'Incomplete Ending of *Daniel*', pp. 49 and 57. See also M.D. Clubb,
Christ and Satan (New Haven, Conn., 1925; repr. 1972), pp. xiv-xv,
for evidence that the poem was a separate manuscript, and R.E.
Finnegan, *Christ and Satan* (Waterloo, Ont., 1977), pp. 4, 9 and 10,
for the view that *Christ and Satan* probably formed part of the original
plan for the manuscript.

[5] Gollancz, *Caedmon Manuscript*, pp. l-lii, suggests that the two
remaining leaves were nos. 5 and 7 of the original gathering and that
parts of the gathering were lost at the time the manuscript was written,
perhaps as the result of 'some error of transcription, or some change
of plan'. Timmer, *Later Genesis*, pp. 13-15, like Gollancz, suggests
that some at least of the missing leaves were lost at the time of writing,
probably as the result of the interpolation of *Genesis B* into *Genesis A*,
but he considers the present leaves to be nos. 4 and 6. Doane, *Genesis
A*, pp. 7-10, argues that they were nos. 2 and 6 and that there was a
gap of three folios rather than one at *Genesis*, line 205.

copied partly on vellum prepared in connection with the end of *Daniel*. Evidence will be brought forward about the number of missing folios and the dates at which they were lost and it will be argued that the losses from gathering 2 are not related to the interpolation of *Genesis B*.

Physical Description of the Manuscript

COLLATION

The present manuscript consists of 116 vellum folios paginated 1-229 in a seventeenth-century hand identified by Timmer as that of Francis Junius; the first folio, which contains a full-page drawing on its verso, and 116v are not included in this pagination. The manuscript consists of seventeen gatherings, mostly regular quires of eight. Twenty-seven folios are missing and had already been lost when the pages were numbered in the seventeenth century. The collation is as follows:

1^8 (lacks 1, 2 and 3), 2^2 (1 and 2 are singletons, perhaps the remnants of an original quire of 8), 3^8 (lacks 6 and 7), $4\text{-}6^8$, 7^8 + one leaf after 7 (pp. 87/88), 8^8 (lacks 3), 9^8 (lacks 3 and 5), 10^8 (lacks 1 and 5), 11^8 (lacks 4), 12^8 (lacks 4 and 5), 13^8 (lacks 6), 14^8 (lacks 4 and 8), 15^8 (lacks 2), 16^8, 17^{14} (lacks 2, 5, 9 and 13).

This collation differs from that by Ker in gatherings 8, 14, 15 and 17;[6] evidence will be brought forward to show that leaves have been lost at these points even though there are no gaps in the text.

The manuscript consists of two parts. Part I runs from p. 1 to p. 212 and comprises the whole of gatherings 1-16 together with the first folio of gathering 17. This section of the manuscript was written by one scribe and is elaborately decorated with line-drawings and large initials–some decorated, some plain. It contains three poems: *Genesis*, *Exodus* and *Daniel*. Part II comprises pp. 213-29, that is, fols. 2-10 of gathering 17. It was written by two scribes, of whom the first wrote

---

[6] Cf. Ker, *Catalogue*, pp. 407-8. Ker argues that these leaves were originally singletons, whereas I argue that leaves have been lost.

pp. 213-15 and the second pp. 216-29, and contains one poem, *Christ and Satan*.[7] This part of the manuscript contains no illustrations or spaces for them, though–as will be shown later–it is probable that space was originally provided for illustrations. There is one ornamental initial (p. 226) and there are two designs which have no connection with the text (p. 225 and the verso of p. 229). This second part of the manuscript ends with the words 'Finit Liber II. Amen.' (p. 229); there is no corresponding explicit to Part I as it exists at present.

STITCHING

The most important fact to emerge from re-examination of the manuscript is that it has been completely re-sewn. The present stitching is on three bands, plus head- and tail-bands, at distances of about 70, 165 and 260 mm from the top of each page, with kettle-stitching at about 35 and 290 mm from the top (see fig. 1). Holes from earlier stitching are visible at the centre of all gatherings and on the stubs of all except five of the singletons at distances of approximately 55, 95, 160, 230 and 265 mm from the top of each page; the marks of this earlier stitching can be seen particularly clearly on the stub of pp. 109/110 in gathering 9. The centre of the last gathering, which contains *Christ and Satan*, shows the same two sets of stitch-marks as the rest of the manuscript; it can therefore be inferred that *Christ and Satan* had already been added to the rest of the manuscript by the time it was first sewn and that if this text had an earlier, independent existence, as Lucas has claimed, it was used unstitched.

The manuscript now contains twenty singletons (see Appendix I). One of these (pp. 87/88) was probably always a single leaf. Gathering 7, in which it occurs, already contains the normal four bifolia; moreover, the single leaf, which has full-page illustrations on both

---

[7] It is usually claimed that p. 229 was written by a third scribe. This hand is very close to that of pp. 216-28–the main difference is that the *y* is not dotted–and the late Francis Wormald believed that the hands were the same (private communication). The identity of the hands is not crucial to my argument that *Christ and Satan* was not originally a separate manuscript.

Original stitch-marks	Present stitching	Slots in front cover	Slots in back cover
	35 mm		
55 mm	kettle-stitching	62 mm	63 mm
	70 mm		
95 mm			
160 mm	165 mm	158 mm	163 mm
230 mm			
		258 mm	
	260 mm		262 mm
265 mm			
	290 mm		
	kettle-stitching		

Fig. 1   The location of the stitching-holes in folios of Junius 11 (measurements are given from the top of the folios; not-to-scale).

sides, has never been ruled and there is no evidence such as stitch-marks on the stub to indicate the existence of an earlier conjugate leaf. Of the other nineteen singletons, four (nos. 2-4 and 9 in Appendix I) have no stubs, the missing leaves having been cut out close to the present stitch-line. The remaining fifteen have traces of earlier stitch-marks on their stubs, implying that an earlier conjugate leaf has been lost at each of these points, even though in five cases there is no gap in the text (nos. 10 and 17-20 in Appendix I). These five leaves must have been intended for pairs of full-page illustrations, and as two of them occurred in the text of *Christ and Satan*, illustrations must have been planned for this poem.

The position of the stitch-marks on the stubs of the singletons shows that the missing leaves were cut out deep in the gutter of the manuscript, either on the original stitch-line or close to it. When the resulting singletons were re-sewn they were moved further into the manuscript in order to provide a stub through which the new stitching could pass. In consequence, these leaves are either narrower than the adjacent leaves or, if they are the same width, their outer margin is wider. Those leaves where the outer margin is wider than that on the adjacent leaves represent the remaining halves of bifolia of which the missing halves were lost before the manuscript was re-sewn and trimmed to its present size. Single leaves where the outer margin is the same width as on the adjacent pages but the pages themselves are narrower represent the remaining halves of bifolia of which the other halves were lost after the manuscript was re-sewn and trimmed to its present size.

The three folios missing from the beginning of gathering 1 were cut out close to the present stitch-line: there are no stubs, and the leaves have not been moved inwards as would have been the case had the leaves been lost before the manuscript was re-sewn. These three leaves, therefore, were lost after the re-sewing. The leaves missing from gatherings 2 and 3 were likewise lost after the manuscript had been re-sewn, but in this case the single leaves have been re-sewn independently of the main stitching of the manuscript.

Gathering 2 (pp. 9-12) now consists of two singletons, both cut on the original stitch-line and re-stitched further in, the edges overlapping and strengthened by a binding strip carrying pen-trials in a hand of the late thirteenth century or the early fourteenth.[8] Two pieces of evidence indicate that the repair to this gathering did not form part of the general re-stitching of the manuscript. First, the outer edges of the two singletons are not level with those of the rest of the manuscript and were not trimmed in the same operation; secondly, the two leaves and their binding strip are not attached to the head- and tail-bands but merely to the top kettle-stitching and the second and third of the three main bands. The only holes in the binding strip are those corresponding to the present stitching and there are no indications that it was ever attached to the top band or to the lower kettle-stitching. The leaves which were originally attached to the present singletons must, therefore, have been lost after the manuscript had been re-sewn. The two remaining leaves come from different bifolia and are usually thought to be from different halves of the gathering, with a gap between them. The second leaf certainly belongs to the second half of the gathering because it is ruled on the verso and has not been re-ruled; the rulings are not particularly distinct, so it is unlikely to be the outer leaf. The first leaf, pp. 9/10, is ruled on the recto, suggesting a position in the first half of the gathering. This looks like a re-ruling, however, particularly since the margins are marked by a single vertical line whereas on all other pages up to p. 95 the margins are indicated by double vertical lines. The top outer corner of each of the two leaves was cut away at some time before the pages were numbered in the seventeenth century; this cutting was done independently of the trimming of the manuscript for binding, and careful comparison of the indentations on the edges shows that the two leaves were cut simultaneously. It seems likely, therefore, that the leaves were adjacent and that both belonged to the second half of the gathering. There is no obvious gap in the text at line 205 to argue against this being the case: the text on p. 10 ends part-way across a line, showing that the account of God's blessing of man (Genesis I.28-30) was thought to be complete even though some of the biblical details are

---

[8] The texts are fairly well known: 'Amen dico vobis quoniam super omnia bona sua constituet eum' (Matthew XXIV.47); 'Domine Dominus noster quam admirabile est nomen tuum in universa terra' (Psalm VIII.2); 'Confitemini Domino quoniam bonus quoniam in saeculum misericordia eius' (Psalm CVI.1); and 'Sciant presentes et futuri' (a formula frequently found at the beginning of charters).

omitted, and p. 11 continues with a paraphrase of Genesis I.31, describing God surveying his work.

Gathering 3 (pp. 13-24) consists of two bifolia, pp. 13/14-23/24 and 19/20-21/22, and two singletons, pp. 15/16 and 17/18 (see fig. 2). There is a gap in the text between pp. 22 and 23 (at *Genesis* 441) but the stubs of pp. 15/16 and 17/18 appear before pp. 19/20 and not after pp. 21/22 as one would expect. The missing pages were cut along the original stitch-line and marks of cutting are visible near the top of the gutter between pp. 20 and 21. This gathering, quite exceptionally, has two sets of stitching. The first is at the centre of the gathering, between pp. 20 and 21, and is at the normal five points; the second holds the two singletons to the head- and tail-bands and to the second and third of the three main bands; there are no stitches or holes corresponding to the kettle-stitching or the upper of the three main bands, but there is an extra stitch about 7 mm from the bottom of the leaves and there is a similar extra stitch at pp. 20-1. The fact that the main stitching does not pass through the stubs of the single leaves implies that the missing leaves were cut out and the resulting single leaves re-attached after the main stitching of the manuscript was done. This is confirmed by the fact that the outer margins of the two single leaves are the same width as those of the other leaves in the gathering and the leaves themselves are narrower, showing that they were moved inwards after the manuscript had been trimmed to its present size.

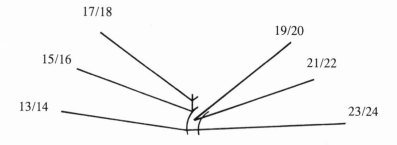

Fig. 2 The construction of gathering 3 of Junius 11

Evidence from these two gatherings provides a *terminus ante quem* for the re-stitching of the manuscript. As was said above, the binding strip in gathering 2 contains texts written in a hand of the late thirteenth or early fourteenth century. The repair involving this binding strip was made after the manuscript as a whole had been re-sewn; the re-stitching must therefore date from before c. 1300. The evidence also shows that Gollancz's suggestion that gathering 2 'when bound already consisted for the most part, if not wholly, of separated leaves' cannot be true.[9] It is clear from the position of the original stitch-marks on pp. 9-12 and from the re-sewing that the bifolia to which these two leaves belonged were complete not only when the manuscript was first sewn but at the time of the re-sewing. It is not possible to say with any certainty when the other two bifolia were lost from the gathering, although the looseness of the spine at this point suggests that they too were lost after the re-sewing of the manuscript. If this is so, the gathering was still complete at the time of the re-stitching.

Analysis of the structure and contents of the gathering shows that they give no support to Gollancz's suggestion, further developed by Timmer, that *Genesis B* was first added to *Genesis A* in the present manuscript.[10] If it is accepted that the two leaves which remain from gathering 2 came from the second half of the gathering and were adjacent, the gathering can be reconstructed in one of two ways (see fig. 3). Gathering 1 (pp. 1-8) contains an account of the creation up to the appearance of dry land, based on Genesis I.1-10 (*Genesis A* 112-68). The text on pp. 9/10 (*Genesis A* 169-205) describes the creation of Eve. It is based on the second of the two biblical accounts of the creation (Genesis II.18 and 21-3), but it is clear that this has been conflated with the earlier account (Genesis I.26-7), because the text continues with a paraphrase of the blessing of Adam and Eve, based on Genesis I.28-30. The leaves missing from the beginning of gathering 2, between pp. 8 and 9, must therefore have contained material dealing with the rest of the creation story up to and including the creation of Adam (Genesis I.11-27 and possibly II.7). The poem called *Genesis B* begins on the first page of gathering 3 (p. 13), with a reference to the prohibition. This is based on Genesis II.16-17 but with the

---

[9] Gollancz, *Caedmon Manuscript*, p. lii.

[10] *Ibid.* p. liii, and Timmer, *Later Genesis*, pp. 14-15.

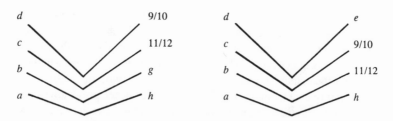

Fig. 3 Alternative reconstructions of gathering 2 of Junius 11

important difference that the prohibition is made to both Adam and
Eve, not to Adam alone as in the bible. In the original version of the
poem (in Old Saxon) these lines must have been preceded by some
account of the creation of Adam and Eve and of the garden; the poem
could also have included the rest of the creation material from Genesis
I and II. There is no direct evidence on how much of this material was
copied into Junius 11, but it is likely that the amount was slight: at
most four manuscript pages of text and probably much less. On the
other hand there must have been something to link the description of
the four rivers (p. 12) to the incomplete opening of *Genesis B* (p. 13).
It is inconceivable that the scribe should have begun the interpolation
in mid-speech, as Gollancz implies. In view of the small amount of
text needed to fill this gap, the second of my suggested reconstructions
(fig. 3) is the more likely, with the arrangement of the biblical material
as set out in Appendix II below, p. 275.

If one accepts Gollancz's (and Timmer's) argument that pages were
cut out in order to avoid duplication of material, one must conclude that
the lines from the Old Saxon *Genesis* which were used in Junius 11 did
not include the creation of Eve, since this is preserved in the *Genesis
A* version on pp. 9/10; nor did they include the creation of Adam,
which must precede that of Eve. The only material which could have
filled the gap between pp. 12 and 13 is a reference to the introduction
of Adam into the garden of Eden (Genesis II.8 and 15) and possibly
some reference to the two trees (Genesis II.9), which are not mentioned
at the appropriate point on p. 12. None of this material could have
overlapped with the contents of the leaves now missing from the
beginning of gathering 2. The fragmentary state of gathering 2,
therefore, cannot be used as evidence that *Genesis B* was first combined
with *Genesis A* in Junius 11.

The losses discussed so far–those from gatherings 1-3–occurred after the manuscript had been re-sewn. By contrast, eleven of the twelve singletons missing from gatherings 8-17 were lost at an earlier stage. Marks of earlier stitching on the stubs of these eleven leaves show that they have all been moved inwards from their original position; in addition, the outer margin of all except the two singletons in gathering 17 (see fig. 4) is about 5 mm wider than that of the adjacent leaves, showing that they were moved before the manuscript was trimmed to its present size.[11] The twelfth leaf missing from this part of the manuscript, namely the folio missing after p. 180 in gathering 14, was cut out close to the present stitch-line and was therefore lost after the manuscript had been re-sewn.

Evidence that singletons have been lost is supplied by the presence of marks of earlier stitching on the stubs of the remaining leaves. Evidence for the loss of complete bifolia comes from gaps in the text. Gaps in the text at *Genesis* 168 and 234 indicate that folios are missing from the beginning and end of gathering 2. Since the present gathering consists of the remains of two bifolia it is likely that two complete bifolia are missing. A bifolium is also missing from the centre of gathering 12, between pp. 148 and 149, because there is a gap in the text at *Exodus* 141. The only other place where a bifolium may have been lost is in gathering 17, after pp. 211/212 (see fig. 4). There is no conclusive textual evidence that part of *Daniel* has been lost, but there is a cut on the original stitch-line of pp. 211/212 (these pages were moved sideways when the manuscript was re-sewn) and this implies that a leaf was cut out at this point while the original stitching was in place. The addition of a bifolium between pp. 212 and 213 would restore the normal hair-to-hair and flesh-to-flesh (HFFH) arrangement of the pages, whereas at present a flesh side (p. 212) faces a hair side (p. 213). Further evidence for the loss of a bifolium at this point comes from the note in a twelfth-century hand on p. 212: 'en rex venit mansuetus tibi sion filia'. The note is smudged but there is no offset on the opposite page as one might expect; presumably the offset was to be found on a page of the (now lost) bifolium.

---

[11] The width of the margins in gathering 17 varies a good deal, and it is not possible to say with any certainty whether the margins of pp. 217/218 and 223/224 are wider than those on the adjacent pages or not.

The evidence from the stitching leads to several important conclusions. First, it is possible to date most of the losses from the manuscript, at least within broad limits. The leaves missing from gatherings 8-17, with the exception of the folio lost after p. 180, must have been lost at an early stage because they were cut out before the manuscript was re-sewn; the re-sewing in turn predates the late-thirteenth- or early-fourteenth-century repair to gatherings 2 and 3; the leaves missing from gatherings 1-3 on the other hand were lost after the re-sewing but, at least in the case of the massive losses from gatherings 2 and 3, before *c.* 1275 x 1325 (s. xiii/xiv), the approximate date of the repair. The division between these two groups of losses parallels exactly the division between the illustrated and unillustrated parts of the manuscript, a point which will be taken up later. Evidence that the two leaves which survive from gathering 2 both came from the second half of the gathering and were still bifolia when the manuscript was re-sewn, together with evidence from the contents of these leaves, indicates that the arguments used by Gollancz and Timmer to support their view that *Genesis B* was first added to *Genesis A* in the present manuscript cannot be sustained. Evidence that a leaf is missing between pp. 212 and 213 supports the view of Ker, Hall and Lucas that

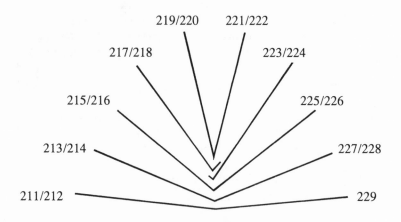

Fig. 4 The construction of gathering 17 of Junius 11

the end of *Daniel* has been lost. Finally, the fact that *Christ and Satan* was included in the manuscript as originally sewn and that it has not been sewn independently suggests very strongly that it was not originally a separate manuscript (as Lucas has argued). Evidence that space was provided for at least four and probably six full-page illustrations in this poem shows that it was intended to resemble the other poems in the manuscript in decorative appearance; this too supports the view that it was copied into the manuscript as a continuation of the three Old Testament poems rather than being bound in after a separate existence. Further evidence on this point will be brought forward later.

BINDING

The fact that the manuscript has been re-sewn means that it cannot be in its original binding. In the first place, the leaves of the manuscript were originally at least 5 mm wider than they are at present; this is shown by the fact that the outer margins of some of the singletons are 5 mm wider than those of the adjacent leaves and also by the fact that parts of the marginal inscriptions on pp. 3 and 6 have been lost. The edges of the boards are flush with the edges of the leaves and would therefore have been too narrow for the original manuscript. In the second place, the slots through which the manuscript is attached to the boards correspond to the present stitching and could not have been used for the original stitching (see fig. 1). There are no other slots in the boards, so they must have been prepared for the present stitching of the manuscript. The re-stitching of the manuscript has been shown to predate the repair to gathering 2, which, in turn, can be dated to the late thirteenth century or the early fourteenth. For a more precise date it is necessary to consider the style of the binding.

The binding is of oak boards covered in whittawed leather; the spine has been repaired with a strip of brown calf-skin inserted under the original leather. There is no record of when the repair was made, but it probably dates from between 1950 and 1965. The boards measure approximately 195 x 320 mm and have bevelled edges which are flush with the leaves of the book. The book is attached to the boards by three thongs plus head- and tail-bands of thong, oversewn in green and beige silk. The head- and tail-bands were sewn in the same operation as the three main bands. The thongs pass through tunnels about 5 mm long in the thickness of the boards to grooves about 23 mm long on the outside of the boards, and then through slots to the inside, where they are fixed by wooden pegs. The slots, together with their pegs, are visible on the inside of both covers, 28 mm from the edge and about 62, 158 and 258 mm from the top of the boards, and the outer grooves can be felt through the leather of the front cover; those at the back cannot be felt because of the modern repair. The head- and tail-bands are attached to the boards through tunnels in the thickness of the boards, or possibly through grooves on the outside of the boards, emerging on the inside of the boards through small circular holes; the head- and tail-bands are broken at both back and front and the cord used for stitching the book to the tail-band has been taken through the tunnel at the bottom of the front board and knotted on the inside. The mitres at the corners of the skin covering the boards are cut with a central tongue (Pollard's 'third mitres') and the skin is pasted to the boards.[12] The spine of the manuscript has five ridges, but it seems likely that before the modern repair the spine was flat. There are no tabs, and no trace of the title which M.R. James said was written in fourteenth-century capitals on the back of the book.[13] The inside of the back cover shows an offset from a paste-down, now lost; the text (parts of Matthew III.11 and Luke III.21-3) is from a gospel harmony written in an Anglo-Caroline hand dated by Ker to the eleventh century; traces of writing are visible on the turn-over of the binding leather as well as on the board.[14]

The book was fastened by three straps which passed from the front cover to pins on the back cover of the manuscript. The outer straps and pins have disappeared but the grooves for the straps are visible on the outer surface of the front board, about 10 mm wide and about 70

---

[12] For the term 'third mitres', see Graham Pollard, 'Describing Medieval Bookbindings', *Medieval Learning and Literature: Essays presented to R.W. Hunt*, ed. J.J.G. Alexander and M.T. Gibson (Oxford, 1976), pp. 50-65, at 59.

[13] M.R. James, *The Ancient Libraries of Canterbury and Dover* (Cambridge, 1903), p. xxv.

[14] Timmer, *Later Genesis*, p. 3, and Ker, *Catalogue*, p. 408. The strip of vellum which projects between pp. 210 and 211 may be the remains of this paste-down; there is a similar, though narrower, fragment of vellum at the back of gathering 1.

and 245 mm from the top of the board, and there are two holes in the back cover where the pins were fixed, 85-87 mm from the edge and 72 mm from top and bottom.   The pin for the central strap is still preserved, projecting 8 mm from the centre of the back cover, and there are remains of the strap at the centre of the front cover, fixed in a groove about 25 mm wide.   There is a scar inside the front board at the centre of the upper edge, suggesting that the book may at one time have been chained.

This binding must date from the period 1100 x 1250.   The arrangement of three bands carried straight across the boards with head- and tail-bands threaded at 45° to the corners is typical of twelfth-century bindings.   The way in which the bands are laced to the boards is quite different from that of any of the Anglo-Saxon bindings described by Pollard: in particular, there is no sign of the triangular grooves which were typical of bindings before about 1100.[15]   On the other hand, the bands are still threaded through tunnels in the thickness of the boards, whereas after about 1230 the bands were normally carried round the outer edge of the board and along grooves in its outer surface.   Two details suggest a date in the later part of the period.   The boards have a sharp bevel on the edges, a feature more typical of the late twelfth century than of the earlier period, when boards were usually cut square.   In addition, the leather covering is pasted to the boards and there is no indication that the mitres were stitched as they were on many twelfth-century bindings.

The fastenings of the manuscript may not all be of the same date.   The grooves for the three straps are not all of the same width.   Moreover, while there are numerous illustrations in twelfth-century manuscripts of books fastened with one strap, and in thirteenth-century manuscripts of books fastened with two, there seem to be no examples of three straps.   The pin which projects from the back cover suggests that the manuscript was stored flat, resting on its front cover, a point which is confirmed by the absence of tabs (designed for pulling books

---

[15] Pollard, 'Bookbindings', pp. 54-6; the Junius 11 binding is closest to Pollard's fig. 3 on p. 57.   In view of Lucas's claim that the binding is Anglo-Saxon it should perhaps be pointed out that Pollard did not include Junius 11 in his study 'Some Anglo-Saxon Bookbindings', *Book Collector* 24 (1975), 130-59.

out of chests) and by the position of the chain-mark. Books chained at
the top of the cover were kept on lecterns, usually with a bar running
across the top, whereas books chained in presses like those at Hereford
or in the Bodleian Library had the chain fixed to the front edge of the
cover.[16]

Stylistic and technical evidence therefore suggests that the present
binding dates from the early thirteenth century, not, as has previously
been argued, from the fifteenth century or from the Anglo-Saxon
period. The early loss of eleven singletons and probably also of some
bifolia from the manuscript explains why it was necessary to rebind it.
What is puzzling, however, is that it was necessary to cut new boards,
for the normal practice seems to have been to turn the old boards round
and recut them, as was done in the case of four out of the fifteen
Anglo-Saxon bindings described by Pollard.[17] One can only speculate
on the reason for the new boards in the case of Junius 11. Perhaps the
old boards were too damaged to be re-used, or possibly the manuscript
was bound originally in limp covers (*in pargameno*) instead of in
boards (*in asseribus*) as was the case with many of the manuscripts
listed in the fragmentary late-twelfth-century catalogue of Christ
Church, Canterbury.[18]

PRICKING AND RULING

Throughout most of the manuscript, pages are pricked in both margins,
although the outer row of prickings was lost in many cases when the
manuscript was trimmed. The position of the prickings shows that they
were made a gathering at a time with the pages already folded. Ruling
was done with a dry point, a gathering at a time, on the outside of each
gathering; the pages were not re-arranged after ruling. Gatherings 1-7

---

[16] The Hereford library is illustrated in B. H. Streeter, *The Chained
Library* (London, 1931), p. 59. For the different positions of the
chaining mechanism, see N. Ker, 'Chaining from a Staple on the Back
Cover', *Bodleian Lib. Record* 3 (1950-1), 104-7.

[17] Oxford, Bodleian Library, MS. Auct. F.1.15 and MS. Bodley
97; London, British Library, MSS. Add. 37517 and 34890, nos. 4, 7,
8 and 9 in Pollard, 'Anglo-Saxon Bookbindings', pp. 144-5 and 148-
51.

[18] James, *Ancient Libraries*, pp. 7-12.

(pp. 1-90) were ruled with the sheets flat, and the rulings therefore appear on the outside of each sheet, that is, on the recto of folios in the first half of the gathering and on the verso of those in the second half. Gatherings 9-16 (pp. 105-210), on the other hand, have the rulings on the recto of each folio; the marks suggest that each of these gatherings was ruled as a single folded pile, some of the later folios in each gathering being re-ruled later. Pages were ruled with twenty-six lines on an area approximately 120 mm wide; margins are normally indicated by pairs of vertical bounding-lines, except for pp. 95/96-211/212 which have single bounding-lines. The position for the vertical rulings is marked by pairs of prickings about 10 mm apart.

There are numerous exceptions to this general pattern. Gathering 4 (pp. 25-40) is pricked for twenty-eight lines though only twenty-six are ruled. In gatherings 9, 10, 14 and 15 (pp. 105-28 and 169-94), the position for the vertical rulings is marked by various arrangements of two, three or four prickings, instead of the normal pairs. Gathering 8 (pp. 91-104) is ruled with double vertical bounding-lines up to p. 94 and with single lines thereafter; it cannot, therefore, have been ruled in a single operation. The main exceptions, however, occur in the last gathering of the manuscript (pp. 211-29).

Superficially, the inner part of this gathering (pp. 213-28) is very different from the outer bifolium (pp. 211/212 and 229) (see fig. 4). The first folio in the gathering (pp. 211/212) is ruled with twenty-six lines, although it is pricked for twenty-seven; the other folios are ruled with twenty-seven lines. The outer bifolium, pp. 211/212 and 229, has a writing-area approximately 120 mm wide like the rest of the manuscript; the writing-area in the central part of the gathering is about 140 mm wide. The first folio has single vertical bounding-lines; the rest of the gathering has double ones. In addition, pp. 213-29 are not written by the scribe of the main part of the manuscript, whereas the first folio of the gathering is. These differences, together with evidence that the inner part of the gathering has been folded horizontally, have led Lucas to suggest that the central part of this final gathering was originally a separate, folded booklet, subsequently bound into the last gathering of the main manuscript, during which process part of it was lost.[19] Careful examination of the gathering shows that

---

[19] Lucas, 'Incomplete Ending of *Daniel*', pp. 49 and 57.

the situation is more complex than Lucas suspected.

Although the outer bifolium appears at first sight to be quite different from the rest of the gathering, evidence from the pricking and ruling shows that the real division is between the outer three bifolia (pp. 211-16 and 225-9) and the inner sheets (pp. 217-24). The three outer bifolia were pricked in both margins like those in the rest of the manuscript; the central bifolium (pp. 219-22), on the other hand, is pricked in the outer margins only. The two singletons (pp. 217/218 and 223/224) were probably pricked in the outer margins only, but it is not possible to be absolutely certain of this because both leaves were moved inwards when the manuscript was re-stitched and it is possible that prickings in the inner margins are hidden in the gutter of the manuscript. The prickings for the vertical rulings show that pp. 213-16 and 225-8 were intended to have a narrower writing-area than that now covered by writing. The prickings on pp. 213/214 and on the conjugate pp. 227/228 define a writing-area of 112-120 mm like that on the outer bifolium; pp. 215/216 likewise have prickings at the inner edge of the bottom margin which are independent of the present vertical ruling; in all cases these prick-holes correspond exactly to the prick-holes on the outer bifolium of the gathering. By contrast, the inner leaves of the gathering (pp. 217/218 and 219-22), which are also pricked for a narrower writing-area than was actually used, have their prickings in a quite different position: the holes at the bottom of pp. 217/218 are 48 and 55 mm from the gutter and those on pp. 219-22 are 40 and 45 mm from the gutter; those on the outer three bifolia, on the other hand, are 21 and 30 mm from the original gutter. Finally, the angle of the outer row of prickings for the horizontal rulings on pp. 227/228 is identical with that of the prickings on p. 229. It seems certain, therefore, that the three outer bifolia of gathering 17 were pricked simultaneously and formed part of the original gathering prepared for the end of *Daniel*, whereas the inner leaves (pp.217-222) did not. There is no evidence to indicate whether the single leaf (pp. 223/224) belonged to the original gathering or not, but the likelihood is that it did not. If, as was suggested earlier, a bifolium has been lost after pp. 211/212, only three other bifolia would originally have been needed to make up a normal gathering, namely the present pp. 211-16 and 225-9.

The evidence of the ruling, like that of the prickings, links pp. 213/214 with the outer bifolium of the gathering. If pp. 213-28 were originally a separate manuscript, as has been suggested by Lucas, one would expect to find evidence that they were pricked and ruled together. In particular one would expect to find the primary ruling for the gathering on p. 213, the outer sheet of the supposed separate manuscript. In fact the rulings on p. 213 are barely visible apart from the bottom line and the two vertical bounding-lines marking the outer margin, which are quite sharp. It is clear therefore that p. 213 was ruled originally with only twenty-six lines, the twenty-seventh line and the vertical bounding-lines for the outer margin being added later, and that at the time when it was originally ruled it was not the outer page of a gathering. The top twenty-six lines on p. 213 are in fact exactly level with the corresponding lines on p. 212, suggesting that the two pages were ruled together and confirming the evidence brought forward earlier that they were pricked together. The ruling of the inner leaves of the gathering, like their pricking, distinguishes them from the outer part of the gathering. The vertical rulings on the first of the two singletons (pp. 217/218) are completely out of alignment with those elsewhere in the gathering, resulting in an outer margin which is only 32 mm wide at the bottom and 45 mm wide at the top. The central bifolium of the gathering (pp. 219-22) also differs strikingly from the rest of the gathering: the lines on the two central pages (pp. 220-1) are not opposite each other and the writing-area of p. 220 measures 5-6 mm less vertically than that on the opposite page or in the rest of the manuscript. It is clear that these pages cannot have been ruled at the same time as the outer three bifolia of the gathering.

If, as seems certain, the outer three bifolia of the last gathering were prepared in connection with the end of *Daniel*, whereas the inner singletons and bifolium were inserted when *Christ and Satan* was added to the manuscript, some explanation is necessary for the crease, which affects the added portion together with two of the three original bifolia. The crease is in precisely the same position on all leaves. It lies exactly half-way down the page and is much looser at the edges of the leaves than it is near the spine, showing that it was made from the spine outwards. The outer two bifolia in the gathering were moved sideways when the manuscript was re-sewn and the original stitch-line on these sheets is now about 5 mm to the left of the stitching. The tightest part of the crease lies across this area, showing that the crease was made after these sheets had slipped sideways. The crease must therefore date from the time of the re-sewing of the manuscript. Why this part of the manuscript should have been folded remains a mystery. There can be no doubt, however, that *Christ and Satan* was written partly on vellum prepared for the last gathering of *Daniel*: the evidence from the pricking and ruling demonstrates this quite conclusively and confirms what had already been suggested by the collation. The seemingly attractive suggestion that it was an independent manuscript of the folded booklet type must therefore be rejected.

The Production and History of the Manuscript

Evidence has been brought forward earlier in this article on four specific points: the extent and date of the losses from the manuscript, the interpolation of *Genesis B* into *Genesis A*, the date of the binding, and the addition of *Christ and Satan*. Examination of the manuscript also allows one to make some more general inferences about its production, appearance and history.

The original plan included only the Old Testament poems. Seventeen gatherings of eight folios were prepared for this purpose, and provision was made for extensive illustration. The manuscript ended on the second folio of gathering 17, the other six folios being left blank. One notable point about the manuscript was the large number of full-page illustrations or of spaces allocated for them: fourteen still remain in *Genesis*, seven in *Exodus* and three in *Daniel*, and the new evidence from the collation shows that the number of spaces left for full-page illustrations must have been even greater. This is of particular interest for three reasons. First, the provision of space for two pictures between pp. 94 and 95 would relieve an exceptionally long stretch of unbroken text, extending from p. 89 to p. 96. Secondly, the two pairs of picture-spaces in *Daniel* (p. 174-5 and 182-3) would bring the allowance in the earlier part of the poem nearer to that at the end where there are three full-page spaces. Thirdly, the provision of six spaces for illustrations in *Christ and Satan* means that this text must have been intended to match the earlier poems in the manuscript in appearance.

As often happened, the blank pages at the end of the manuscript were used for rough sketches. The design on p. 225 was certainly present before the text of *Christ and Satan* was copied, because the double line marking the bottom of the text was ruled above the sketch instead of at the bottom of the page and the outer edge of the text itself curves inwards towards the drawing. The style of this drawing (a repeating design of acanthus rosettes and Ringerike) and of that on the verso of p. 229 (consisting of two oval Ringerike patterns) shows that they must be roughly contemporary with the original drawings in the earlier part of the manuscript. Their position in the gathering, especially that of the first at the centre of the original gathering, shows that at the time they were done there was no intention of continuing the text after the end of *Daniel*. *Christ and Satan* was an afterthought, therefore, but a fairly early afterthought, as is shown not only by its script but by the fact that it was added before the manuscript as a whole had been sewn. The evidence from the pricking and ruling reveals that space was made for the poem by adding three bifolia to the centre of gathering 17, making a final gathering of fourteen folios. It is not unusual for the last gathering of a manuscript to be longer than the others. A gathering of fourteen is rather exceptional, but there are parallels from the Anglo-Saxon period: London, British Library, MS. Cotton Nero A.i (s. xi[1]) includes three gatherings of fourteen.[20] Still, one might have expected the material to have been accommodated in two gatherings, one of eight and one of six. The drawings on the last page of the gathering may provide an explanation of why this was not done. If *Christ and Satan* had been copied on to two gatherings these drawings would have come in the centre of the poem, after eight and a half of the present sixteen pages of text, and this would have interfered with the sequence of text and pictures which was necessary to make the addition match the earlier part of the manuscript. As it is, the scribes seem to have had problems in fitting the text into the available space. As a first measure the ruling was touched up on the original sheets to give a wider writing-area and the added sheets were ruled to a similar width. In addition, the second of the two scribes started to compress his writing half-way down p. 227, reverting to a more normal spacing half-way down p. 228, presumably when it became clear that it would be necessary to continue on p. 229.

Once *Christ and Satan* had been added the manuscript was sewn and probably also bound. How it was used is not known, but it was still being read up to the end of the twelfth century. There are two marginal notes in hands of the twelfth century (on pp. 212 and 219)

---

[20] Ker, *Catalogue*, no. 164.

and, more importantly, two twelfth-century drawings. The first of these (p. 31) is not related to the text but that on p. 96 shows the messenger telling Abraham about the capture of Lot, an incident described on p. 94 of the manuscript (*Genesis A* 2018-23). The drawing dates from the second half of the twelfth century and shows that the text was still considered to be of interest at this date.

By the thirteenth century Old English texts and books written in Insular script were less valued. A Glastonbury catalogue dating from 1247-8 describes several books written in Old English as 'old and useless', and the writer of a book-list of 1327 from Exeter states that he has not set a price on many old books in French, English and Latin because they were considered to be valueless.[21] There is no evidence that Junius 11 was being read in the thirteenth century: in fact all the evidence is against it, for six of the single leaves cut out before the manuscript was re-stitched contained sections of text. Moreover, the extraordinarily dirty and crumpled state of the last gathering suggests that the manuscript was seriously ill-treated at this time. Nevertheless it was considered worth rebinding, even though it was a vernacular text and even though the binding was done in a fairly crude way. This fact, together with the close correlation between the early losses and the unillustrated part of the book, suggests that it was valued primarily for its pictures. It may have been the loss of some of these pictures from gatherings 2 and 3 at an early date after the rebinding that prompted the owners to chain the book. As was said above, the chain-mark is at the centre of the top edge of the front cover, showing that the manuscript was displayed on a lectern. It is possible that the work belonged to an institution whose library was arranged on a lectern system similar to that at Zutphen,[22] a point which could ultimately be of importance in determining its provenance. Alternatively, the book could have been chained in the church, like two psalters at Reading, or in the cloister, like the books chained on desks outside the chapter-house at Cîteaux in the fifteenth century.[23] In this case it would almost certainly not have

---

[21] *Ibid.* pp. xlvi-xlvii.

[22] Streeter, *Chained Library*, pp. 9-12.

[23] F. Wormald, 'The Monastic Library', F. Wormald and C.E. Wright, *The English Library before 1700* (London, 1958), pp. 15-31, at 17, and J.W. Clark, *The Care of Books* (Cambridge, 1901), p. 105.

been included in the main library collection and one would not expect it to contain any shelf-marks.[24]

Conclusions

Many questions about the sources, place of origin and history of Junius 11 still need to be answered. The evidence of codicology has, however, settled two long-standing arguments conclusively. It has been shown that the binding is not Anglo-Saxon as has recently been claimed by Lucas; nor does it belong, as is more usually claimed, to the fifteenth century. It can now confidently be assigned on technical and stylistic evidence to the early thirteenth century. Secondly, it is clear that the suggestion put forward at intervals since 1925 that *Christ and Satan* was an independent manuscript bound in with the other poems after a separate existence cannot be correct. It was an addition to the original plan, but an addition copied for the most part on vellum already prepared for the last gathering of the original manuscript.

---

[24] Wormald, 'Monastic Library', p. 17.

APPENDIX I

List of Missing Leaves

Gathering Pages		Position of lost leaf	Text reference	Comments
1. Single leaves (20)				
a. Probably always a single leaf (1)				
(1) 7	87/88	74-5	*Gen 1520*	*no gap in text;* no earlier stitch-marks on stub; leaf not ruled
b. Lost after the manuscript was re-sewn (8)				
(2) 1	3/4 ⎫	before	-	no stubs; missing folios cut out on
(3)	5/6 ⎬	frontispiece		present stitch-line
(4)	7/8 ⎭			
(5) 2	9/10 ⎫	see above	*Gen 168-235*	margins of normal width; leaves
(6)	11/12 ⎭	discussion,		narrower and held together by binding
		pp. 262-5		strip; position in gathering not clear
(7) 3	15/16 ⎫	22-3	*Gen 441*	stubs now at pp. 18-19; leaves re-sewn;
(8)	17/18 ⎭			margins normal width; leaves narrower
(9) 14	169/170	180-1	*Dan 177*	no stub; missing folio cut out on present stitch-line
c. Lost before the manuscript was re-sewn (11)				
(10) 8	99/100	94-5	*Gen 2045*	*no gap in text;* margin wider; leaf same in width as others
(11) 9	109/110	110-11	*Gen 2418* ⎫	
(12)	111/112	108-9	*Gen 2381* ⎪	
(13) 10	121/122	122-3	*Gen 2599* ⎬	gap in text; margins wider; leaves same
(14)	127/128	116-17	*Gen 2512* ⎪	in width as others
(15) 11	135/136	134-5	*Gen 2806* ⎭	
(16) 13	159/160	164-5	*Ex 446*	*no apparent gap in text*; margins wider; leaf same in width as others; probably the whole of section xlviii lost
(17) 14	175/176	174-5	*Dan 70* ⎱	*no gap in text;* margins wider; leaves
(18) 15	191/192	182-3	*Dan 208* ⎰	same in width as others
(19) 17	217/218	222-3	*C & S 430* ⎱	*no gap in text;* leaves same in width as
(20)	223/224	216-17	*C & S 171* ⎰	others; width of margins in this gathering varies considerably
2. Bifolia (4)				
(21) 2 (2)		9-13 exact	*Gen 168*	see discussion above, pp. 262-5
(22)		position not	234	
		clear		
(23) 12		148-9	*Ex 141*	gap in text
(24) 17		212-13	*Dan 764*	*no obvious gap in text*
		228-9	*C & S 709*	*no gap in text*

APPENDIX II

Suggested Arrangement of the Biblical Story in the First Two Gatherings of Junius 11

Gathering 1,	pp. 1-8	Genesis I.1-10	= *Genesis A* 112-68

Gathering 2, *a-e* Genesis I.11-27 (possibly expanded by II.7)

pp. 9/10 Genesis II.18 and 21-3
(expanding Genesis I.27) ⎫
Genesis 1.28-30 ⎭ = *Genesis A* 169-205

pp. 11/12 Genesis 1.31
Genesis II.5-6 and 10-14 ⎫ = *Genesis A* 206-34
h Genesis II.8-9 and 15 ⎭

Gathering 3, p. 13 Genesis II.16-17 = *Genesis B* 235-6

The Eleventh-Century Origin of *Beowulf* and the *Beowulf* Manuscript*

Kevin S. Kiernan

Until now no one has investigated the possibility that *Beowulf* was composed at the time of its only surviving manuscript. Indeed, since the inauguration of *Beowulf* studies in the early nineteenth century, scholars have shown surprisingly little interest in the unique *Beowulf* manuscript.[1] Facsimiles have been available for the past century, seemingly belying this assertion, but to a large extent they have only

---

* This article is a summary of the relevant palaeographical and codicological arguments in Kevin S. Kiernan, *Beowulf and the Beowulf Manuscript* (New Brunswick, N.J. 1981). My initial investigation of London, British Library, MS. Cotton Vitellius A.xv was made throughout April 1977. I carefully rechecked all palaeographical and codicological descriptions against the MS in March, 1979, after my book was written. I am extremely grateful to the officials in the Department of Manuscripts in the British Library for giving me daily and unlimited access to the MS during these periods.

[1] Prior to 1981, the only extensive description of the entire codex, BL MS. Cotton Vitellius A.xv, was Max Förster's *Die Beowulf-Handschrift*, Berichte über die Verhandlungen der sächsischen Akademie der Wissenschaften zu Leipzig, phil.-hist. Klasse 71 (Leipzig, 1919). The few major studies of the part known as the Nowell Codex, which includes the *Beowulf* MS, are in Stanley I. Rypins, *Three Old English Prose Texts in MS. Cotton Vitellius A.XV*, EETS 161 (London, 1924) pp. vii-xxix; Kenneth Sisam, *Studies in the History of Old English Literature* (Oxford, 1953) pp. 51-96; and Kemp Malone, *The Nowell Codex (British Museum Cotton Vitellius A.XV. Second MS)*, EEMF 12 (Copenhagen, 1963). The only thorough palaeographical study of the *Beowulf* MS per se is Tilman Westphalen, *Beowulf 3150-55: Textkritik und Editionsgeschichte* (Munich, 1967).

impeded a real understanding of the manuscript.[2] They are surely unreliable, if not actually worthless, as primary sources for detailed palaeographical and codicological research. The curious neglect of the *Beowulf* manuscript is owing not so much to the early accessibility of the facsimiles, however, as to the earlier theory that relegated the manuscript itself to the status of a poor facsimile. The manuscript was universally presumed to be, at best, a reproduction of a reproduction, the last fuzzy stage of an incalculably long and complicated transmission of the original text. This theory is founded on linguistic and historical assumptions that many scholars now consider fallacious.[3]

---

[2] Most eds. are founded on Julius Zupitza's facsimile, *Beowulf: Autotypes of the Unique Cotton MS. Vitellius A.XV in the British Museum, with a Transliteration and Notes*, EETS o.s. 77 (London, 1882); 2nd ed., *Containing a New Reproduction of the Manuscript with an Introductory Note* by Norman Davis, EETS 245 (London, 1959; repr. 1967). Indeed, though most editors have of course consulted the MS for specific readings, I know of no modern ed. founded on the MS itself. The facsimile achieved its special status not because scholars had been convinced that it was a uniformly reliable reproduction of the MS (it is not), but because Zupitza's 'transliteration' is actually a convenient restoration, incorporating Thorkelin readings wherever the MS was defective. As Zupitza himself said, 'The transliteration contains more than can be read in the Facsimile or even in the manuscript, inasmuch as it has been my endeavour to give the text as far as possible in that condition in which it stood in the manuscript a century ago' (p. xviii). Thus by 1882, Zupitza had seemingly preempted the need to study the MS at first hand. Editors have neglected the Thorkelin transcripts for the same reason.

[3] In addition to many of the articles in this volume, see Ashley Crandell Amos, *Linguistic Means of Determining the Dates of Old English Literary Texts*, Medieval Academy Books 90 (Cambridge, Mass., 1980); N.F. Blake, 'The Dating of Old English Poetry' in *An English Miscellany Presented to W.S. Mackie*, ed. Brian S. Lee (London, 1977) pp. 14-27; Nicolas Jacobs, 'Anglo-Danish Relations, Poetic Archaism, and the Date of *Beowulf*: A Reconsideration of the Evidence', *Poetica* (Tokyo) 8 (1977), 23-43; and J.D. Niles 'The Danes and the Date of *Beowulf* ', a paper read at the meeting of the

Linguistic and historical arguments can, at any rate, serve a late date of composition at least as well as an early one, and thus can dissolve the biases that have so far precluded any serious interest in the manuscript. There is reason to be interested, for the palaeographical and codicological features of the *Beowulf* manuscript consistently suggest that *Beowulf* is contemporary with its extant manuscript.

Neil R. Ker, the acknowledged authority on Anglo-Saxon palaeography, dates the *Beowulf* manuscript by its script alone at the beginning of the eleventh century.[4] Though his dating code for the manuscript, 's. X/XI,' is usually reduced by scholars, for convenience, to 'around the year 1000,' Ker in fact warns us that approximate year-numbers like these are 'not satisfactory dates for manuscripts datable only by their script and decoration unless we remember how approximate they must be' (p. xx). He prefers to assign half-century limits for such manuscripts so that 's. X/XI' is best interpreted as (roughly) 975-1025. However, the nature of the the *Beowulf* text and the political history of the period make it possible to reduce these limits considerably. Through the long, calamitous reign of Æthelred Unræd (978-1014), England was mercilessly attacked and plundered by vikings, most ferociously and effectively by Danish Scyldings under Sveinn Forkbeard.[5] Since the opening lines of *Beowulf* unabashedly celebrate the founding of the Danish Scylding line, it is difficult to imagine Anglo-Saxon scribes placidly copying the *Beowulf* manuscript during Æthelred's reign. By 1016, however, the political situation had

---

Medieval Association of the Pacific on 28 March 1980.

[4] *Catalogue of Manuscripts Containing Anglo-Saxon* (Oxford 1957) pp. xvii, 281. Ker states that a date 'at the beginning ... of the half-century would be expressed as s. x/xi' (p. xx), the date he assigns the *Beowulf* MS.

[5] The Chronicle for these years reads like a list of viking depredations; see *Two of the Saxon Chronicles Parallel*, ed. John Earle (1865), rev. Charles Plummer, I (Oxford, 1892). Sveinn Forkbeard began tormenting England in 994, when he and Olafr Tryggvason of Norway descended with a fleet of 94 warships, in what Frank M. Stenton has called 'the most formidable invasion which England had experienced for half a century'. *Anglo-Saxon England*, 3rd ed. (Oxford, 1971) p. 378. Sveinn conquered England in 1014.

changed completely. England had by then become the centre of the Danish Scylding dynasty, under the strong and peaceful rule of Knut the Great (1016-35), son of Sveinn and descendant of the legendary Scyld.[6] The most probable time of the manuscript, then, is sometime after 1016, when the genealogical panegyric was a compliment, rather than an insult, to the reigning king. Knut's reign is also an eminently appropriate time for the composition of *Beowulf*, providing as it does a splendid confluence of Anglo-Saxon poetry and Scandinavian lore.

The nature of the palaeographical and codicological evidence supporting an eleventh-century provenance for both Beowulf and the *Beowulf* manuscript requires a meticulous distinction between the manuscript and its facsimiles. The caveat is applicable to all studies of manuscripts, of course, but it has particular relevance in this case. Most of the evidence can be gathered only by direct access to the manuscript, while some spurious evidence, derived from facsimiles alone, vanishes by looking in the manuscript. Thus John Pope, who relied on ultraviolet photographs for his first edition of *The Rhythm of Beowulf*, was misled by a hole, some shine-through, and some dirt on the last page of the *Beowulf* manuscript; after examining the manuscript itself in 1964 for the second edition, he withdrew several suggested readings, supported by the photographs but not by the manuscript.[7]

---

[6] For the Norse genealogy from Scyld to Knut, see the Latin abstract of the *Skjǫldunga saga* in *Arngrimi Jonae opera*, ed. Jakob Benediktsson (Copenhagen, 1950), pp. 333-86; the well-known West-Saxon genealogy that includes Scyld does not, of course, list the later Danish kings, like Healfdene and Hrothgar. Obviously, ll 1-63 of *Beowulf* follow the Norse line. See *Chronicle A* s.a. 855, and *The Chronicle of Æthelweard*, ed. Alistair Campbell (New York, 1962) pp. 32-3. All references to an edited text of *Beowulf* are from Frederick Klaeber, *Beowulf and The Fight at Finnsburg*, 3rd ed. (Boston, 1950).

[7] 'Preface to the 1966 Edition' (New Haven, 1966), pp. xxiv-xxxi. As Pope's experience implies, there is a great difference between studying an ultraviolet photograph and studying the MS under ultraviolet light. Note that both Malone and Davis favour an ordinary photograph over an ultraviolet one for the last page of the MS (*Nowell Codex*, p. 120, and Zupitza-Davis, *Beowulf*, p. v), while both make use of A.H. Smith's transcription (pp. 105-8, vii-xii), which Smith says he

Kemp Malone, who of course had extensively studied the manuscript in preparing his facsimile of the Nowell Codex, nonetheless relied on a facsimile alone for the reading 'faer (?),' supposedly written 'in a much later hand' above line 2 of folio 179v; in the manuscript this 'reading' is nothing more than a smudge of dirt on the vellum.[8] And C.L. Wrenn, who established *wun[d]ini* as a proof of the early date of *Beowulf*, unfortunately based his reading on a facsimile, too, for the *d* he believed to be lost was in fact merely covered by the paper mounting, and the *-ini* is clearly *-mi* in the manuscript.[9] In short, facsimiles can be dangerous, and scholars and editors of *Beowulf* have not always used them with due caution. Modern technology has yet to produce a facsimile of *Beowulf* that can furnish uniformly reliable information on such vital details as scribal proofreading, changes in ink, the texture and discolouration of vellum, sheet collations, drypoint rulings, measurements, erasures, and palimpsests.[10] With time, care,

---

'derived from panchromatic and ultra-violet fluorescence photographs and the visual examination of fluorescence effects under the ultra-violet light.' 'The Photography of Manuscripts,' *London Mediaeval Studies* 1 (1938) 202.

[8] See *Nowell Codex*, p. 85, under fol. 182v. Like Zupitza, I adhere to the old foliation numbers still visible on the vellum leaves of the MS. For the many advantages of the MS foliation over the 1884 foliation Malone follows, see 'The History and Construction of the Composite Codex' in *Beowulf and the Beowulf Manuscript*, pp. 65-169, esp. 71-110.

[9] *Beowulf with the Finnesburg Fragment*, 3rd ed. rev. W. F. Bolton (New York, 1973), p. 130 n. As Zupitza says, letters covered by the paper mounting can normally be seen by holding the vellum to the light (Zupitza-Davis, *Beowulf*, p. xix). In the case of *wun/dmi* on fol. 160v 4-5, the *d* can now be seen in the new facsimiles because the paper that once covered it was trimmed. The *m*, too, is clear in the new facsimiles, though its first minim is distorted by shine-through.

[10] Some of these features, to a large extent readily discernible by the naked eye in the MS but obscured by black-and-white facsimiles, can be reproduced in colour photographs. See, e.g., the colour facsimile of fol. 179r, the frontispiece of *Beowulf and the Beowulf Manuscript*. For other technological means that may yet produce better

good eyesight, and an open mind, the student of the manuscript itself will not be fooled, as one can easily be with facsimiles, by holes, tears, dirt, stains, shadows, wrinkles, shine-through, off-prints, burns, or the paper mountings.

A collation of the vellum leaves of the entire Nowell Codex reveals that, in all probability, *Beowulf* was originally copied as a separate book that was later added to the prose part of the codex. Though the threads, folds, and prick-marks from the original gatherings were all destroyed in the Cottonian Library fire of 1731, a collation of the hair and flesh sides of the separate vellum leaves can determine which leaves were probably conjugate and which leaves were certainly not. The collation shows that *Beowulf* could have begun either on the seventh leaf of a quarternion (the traditional view) or on the first leaf of a new gathering. In the absence of the prick-marks, the rulings themselves are not sufficient to confirm either view, however, since the sheets were ruled separately for the most part. Even with the same prick-marks it would have been impossible for the scribe to rule all of the separate sheets invariably alike, and in fact there are often noticeable discrepancies in the rulings within discrete gatherings of the *Beowulf* manuscript. As a result, though the width and length of the writing grid for the first leaf of *Beowulf* differs slightly from those of the preceding leaf, it would be unsafe to use this evidence as definitive proof that *Beowulf* began a new gathering. Nonetheless, since the second gathering of the prose codex is certainly a trine, while the third and fourth gatherings are trines expanded to quires by the addition of half-sheets, it is reasonable to conclude that the fifth gathering was also a trine, all that was needed to finish copying the prose texts, and that *Beowulf* thus began on a new gathering.

This conclusion is well supported by other palaeographical and codicological evidence. On the first page of *Beowulf*, for instance, the unusually heavy rulings, which have split the vellum at both margins,

---

facsimiles of the *Beowulf* MS, see *Applied Infrared Photography*, Eastman Kodak Publication no. M-28 (Rochester, N.Y., 1977); and J.F. Benton, A.R. Gillespie, and J.M. Soha, 'Digital Image-Processing Applied to the Photography of Manuscripts: With Examples Drawn from the Pincus MS. of Arnald of Villanova', *Scriptorium* 33 (1979) 40-55.

suggest that the page was on the outside of its gathering; in the bottom margin the worn signature, *Vi[tellius] A 15*,[11] indicates that the poem was a separable part of the codex; in the first line the sudden and remarkable change in the scribe's way of drawing capitals suggests a new codex; and in the bottom third of the page the damage to the text was most likely caused by sweat and friction when the page served as an outside cover.[12] There is more pervasive corroboration, too. An exhaustive study of the scribal proofreading throughout the Nowell Codex reveals that only *Beowulf* was thoroughly and repeatedly proofread and intelligently corrected by both scribes. The second scribe even corrected the first scribe's work in *Beowulf* (but not in the preceding prose texts), and in addition to making some needed corrections made a few unnecessary emendations, apparently to standardize the two scribes' divergent orthography.[13] The second scribe's special connection with the *Beowulf* manuscript, moreover, was not limited to copying, proofreading, and making selective emendations. The manuscript must have remained in his possession, for he continued to work with it long after he had first copied his part of the poem. He later restored readings which had been damaged by

---

[11] [Despite repeated efforts, including the use of an ultraviolet lamp and of digital image-processing equipment, I have been unable to bring out any lettering whatsoever after the *Vi*. For the possibility that *Vi* is an early-modern quire signature, see Kiernan, 'A Long Footnote for J. Gerritsen's "Supplementary" Description of BL Cotton MS Vitellius A. xv', *English Studies* 72.6 (1991), 489-96.]

[12] Both Thorkelin transcripts confirm that the damage was not done by modern readers of the MS. See *The Thorkelin Transcripts of Beowulf*, ed. Kemp Malone, EEMF 1 (Copenhagen, 1951), pp. 1, 1a. As far as it goes, Humfrey Wanley's transcript confirms this conclusion, for Wanley copies *aldor[le]ase* as *aldor ... ase* in 1705. *Antiquae literaturae septentrionalis liber alter, seu Humphredi Wanleii librorum veterum septentrionalium ... catalogus historico-criticus ...* (Oxford, 1705), repr. *English Linguistics: 1500-1800*, 248 (Menston, England, 1970), p. 219.

[13] E.g. he emends *-scaðan* to *-sceaðan* on fol. 140v14 and *-þeo* to *-þeow* on fol. 144r5, though the original spellings are not wrong, and indeed occur frequently in the first scribe's section of the MS.

accident (*eowrū cynne*, for example, on folio 192v2) or by ordinary wear and tear (most notably on the last page of the manuscript, where he freshened up a badly faded text). There can be no doubt, at least, that both scribes understood *Beowulf* and treated the *Beowulf* manuscript as if it were a separate, and important, codex.

The most extraordinary example of the second scribe's special connection with the *Beowulf* manuscript is that he later copied a new text on a palimpsest of folio 179. The palimpsest accordingly provides us with startling palaeographical and codicological evidence that part of *Beowulf* was actually revised in the course of the eleventh century, long after the original text was copied. The discovery of the palimpsest was made by Tilman Westphalen, who published his stunning findings in 1967.[14] A century ago Zupitza, presumably observing the unusual condition of the vellum and the strange appearance of the script on the folio, had concluded without due explanation that 'all that is distinct in the FS. in folio 179 has been freshened up by a later hand in the MS'.[15] A codicological study of the manuscript alone shows quite convincingly that folio 179 is a palimpsest. The sheet collation shows unequivocally that it and folio 188 formed the outside sheet of the penultimate gathering of *Beowulf*, yet it is equally clear that only folio 179 was subsequently washed down and heavily scoured, without affecting the conjugate leaf.[16] Hence the original text on folio 179 was erased. Westphalen showed that the folio was a palimpsest by a systematic palaeographical study, a letter-by-letter comparison of the script with the second scribe's handwriting in the rest of the manuscript. His brilliant discussion of Zupitza's 'freshening up' theory reveals that the scribe's handwriting on this folio had evolved into a more modern script, similar in some ways to the first scribe's.[17] The evolution of the second scribe's *a*, from a four-sided angular letter to

---

[14] See n. 1.

[15] Zupitza-Davis, *Beowulf*, p. 102.

[16] The black-and-white facsimiles very inadequately represent the marked difference in texture and colouration, caused by the palimpsesting of fol. 179, between fols. 179 and 188. The apparent similarity between fols. 179v and 188r, the flesh side of the sheet, is especially misleading.

[17] *Textkritik*, pp. 41-109.

a three-sided rounded one, is particularly illustrative.[18] Westphalen reasonably estimated that this kind of development in a professional scribe's handwriting must have taken a long time, up to twenty years.

The palimpsest and the later script of folio 179 are by definition incompatible with the old belief that the *Beowulf* manuscript is a late, purely mechanical copy of a much earlier poem. In his effort to reconcile them, Westphalen subordinated the facts he had discovered to the theories that the poem was early and that the text on folio 179 was necessarily the original text, freshened up. This unnatural union accounts for his uncharacteristically diffident hypothesis that someone in need of vellum must have randomly chosen the *Beowulf* manuscript as a good source for palimpsests;[19] and that the second scribe, ten to twenty years older, luckily discovered the vandalism and restored what he could still see of the original text. The evidence, however, does not well support this part of Westphalen's otherwise splendid refinements of Zupitza's 'freshening up' theory, and points instead to the conclusion that the second scribe himself made the palimpsest for the customary purpose of providing vellum for a new text, in this case for a late revision of *Beowulf*. As A.H. Smith says, the script on the folio does not display 'that hesitation and lack of coincidence usually associated with freshening up, forgery, and the like'.[20] Surely the evolution of the scribe's letter-forms could not have been so convincingly documented by Westphalen if the scribe had in fact been laboriously restoring the erased original, for then he would have been tracing over his old letter-forms. Moreover, some of the supposedly freshened up material cannot be logically attributed to the original. It is hard to believe, for example, that the scribe restored the mistake and the superscript correction of it at the end of line 9 on the recto. It is equally unlikely that the many strange spellings, unparalleled in the rest of the manuscript, were original readings. In a late revision, on the other hand, the scribe's mistake and correction are no cause for wonder, while his anomalous spellings, like *hard* for *heard* in line 15 on the verso, can be consistently explained as natural signs of attrition in the late West-Saxon literary dialect, which began to break down in

---

[18] *Ibid.*, pp. 65-7.

[19] *Ibid.*, p. 96.

[20] 'Photography of Manuscripts', p. 200.

non-West-Saxon territory as the eleventh century advanced.[21] Finally, a close look at the badly damaged condition of the text on the palimpsest, particularly at the textual lacunas, shows conclusively that we are faced with a revision, not a mere restoration of the original text. The text we now have is shorter than the original, for the erased first line on the verso was almost certainly a dittograph in the revision from r20-21: [b]*roga ... sceapen* can be read with confidence. As this line also illustrates, parts of the revised text were later erased. In fact, most of the gaps on the recto are erasures made after the new text was copied,[22] not parts of the original text, which the scribe was unable to freshen up. Thus a full restoration of the *revised* text, not of the original one, was never completed.

The incipient state of the text on the palimpsest, and the fact that it displays in any case a later script than the rest of the manuscript, opens the possibility that the *Beowulf* manuscript amounts to an unfinished draft of the poem. As incredible as an extant draft of *Beowulf* may seem to some readers, there is considerable palaeographical and codicological support for the view that the *Beowulf* manuscript in fact preserves for us the last formative stages in the creation of the epic. Three lines of text thematically related to the new text on the palimpsest have been imperfectly but deliberately deleted on the next folio, 180v1-3.[23] The erasing was never finished, though it

---

[21] See Sisam, *Studies*, p. 153. For the first modern grammar of late West-Saxon, or 'the Classical Old English of about A.D. 1000', see Randolph Quirk and C.L. Wrenn, *An Old English Grammar*, 2nd ed. (London 1957; repr. 1979), p. vii.

[22] The erasure made between *hea* and *hord* in l. 5 left a filmy residue on the *a* of *hea*, thus proving that the erasure was made after the new text was copied on the folio. The erasures in these gaps on the recto were evidently made while the vellum was damp, for the skin in these areas is unusually rough, with a grey discolouration that becomes fluorescent under ultraviolet light.

[23] The black-and-white facsimiles show the damage to the text on fol. 180v, but the MS shows that the first three lines were intentionally rubbed off. Both Thorkelin transcripts, moreover, confirm that the damage is not modern: Thorkelin's copyist did not attempt to transcribe them (p. 67), while Thorkelin himself wrote in the margin

seems likely that the vellum was being prepared for a new text as well. Presumably both folios 179 and 180v1-3 are part of the same revision-in-progress. An analysis of the construction of the *Beowulf* manuscript provides a possible explanation for the purpose of this revision. As we have seen, the palimpsest is the first leaf of the last two gatherings of the manuscript, and as such begins a self-contained unit of the manuscript. Moreover, the number of sheets in these last two gatherings, the manner in which the sheets are arranged, the number of rulings, and the width of the writing grid, are all features that differ sharply from the established format of the rest of the *Beowulf* manuscript. It is therefore possible that this part of the manuscript formerly existed separately, and was artificially appended to the extant manuscript by the second scribe.[24] If so, the revised text on the palimpsest may have been written (or copied) by this scribe at a later time to provide a smoother, more natural transition between two, originally distinct, and perhaps even totally unrelated manuscripts.

The theory of a composite manuscript is substantiated by other palaeographical and codicological facts in both scribes' sections of the manuscript. Before considering this evidence, however, one ought to note the relevant textual context in which it is found. The main palaeographical and codicological evidence, which can be characterized as unprecedented signs of extemporizing in the copying of the manuscript, is all found in the section of the text known as 'Beowulf's Homecoming', a narrative unit that makes the vital transition between Beowulf's youthful exploits in Denmark and the confrontation in his old

---

of his copy, 'Hic lacuna trium linearum sive 15 versuum incidit qui in autographo defuisse videntur et enim membrana, ex qua hoc apographum desumptum hic vacua est' (p. 104a).

[24] In his review of Förster's *Beowulf-Handschrift*, Wolfgang Keller suggested that the bad condition of fols. 179r and 198r could be explained by assuming that this part of the MS, containing the Dragon episode, was used separately, so that the two pages served as outside covers. The explanation ignored, however, the bad condition of fol. 179v. *Beiblatt zur Anglia* 34 (1923), 4-5.

age with the dragon in Geatland.[25] The first scribe copied all of the section on Beowulf's youthful exploits in the first five gatherings of the *Beowulf* manuscript, and in the first fourteen lines of the next gathering (up to line 1887); the second scribe copied all of the section on Beowulf's last fight, from the last six lines of this same gathering (from line 2200) to the end of the manuscript. The two scribes divided the copying of the transitional gathering, containing the transitional text of Beowulf's Homecoming (lines 1888-2199), with the second scribe taking over in the middle of line 1939b. The scribes' division of labour was neither by episode, nor by gathering, folio, page, or even by half-line of verse. The transition in the script is as abrupt and unplanned as Beowulf's decision to go home. Unless it is only a remarkable coincidence that the palaeographical transition and the textual transition were achieved in the same gathering, Beowulf's Homecoming may well have been first composed to join together two different *Beowulf* manuscripts and first copied in our surviving manuscript.

The exceptional nature of the transitional gathering as the essential link between two otherwise disparate palaeographical and codicological units is well illustrated by considering the aspect of the manuscript without this gathering. Without it, scholars would have been led to conclude that the two gatherings preserving Beowulf's fight with the dragon had been copied many years before the five gatherings preserving Beowulf's youthful fights with Grendel and Grendel's dam. The relatively archaic script of the second scribe, in which insular letter-forms like the low *s* still effectively compete with the high

---

[25] The textual transition was first interpreted as a separate creation by Karl Müllenhoff in 'Die innere Geschichte des *Beovulfs*', *ZfdA* 14 (1869) 193-244; a more recent version of the theory was propounded by F.P. Magoun, in '"*Béowulf A*": A Folk Variant', *Arv: Tidskrift för Nordisk Folkminnesforskning* 25 (1958), 95-101; and '*Béowulf B*: A Folk-Poem on Béowulf's Death' in *Early English and Norse Studies: Presented to Hugh Smith in Honour of his Sixtieth Birthday*, ed. Arthur Brown and Peter Foote (London, 1963), pp. 127-40. Though most scholars reject or ignore these 'dissection' theories, the essentially episodic structure has been obvious to many; compare, e.g., Klaeber's description of the structure (*Beowulf*, pp. ix-xii).

Caroline *s*, would be grounds enough to argue that the second scribe's work was somewhat older than the first scribe's, in which the Caroline influence is more advanced.[26] It would seem most probable as well that the two *Beowulf* manuscripts derived from different scriptoria, judging by the marked difference in format: specifically, the first scribe regularly uses four-sheet quires, ruled with a narrower writing grid about 10 cm. wide for 20 lines of text per page, and with sheets generally arranged so that hair faces hair and flesh faces flesh; the second scribe uses five-sheet gatherings, ruled with a writing grid over 11 cm. wide for 21 lines of text per page, and with sheets invariably arranged with hair sides facing out, so that hair faces flesh within the gatherings. In short, without the palaeographically and codicologically transitional gathering, scholars would have reasonably concluded that two virtually complete *Beowulf* stories had been preserved in two unrelated manuscripts, attesting to a rather lively *Beowulf* tradition in different parts of England in late Anglo-Saxon times. Surely it would have been a reckless theory, attacked from all sides, to propose that the first scribe's manuscript and the second scribe's manuscript were parts of the same manuscript, or even that the two stories were parts of the same original poem.

The second scribe takes over copying in the transitional gathering on the second leaf, folio 172v4, but since the first scribe began copying in it, the gathering was of course made up in the first scribe's manner:[27] there are four sheets to the quire, rulings with the narrower writing grid for twenty lines of text per page, and the first two sheets

---

[26] See Ker, *Catalogue*, p. 282 and Westphalen, *Textkritik* pp. 69-82. As we have seen, Westphalen observed that the second scribe's later script on fol. 179 had evolved into a slightly more modern style, more like the first scribe's, and had perhaps been influenced by it (p. 82).

[27] We must assume that the scribes themselves arranged the sheets of their respective gatherings, in view of their manifest disagreement over the aesthetics of sheet arrangement. The first scribe, through the prose texts and his part of *Beowulf*, consistently tries to obscure the contrast between hair and flesh sides, while the second scribe, through his part of *Beowulf* and the *Judith* fragment, consistently displays the contrast.

are arranged with flesh facing flesh, the second two with hair facing hair. Presumably the first scribe fully expected to finish copying the gathering, if not the entire poem. Because the handwriting of the two scribes is so ill-matched, it is clear that they did not plan in advance a place for the second scribe to take over the copying. If they had, the change in handwriting could have been obscured by the first scribe stopping at the end of folio 172r, rather than after three lines on the verso. There is convincing palaeographical and codicological evidence that the first scribe suddenly halted where he did, and the second scribe took over, because by that point the decision had been made to join two originally distinct manuscripts, and perhaps two originally distinct poems.

The evidence indicates that the second scribe may well have copied his part of the transitional gathering containing Beowulf's Homecoming after he had already copied the last two gatherings of the manuscript, those containing the fight with the dragon and Beowulf's death. What so strongly suggests that he copied this gathering last is that he resorted to various extreme measures to fit far more text within the gathering than it was originally designed to hold. Most notably, he squeezed four extra lines of text, in disregard of the original rulings made by the first scribe, on folios 174v though 176r. This extraordinary recourse would not have been necessary if the scribe had at least two extra gatherings of unused vellum (and uncopied text) ahead of him. The squeezing in of 21 lines of text per page, at this early stage, on four successive folios clearly ruled for 20 lines of text per page, can only mean that the scribe did not have vellum available after this gathering. Otherwise he could have easily fit the text of four extra lines simply by adding a few extra letters per line in the course of copying the last three gatherings of the poem. Unless he was compelled to squeeze the extra material into the transitional gathering, it was far too early in the copying for the scribe to be worrying about running out of vellum. If he really had over twenty empty folios remaining on which to copy, the scribe's desperate recourse of ignoring the rulings of the transitional gathering is inexplicable. The last two gatherings of the poem, then, evidently had been copied already.

It should be stressed that the four extra lines on folios 174v through 176r could not have been added inadvertently. These folios do not constitute a separate sheet of vellum, and so it is out of the question that one sheet of the quire was unintentionally ruled for 21 rather than 20 lines. The third sheet of this gathering consists of folios 173 and

176, while the innermost sheet consists of folios 174 and 175. Rulings were made with an awl, making furrows that provided rulings for recto and verso simultaneously. Thus the third sheet cannot have been ruled by mistake for 20 lines on folio 176v, but for 21 lines on the recto; and the innermost sheet cannot have been ruled for 20 lines on folio 174r, but for 21 lines on the verso. The extra lines of text on these four consecutive pages, folios 174v-176r, are obviously not there by accident. On the contrary, the second scribe tried to camouflage his additions. He did not simply rule extra lines at the bottom of each page; instead, he managed to maintain a uniform written space (about 175mm., from the first ruling to the last) by deliberately ignoring the first scribe's inner rulings, and by carefully spacing the lines of his own text so that he would progressively pick up enough room for an extra line of text per page. The Zupitza-Davis facsimile of folio 174v is faithful enough to illustrate his method, for it faintly reproduces the first scribe's rulings. Starting at line 3, the second scribe began lifting the line of text away from the ruling, until, at line 17, an entire line of text had been added, and his copy could once again coincide with the first scribe's rulings. Thus, if one counts the rulings in the facsimile there are 20, despite the fact that there are 21 lines of text. This decidedly difficult way of including extra material on the folios virtually proves that, for some reason, the second scribe was compelled to fit it all within the transitional gathering.

There are other sure signs of his need to fit more text in than the gathering was designed to hold. On folio 174v, the same page on which the scribe began squeezing in an extra line of text in disregard of the rulings, he omitted fitt number XXX for lack of space. It is not surprising that he did not squander the line he had so laboriously gained on a fitt number, and that he drew the large capital *O* outside the area of the text. He garnered a good deal more space throughout the gathering by ignoring the first scribe's margins, or bounding-lines, which permitted him only about 10 cm. of text per line. The second scribe added about 1 cm. of additional space per line by ignoring one or both of the first scribe's margins. Again, folio 174v provides a good example, because of the clarity of the rulings: the right bounding-line can be clearly seen in the facsimile in line 10, between *hryre* and *lytle*. By ignoring the margin on this one page, the scribe added outside the margin over 60 characters, the equivalent of at least two whole lines, to his text. The scribe normally ignored the right margin,

as in this example, though a few times he disregarded the left
bounding-line too. We can even see in the facsimile the point at which
the scribe knew that the remainder of his text would fit into the
gathering without further violating the bounds of the first scribe's
writing grid. By folio 176v he stopped squeezing in an extra line of
text in disregard of the rulings; on the next page, folio 177r, though he
ignored the first scribe's left margin for the first 18 lines, he used the
margin for the last two lines, and thereafter generally adhered to the 10
cm. boundaries until the last page of the gathering (fol. 178v). His
lack of consistency clearly shows that he did not simply abandon the
first scribe's format to follow his own standards, or he would have
continued with 21 lines of text and 11-cm. bounding-lines throughout
the gathering. The scribe undeniably went to great lengths to fit a
certain amount of text within the transitional gathering. It seems most
likely that he was obliged to do so because he had already copied the
last two gatherings of the poem.

Thus a clear pattern emerges from all of the unusual
palaeographical and codicological data associated with the second
scribe. He has not only made emendations and corrected errors in his
own and in the first scribe's part of the *Beowulf* manuscript, and
restored damages as age and use deteriorated the manuscript. His part
of the manuscript provides persuasive palaeographical and codicological
evidence that he helped copy a new episode, Beowulf's Homecoming,
designed to fuse two different manuscripts about Beowulf's Danish and
Geatish exploits into a unified epic. Apparently, many years later, he
was still working towards a better fusion of these parts on the revised
text of the palimpsest.[28] There is also some palaeographical and

---

[28] That this fusion was still perhaps in its early stages can be
illustrated by the last seven lines on fol. 178v, immediately following
Beowulf's Homecoming and preceding the palimpsest. Klaeber's ed.
highlights how abruptly they lead to Beowulf's kingship, the text on the
palimpsest:

Eft þæt geiode   ufaran dogrum
hildehlæmmum,   syððan Hygelac læg,
ond Hear[dr]ede   hildemeceas
under bordhreoðan   to bonan wurdon,
ða hyne gesohtan   on sigeþeode

codicological evidence that the first scribe participated in the revision that fused the two stories and the two manuscripts. There are indications, at least, that the text immediately preceding the transitional gathering underwent major revisions after the first scribe stopped copying and the second scribe replaced him. And if the second scribe was indeed copying an entirely new text in the transitional gathering, and later had to revise the first folio of the next gathering (fol. 179, the palimpsest), as well as delete three lines from folio 180v, it should not be surprising that the first scribe might also need to revise part of the text preceding the transitional gathering to accommodate the new direction of the narrative. Together, the anomalous rulings of the preceding gathering (fols. 163-170), and the fitt numbers that run through it and the transitional gathering (fols. 171-178), furnish solid palaeographical and codicological support for positing such a revision.

The first scribe ruled all of his gatherings, except the one in question, for 20 lines of text to the page. His total uniformity in this respect, not only in *Beowulf* but in the prose texts of the Nowell Codex as well, renders the 22-line rulings for folios 163-170 decidedly suspicious. The most obvious explanations are that the scribe had more material to copy in the gathering than he originally had planned for it (an explanation consonant with revision) or that the gathering was ruled anomalously by mistake. The latter explanation can be safely dismissed. The scribe made sure that his anomalously ruled gathering would not look much different from the rest of his gatherings by

---

hearde hil*d*frecan,   Heaðo-Scilfingas,
niða genægdan   nefan Hererices -:
syððan ....   (ll. 2200-07a)

'Again it came about in later days, in the crash of battle, after Hygelac lay dead, and battle-swords became the slayer of Heardred under his shield, when fierce warriors, the Battle-Scilfings, sought him out among his victorious kin, with force assailed the nephew of Hereric-: after ...'. Beowulf's rule and the Dragon episode are not very well introduced by these lines, which seem to be leading to other events. Klaeber's note, '2207. *syððan* is used, in a way, correlatively with *syððan* 2201', stresses rather than reduces the syntactic and textual leaps one must make in the middle of the half-line 2207a, from the end of fol. 178v to the beginning of the palimpsest.

keeping the writing space identical (about 175mm.), despite the two
extra rulings. It is not extraordinary in itself, of course, that the scribe
ruled his gathering in accord with the amount of text he had to copy.
What is remarkable is that, for some reason, he was obliged to restrict
the extra rulings to this gathering: it is strange that he ruled it for 22
lines per page, and then the next gathering for 20 lines, instead of
ruling both for 21 lines, like the last two gatherings of the poem. The
apparent reason is that the scribe had to copy more material on the first
of these quires than he had initially planned for it, and curiously could
not spread the additional material over two gatherings. As in the
similar case of the second scribe in the transitional gathering, this kind
of restriction may imply revision in the circumscribed area. It can be
argued, then, that the first scribe, after being replaced by the second,
went back and copied a revised text on the preceding quire.

This hypothetical revision, it follows, was either considerably
shorter or somewhat longer than the original text. At first glance, it
would appear that the revised text was longer, since it required a
gathering ruled for 22 lines per page, while the original text only
needed 20 lines per page. In other words, the revised text was about
32 lines longer (two lines added for 16 consecutive pages) than the
original text. But these appearances are probably deceiving. Evidence
from the fitt numbers indicates that the poem was shortened, which
could mean that a gathering ruled for 22 lines replaced two original
quires ruled for the customary 20 lines. In this case the revision is
quite radical, for it means that about 288 lines (the difference between
the two quires ruled for 20 lines and one quire ruled for 22) were
deleted from the poem. However, it is unrealistic to conceive of a
major revision as simple addition or subtraction of lines. If there was
a major revision, parts of the text no doubt were deleted while other
parts were expanded. The fitt numbers suggest that an entire fitt may
have been deleted from the poem, but aside from this clue the precise
nature and scope of the presumptive revision of the text in this
gathering remain a mystery.

The fitt numbers indicate that the twenty-fourth fitt of the original
text was deleted in its entirety. Accordingly, they independently
corroborate the conclusions reached on the basis of the anomalous
rulings. All of the fitt numbers in *Beowulf* from I to XXIII are in
perfect order, and have not been tampered with in any way. But
beginning with the second number of the gathering anomalously ruled

for 22 lines, and continuing through the transitional gathering to number XXXI, all of the fitt numbers either have been altered or were never written in the first place. The scribe mistakenly wrote XXV, instead of XXIIII, for the second number in the anomalously ruled quire, and thereafter he and the second scribe held to the new erroneous sequence for the remainder of the poem. A later alterer made an abortive effort to correct the number sequence, but in the process obscured the first scribe's error, and left the false impression that the second scribe had made a series of errors. In all, five fitt numbers were altered: of the first scribe's numbers, XXV was changed rather sloppily to XXIIII by the alterer writing two of the four I's over the V (the inept imitation of the scribe's I's shows that neither scribe was the alterer); XXVI, XXVII, and XXVIII were changed to XXV, XXVI, and XXVII, simply by erasing the last I of each number. Similarly, the second scribe's number XXVIIII, the only one of his that was altered, was changed to XXVIII by erasing the last I.

The spurious alteration of these numbers has led to some unwarranted conclusions about the number of fitts in the poem. The second scribe wrote only two fitt numbers in the transitional gathering, XXVIIII on folio 173r and XXXI on folio 177r. As we have seen, he did not write XXX on folio 174v for lack of space. He did, however, clearly mark the beginning of the new fitt with a large capital *O* in the margin. But when the alterer changed XXVIIII to XXVIII by erasing the I, he left the false impression (followed by most modern editors) that the second scribe had failed to write in *two* fitt numbers, XXVIIII and XXX, and worse, that he had failed even to mark the beginning of one of the fitts with a capital letter. Thus the alterer ingenuously shifted the first scribe's mistake over to the second scribe, for the illusion that two fitt numbers are missing here can be directly traced back to the first scribe's error of skipping number XXIIII, and writing number XXV instead. The second scribe, who relied on the accuracy of the first scribe's number sequence, continued numbering the fitts where the first scribe left off. Hence the disarray in the fitt numbers of the anomalously ruled quire and of the transitional gathering, as well as the confusion over the actual number of fitts in the poem, can all be reduced to the first scribe's omission of XXIIII. If one ignores the spurious alterations, the fitts were numbered from I to XXIII, and then from XXV to XLIII, indicating that there are 43 fitts in the poem, whereas in fact there are only 42.

The two scribes' number sequence before the alterer obfuscated the evidence is quite significant. It effectively proves that the fitts of the poem had not been numbered in this way before the extant manuscript, and a first numbering of the fitts is in keeping with a contemporary manuscript. At the very least, the omission of XXIIII implies that the first scribe was numbering the fitts of *Beowulf* for the first time, without the aid of numbers in his exemplar, and that he omitted a number by mistake. The first scribe undoubtedly wrote his fitt numbers after he copied the text, for the numbers up to folio 168r9 were written by him with a much finer quill tip than the one he used to copy the text. Presumably he wrote the numbers later because, without numbers in his exemplar, he felt he could not easily keep track of the sequence while copying. The first scribe's mistake also shows that the second scribe did not have numbers in his exemplar, for his numbers ingenuously perpetuate the first scribe's erroneous sequence. Moreover, there are clear signs that the second scribe tried, with indifferent success, to leave space for fitt numbers that would be added later. In the last two gatherings he remembered to leave a line free on folio 183r8, and in other cases there was usually enough space, whether he remembered or not, for fitt numbers at the end of the preceding fitts. However, there was no space at the end of fitt XXXVII, folio 189v16, and the scribe forgot to leave a line free. He realized his oversight part way through the first line of the new fitt, and remarkably improvised space by cutting off the name *Wihstanes* after writing only *wih-*. On folio 191r12 he no doubt thought he had left room for a fitt number, but apparently he did not yet know that the number would be XXXVIIII, too long to fit the space, which he ultimately left blank.[29]

---

[29] *Judith*, too, was numbered after it was copied, but by someone other than the second scribe, as the distinct palaeographical style of the *X*s proves. For a study of the implications of the number sequence in *Judith*, and of the way in which the *Judith*-fragment was added to the Nowell Codex in early modern times, see my *Beowulf and the Beowulf Manuscript*, pp. 150-67. As *Judith* helps illustrate, the spaces the second scribe left for fitt numbers in his part of *Beowulf* have no bearing on the theory of a composite MS, since they could be filled by any number sequence, including seriatim numbering with unrelated texts.

All of the facts, then, point to the conclusion that *Beowulf* was numbered for the first time in the extant manuscript. But the first scribe's blunder, his omission of XXIIII, may tell us more than that the number sequence is contemporary with the manuscript. The numbering could have been initially thrown off if a revised text of the anomalously ruled quire in part entailed the deletion of the original twenty-fourth fitt. The first scribe's numerical oversight is easily explained if one assumes that the revisions were made on the quire or quires replaced by the anomalously ruled one. If it was his practice to number the fitts as soon as he finished a gathering, the first scribe could have mechanically copied the fitt numbers he had supplied for his first copy when he transcribed the revision. To this extent the fitt numbers enhance the possibility, first suggested by the anomalous rulings, that folios 163-170 contain part of a late revision of *Beowulf.*

My investigation of the *Beowulf* manuscript began as a palaeographical and codicological description of a neglected Anglo-Saxon codex. From the start it was obvious that nearly all unusual features in the codex, features that implied something other than mechanical copying of five Old English texts, had not been adequately described before. If my investigation has ended as an interpretation of palaeographical and codicological data, it is because so much of the unusual data, alone and combined, seemed to imply that the *Beowulf* manuscript was contemporary with the poem: apparently it was copied as a separate codex; without doubt it was thoroughly, repeatedly, and intelligently proofread by the scribes; it was dutifully repaired by the second scribe as time and use damaged it; and most importantly, a wide range of evidence persistently suggests that it was revised by both scribes in one specific, and seemingly relevant, section of the manuscript, between folios 163 and 180, and especially between folios 171 and 179. The evidence of revision implies as well that the *Beowulf* manuscript is an unfinished draft of the poem, and that it preserves for us the artistic fusion of two originally distinct *Beowulf* narratives. A truly objective description of the codex would not completely overlook or ignore the possible significance of such features as a signature of ownership on the first page of *Beowulf,* marked changes in format, discrepancies in the rulings, erasures and corrections, pages that contain more lines of text than rulings, a later script, a number sequence almost certainly originating with the extant manuscript, three deliberately deleted lines, and a palimpsest. It seems more likely that all previous descriptions of the codex were begun with the presumption that such evidence was not worth describing in a very late manuscript of a very early poem.

Palaeography and codicology, in any case, do not support the theory that the *Beowulf* manuscript is a late copy of an early poem. On the contrary, they support the view that *Beowulf* is an eleventh-century composite poem, and that the *Beowulf* manuscript is a draft, the archetype of the epic as we now have it. With this new light on the problem of dating the composition of *Beowulf*, it is not hard to imagine how Anglo-Saxon poems like *Beowulf* might have emerged during the reign of Knut the Great as an aesthetic aftermath of the Danish Conquest. As Roberta Frank shows in her contribution to this volume,[30] there are remarkable affinities between the *Beowulf* poet and the Norse skalds and storytellers who thrived in the age of Knut. On its most basic level, the subject-matter of *Beowulf* is thoroughly Scandinavian, and may well have been composed by an Anglo-Saxon poet who grew up in the Danelaw. The poem begins with a dedicatory salute to the founding of Knut's royal Scylding dynasty. As Alexander Murray argues in his article below,[31] the Scylding line had been appropriated by the West-Saxon kings from the ninth century on. But the genealogy in *Beowulf* leads unequivocally and triumphantly to Danish kings, not English ones, and the Anglo-Saxon and Danish Scyldings were incompatible before Knut married Æthelred's widow, Emma. Surely Hrothgar, the dominant power in Scandinavia, could have been modelled on Knut the Great, the reigning Scylding *þeodcyning* of a vast northern empire. The Anglo-Saxon poet who created the exploits of Beowulf in Denmark was content to suggest that even the mighty Danish Scyldings, led by a wise and noble king, were not immune to irrational disaster. Knut would not have been offended by the implication that everything in this life is transitory, or that God ultimately rules the universe.

But if there were two poets of *Beowulf*, the one who created the Dragon episode was more poignant than the first. The poet of the

---

[30] 'Skaldic Verse and the Date of *Beowulf* ', *The Dating of Beowulf*, ed. Colin Chase (Toronto, 1981), pp. 123-139.

[31] '*Beowulf*, the Danish Invasions, and Royal Genealogy', *The Dating of Beowulf*, pp. 101-111.

Dragon episode traces the actual disintegration of a dynasty, which culminates in the death of a glorious hero and implies the subsequent extinction of an entire race. This poet had for his model the fall of the house of Alfred, and the subsumption of his homeland and his race in the Danish empire. If he knew Anglo-Saxon history from the *Chronicle*, he might have remembered that fiery dragons first portended the viking invasions of England in the year 793; at any rate, he would have known that many Anglo-Saxon thanes deserted their lords when the dragon ships came in the eleventh-century Danish Conquest. This poet's mood is elegiac and, in view of eleventh-century events, unbearably sad. The poet himself is a 'last survivor of a noble race', who was left an enormous legacy after the death of his lord. If the last poet of *Beowulf* was the second scribe, as the palaeographical and codicological evidence encourages one to believe, he increased and continued to polish an Anglo-Saxon treasure during the reign of a Danish Scylding lord.

The Structure of the Exeter Book Codex (Exeter, Cathedral Library, MS. 3501)

Patrick W. Conner

Exeter Cathedral Library MS. 3501 contains the largest and most varied collection of Old English poetry extant. The manuscript, commonly known as the Exeter Book, was most probably written in the third quarter of the tenth century, and it has remained at Exeter since at least the end of the eleventh century.[1] The Exeter Book we now have, however, and which we usually think of as an extensive but organized collection of miscellaneous verse forms from the Anglo-Saxon period, is most probably not the volume envisioned by the scribe who wrote it. This study presents and interprets codicological and

---

[1] The earliest reference to the manuscript is taken to be a description in Bishop Leofric's eleventh century inventory of church properties at Exeter. The best editions of Leofric's inventory are Max Förster, 'The Donations of Leofric to Exeter', *The Exeter Book of Old English Poetry*, ed. R.W. Chambers, Max Förster and Robin Flower (London, 1933), pp. 10-32, esp. 28; and Michael Lapidge, 'Surviving Booklists from Anglo-Saxon England', *Learning and Literature in Anglo-Saxon England: Studies Presented to Peter Clemoes on the Occasion of his Sixty-Fifth Birthday*, ed. Michael Lapidge and Helmut Gneuss (Cambridge, 1985), pp. 64-9, reprinted in the present volume. The accepted date of the Exeter Book's compilation is based on the date of its script. This has been most completely studied by Robin Flower ('The Script of the Exeter Book', *The Exeter Book of Old English Poetry*, ed. R.W. Chambers, Max Förster and Robin Flower [London, 1933], pp. 83-90) who dates the hand 970-990; Neil Ker (Neil R. Ker, *Catalogue of Manuscripts Containing Anglo-Saxon* [Oxford, 1957], p. 153) concurs in dating the manuscript 's. x^2'. My own investigations of the hand suggest that it is not likely to have been written later than 975.

palaeographical evidence which indicates that the Exeter Book codex is
a compilation of three manuscript booklets. The contents of these
booklets are shown in the following table.

Table 1: Contents of the Three Proposed Booklets

First Booklet: [8r -52v]

Christ I	*Guthlac A*
Christ II	*Guthlac B*
Christ III	

Second Booklet: [53r -97v]

Azarias	*Widsith*
Phoenix	*Fortunes of Men*
Juliana	*Maxims I*
Wanderer	*Order of the World*
Gifts of Men	*Riming Poem*
Precepts	*Panther*
Seafarer	*Whale*
Vainglory	*Partridge* [lines 1-2a]

Third Booklet: [98r-130v]

Homiletic Fragment III	*Descent into Hell*
[lines 3-16 of 'The Partridge']	*Almsgiving*
Soul and Body II	*Pharaoh*
Deor	*Lord's Prayer I*
Wulf and Eadwacer	*Homiletic Fragment II*
Riddles 1-59	*Riddle 30b*
Wife's Lament	*Riddle 60*
Judgment Day 1	*Husband's Message*
Resignation A	*The Ruin*
Resignation B	*Riddles 61-95.*

Divisions among the booklets are supported by the intersection of
several kinds of evidence. One indication in an ancient manuscript of
the separate existence implied in the identification of booklets is the

presence of a soiled first folio.[2] The first such folio in the Exeter Book is 8r, the first page of the poetic texts, but that folio may only prove that the whole codex existed for a period without boards. The feature of a discolored initial page is more useful in identifying the second booklet, however. The whole first quire of the second booklet is slightly browner than those gatherings which precede it, and its first leaf is a bit more soiled. In fact, because the top two and one-half inches, containing material presumably connected with 'Azarias', have been cut from 53r, that same amount of space on 54r is soiled to the same degree as the remainder of the preceding folio. This suggests that 'Azarias' was mutilated before the booklets were bound together, and that the exposed membrane of 53r and 54r served to front the booklet at some period in its history. The third booklet does not offer evidence of a soiled page for its independent existence, but the homiletic fragment which in the past has been taken to be a part of 'The Partridge' is the end of a poem whose beginning is now lost, and this mutilation accounts for the absence of a soiled first page here.

Furthermore, the division of the manuscript is supported by three different grades of limp membrane, each grade restricted to one of the three booklets. Julian Brown has discussed the distribution and differences between what he called insular membrane and continental membrane in manuscripts made, for the most part, much earlier than the Exeter Book. Insular membrane, he says, 'is rather thick; it has a kind of rough, suede-like finish. You can generally see the mark of the scraper on both hair and flesh side; and the hair-side and the flesh-side

---

[2] P.R. Robinson, 'The "Booklet": A Self-Contained Unit in Composite Manuscripts', *Codicologica 3: Essais typologiques*, ed. A. Gruys and J.P. Gumbert (Leiden, 1980), p. 48; also see Robinson, 'Self-Contained Units in Composite Manuscripts of the Anglo-Saxon Period', *ASE* 7 (1978), 231-8, reprinted in the present volume. It should be noted, however, that while soiled pages may indicate that a unit did indeed exist as a separate booklet, the condition is sometimes counterfeited by folia in certain manuscripts which have long lain open at one spread in display cases. For example, in the Exeter Book, the spread on 84v/85r , the opening of 'Widsith', is slightly soiled, apparently because in the past it was regularly displayed on this spread.

are very alike in surface as well as colour'. This is a most apt description of one sort of membrane which is used throughout the Exeter Book. While it varies slightly from booklet to booklet, I should be unwilling to submit so subtle and subjective an evaluation of this variation as evidence of a three-booklet division if it were not further supported by the inclusion in each of the three divisions of strikingly different grades of limp membrane which match Brown's description of continental membrane: 'much thinner, and much smoother (that is, without a nap), ... and with hair sides more yellow in colour, the flesh sides more white than insular membrane, where the distinction is not at all obvious'.[3] Whether this membrane originated on the continent or not, it nevertheless represents a different grade of membrane with its own range of variation, and as such can be used to help trace booklet divisions.

In the first six gatherings, there are nine sheets of this particular membrane, distributed through gatherings two through five. Its flesh side has been heavily pounced, or rubbed with a chalky, white, farinaceous substance, which makes this particular type of membrane very identifiable in good light. It does not appear elsewhere in the Exeter Book manuscript, although it does occur at least once in London, Lambeth Palace Library, MS. 149, Bede's *Super Apocalypsim* and Augustine's *De adulterinis coniugiis*, written in the same hand, and—as Dorothy Coveney has demonstrated—probably in the same scriptorium.[4]

In the second six gatherings, limp membrane is not widely distributed, but does comprise the whole of the eleventh gathering. This membrane is not so well prepared as the limp membrane noted in the first booklet. It lacks the white pouncing on the flesh side which we found earlier, and there is a flaking of the hair side preparation which I have not noted elsewhere in the manuscript. The limp

---

[3] T.J. Brown, 'The Distribution and Significance of Membrane Prepared in the Insular Manner', *La Paléographie hébraïque médiévale*, ed. Jean Glénisson and Colette Sirat (Paris, 1974), p. 128.

[4] Dorothy K. Coveney, 'The Ruling of the Exeter Book', *Scriptorium* 12 (1958), 55; the identification of the hand in Lambeth 149 was made by Kenneth Sisam, as reported by Robin Flower, 'The Script of the Exeter Book', p. 85.

membrane of the last five gatherings is restricted to quires thirteen and fifteen. It is thin, uneven in color generally, being very yellow on the hair side and, evincing a crinkled or cockled nature on the flesh side, gives the impression of not having been at all well prepared. Each of the identifiable types of limp membrane is restricted to one of the three booklets.

As to ruling procedures, all of the gatherings were made up, folded, pricked on a ruled line, opened out and ruled horizontally. Because the membrane varies greatly in thickness, this set of rulings was not sufficient to allow the scribe to enter text on a guideline through the whole gathering without several auxiliary rulings. The difference among the booklets is dependent on the procedure used to add rulings. In gatherings one through six, the auxiliary rulings are made on the rectos of the first folio to need them in quires composed of four bifolium sheets, and on a verso/recto spread in the two quires employing singletons in the format. However, in the second booklet, gatherings seven to twelve, the reruling always takes place on a spread, either the center spread, or the spread between the third and fourth leaves. In gatherings thirteen through seventeen, these added rules are made only on the rectos of the first folio to need them, which is usually the fourth or fifth folio of the gathering. Thus a study of the auxiliary rulings indicates three habitual techniques which correlate exactly with the booklet divisions. [5]

Other evidence to be considered concerns the manuscript's ornamentation, all of which is made in the ink of the text, apparently with the text pen, and—I conclude—by the scribe, himself. The decorative initials of the first six gatherings are truly well made. They are most carefully drawn, with a smoothness of line indicative of a competent craftsman. This is a judgment which cannot be readily demonstrated in the facsimile, but it can be seen in a good light at Exeter. More obvious, perhaps, is the difference in the scribe's technique with respect to the capital or uncial form of the eth: Ð. On

---

[5] An excellent study demonstrating the value of analyzing auxiliary rulings is J. Leroy, 'Quelques systèmes de réglure des manuscrits grecs', *Studia Codicologica*, ed. Kurt Treu, Texte und Untersuchungen zur Geschichte der Altchristlichen Literatur 124 (Berlin, 1977), p. 291-312.

51v an ornate eth opens the final section of 'Guthlac B'. This letter is carefully designed and executed with a sure stroke. The cross bar is neatly balanced on both the vertical and horizontal axes of the letter, and its placement reflects the scribe's developed sense of layout. The first eth encountered in the second booklet, however, is on 57r, and does not reflect nearly the degree of skill that the same letter demonstrated just six folia earlier. The problem is not that this second eth lacks the ornamental strokes of the earlier form, for that might well be intentional, the alteration of initial patterns apparently serving to allow a reader to find his place in the manuscript. The problem with this eth is that it could not have been made by as skilled a hand as made the eth on 51v. The crossbar is unbalanced, and the letter does not sit squarely on its line, but leans topheavily toward the left. The next eth in the proposed second booklet, f. 58, is unique in the manuscript: the scribe has ornamented the D-form on which the eth is based in such a way as to preclude drawing in the crossbar, so he crossed the top of the loop in what looks like an afterthought. The heavy-handed attempt at ornamentation here, as well as the misplaced crossbar, indicate a scribe who simply has not mastered this initial form. The eth on 63r is a bit better, but the crossbar is slightly unbalanced toward the interior of the letter, and the whole again tips a bit toward the left. On 69r the scribe seems still to be experimenting with the form, and chooses to include ornamentation on the vertical line above the crossbar, but not below it. The design is simply unattractive and, I think, reflects a scribe who is not used to working with a capital eth. On 72r and 80r barely-ornamented, split line versions of the letter appear, the second of which is the perfected version of the former in design and execution.

It is possible that the scribe's copying tasks were dominated by Latin texts where he would have had no occasion to make initial eths. If, as the analysis of ligatures below suggests, the booklet were the earliest of the three to have been copied, we may well be able to see there the scribe's experimentation with this new capital form. This letter occurs as a capital initial only once in the proposed third booklet, f.100r, and it is made on a smaller scale and completely without ornamentation, yet it is more nearly balanced than anything in the second booklet, and the characteristic tip toward the left has been corrected.

In the hypothetical third booklet, square, unadorned capitals open many sections, in some cases riddles, and the so-called stanzas of

'Deor' in addition to the decorated initials typical of the rest of the codex. These are the same capitals which we find used after decorative initials in the rest of the manuscript, but which are not used alone elsewhere to initiate a section, with a few exceptions, such as the three bestiary poems, where they are written on a much larger scale. In fact, the scale of the initials throughout the third booklet is generally smaller than that used in the previous two booklets, although this could have been conditioned by the shorter length of the riddling texts. A further indication that a changed sensibility is at work initialing the poems of the last booklet lies in the fact that the initials of riddles 62, 64, 65, and 66 were touched in red lead, which is now badly deteriorated. A similarly deteriorated red also occurs throughout Lambeth 149, written in the same hand. The red, then, particularizes the third booklet by adding a feature to its history not shared by the other two booklets.

Any consideration of the decoration in the Exeter Book must also take into account the drypoint drawings which occur mostly in the margin on seven separate folia. In the facsimile, Förster claimed that the drypoints were added much later, dating them well after the writing of the manuscript on the basis of the costuming of one figure drawing.[6] But such a dating is irrelevant once it is noticed that the writing goes over the drypoint lines in four of the drawings. This proves conclusively that these drypoints and surely others in the same styles were on the parchment first, which—given the accepted dating of the hand—must have been before the third quarter of the tenth century. Table 2 indicates how the drypoints support the tripartite division of the manuscript.

There are no drypoint drawings in the first booklet. The second booklet, however, is remarkable in the number of drypoints it contains. Indeed, there is at least one in every gathering except the ninth, and the ninth is clearly missing both leaves of its second sheet, which may well have held a drypoint.[7] Whether it did or not, however, the second booklet alone is rife with these sometimes rough, sometimes charming drawings incised in the membrane.

---

[6] Max Förster, 'General Description of the Manuscript', *The Exeter Book of Old English Poetry*, ed. R.W. Chambers, Max Förster and Robin Flower (London, 1933), p. 60.

[7] Ibid., p. 58.

Table 2:   Drypoint Drawings in the Exeter Book

Quire	Folio	Description
7	59v	a series of diagonals arranged in left margin as mirror images of one another; *writing crosses design*
8	64v	a foliate design; *writing crosses design*
10	78r	head of an angel, with wings
	80r	the letter *D* outlined twice
11	87v	standing robed figure with book
12	95v	the letter *P* outlined twice; two draped hands, extending down; *writing crosses design*
16	123r	man on horse; the whole figure inverted; *writing crosses design*

The drypoint drawings of the second booklet are treated very differently from the one drypoint in the third booklet. Throughout the second booklet, the drypoints are allowed to stand in the outer margins of the texts, although whether as purposeful decorations or as insignificant blemishes on the membrane is not clear. In any case, these drawings were not considered by the scribe of this part of the manuscript to be sufficiently intrusive to be hidden or rubbed out. The bifolium sheet containing f. 123 has been turned so that this miniature of a horse and rider is upside down at the bottom of the page, and the central portion of the drawing has been rubbed until it is quite thin. Perhaps because this rubbing has not succeeded in removing the drawing, it has been abandoned. But the fact that the page is turned, resulting in obscuring the drawing further, indicates that again, as with the use of the larger capitals for smaller sectional divisions, the sensibilities operant in the third booklet are very different from those at large in the second booklet.

The codicology of the Exeter Book supports the division of the manuscript into the proposed booklets. Nor is paleographical support for the hypothesis lacking. In the 1933 facsimile volume, Robin Flower claimed that 'despite the general identity of letter forms, [there is] such variety in the quality of the script that we must suppose several scribes to have been employed on the writings'; both Neil Ker and

Kenneth Sisam demurred, claiming that one scribe wrote the whole manuscript.[8] The fact of the matter, I think, lies between the two positions. One scribe probably did write the manuscript, but at different times.

Table 3 indicates a definite distinction in the way the long *s* is ligatured with a following *t*, *p*, or *wynn* which accords exactly with the proposed booklet divisions.

Table 3: Distribution of Ligatures with Long *S*

Quire	S+T		S+P		S+Wynn	
	no lig.	*lig.*	*no lig.*	*lig.*	*no lig.*	*lig.*
1	24	17	8	5	2	2
2	21	37	7	9	1	2
3	17	26	6	9	4	0
4	17	30	5	10	3	1
5	15	18	9	4	4	0
6	16	38	15	16	4	5
7	1	70	0	38	0	8
8	0	49	0	42	0	13
9	1	53	0	29	0	10
10	1	59	0	23	0	10
11	0	43	0	33	0	5
12	0	61	0	29	0	4
13	2	86	6	43	2	8
14	1	44	0	39	0	6
15	2	54	2	20	1	4
16	0	48	1	15	1	7
17	1	54	0	13	0	1

---

[8] Flower, 'Script of the Exeter Book', p. 85; Neil R. Ker, *Catalogue of Manuscripts Containing Anglo-Saxon*, p. 153; Kenneth Sisam, 'The Exeter Book', *Studies in the History of Old English Literature* (Oxford, 1953), p. 97.

In the first six gatherings of the Exeter Book, long *s* is almost as often not ligatured as it is ligatured. In gatherings seven to twelve, on the other hand, I have found but three incidences where long *s* is not ligatured with a following *t* out of 565 incidences where it might have been written without a ligature. In gatherings thirteen to seventeen the non-ligatured long *s* is present, but not nearly in so great a concentration as in the first six gatherings: in the last booklet, it occurs 21 times out of 461 possibilities.

A ligature, of course, is as much a part of the calligraphic design of the script as the letter forms themselves. We cannot expect a scribe, who has exhibited freedom with regard to the *s* ligature in six gatherings, suddenly to restrict himself from an established alternative any more than we would expect him suddenly to change an established letter form. The change of habit, then, on f. 53r indicates a textual break which, since a change of scribe is not otherwise evident, must indicate a lapse in time during which this detail of the script was changed. After the second break, between gatherings twelve and thirteen, the scribe is significantly more disposed not to make the ligature than he had been in the second six gatherings, and if the first six gatherings had been written last, we would see the orderly development of this scribal habit from always ligaturing the long *s* with the following *t*, *p*, or *wynn* in gatherings six to twelve, through gatherings thirteen to seventeen, where the scribe occasionally misses a ligature, to the present first six gatherings where he shows what amounts to freedom to ligature or not to ligature. Lambeth 149, written in the same hand, shows the continuity of this development. A count there of the ligatures with long *s* shows that in 776 out of 797 occasions where long *s* and *t* fall together, the ligature was not made. Nor is the ligature ever made with the long *s* and *p* in Lambeth 149. Oxford, Bodleian Library, MS. Bodley 319, Isidore's *De miraculis Christi* also in the same hand, shows only one ligature with this form of the long *s* and *t*.[9] Thus, Bodley 319 may well represent the most

---

[9] The relationship of Bodley 319 to the Exeter Book was first noted by Neil R. Ker, 'Rev. of *The Exeter Book of Old English Poetry*', *Medium Ævum* 2 (1933), 230-31. A carolingian form of the long *s* occurs three times ligatured with *t* in Bodley 319 [fols. 11v, 14r and 62v], and three times in Lambeth 149 [fols. 52v, 82v and 120v], but

recent example of this scribe's work. Because the habits of ligature differ in these latter manuscripts whose integrity as self-sufficient units can hardly be challenged, the three habits of ligature in the Exeter Book support the suggestion that three separate texts have been copied at different times and bound into one codex.

Confirmation of this pattern is offered by a study of the scribe's patterns of choice with regard to the letter *Y*. The script design permits three forms of the letter: an *F*-shaped *Y*, common in the great insular gospel books of the seventh and eighth centuries; a curved *Y* typical of square minuscule; and a straight-sided *Y*. Table 4 indicates the pattern of distribution.[10]

I have been able to determine no linguistic correlations with the use of these forms; there seems to be no particular word nor combination of letters where one is more likely to get one form of the *Y* rather than another. Table 4 indicates the same preference for the curved *Y* as the old *F*-shaped *Y* in the first and third booklets. Again, as with the ligatures, the second booklet is anomalous. The first two gatherings of that booklet show a marked preference for the *F*-shaped *Y* over the curved form. The remaining gatherings in the booklet approximate the distribution of *Y*-forms in the first and third booklets, but with a significantly lesser proportion of the straight-sided *Y*. Indeed, there are but 7.5% of straight-sided *Y*-forms in the whole second booklet, as opposed to 11% and 12% in the other booklets.

Again, a lapse in time between the copying of each booklet will explain the anomalies in the *Y*-forms as well as the ligatures. In the second booklet, the scribe's preferences are in a state of flux. After a hiatus, during which he may have written other things in this hand, he

---

this is a very different construction of the ligature from the one under examination.

[10] In this article's first appearance in *Scriptorium*, I included the frequencies of the ∝ form of the letter *A* in table 4. Bernard Muir, 'A preliminary report on a new edition of the "Exeter Book" ', *Scriptorium* 43 (1989), 274, provides a more accurate count of this form than I; thus, I have removed my count. Moreover, all of the evidence presented here has been reconsidered and the same conclusions are confirmed in my study, *Anglo-Saxon Exeter* (Woodbridge, 1993), pp. 110-47. [PWC]

wrote the third booklet, having developed and internalized a habitual distribution for the *Y*-forms.

Table 4: Distribution of Special Letter Forms

Quire	ſ	ɣ	ẏ
1	84	28	105
2	81	29	123
3	112	33	129
4	77	30	158
5	82	25	132
6	72	18	150
Total	498	163	797
	[34%]	[11%]	[55%]
7	171	24	83
8	148	27	104
9	81	17	105
10	97	20	121
11	91	9	114
12	85	11	125
Total	673	108	652
	[47%]	[7.5%]	[45.5%]
13	74	15	128
14	54	25	101
15	74	45	113
16	66	14	111
17	27	9	48
Total	295	108	501
	[33%]	[12%]	[55%]

If the first booklet were written after the third, as the patterns of ligature and the development of the initial eth suggest, we should not be surprised to find a similar pattern of the *Y*-form distribution. While we do not need to explain the evidence by positing a different scribe for each booklet, we must posit a significant lapse of time following the writing of each section in order to explain both how it is that the habits in ligaturing vary in the way they do, and why the varied distributions of the Y-forms respond to the same boundaries. Such lapses in time do not, of themselves, require us to posit booklet divisions; surely it was possible in the medieval scriptorium to lay one thing aside and come back to it. But a lapse in time which coincides with other indications of booklets—the handling of the initials and drypoints, the soiled outer leaf of the second booklet, the distribution of identifiable types of membrane, and the variation in ruling procedures—very strongly asserts the validity of the hypothesis.

Once the booklets are verified by the physical evidence of the manuscript, we need to survey the effect of this manuscript structure on our perceptions of the poetry contained within it. P. R. Robinson points out that the fundamental criterion for determining a booklet is that its 'contents form a self-sufficient unit'; that is, any part of a codex designated as a booklet must display a form and function quite independent of its context within the codex.[11] In short, while there must be codicological reasons to identify a unit as a booklet, there must also be literary reasons to support that unit's integrity as a booklet. Such literary justification for a booklet's boundaries may be a relatively simple matter where its contents are homilies following a liturgical rationale, or copies of charters unified by references to a single locale, royal personage, or religious foundation, or especially where the booklet is constituted of a single work. Literary justification for a unit's self-sufficiency is more difficult to assess where a great deal of variation exists among the contents, and very much more difficult where the contents are, like those of the Exeter Book, primarily works of art without discernible utilitarian functions to unify them, such as homilies and charters have. Certainly the effect of the hypothesis set forth here will be to challenge scholars and critics of Old English literature to reconsider these poems anew from the standpoint of the more restricted collections in which they are contained. The new alliances thus formed by the booklet divisions should provide particularly interesting material for scholars seeking to apply contemporary literary critical theory in which the very definition of 'a text' is at issue. It is likely, then, that any final agreement about the

---

[11] Robinson, 'The Booklet', p. 47.

homogeneity of the texts in each of the booklets will take several years to formulate fully.

At present, then, I shall venture but a few general observations about the literary relationships among the poems of the three proposed booklets to justify them as 'self-sufficient units'. The first three works in the first booklet are organized respectively around the incarnation, the ascension, and the second coming of Christ; the next two pieces are based on the holy living and holy dying of St. Guthlac. Each of these five sub-sections employs its own source materials. Thus, biographical chronology seems to have provided the informing principle of selection for the poems in the first booklet, and its repetition in the 'Christ' and 'Guthlac' collections certifies that booklet's essential unity. The third booklet, on the other hand, is unified by the large collection of riddles which runs through it. The fact that all of the shorter Exeter Book poems which also occur elsewhere in apparently related texts—'Soul and Body II', 'The Judgment Day I' and 'The Lord's Prayer I'—are poems of the third booklet, suggests a textual history for the third booklet which is not shared by the other two booklets, and creates a powerful argument for the third booklet as a self-sufficient unit. James Anderson's study of several riddles and poems unified in this part of the manuscript through references to Easter imagery in a 'riddlic' mode makes an even stronger case for the booklet's literary integrity.[12] The poems in the hypothetical second booklet do not make so coherent a collection as the works of the first and third booklets, although such poems as 'The Wanderer' and 'The Seafarer'; 'The Gifts ...' and 'The Fortunes of Men'; and 'The Panther', 'The Whale' and what remains of 'The Partridge' are all maintained in the one booklet. I have briefly suggested elsewhere that the ten shorter poems following 'Juliana', from 'The Wanderer' to 'Widsith', constitute a sequence which builds upon the dual themes of exile and gleomanry.[13] This booklet, then, might be seen to consist of three long poems (if we assume 'Azarias' was longer than what remains of it) followed by two sequences, the

---

[12] James Anderson, *Two Literary Riddles in the Exeter Book: Riddle 1 and the Easter Riddle* (Norman, Ok., 1986).

[13] Patrick W. Conner, *A Contextual Study of the Old English Exeter Book* (unpubl. Ph.D. dissertation, University of Maryland, 1975), pp. 70-103.

'Wanderer/Widsith' sequence and a sequence of bestiary poems. Such an analysis notwithstanding, the texts of the second booklet could certainly have existed as a separate collection of miscellaneous poems. The earliest reference to the collection, its description in Leofric's inventory, identifies the whole codex as a 'mycel englisc boc be gehwylcum þingum on leoðwisan geworht', that is, a 'great English book with everything composed in verse'.[14] There is nothing improbable, then, in the second booklet's having been a smaller English book with all sorts of things composed in verse.

The advantage, therefore, of recognizing the three-booklet structure of the Exeter Book is that it allows students of Old English poetry to examine and exploit the juxtaposition of poems within each booklet without having to account for the relationship of apparently disparate texts in different booklets. But perhaps even more interesting for the student of medieval manuscripts is that such recognition establishes the Exeter Book in a parallel relationship to the other three major poetic codices in Old English: they all exist in composite manuscripts. Oxford, Bodleian Library, MS. Junius 11 clearly contains two booklets; the Nowell Codex contains several booklets, and *Beowulf* itself may have existed as a single, unbound booklet; the Vercelli Book was apparently developed over a period of time in booklets, by one scribe.[15] Future refinements in the dating and locating of Old English poetic texts may well depend on our development of the implications of this fact.[16]

---

[14] For references to Leofric's inventory, see above, note (1).

[15] The most thorough recent studies of these manuscripts are, respectively: Peter J. Lucas, 'MS. Junius 11 and Malmesbury', *Scriptorium*, 34 (1980), 197-220 and 35 (1981), 3-22; Kevin S. Kiernan, *Beowulf and the Beowulf Manuscript* (New Brunswick, N.J., 1981); D.G. Scragg, 'The Compilation of the Vercelli Book', *ASE*, 2 (1973), 189-207, reprinted in the present volume.

[16] I am most grateful to the Dean and Chapter of Exeter Cathedral for permission to examine the Exeter Book extensively during the summer of 1984, and to Mrs. Audrey Erskine, Archivist of the Exeter Cathedral Library, for her interest in and support of this project.

The Compilation of the Vercelli Book

D.G. Scragg

The Vercelli Book, as is well known, is a codex of the late tenth century containing a selection of religious prose and verse in Old English. Of the manuscript's twenty-nine items (some of which are defective owing to loss of leaves), six are alliterative poems and the rest prose homilies. There seems little doubt that one scribe (henceforth referred to as V) was responsible for writing the whole of the codex, even though the size of the writing changes considerably at various points, particularly towards the end of the volume where the lineation also changes.[1] As the earliest of the four extant poetic

---

[1] A full description of the manuscript is to be found in N.R. Ker, *Catalogue of Manuscripts Containing Anglo-Saxon* (Oxford, 1957); cf. also the facsimile of the manuscript, *Il Codice Vercellese* (Rome, 1913), with an introduction in Italian by Max Förster (the facsimile foliated to reproduce the manuscript). The publication of a new facsimile in EEMF, with an introduction by Celia Sisam, appeared as volume 19 in 1976.

The most convenient edition of the poetry in the Vercelli Book is *The Vercelli Book*, ed. George Philip Krapp, The Anglo-Saxon Poetic Records 2 (New York, 1932), from which the titles used in this paper are taken. Not all of the prose has yet appeared in a modern edition, and references to it are therefore to folio and line of the manuscript. Max Förster's definitive edition of the homilies was interrupted by the second world war, and only the first eight, together with the opening of the ninth, were published (*Die Vercelli-Homilien*, Bibliothek der angelsächsischen Prosa 12 [Hamburg, 1932; rptd without homily IX Darmstadt, 1964]). Another volume, set up in type but not printed, was lost during the war, and Förster handed the project and his materials over to Rudolph Willard of Austin, Texas, before his death

317

codices and the earliest surviving collection of homilies in the
vernacular, the book is potentially a most important source of
knowledge of tenth-century English; most linguistic studies which range
over Old English as a whole have included some reference to it. Yet
the language of the manuscript is a relatively neglected subject of
study, the place of its composition has not been established and the
circumstances of its compilation have not been fully explained.[2] This
paper seeks to learn more of the book's origin in two ways: firstly, by
examining its make-up in an attempt to determine the number and the
nature of the sources that V used, and, secondly, by considering the
distribution of distinctive linguistic forms in the manuscript in order to
find out more about the nature of V's exemplars and about his
background and training as displayed in his attitude to the language of
his exemplars.

It is difficult to discern any principle of arrangement in the items
of the collection. No attempt is made to follow the order of the church
year, and the poems are distributed amongst the homilies in a way that

---

in 1955. On the assumption that Willard will not now publish, a new
edition is in course of preparation by Paul Szarmach (see Postscript, p.
343). Meanwhile, homilies IX, XV and XXII are available in Max
Förster, 'Der Vercelli-Codex CXVII nebst Abdruck einiger
altenglischer Homilien der Handschrift', *Festschrift für Lorenz
Morsbach*, ed. F. Holthausen and H. Spies, Studien zur englischen
Philologie 50 (Halle, 1913), 20-179; and homily XI is available in
Rudolph Willard, '*Vercelli Homily XI* and its Sources', *Speculum* 24
(1949), 76-87; homily XIII in R. P. Wülker, 'Über das Vercellibuch',
Anglia 5 (1882), 451-65; and homily XXIII in Paul Gonser, *Das
angelsächsische Prosa-leben des hl. Guthlac* (Heidelberg, 1909; rptd
Amsterdam, 1966).

[2] On the language of the manuscript see below, p. 326, n. 16.
With regard to the book's origin, P.O.E. Gradon in *Cynewulf's Elene*
(London, 1958), pp. 3-5, discounts the earlier view of Förster that it
was written in Worcester and, by implication, Vleeskruyer's suggestion
that it is Mercian compilation (*The Life of St Chad* [Amsterdam, 1953],
p. 58). She concludes: 'further research ... might usefully start from
the hypothesis that it is a Winchester or Canterbury book (perhaps with
Glastonbury antecedents)'.

is difficult to understand. Amongst the prose items there is considerable overlap, there being two Christmas homilies (V and VI, not consecutive but divided by two poems) and a number of Rogation pieces (XI, XII and XIII in a series for the three days of the festival, X independent of those three, and XIX and XX, again intended to be read consecutively but independent of the other Rogation items). The fact that the second half of homily XXI is a version of homily II suggests that the compiler of the collection was working so haphazardly that he inadvertently repeated material. Nevertheless some of the items have a deliberate relationship (e.g. the three Rogation homilies XI-XIII, and homilies VIII and IX for the first and second Sundays after Epiphany), and there is evidence that the compiler drew upon at least one existing sequence of homilies in that homilies VII-X are numbered *ii-v*.[3]

It cannot be assumed that the items of the collection were copied in the order in which they now stand. The present order of quires was probably the final decision of V, whatever the order in which items and quires were written, for the quire signatures are contemporary, almost certainly in V's hand. But the end of a quire coincides with the end of an item twice in the volume, at fol. 24 (quire 3, homily IV) and at fol. 120 (quire 17, homily XXII), in each case a blank half page now remaining. The last leaf and the concluding signature of quire 3 are missing, and since there would not be room for a complete item on a single leaf, it is to be presumed that the lost leaf was blank except for the signature. Thus homily V, which begins at the head of quire 4, was not originally intended to follow homily IV; the writing of quire 4 had already begun (or was complete) when the two quires were placed together, otherwise the final blank leaf of quire 3 would have been utilized. There is no proof of the relative order of copying of the two quires,[4] and homily V may well have been planned as the opening

---

[3] See discussion below, p. 322-4.

[4] Quire 4 is unique in the manuscript in having twenty-nine lines to a page. Throughout the volume lineation varies according to gathering, but there is a basic division between quires 1-14 (excluding 4) with twenty-four lines (increased to twenty-five in quires 2 and 7) and quires 15-19 with from thirty-one to thirty-three lines. Differences in the size of script consequent upon lineation changes led Richard P. Wülker

item of a collection; it is a Nativity homily, and as such would be a
suitable opening item for a collection following the order of the church
year. (The homily survives in two other collections, Cambridge,
Corpus Christi College, MS. 198, and Oxford, Bodleian Library, MS.
Bodley 340, in each case as the opening item.)

Quire 17 is not a full quire but consists of two single leaves (fols.
119 and 120); at least one more leaf must have been present when the
manuscript was assembled, for the concluding signature of the quire is
missing. The likelihood is that quire 17 has lost a number of leaves,[5]
probably blank but perhaps containing another item. In either case, the
two items now juxtaposed in the Vercelli Book, homily XXII which
concludes on the two surviving leaves of quire 17, and the poem *Elene*
which begins on the opening leaf of quire 18, are unlikely to have been
consecutive in a source used by V. If, as seems probable, the lost leaf

---

(*Grundriss zur Geschichte der angelsächsischen Litteratur* [Leipzig,
1885], p. 239) to postulate a second scribe for quires 15-19, and even
to suggest the possibility of a third for quire 4. The major change in
lineation after quire 14 is acceptable as a basic change of policy on the
scribe's part, but the change to twenty-nine lines in quire 4 and then
back to twenty-four/twenty-five subsequently shows a curious
inconsistency. If, however, quire 4 was ruled (and perhaps partly
written) before quires 1-3, the number of radical changes in lineation
is reduced to the minimum of three.

[5] Eleven quires in the codex consist (or consisted before the loss of
odd leaves) of four sheets of parchment folded to make eight leaves.
Three more have an extra leaf inserted, making nine leaves, one has
only three bifolia (six leaves), two have three bifolia and a single leaf
(seven leaves), and one has five bifolia (ten leaves). It is thus unlikely
that quire 17 when constituted had less than six leaves. It is clear that
the two single leaves do not belong to an adjoining quire but are the
remains of a separate one because the Vercelli Book is unusual in
having two signatures to each quire, a numeral at the head of the first
page and a letter at the foot of the last. Quire 17's opening numeral
remains, though its conclusion is lost.

or leaves were blank, then the hiatus is similar to that between quires 3 and 4.[6]

Three blocks of quires have now been defined: A, quires 1-3, containing homilies I-IV; B, quires 4-17, containing homily V, *Andreas*, *Fates of the Apostles*, homilies VI-XVIII, *Soul and Body I*, *Homiletic Fragment I*, *Dream of the Rood* and homilies XIX-XXII; and C quires 18 and 19, containing *Elene* and homily XXIII. The divisions between the blocks mark points at which the copying of items was not consecutive, and it is likely that at each of these points V turned to a different source. Differences within block B point to the use by a compiler of further sources for that block, though it cannot be shown definitely that material from some or all of them had not been combined already in a source used by V.

Sections A and C are each homogeneous palaeographically. The three quires of A are of similar length,[7] with twenty-four or twenty-five lines to a page, and the four homilies they contain are more or less uniform in presentation (e.g. each begins at the head of a page, each opens with an initial capital spread over two lines [except for homily I, the opening of which is obscured], and each has a letter or letters in square capitals following the initial, in homily II the capitals continuing for the full length of the first line). Section C has two quires of uniform length (eight leaves, except that the last leaf of the final quire, probably blank except for the signature, has been lost). The first item of C, *Elene*, is divided into numbered fitts, each separated by a blank line, and each opening with a large capital. Similarly, the only other item of C, homily XXIII, is separated from *Elene* by a blank line, and it too opens with a large capital.

---

[6] As with quires 3 and 4, there is no proof of the relative order of writing of quires 17 and 18, but two features make it probable that they were consecutive: the increase in number of lines per page which occurred in quire 15 is maintained throughout the rest of the book, and a sequence of four pen trials made by V, which take the form of the abbreviation *xƀ* (cf. Kenneth Sisam, *Studies in the History of Old English Literature* [Oxford, 1953], pp. 109-10), begins in quire 17 and continues in quire 18.

[7] Quires 1 and 2 have four bifolia plus one leaf and quire 3 has three bifolia plus one leaf.

Section B, however, contains a number of marked subdivisions. The section opens with homily V which, unlike the homilies of section A, is headed by a minuscule title in English and Latin (*To middan wintra. Ostende nobis domine*); the first word of the homily proper is capitalized, with the initial covering two lines. A half page is left blank at the end of the homily. The next item, *Andreas*, has sectional divisions separated by a single blank line, each section beginning with a capitalized word, the initial letter of which is larger than the rest. Two of the initials are slightly ornamented (on 47v and 51r) and that on 49r is a fine zoomorphic *H*. *Fates of the Apostles* is the first item in the codex which does not begin at the head of a page; instead, it is divided from *Andreas* in the same way that sectional divisions of the longer poem are separated. The first word of *Fates of the Apostles* lacks its initial (*H*) but in the space left for it and in the margin alongside, the faint outline of a zoomorphic design similar to that on 49r may be seen.[8] The manuscript presentation has been put forward as an argument in favour of the theory that the poem with its runic acrostic is an epilogue to *Andreas*,[9] but such a view is not supported by comparison with *Elene*, at the end of the Vercelli Book, where homily XXIII which follows it is presented like a section of the poem. Nevertheless there may be justification for seeing *Andreas* and *Fates of the Apostles* as having a longer manuscript history in common with each other than either has with neighbouring items in the Vercelli collection.

It has already been observed that homilies VII-X are connected by the numerals *ii-v*. Superficial resemblances in the presentation of these items add to the impression that they form a collection which antedates

---

[8] The ascender with a 'knucklebone' at the top and bulbous decoration half-way down is the most obvious, though itself faint. Also visible is the rounding of the bow. The lines are thin, but very black, a slight surrounding dusting of the parchment possibly suggesting a form of crayon- or pencil-work rather than ink. The marks appear not to have been noted previously and cannot be seen in Förster's facsimile. Together with the 'practice' initial on 109v (and another on 112r which is more likely to be the work of a later copyist), they offer interesting material for the study of manuscript illumination.

[9] Cf. Ker, *Catalogue*, p. 461.

the Vercelli one: each homily ends part way down a page and is followed after a break of one or two lines by new material; each has its introductory numeral on the blank line between it and the preceding item. Homily VI, preceding this group, begins at the top of a page, and has two lines of Latin title in minuscule; then, after a single-line break, the homily opens like those of the following group, with the first word capitalized and the initial letter of it larger. Thus this homily might be number 1 of the series. Ker's *Catalogue* mentions a numeral *i* attached to this homily. Miss Gradon has suggested that it is perhaps visible at the foot of the preceding page (54r), after the blank space left at the end of *Fates of the Apostles*,[10] but this is not so, as what can be seen in the Förster facsimile at this point is a reagent stain which shows through from the foot of 54v.[11] No numeral *i* exists, though this, it should be added, does not preclude homily VI from being the first of the numbered series. At the end of the group VII-X the numeral *vi* appears immediately after the close of homily X. The item which is so numbered might be expected to begin on the following line if the pattern of homilies VII-X were to be followed, but instead the rest of the page (about two-thirds of the whole) is left blank, homily XI, the next item, starting at the top of the next page (71v). Since no further numeral occurs in the codex, it is possible that homily XI on the new page represents the beginning of material taken from a fresh source, and is not the homily referred to by the numeral *vi*, especially as homily XI is clearly closely related to those that follow it, which are without numerals. The explanation for the homily numbered *vi* (whether it is the present XI or not) not being copied when the numeral was written may lie in the fact that homily X ends half way down the

---

[10] *Ibid.*; Gradon, *Cynewulf's Elene*, p. 5, n. 3.

[11] A number of pages in the manuscript are marked by discoloured areas which coincide with parts of the text which its first known modern transcriber, a German scholar called Maier, found difficult to read. It is normally assumed that reagent was applied by Maier to bring up faded passages, e.g. fol. 1, probably exposed before the present nineteenth-century binding was added, but it should be noted that reagent has sometimes been applied to words which had been scratched out, either by V or by a near-contemporary reader, e.g. at 65r15.

recto of the last sheet of a gathering: perhaps the scribe reached the end
of the homily and wrote *vi*, fully intending to copy another homily
immediately, without a break, as he had done with the preceding items,
but broke off to prepare a new gathering, and, when returning to
writing, began at the top of a fresh page either because the material
was no longer what he would have copied as *vi* or because he had
forgotten his earlier plan.[12]

Homilies XI-XIII are related by their similarly worded minuscule
rubrics: *Spel to forman, ðam oðrum* and *þriddan gangdæge*. Each
homily ends part way down a page and is followed without a break by
new material. Each, too, has its opening word in capitals with the
initial letter over two lines. Homily XIV seems to be related to them,
as it is the only other homily in the codex with a rubric, this time
Larspel to swylcere tide swa man wile, which is written partly on the
half line left at the end of the preceding homily, the only indications
that it is the start of a fresh item being in the colour of the ink (not
visible in the facsimile) and in the rather wider spacing of the letters in
the rubric as compared with those in black ink. Again the opening
word of the homily is in square capitals with the initial letter over two
lines. In all four homilies the opening word or letter of the homily is
in red also, and *a e n* of *amen* at the end of homily XIII are shaded in
red. No colouring appears anywhere else in the manuscript.

Homilies XV-XVIII all follow on from each other and from the
preceding item (homily XIV) without any space left in the manuscript,
even to the extent, in homily XVIII's case, of the new piece beginning
on the last line of a page. But the headings to these four are quite
different from those to all other items in the collection, and yet are
sufficiently uniform in themselves for the assumption to be made that
they form another group from a single source: all four have Latin
headings in square capitals and each opens with a capitalized

---

[12] Professor Clemoes, to whom I am grateful for a most helpful
commentary on the first draft of this paper, has suggested to me that
the numbers *ii-vi* may refer to the homilies *above* them. This solves
the difficulty of the missing homily *vi* and also explains the absence of
a number *i* at the beginning of the sequence, but leaves the odd
circumstance that the scribe copied a sequence beginning with a homily
numbered *ii*.

abbreviation (M̄) extending over two lines. The abbreviation is in itself distinctive, standing as it does for *Men þa leofestan*, a formula which elsewhere in the manuscript is either written in full or abbreviated with more indication of the whole phrase (e.g. *men þa ł, m̄ þa leofestan*).[13] Homily XVIII is followed by three short poems, *Soul and Body I*, *Homiletic Fragment I* and *Dream of the Rood*. A lost leaf after fol. 103 contained the end of the first poem and the beginning of the second, so that it is not possible to associate the three on grounds of manuscript presentation. *Dream of the Rood* begins on the last leaf of quire 14 and continues in quire 15; it is with the latter quire that the considerable increase in lines per page noted above[14] occurs.

Homilies XIX-XXI form a distinct group. The first and last have zoomorphic initial letters, while XX has a space for an ornate initial capital although no letter is omitted from the text. Partly filling the blank space are two early attempts at the opening letter (a large square *M*) and also one of the second letter (*E*); all three have been somewhat sketchily erased. At the foot of the page (not visible in the facsimile) is a faint outline of a zoomorphic initial. The hesitation expressed in the erasures, the space ultimately left for an initial decoration, and the apparent practice outline of a zoomorphic design below suggest that the scribe felt bound to reproduce some decorative work but was in some way defeated by it.[15] Had a zoomorphic device been completed for homily XX, all three items would have had identical openings, being otherwise similar now (e.g. in having the opening word or phrase completed in large square capitals extending over two lines). Homily XXII, which is without any initial decoration, cannot be definitely

---

[13] The abbreviation *m̄* for the whole phrase also occurs frequently (ten times) within these four homilies. It is interesting to note the repetition of two opening formulae following the *M*-abbreviation in these items. Homilies XV and XVII have variations on one theme: 'Sægð us on þyssum bocum hu ...' (XV) and 'Sægeð us 7 myngaþ þis halige godspelle be ...' (XVII); while XVI and XVIII have another: 'Sceolon we nú hwylcumhwegu wordum secgan be ...' (XVI) and 'Magon we nu hwylcumhwego wordum asecgan be ...'(XVIII).

[14] P. 319, n. 4.

[15] Cf. the discussion on the decorated initial to *Fates of the Apostles* above p. 322 and n. 8.

associated with the group XIX-XXI. It does not begin with the formula
Men þa leofestan as they do, and the writing at its opening consists of
finer strokes and slightly smaller letters than does that at the end of
homily XXI (though this may be due merely to the scribe's use of a
newly sharpened pen). It does, however, begin on the half page left
blank at the completion of homily XXI.

The following are tentative groupings of the items in the codex,
perhaps reflecting separate sources for the material. It is emphasized
that these represent a useful working hypothesis rather than a definitive
statement. The groups are separated on the basis of the evidence so far
presented, dubious divisions being indicated by the use of lower case
letters.

Group A   Homilies I-IV

Group B   1a   Homily V
             1b   *Andreas* and *Fates of the Apostles*
             2a   Homilies VI-X
             2b   Homilies XI-XIV
             3   Homilies XV-XVIII
             4a   *Soul and Body I, Homiletic
                  Fragment I* and *Dream of the Rood*
             4b   Homilies XIX-XXI
             4c   Homily XXII

Group C   *Elene* and homily XXIII

The point has now been reached at which it is possible to consider the
language of the codex. There is insufficient scope within the bounds
of this paper to consider the language of individual items in the
collection in detail; this has already been done for some of them,[16]

---

[16] Cf. for the poetry, Gradon, *Cynewulf's Elene*; *Andreas and the
Fates of the Apostles*, ed. Kenneth R. Brooks (Oxford, 1961); *The
Dream of the Rood*, ed. Michael Swanton (Manchester, 1970); Sisam,
Studies, pp. 119-39; and Jane Weightman, *The Language and Dialect
of the Later Old English Poetry* (Liverpool, 1907). On the prose, apart
from the scattered comments of Förster, there are brief but accurate

and publication of more thorough investigations may profitably await the appearance of a complete edition of the prose. But relevant to the question of the compilation of the manuscript is the linguistic conformity, relatively speaking, which exists within some of the groups defined above. Furthermore, V's language (and perhaps the manuscript's origin) may to some extent be detected from an analysis of these separate groups. It can easily be seen that no scribe interested in the normalization of language has ever copied the whole of the Vercelli Book material; for the most part, V copied mechanically, and in doing so preserved invaluable linguistic material from his exemplars. But no professional copyist could avoid imposing his own forms on words of very frequent occurrence in a task as lengthy as the compilation of this codex. Clearly the dative article form *þam* is V's preferred spelling, for no variant occurs;[17] yet it cannot be assumed from this that no variant occurred in the exemplars. The imposition of a scribe's form is appreciable when the form is invariable, but it may occur when more than one spelling is regular also. V wrote the pronoun *heo* fifty-five times in the course of the manuscript, and *hio* sixty-nine times; it is not now possible to say which of these he preferred, if indeed he had a preference, but it is possible that in many of the instances he changed an exemplar *heo* to *hio* or vice versa without being aware that he had done so. It is even possible that he changed his practice at some point during the copying, since he changed other mechanical things like the number of lines to a page more than once, on one occasion radically.[18] Such self-evident observations are iterated to emphasize that the task of isolating V's

---

observations by Vleeskruyer, *St Chad*, valuable pointers by Hans Schabram, *Superbia* (Munich, 1965), pp. 77-87, and a circumscribed study of the unpublished homilies by Paul W. Peterson, 'Dialect Grouping in the Unpublished Vercelli Homilies', *Studies in Philology* 50 (1953), 559-65.

[17] It is assumed that *ðam* is not a variant *spelling*. *ð* and *þ* are allographics of one grapheme, with a partial complementary distribution in the codex (*þ* is preferred in initial positions), just as long, low and round *s* are part of the grapheme <s> (and again one of them, the long form, is preferred initially).

[18] See p. 319, n. 4.

forms from those of his exemplars is not easy, and that the conclusions which follow are necessarily tentative. They rely on an accumulation of relatively minor points, with disproportionate weight attached to a few forms and with very great danger of being misled by a scribe's mechanical error.

The value of the linguistic evidence and some of its attendant problems may be illustrated by considering first, in isolation, the occurrence of a single linguistic feature throughout the codex: the distribution of examples of the digraph *io*. The two sequences *io* and *eo* occur in Old English in words with Common Germanic (CG) *eu* and *iu*, and also in those with CG *e* and *i* in certain contexts (i.e. when subject to breaking or back mutation). The pattern observed in Old English texts is as follows: in Northumbrian *eo* is in general the reflex of CG *e* and *eu*, and *io* that of CG *i* and *iu*; Mercian (the Vespasian Psalter) shows a preference for *eo* for CG *e* and *i*, but confuses *eo* and *io* for CG *eu* and *iu* (in Rushworth[(1)] the spread of *eo* is even more pronounced); in West Saxon *eo* is generally preferred, though *io* occasionally appears in early West Saxon (especially in the *Cura Pastoralis*) for CG *i* and *iu*; in Kentish *io* is almost universal for CG *eu* and *iu* but both digraphs appear for CG *e* and *i*.[19]   Although theoretically *io* is a useful guide to a manuscript's origin, in practice it has rarely proved so; for example, Dr Sisam's masterly study of the compilation of the *Beowulf* codex (from which the present paper has benefited greatly) failed to explain the distribution of *io* instances.[20] In the Vercelli Book the phenomenon has proved no less puzzling: as Sisam observed, 'most of the pieces have some *io* forms, but they cluster or thin out in a way that is hard to explain'.[21]   But in table 1, showing the distribution and etymology of all the *io* words in the codex, a certain patterning may yet be discerned. The distribution of forms argues against them being in the main the introduction of V. The items after homily XV, with the exception of homily XXII and *Elene*, have few examples, yet since there are frequent instances in these two items, it cannot be assumed that V changed his practice after

---

[19] Cf. A. Campbell, *Old English Grammar* (Oxford, 1957), §§ 293-7, for further details.

[20] *Studies*, pp. 65-96 (esp. p. 93).

[21] *Ibid*. pp. 104-5.

Table 1. *Distribution of the digraph* io *in the Vercelli Book*

Groups…	A			B1a		B1b	B2a					B2b				B3				B4a	B4b			B4c	C		
Items…	I	II	III	IV	V	Andr.Fates	VI	VII	VIII	IX	X	XI	XII	XIII	XIV	XV	XVI	XVII	XVIII	Poems 1 2 3	XIX	XX	XXI	XXII	Elene	XXIII	Total
io as a reflex of																											
CG ě	—	—	—	3	—	2	1	8	8	8	15	9	8	5	5	5	—	—	—	2 —	—	—	1	1	2	—	77
CG eu	—	3	1	4	3	3	—	5	4	6	3	1	1	—	—	3	—	—	—	—	—	—	—	—	3	—	24
CG y̌	4	—	1	—	1	3	5	1	1	3	6	1	1	—	3	—	—	—	—	—	—	—	—	—	2	—	40
CG ī	—	—	—	—	—	—	1	1	—	—	1	1	—	1	3	—	—	—	—	—	—	—	—	—	1	—	9
CG iu	12	17	44	52	24	7	10	22	11	27	30	13	11	—	22	23	2	1	4	1 1	—	1	—	25	33	1	393
CG iu+i/j	—	—	—	—	—	—	—	1	—	1	—	2	1	1	—	—	—	—	—	1	—	—	—	1	1	—	5
CG jū	—	—	—	—	—	1	—	—	—	1	3	—	—	—	—	—	—	—	1	—	1	—	—	—	—	—	9

Poems 1, 2 and 3 are respectively *Soul and Body I*, *Homiletic Fragment I* and *Dream of the Rood*

Also with io are *giomrunga*, 'lamentation', homily X/68r11 (CG *g*+*æ̃*+nasal), and three words of obscure etymology: *diogol*, 'secret', 1/2v20 (CG *au+i/j* and suffix substitution -*ol* for -*il*?); *gebiorđor*, 'birth', X/65v20 (CG) *e*? perhaps an ablaut variant of CG -*burþi*-, OE *gebyrde*); and *scionesse*, 'incitement', XXII/119r31 (CG *sc*+*ā* or *ū*).

Table 2. *Distribution of* eo *and* io *in four common words in the Vercelli Book:* beon, *'be'*; seo, *'the'*; heo, *'she'; and* deofol, *'devil'*

Groups…	A			B1a		B1b	B2a					B2b				B3				B4a	B4b			B4c	C		
Items…	I	II	III	IV	V	Andr.Fates	VI	VII	VIII	IX	X	XI	XII	XIII	XIV	XV	XVI	XVII	XVIII	Poems 1 2 3	XIX	XX	XXI	XXII	Elene	XXIII	Total
eo:																											
parts of *beon*	4	6	4	11	—	4	—	—	—	—	—	—	—	1	1	14	7	7	4	4 2	1	7	19	11	3	2	112
seo	1	2	2	1	—	6	—	—	—	—	—	—	—	—	—	2	8	1	—	— 1	3	16	12	3	11	1	70
heo	—	1	15	1	6	—	—	—	—	—	—	—	—	—	—	2	4	10	—	—	—	20	1	4	12	—	55
deofol	1	—	1	—	2	7	—	—	—	—	—	—	—	—	1	—	—	—	7	1	8	8	8	5	5	3	65
io:																											
parts of *bion*	6	3	7	32	11	1	—	—	—	9	13	9	1	2	4	17	1	1	1	1 1	—	—	—	6	1	—	142
sio	5	3	17	8	7	4	4	9	1	9	9	1	2	4	1	2	2	—	—	—	—	—	—	—	10	14	119
hio	—	1	15	4	6	—	4	5	—	—	—	2	4	1	1	2	—	—	—	—	—	—	—	—	7	18	69
diofol	—	9	5	8	—	2	2	3	6	2	2	4	—	—	—	4	4	—	—	—	—	—	—	3	2	—	56

heo and *hio* appear in *Elene* for 'they' as well as for 'she'; the numbers are inclusive.

homily XV. The inevitable conclusion is that he was in some way influenced by the distribution of *eo* and *io* in his exemplars, a conclusion which may be tested against the separate exemplars defined in the groups stipulated above. Certainly there are significant differences in the distribution of forms in the various groups. For example, the greatest number of instances of *io* as the reflex of CG *e* and *eu* occurs in group B2, whereas groups B3 and B4b are completely free of them. Group B4b, in fact, has only one instance of *io*, and in group B3 they are scarce except in the first item of the group.

Table 2, which shows the comparative distribution of *eo* and *io* in some common words (all with CG *iu*), may make the situation clearer. Particularly noticeable are the complete absence of *eo* in group B2a and its scarcity in B2b. Furthermore the comparatively large number of instances of *io* for CG *iu* shown by table 1 to occur in homily XV, the first item of group B3, is seen to be confined to the four words of table 2, and is balanced by an equal number of instances of *eo* in the same words. If group B3's other linguistic evidence is reliable, its contents were derived by V from a Mercian source.[22] Yet in Mercian texts *io* forms ought to be rare, or at least not as frequent as they are in homily XV. Is it justifiable to see *io* in this homily as V's introduction? The twenty-six instances of *io* in the homily occur only in common words: parts of *bion*, *sio*, *diofol* and three examples of the possessive adjective *hiora*. With the exception of the last, these are words which occur very frequently with *io* in group B2, which V copied immediately before homily XV, and even in the case of *hiora*, a form almost never used in group B2 where *hira* and *hyra* are usual, there is the parallel of the pronoun *hio*. After homily XIV, instances of the digraph *io* in the codex reduce gradually until they disappear entirely in homilies XX and XXI. It is, then, reasonable to see all instances after homily XIV as having been introduced by V, who slowly forgot the digraph he became so accustomed to in the copying of group B2 and reproduced only the *eo* spelling of his exemplars for the material from homily XV to homily XXI. In homily XXII and *Elene*, *io* reappears in considerable numbers, presumably because once again *io* was used in the exemplars.

---

[22] Cf. below, p. 335.

In group B4b there occurs a single instance of *io* in *bion*, 'bees' (107v26, homily XIX), a form that baffled Sisam when he tried to determine the compilation history of the Vercelli Book.[23] But the form is explicable as long as it is recognized that V frequently copied mechanically and unintelligently, to the extent that he showed no grasp of the contextual meaning of words copied.[24] It is proposed that the fairly large number of *io* instances in homily XV were introduced by V, i.e. he changed his exemplar *beon, seo, deofol* and *heora* to *bion, sio, diofol* and *hiora* almost as often as he retained the exemplar spelling.[25] Subsequently, in homilies XVI-XVIII, *io* occurs only eight times: *sio* twice, *diofol* three times, *giogoðhade* once, and once each *bioð* and *bion*, 'be'. In the poems which follow homily XVIII, *siofa(n)* appears twice and there are two instances of *bioð*. Hence in more than twenty-two folios from the end of homily XV to the beginning of homily XIX, V wrote *io* only twelve times. Some of the instances, particularly *giogoðhade* and *siofa*, may be exemplar spellings, but it is not likely that *io* was used regularly in the exemplars (i.e. more often than it appears here) because V was not interested in removing it, as may be seen by other parts of the codex, copied both earlier and later. It is very probable that at least nine instances of *io* here were introduced by V himself into words with which he was especially familiar, and that he further introduced *io* into *bion*, 'bees', of homily XIX under the impression that this again was the common substantive verb.

The distribution of words with *io* has shown that some of the groups isolated by examination of the foliation and manuscript presentation have a measure of internal linguistic consistency. It may now be seen how far such consistency is maintained.

The four homilies of group A have nothing in common linguistically which they do not share with the rest of the codex, except such negative evidence as the fact that all four have frequent *io* spellings as well as many words with *eo*. There is slight evidence of

---

[23] *Studies*, pp. 104-5

[24] Cf. *hio dæleð* 62v7 written for *he todæleð*.

[25] Only *almost* as often, for though he wrote equal numbers of *eo* and *io* spellings in the first three words, he wrote *heora* ten times and *hiora* only three times.

a division between homilies I and II on the one hand and III and IV on the other; for example, in present tense verb inflexions the former have mainly unsyncopated second and third person endings (e.g. *bebeodeð*, *cymeð*, *forgifeð* and *frinest*) while the latter have mainly syncopated ones (e.g. *cwyð*, *cymð*, *gifð* and *stent*).[26] Equally slight are occasional rare spelling variants which occur in both I and II (*scile* and *sin* for *scyle* and *syn*).[27]

Present tense verb inflexions mark off the first item of group B1, homily V, from the concluding items of A: homily V has no example of syncope other than *gefehð* (invariably contracted in Old English), unsyncopated forms appearing fourteen times (e.g. *cymeð*, *eteð*, *gifeð* and *læreð*). Again, no linguistic feature clearly links the items of group B1 (homily V, *Andreas* and *Fates of the Apostles*), though it should be noted that a slight emphasis on *o* rather than *a* before a nasal which distinguishes the homily (*gelomp, mon, monige* and *wommum*) also appears in the poems (*bona, con[n], geblond, gong, mon, wong* and *wonn*).[28]

The regular use of *io* in the homilies of group B2 has already been shown to mark these items off from those of preceding and succeeding groups, but it has also been shown in the distribution of *io* and *eo* in the four common words of table 2 that there are slight differences between homilies VI-X (classified B2a) and homilies XI-XIV (B2b). Consequently it will be best to examine the two groups separately. The first point to note about group B2a is that, despite the occurrence of distinct and significant linguistic features, there is not total consistency

---

[26] On the value of such verb inflexions for the study of dialect origins, cf. Sisam, *Studies*, pp. 123-6.

[27] Cf. Karl Brunner, *Altenglische Grammatik nach der angelsächsischen Grammatik von Eduard Sievers*, 3rd ed. (Tübingen, 1965), § 31, n.2, and § 427.1.

[28] Except in common forms like *þone* and *þonne*, *o* for CG *a* before a nasal occurs only sporadically in the codex. A high proportion of the occasional forms in the prose appears in homily V, but the use is perhaps not regular enough for a definite conclusion on it as an exemplar spelling. Instances in *Andreas* and *Fates of the Apostles* are also slightly above average, though the spelling is not unusual in poetry.

of language within the group. For example, though *io* for CG *e* and *eu* occurs very frequently, and the use of it in parts of *bion, si, hio* and *diofol* is invariable, the preposition *in* appears frequently in only two of the items (homily VIII: *in* fifteen times, *on* fifteen times; homily X: *in* twenty-four times, *on* thirty-seven times) but rarely elsewhere (never in VI, three times in VII and twice in IX). It seems likely that V in the main reflected his exemplar with regard to *in/on* throughout the composition of the Vercelli Book,[29] and we have seen that the use of *io* in group B2a is probably also taken from the exemplar. This leads to the conclusion that whoever introduced the frequent examples of *io* in this group was less interested in regularizing either *in* or *on*, and a similar selective normalization is apparent in other linguistic forms. The sequence *-fn-* never appears in the group, giving way to the variant *-mn-* (*emne* and *stemne*) in the twelve instances that occur (all in homilies VIII-X). The consistency with which *-mn-* is maintained in these homilies is remarkable when it is compared with an equally consistent use of *-fn-* in other parts of the codex, e.g. homilies I and IV which each have it seven times; the appearance of only one or the other of the spellings within individual homilies suggests a faithful reflection of the exemplars. The spelling *-mn-* is West Saxon according to the grammars, being the dominant form in early and late West Saxon;[30] all the early non-West Saxon texts preserve *-fn-*, and this is the spelling which predominates in late manuscripts with non-West Saxon associations (the Blickling Homilies and the Old English Bede). The only major non-West Saxon text with *-mn-* is Rushworth[(1)], where it is

---

[29] Cf. for example the complete exclusion of *in* from homilies XIX-XXI, which is consistent with late West Saxon practice and confirms the late West Saxon exemplar of the three homilies as postulated below, pp. 336-8.

[30] Sievers-Brunner, § 193.2 and Campbell, § 484. The position is confirmed by an examination of the Ælfric material in *Homilies of Ælfric*, ed. John C. Pope, Early English Text Society 259-60 (London, 1967-8), where the ten instances of *-fn-* (against a great many of *-mn-*) are confined to four manuscripts associated with the south-east which have other occasional non-West Saxon forms (Cambridge, Corpus Christi College, MSS. 162 and 303; London, British Library, MS. Cotton Vitellius C.v; and Oxford, Bodleian Library, MS. Bodley 343).

probably due to West Saxon influence. Luick states that *-mn-* is
Kentish as well as West Saxon and indicates its appearance in Middle
Kentish (*Ayenbite* and William of Shoreham)[31] but all commentators
are agreed that it is non-Anglian. It is odd to find, then, that the
homilies of group B2a have clear evidence of Anglian origin. All have
a number of Anglian lexical items (e.g. *fylnes, gefeon, mitteðe, nænig,
semninga, unmanig, wea* and *ymbsellan*) and most of the present tense
verb forms are expanded (*cnawest, helpeð, siteð* etc.). It would appear
that the exemplar of group B2a was a collection of Anglian homilies
assembled in the south-east (where else could *io* have been regularized
for CG *e* and *eu*?) by a scribe who was not interested in excluding
Anglian words or inflexions, but who did introduce his own spellings
(*io* and *-mn-*). Putting a date on this collection is not easy; a south-
eastern scribe working before c. 975 (the date of the Vercelli Book)
would not unnaturally be sufficiently free from late West Saxon
influence for the Anglian features mentioned to be perfectly acceptable
to him. On the other hand, he does seem to have been influenced by
late West Saxon in some respects: *y* appears for earlier *i+e* (present
subjunctive of 'be' is *sy[n]* eighteen times and *hy*, 'they', occurs eleven
times), *y* appears for *i* in unstressed positions (e.g. the suffix *-lyc* seven
times) and *þænne* for *þonne* occurs eleven times.[32]   None of these
features is general to the codex and they cannot be attributed to V; they
are exemplar spellings. Thus the homilies of group B2a were drawn
from a south-eastern homiliary (or a south-eastern copy of an Anglian
homiliary) written no earlier than the third quarter of the tenth century.
  The relationship of group B2a to group B2b is difficult to assess.
The homilies of B2b are linked to each other by their rubrics, and their
lack of enumeration might be considered enough to distinguish them
from those of B2a. But there are some linguistic links: *io* is almost as
common in B2b as in B2a, for CG *e* and *eu* as well as for CG *iu*, and
sy(n) appears three times and *þænne* four times. The reduced number
of examples might be explained by the more limited sample available
(group B2a covers seventeen folios, group B2b only nine) were there

---

[31] Karl Luick, *Historische Grammatik der englischen Sprache*
(Leipzig, 1914-40; rptd Stuttgart and Oxford, 1964), § 681 and n.1.
[32] Cf. Sievers-Brunner, §§ 41 and 22, n. 2; and Campbell, § 380.

not contradictory evidence too: *-fn-* appears once in homily XI,[33] and *eo* reappears very occasionally in *beon, seo* and *deofol* in the last two items (cf. table 2). Finally, a practice which associates the two groups is the infrequency with which accent marks appear. In the codex as a whole, accents appear at fairly regular intervals (approximately one every ten lines in prose, rather more frequently in poetry) but in the 800 extant lines of group B2a only six accents occur, and they are hardly more frequent in the 400 lines of group B2b (ten instances).[34] Thus there are linguistic and presentational affinities between groups B2a and B2b, but conflicting evidence makes it unsafe to assume positively that they are from the same exemplar.

The items of group B3 have many more features in common than have the pieces in most other groups. For example, *g* is always preserved before *d* in the homilies of this group (in *-hygd-* and *-sægd-*), the four items have a preponderance of *cwom* forms against normal late West Saxon *com*,[35] weak class II verbs have the past suffix *-ad-* frequently (twenty-seven times), the possessive adjective *heora* is almost confined to this group[36] and the round *s* is used more frequently than in preceding groups.[37] All four homilies have frequent instances of the preposition *in* and many non-West Saxon lexical items (e.g. *nænig, fylnes, gefeon* and *semninga*). There are numerous examples of non-West Saxon spellings and accidental forms (e.g. smoothing in *gefehta*, non-West Saxon front mutation in *cerdest, eð,*

---

[33] But *-mn-* appears once in each of homilies XIII and XIV.

[34] Full details of the accents and their use in the codex may be found in D.G. Scragg, 'Accent Marks in the Old English Vercelli Book', *Neuphilologische Mitteilungen* 72 (1971), 699-710. Evidence is presented there to show that V took his accents from his exemplars.

[35] Sixteen *cwom* forms but only four *com*. Cf. Sisam, *Studies*, p. 103.

[36] Of forty-four instances of *heora* in the codex, thirty-three appear in the homilies of group B3. The variant spelling *hiora* also appears in B3 three times, but is more frequently found elsewhere (especially in group A). The usual spelling of the word throughout, however, is *hira* or *hyra*, occasionally *hiera*.

[37] As against the long and low forms. This may not be dialectally significant, but perhaps shows V influenced by the script of his source.

leg, legeleohte and *hersum*, the Mercian past form *slepte*, and *sege* and
segon as past forms of *seon*). Spelling, accidence and vocabulary
concur in identifying all four homilies as of Anglian, probably Mercian,
origin, and the relative infrequency of late West Saxon features
indicates late transmission into the West Saxon scribal tradition.[38]
The likelihood is that V derived group B3 from a Mercian homiliary.

The three sub-divisions of group B4—the three short poems of 4a,
the three homilies of 4b, and homily XXII in 4c—are linked by their
sharing of a number of late West Saxon features, e.g. loss of *g* in *sarie*
and *werie* (*Soul and Body* and homily XXI), *y* for earlier *i* in *synt* (*Soul
and Body* and all four homilies) and the verb form *miht*(-) (*Dream of
the Rood* and all four homilies). But the poems and homily XXII have
other features which mark them off from the three homilies of B4b,
notably their use of *io* and of some Anglian spellings (e.g. *bledum* and
wergas in *Dream of the Rood* and *seted* and *uneðnessa* in homily
XXII). The items of B4b, homilies XIX-XXI, are intimately linked
linguistically. Of the very many features common to them, but not
found throughout the codex, the following are the most noticeable: the
use of *y* for historical *i* in words with weak sentence stress (*ys* sixty
times, *byð* twenty-eight times, *hyt* eight times and *hym* three times) and
occasionally in unstressed syllables (*ælmys-, æryst, apostolys* and
hwilwendys), the almost universal use of southern verb forms (present
second and third persons singular inflexions with syncope and
assimilation and stem vowels showing mutation, e.g. *cymð, bitt*
['pray'], *swylt* and *wiðstent*, and weak past participles with syncope and
assimilation in stems ending in a dental, e.g. *gelæd* and *gemet*), weak
class II verbs with the past suffix *-ud-*, *lufu* declined as a strong noun,

---

[38] The dialectally significant linguistic forms referred to throughout
this paper are, in the main, those generally agreed, and only limited
references to the grammars are given. In the case of spellings and
accidence quoted here, cf. Campbell, §§ 222, 220, 747 and 743. On
dialect vocabulary, the studies by Jordan, Menner, Rauh, Scherer,
Vleeskruyer and Sisam listed by Campbell, p. 367, have been
cautiously relied upon, together with Schabram, *Superbia*. The work
of Meissner (references in Campbell) is less reliable; some of the
Ælfric 'coinings' he lists, for example, can be paralleled in the Vercelli
Book.

the neuter accusative plural of *eall* inflected *eallu, eallo* and *ealle*, a high proportion of examples of *sceolon* against *sculon*, the element *-sæd-*, 'said', without *g*, and no examples of the preposition *in* which is frequent elsewhere in the codex. Many of the spellings and accidental forms cited are not only West Saxon features but those which appear only in the late Old English period,[39] and the vocabulary too contains many items especially frequent in late West Saxon religious prose: *forðsið, geleaflest, leohtbrædnes, leorningcniht, mannsliht, murcnung* and *ymbscrydan*. But against all this evidence must be set occasional suggestions of non-West Saxon origin for the material: the use of distinctly Anglian vocabulary, especially in homily XXI (*hleoðrian, morðor, sigor* and *wea*), and a few expanded verb forms (e.g. XIX: *bebringeð* and *togecyrreð*; XX: *adwæscit, gecigeð* and *gedrefeð*; and XXI: *cymeð, demeð, ætyweð* and *behylfeð*). It is possible that the explanation for these forms is that all three homilies in group B4b are composite and utilize earlier English material. The second half of homily XXI (about eighty lines of text) is taken almost verbatim from an earlier independent homily which survives complete in a number of versions, one of them being Vercelli homily II. A few sentences of homily XX are drawn from a homily represented in the Vercelli collection by item III, while the opening sentence of XX is a slightly expanded version of that to homily XI. The composite nature of homily XIX has not been shown, for no study of its sources has yet been published, but transitions in the text suggest that it was compiled on the pattern of the two succeeding items.[40] It may be that all three homilies were compiled by the same person, for though the nature of the composition of XX and that of XXI seem rather different (earlier material in XX being rather better incorporated into the plan of the whole than is the case in XXI), the spelling and parts of the accidence in both are made to conform with standard late West Saxon. Compare the following pairs of sentences:

---

[39] That the spellings and accidence are late West Saxon, cf. the following (references are in the order of the features cited): Sievers-Brunner, § 22, n. 2; Sisam, *Studies*, pp. 123-6; Campbell, § 751.3; Sievers-Brunner, § 413, n.2; Vleeskruyer, *St. Chad*, p. 133; Sievers-Brunner, §§ 293, n. 3, 92.2*a* and 214.3; and Campbell, § 767, n.1.

[40] Cf. the rather awkward introduction of *ðas gangdagas* in 107v5.

III: hio geicð þas andweardan god ... 7 hio gemanigfealdaþ
            geara fyrstas (15v24)
XX: heo geycð þa 7weardan ... 7 heo gemænigfylt gear
            (110r31)
II: in þam dæge þa synfullan heofiaþ 7 wepaþ, forþan hie ær
            noldon hira synna betan; ac hie sarige aswæmaþ (9v12)
XXI: on þam dæge þa synfullan heofað 7 wepað, forðan þe hie
            ær noldan hyra synna betan; ac hie þonne sceolon sarie
            aswæman (115r12).

In the codex as a whole, copying errors are fairly frequent, and
some passages are so corrupt that no sense is discernible,[41] the
likelihood being in many cases that the text had become corrupt during
the course of a lengthy transmission. In the homilies of group B4b,
however, there are very few places in which a copyist has blurred the
meaning of a passage, the occasional error being so slight that it is
perfectly acceptable to see it as the work of V.[42] The late West Saxon
features of the group can hardly have been introduced by V since he
shows no preference for such forms elsewhere; they appear to be
indicative of the exemplar language, and suggest that the group is
drawn from a recent exemplar, for only a copy made close in time to
the writing of the Vercelli Book could show so much late West Saxon
influence. Lack of serious error suggests a short transmission, and it
is reasonable to assume that V was able to draw on good copy (perhaps
even an authorial copy) of a series of homilies compiled in the second
half of the tenth century from earlier vernacular material by a writer
thoroughly at home in the standardized language then becoming current
throughout southern England. The fact that the compiler of these
homilies was able to draw on much of the material available to V (the

---

[41] For example, on 14r a contemporary copyist marked a short
section for omission because no sense could be discerned. The excision
marks appear suprascript in lines 23 and 24.

[42] In homily XX, for example, there are only six errors. Two are
dittographic: *weg ge gelædde* 110v12 and *heafod leah leahtras*
110v15; two are minor omissions: of *bið* at 111r8, and of *is* at 111v8;
in 111r9 *eallum forhæfdnes* was written for *eall unforhæfdnes*, and in
the same line *idelne plegan* occurs as a nominative phrase.

use of parts of the homilies which V made his II, III and XI has been mentioned) suggests the possibility, probably incapable of proof, that he was working in the same scriptorium as V.

In conclusion it must be observed that there is no proof that B4a, b and c were all taken from one exemplar by V, and certain features, e.g. the frequent occurrence of *io* in B4c, suggest that whoever imposed late West Saxon order on B4b did *not* copy B4c. But neither can it be shown definitely that the three groups are from separate sources, and they must remain, as yet, sub-divisions of one unit.

The evidence from group C is similarly inconclusive. Both the Cynewulfian *Elene* and homily XXIII, which consists of extracts from two books of the Old English translation of Felix of Crowland's *Life of St Guthlac*, have a few linguistic forms which are reminiscent of the items of group B4 (e.g. in *Elene io* is as common as in homily XXII, and in homily XXIII *miht* and *-ud-* as the past suffix of weak verbs class II associate the item with group B4b), but the two single leaves on which homily XXII is concluded suggest, as has been shown, a copying break between groups B4 and C. The two items of C have little in common with each other linguistically except that they are both of Mercian origin,[43] but they both tell lives of saints, and a common exemplar for them is not improbable.

Three exemplars have now been definitely established for the Vercelli Book material, a south-eastern homiliary of the second half of the tenth century (group B2a), a Mercian homiliary of unknown date (group B3) and a late West Saxon collection (group B4b). At least two other exemplars were used for the material in groups A and B1, and others may have been used for that in B2b, B4a, B4c and C. Attention must now turn from the exemplars to the scribe V. The first thing which can be said with some assurance is that the collection was not planned in its entirety before execution began, and the explanation for the confused order of items, with overlaps in content, is that a number of

---

[43] The Mercian element of Cynewulf's language is now recognized; cf. Gradon, *Cynewulf's Elene*. *The Life of St Guthlac*, an east Mercian saint, was probably translated in that area; Mercian linguistic forms are frequent in the homily, e.g. the lexical items *hleoðrian, stræl* and *unmanig*, and the spelling of *caldan* and *leglican*.

different exemplars were used for the material. Thus the Christmas homily which begins group B2 is preceded by a Christmas homily in B1, and group B2a concludes with a Rogation homily and is followed by three pieces for the same season in B2b and yet more in B4. The second interesting feature of the codex is the extraordinary variety of linguistic forms which occurs: V has preserved good late West Saxon in B4b alongside Mercian forms in B3 and Kentish ones in B2. In part this may be due to the date at which the codex was written; such homilies of the collection as reappear in eleventh-century manuscripts have the majority of the non-West Saxon forms removed. But it is also likely that the Vercelli Book was not written within the West Saxon area; the profusion of instances of *io*, *in* and expanded verb forms does not accord with what is known of, for instance, Winchester practice in the late tenth century,[44] and it seems sensible to begin the search for the scriptorium in which the codex was written outside the heartland of Wessex.

The search may begin, indeed, with the south-east. If the exemplar of group B2a was made in the south-east not long before this section was incorporated in the Vercelli Book, as was suggested above, it is reasonable to assume that the exemplar had remained there. It is also reasonable to expect a scribe to be able to obtain late West Saxon material of recent composition there (or anywhere in the south by that date), and the long association of Kent with the Mercian kingdom could well have facilitated access to a Mercian homiliary. If V were south-eastern trained, he would be very likely to accept non-West Saxon and West Saxon forms alike—the introduction of non-West Saxon forms into Ælfrician material by south-eastern scribes is exemplified throughout the eleventh century[45]—and the introduction of *io* by V into parts of the collection is best explained as the result of his south-eastern training or environment. Attention should also be focused on a scattering of south-eastern spellings found throughout the manuscript,

---

[44] The controlled conditions in Winchester are admirably demonstrated by Pamela Gradon, 'Studies in Late West Saxon Labialization and Delabialization', *English and Medieval Studies presented to J.R.R. Tolkien*, ed. Norman Davis and C.L. Wrenn (London, 1962), pp. 63-76.

[45] Cf. Pope, *Homilies of Ælfric*, passim.

e.g. *e* for *y* in *geðeldelice* 5v17, *wedewum* 18v2, *gerene* 88r20, *sendon* ('are') 88v15, *onherien* ('emulate') 101r11 and *scele* 119r6; and *y* for *e* in *gehyrnes* ('praise') 71r4, *acynned* ('bear') 86v13, *acynde* 91r6, *gefylde* ('feel') 97v24, *gescyndan* ('corrupt') 118v16, *gescyndendra* 120r27 and *brymela* 135r14. Many of these may result from a confusion of sense on the part of a copying scribe, but taken in conjunction with other evidence they may be seen as south-eastern forms. So too might other features which appear sporadically, e.g. the instability of initial *g*. Two marginal items noted by Sisam, while not offering proof in themselves of south-eastern origin, add to the weight of evidence: the use of the *xb* sign common in Canterbury manuscripts and the interpolated word *sclean* with a south-eastern spelling.[46] Finally, minute examination of a corrupt sentence at the end of homily III gives indisputable proof of south-eastern scribal interference which is possibly that of V. The sentence now reads: *Þas þing us gedafenað gefellan mid fæder 7 mid suna 7 mid þam þam halga gaste a in ecnesse þurh ealra worulda woruld aa butan ende.* Joan Turville-Petre's study of this homily and its sources points out that part of the incomprehensibility here is the result of scribal omission of two phrases: *Cristes fultume þe mid* before *fæder*, and *leofað and rixað* after *gaste*.[47] Two linguistic points are significant: Kentish *e* for *y* in *gefellan*, 'fulfil', and the use of *in* rather than *on*, the only instance of *in* in this homily (*on* occurs twenty-eight times). Though *in* is a widespread feature of Anglian dialects, Professor Pope has suggested that it is also likely to be substituted for *on* in the south-east.[48] Although we can never be sure that the lacunae are due to V's carelessness rather than to that of an earlier scribe, and although *gefellan* and *in* might also be forms which occurred in the exemplar, it

---

[46] Cf. Sisam, *Studies*, pp. 109-10 and 113, n.2. Sisam thought that the word *sclean* was not in the hand of the main scribe, but it is not clear if he thought so only because the spelling *scl-* for *sl-* does not occur elsewhere in the manuscript. If the word was written later, it would indicate that the Vercelli Book remained in the south-east rather than that it was written there.

[47] Joan Turville-Petre, 'Translations of a Lost Penitential Homily', *Traditio* 19 (1963), 51-78.

[48] *Homilies of Ælfric*, p. 23, n.3.

would be unreasonable to assume that V could have *copied* the dittography which produced *þam þam* and that he would have reproduced the omission of final *n* in *halga*. Hence some of the corruption of this sentence was introduced by V, and it is more than possible that the lacunae and the Kentish spellings are his too. It is not too wild a guess to see him leaving close scrutiny of his exemplar at this point, tired and bored at the end of a long copying task and believing that he knew the formulae of the traditional concluding sentence sufficiently well. The result is a hopelessly confused text, but also the recording of two forms which are indicative of V's own language.

Many later manuscripts containing parallel texts of homilies in the Vercelli Book have connections with the south-east, particularly those which overlap with the Vercelli Book in items which V appears to have drawn from more than one exemplar. CCCC 162,[49] for example, has four items paralleling those in the Vercelli collection, two in Vercelli group A and two in group B4b. Similarly CCCC 198[50] has four items paralleling ones in Vercelli A, B1 and B2, CCCC 303[51] has three items paralleling ones in Vercelli A and B4b, and Bodley 340[52] has five items paralleling ones in Vercelli A, B1 and B2. None of these manuscripts takes its text from the Vercelli Book, either directly or indirectly. The fact that scribes other than V could draw on the same range of material in the south-east is further proof that a library containing copies of all the homilies involved (I, III, V, VIII, IX, XIX and XX) existed in the Kentish area. At least one of the exemplars V used was south-eastern (group B2a), much of the material he drew upon was available for copying in the same area in the eleventh century

---

[49] On Canterbury connections cf. Ker, *Catalogue*, p. 56, and Pope, *Homilies of Ælfric*, pp. 23-4.

[50] CCCC 198 has Worcester connections, especially in the glosses by the 'tremulous hand', but there is reasonable indication that it originated in the south-east, or at least had 'a south-eastern book ... in its pedigree' (Sisam, *Studies*, p. 155, n.4); cf. also Pope, *Homilies of Ælfric*, p. 22.

[51] CCCC 303 was written at Rochester; cf. Ker, *Catalogue*, p. 105.

[52] Bodley 340 was written at Canterbury or Rochester: cf. Sisam, *Studies* pp. 150-3.

and V himself seems to have introducted a number of south-eastern forms. The conclusion that the Vercelli Book is a Kentish compilation seems inescapable.

POSTSCRIPT

Since 1973 a number of significant advances in the study of the Vercelli Book and its contents have been made. As regards the compilation of the codex, the most important of these is Celia Sisam's introduction to *The Vercelli Book*, Early English Manuscripts in Facsimile 19 (Copenhagen, 1976). Miss Sisam's conclusions differ in a number of respects from mine, and I list here those that I accept: my Group A should be subdivided, since the quiring suggests that the scribe had no plans to add homily II when he finished copying homily I, and none to add homily IV when he finished homily III; and irregularities in the lineation of quire 15 suggest that *The Dream of the Rood* may not have been copied continuously from the same source as the two verse items that precede it. On specific blocks of items, we now know that homilies XIX-XXI all draw much of their subject matter from the Latin collection known as the homiliary of St Père de Chartres (see J.E. Cross, *Cambridge Pembroke College MS. 25* [King's College London, 1987], and that these three pieces were composed by the same preacher (see D.G. Scragg, 'An Old English Homilist of Archbishop Dunstan's Day', *Words, Texts and Manuscripts: Studies Presented to Helmut Gneuss*, ed. Michael Korhammer, et al., [Woodbridge, 1992]). But it is also clear that this author did not draw material from homily III for his homily XX (as is stated above) but that homilies III and XX are independently translating the same Latin source. Finally, a study of an eleventh-century composite homily that draws upon a number of the sources used by the Vercelli scribe (and who was therefore probably working in the same library some half-century later) can be found in D.G. Scragg, '"Wulfstan" Homily XXX: its Sources, its Relationship to the Vercelli Book, and its Style', *ASE* 6 (1977), 197-211. For recent editions of the Vercelli prose, see Paul E. Szarmach, *Vercelli Homilies IX-XXIII* (Toronto, 1981) and D.G. Scragg, *The Vercelli Homilies and Related Texts* EETS 300 (London, 1992). Many of the ideas in the paper reprinted here are further explored in the introduction to my 1992 edition.

from *Ælfric's First Series of Catholic Homilies*
(British Library, Royal 7.C.xii, fols. 4-218)

History of the Manuscript
Origin and Contemporary Correction and Revision

Peter Clemoes

Manuscript evidence for the text of the First Series of *Catholic Homilies*, Ælfric's earliest work, is unusually full. It reveals progressive development in the author's text. It shows that when he sent a copy to the archbishop of Canterbury, explaining his aims and methods and asking the archbishop to give the book the sanction of his authority, considerable revision and correction of the homilies as they had been first composed had already taken place. It shows too that subsequently Ælfric reissued the homilies several times and in the process introduced more changes into his text. For instance, in Cambridge, Corpus Christi College, MS. 188[1] and some other manuscripts certain homilies have an authentically expanded form which they do not have in other manuscripts. Each surviving copy, in fact, represents some stage in the evolution of Ælfric's text. London, British Library, MS. Royal 7.C.xii is a unique witness to the earliest phase of which we know.

Dr Sisam was the first to demonstrate this priority.[2] He did so by calling attention in particular to two corrections entered in the manuscript, which are significant because they involve passages belonging to an early state of the text and appearing in this manuscript but in no other. One of these corrections is in homily XII: on fol. 64r/4-v/4 a passage is separated from the neighbouring text by an enclosing line. In the margin alongside there is a note whose wording

---

[1] See Kenneth Sisam, *Studies in the History of Old English Literature* (Oxford, 1953), pp. 175-8.

[2] *Ibid.*, pp. 171-5.

makes it clear that Ælfric was its author, that he had ordered the cancellation of the ringed passage because he had treated the same subject-matter more fully in the homily for the same day in the Second Series, and that he had given instructions for the cancellation before he composed this note. It may have been when he wrote the Second Series homily or later that he had ordered the cancellation of this passage and it may have been before Royal was written—in which case the scribe disregarded his instructions—or very soon afterwards.[3] Dr Sisam,[4] Professor Pope,[5] Dr Ker[6] and the present editors[7] agree that it was almost certainly Ælfric himself who entered this note in Royal. The other correction to which Dr Sisam called attention is the crossing out of a passage on fol. 211. Homily XXXVIII in which this cancellation occurs consists of two parts—an exposition of the gospel passage appointed for St Andrew's day and an account of the saint's passion. The cancelled passage is shown by its wording to be a conclusion which Ælfric had used before he provided the homily with a passion. When the second part was added the passage ought to have been omitted: it has survived in Royal only through scribal inadvertence. Royal's testimony cannot be far removed from Ælfric's draft.

The wording of this cancelled passage on fol. 211 reminds us that originally Ælfric composed the *Catholic Homilies* for his own use—to provide himself with the preaching material he needed as masspriest at Cerne. To quote Dr Sisam: 'we should think of the *Catholic Homilies* ... as, in the main, a two years' course of sermons actually preached by Ælfric, and later revised and made available for other priests'. When the First Series was ready for general use Ælfric composed the

---

[3] There is evidence that the passage was cancelled in Royal very soon after the manuscript was written, as shown below, p. 358. References to materials elsewhere in *Ælfric's First Series of Catholic Homilies*, ed. Norman Eliason and Peter Clemoes, EEMF 13 (Copenhagen, 1966) will cite the original page numbers.

[4] Sisam, *op. cit.*, p. 173, no. 1.

[5] *Ibid.*

[6] *Catalogue of Manuscripts Containing Anglo-Saxon* (Oxford, 1957), p. 326.

[7] See EEMF 13, p. 19, n. 8.

two prefaces, one in Latin and one in English, which are preserved at the head of the set in Cambridge, University Library, MS. Gg.3.28.[8] The Latin preface, composed, as its wording shows, before the Second Series was ready, is addressed to Sigeric, archbishop of Canterbury, its original purpose being to accompany the now lost copy of the Series which Ælfric sent to the archbishop. In addition the Latin preface is addressed, through Sigeric, to other learned users of the book; the English preface is meant for users of the book at large. Royal does not contain these prefaces. One leaf is missing at the beginning of the manuscript's first gathering,[9] and the first homily begins at the top of what was originally the recto of the second leaf. There would not have been room for both prefaces on the lost first leaf:[10] if they were ever present they must have been at least started on extra leaves preceding the first gathering. While this is an arrangement which might have been adopted if the prefaces were added, it is hardly likely to have been used if they were part of the manuscript from the outset. Probably, as the manuscript was first written, the lost first leaf of the first gathering contained a list of contents[11] or it may have been left blank with the

---

[8] Printed thence by Benjamin Thorpe, *The Homilies of the Anglo-Saxon Church. The First Part, Containing the Sermones Catholici, or Homilies of Ælfric*, 2 vols. (London, 1843-6), I: 1-8.

[9] The condition of the recto of the present first leaf (fol. 4) indicates that the loss occurred in medieval times (cf. EEMF 13, p. 17).

[10] Three leaves would have been needed for them, assuming that the size of their script was the same as that of the script elsewhere in the manuscript. There would have been room on the lost leaf for the Latin preface only—though not for the English preface only—but we have no evidence at all to suggest that Ælfric ever thought of these prefaces as anything but complementary.

[11] Ælfric's note to the effect that a list of contents is unnecessary, preserved in C.U.L. Gg.3.28 at the end of the English preface and printed thence by Thorpe, I: 8, is shown by its wording to have been written after the Latin preface was in being: *Quid necesse est in hoc codice capitula ordinare, cum prediximus quod XL sententias in se contineat ...?*

intention that a list of contents would be entered on it later.[12] If the prefaces were not there from the start it is likely to be because they were not yet written. Consequently we may infer that Royal represents a stage in the set's organization between Ælfric's original composition of the homilies for his own use and his despatch of a copy of the Series to Sigeric while the Second Series was still being prepared.

On general—not specific—grounds we may suppose that when Ælfric composed a homily he first wrote it on wax tablets.[13] But not much material can have been on tablets at any one time and we may assume that his homilies were soon transferred to parchment, either by the author himself or by a scribe. Incomplete words (as first written) in Royal, such as *middan* for *middaneard* (fol. 72v/21), may be due to abbreviations which Ælfric had used on his tablets, and many of Royal's miswritings may have their origin in the difficulties of copying

---

[12] If it remained blank there would have been a motive for its removal.

[13] The terms he used in the general sense of 'to write as an author, to compose'—*scribere, awritan, dictare* and *dihtan*—do not yield evidence for the specific methods he followed. For a *résumé*, with bibliography, of the evidence for the use of wax tablets throughout classical and medieval times, see T. McKenny Hughes, 'On Some Waxed Tablets Said to have been Found at Cambridge', *Archaeologia* 55 (1897), 257-82. So far as is known only one example of an Anglo-Saxon writing tablet survives; see M.H. Longhurst, *English Ivories* (London, 1926), p. 69, a reference which I owe to Professor Whitelock. Preserved (in a damaged condition) in the British Museum, it is considered probably of ninth-century date. It is made of whale's bone, measures 3.75 ins. in length and 2.5 ins. in width and seems originally to have been one of a pair fastened together by leather thongs. In shape it closely follows Roman models. A sunk panel for wax is on the inner side; the outer side is decorated with a square panel of interlace carved in low relief. For reproductions see *Proceedings of the Society of Antiquaries* 19 (1901-3), 41; *British Museum: A Guide to the Anglo-Saxon and Foreign Teutonic Antiquities* (1923), fig. 138; A. Goldschmidt, *Die Elfenbeinskulpturen aus der Zeit der karolingischen und sächsischen Kaiser, VIII.-XI. Jhdt*, vol. 3 (Berlin, 1923), pl. xlviii.

Ælfric's text from wax to parchment (if he did not do that himself). But that is not to suggest that Royal itself might be the first parchment copy. If it were, we should expect it to show signs of having been written at intervals over a period of time; and this it does not do. The text which the scribes had in front of them is likely to have been on parchment.

There is no evidence that the Series was not available to them as a whole when they started. The first scribe (S1) wrote homilies I-III and most of homily IV on gatherings 1-3 and the first five pages of gathering 4; the second scribe (S2) wrote the rest of homily IV and homilies V-VIII on the remainder of gathering 4 and gatherings 5-7; S1 wrote homilies IX-XVIII on gatherings 8-12 and the first ten pages of gathering 13; S2 wrote the rest of the homilies on the remainder of gathering 13 and gatherings 14-29. The only gatherings of originally irregular make-up are the third (two leaves preceding a gathering of four), the fourth (a gathering of four), the seventh (one leaf preceding a bifolium) and the twenty-ninth (a gathering of four).[14] Clearly the twenty-ninth gathering was tailored to fit the amount of material remaining after the twenty-eighth had been written. Similarly the seventh gathering, written by S2, who left the last four lines on its last page blank,[15] looks as though it was constructed to fit in before an already existing eighth gathering, written by S1. This might suggest that the end of homily IV and homilies V-VIII and XIX-XL were not ready when S1 was at work and that S2 wrote these homilies later, but the way in which S2 took over from S1 in the course of homily IV—one scribe stopping in mid-sentence at the end of a page and the other beginning at the top of the next—seems to be against this supposition. Rather it seems that the two scribes took over from one another for reasons which were unconnected with their material and that S1 started again with homily IX while S2 was still at work on the preceding items. If so, the exemplar was not a bound manuscript. I infer that the scribes had before them a parchment copy of the homilies—perhaps the first that had been made—which was not bound.

---

[14] See EEMF 13, p. 17.

[15] The rubric for the homily begun by S1 on the first page (fol. 46) of the eighth gathering was erased from fol. 46/1 and transferred to the foot of fol. 45v when S2 inserted the pericope incipit on fol. 46/1 at the head of S1's work.

The occurrence of the *punctus elevatus* and *punctus versus*[16] in the addition which Ælfric[17] entered in the bottom margin of fol. 105 shows that these punctuation marks were part of his usage when he was writing for formal reading.[18]   There is every reason to suppose that Royal's punctuation substantially represents Ælfric's own practice.   At the same time it would be unsafe to assume without further investigation that the scribes had no influence: Mr Harlow has noticed that, among the five homilies he studied, the punctuation of the two written by S1[19] corresponds to the general pattern of usage less closely than the punctuation of the three written by S2 and differs more from the witness of other copies;[20] in particular Mr Harlow has pointed out the more frequent and sometimes rather different use of the *punctus elevatus* in these homilies.[21]   Royal brings us as close as we can get to the system of punctuation which Ælfric was using when he wrote the First Series of *Catholic Homilies*.[22]

---

[16] On these punctuation marks, see below, p. 362-4.

[17] I.e. the same hand as that which entered the note on fol. 64; see EEMF 13, p. 19, n. 8.

[18] The note he entered on fol. 64 is more lightly punctuated.

[19] Homilies IX and XIII.

[20] C.G. Harlow, 'Punctuation in Some Manuscripts of Ælfric', *Review of English Studies* N.S. 10 (1959), 1-19, at 16.

[21] *Ibid.*, p. 15, n. 1.

[22] It is clear that when Ælfric adopted a rhythmical style of writing he changed his practice.   The system of punctuation which is preserved to a greater or lesser extent by the main surviving copies of the *Lives of Saints*, and which is therefore certainly the author's, employs only a simple point and uses it to mark off the rhythmical phrases from one another.   The opening of a new sentence is marked by a capital. Rhythmical pointing of this kind is found already in some of the earliest examples of Ælfric's rhythmical writing—notably the homily for Palm Sunday and those on the Invention of the Cross and SS Alexander, Eventius and Theodulus in the Second Series of *Catholic Homilies*—as recorded in C.U.L. Gg.3.28, an outstandingly pure text, printed by Thorpe.   This passage from the Palm Sunday homily on the Passion (Thorpe, II: 248/32-6) is an example:

The closeness is such that marked variations in the manuscript's punctuation[23] and punctuation which is anomalous or faulty may be textually significant. This is evidence that needs to be correlated with investigations of the relationship between Ælfric's subject-matter and his sources. Defective or otherwise faulty punctuation may be evidence—like the cancelled passage on fol. 211—of growth and revision of Ælfric's text which had taken place before the manuscript was written. For instance, at fol. 51v/18 Royal has no punctuation after *geset ís* whereas all other manuscripts close the sentence here and start a fresh one with *þeah*. This may well indicate that the qualifying injunction *þeah ðe ... handum* had been an afterthought on Ælfric's part. Similarly at fol. 64v/9 Royal has no punctuation after *andgite* whereas all other manuscripts have a full period. This suggests that

---

Þa genealæhton má. hine meldigende. Ac petrus wiðsóc.
gyt ðriddan siðe. 7 se hána sona. hlúdswege sang; Ða becyrde
se hælend. 7 beseah to petre. 7 he sona gemunde. his micclan
gebeotes. 7 mid biterum wope. his wiðersæc behreowsode;

In Gg.3.28's First Series items the punctuation corresponds basically in positioning to Royal's but it does not use the *punctus elevatus*, the point being the only mark within the sentence. The available manuscript evidence does not make it as easy to come close to the punctuation which Ælfric gave his late compositions. But it may be significant that in C.C.C.C. 188, another pure text of the First Series of *Catholic Homilies*, authentic passages which augment certain homilies (notably those for the first and second Sundays after Easter and for the first Sunday in Advent) have only the point as punctuation within the sentence (although not to mark the rhythmical phrasing), whereas this manuscript's texts corresponding to Royal's show use of the *punctus elevatus* in general (cf. Harlow, *loc. cit.*, p. 6). It is worth noticing also that in London, British Library, MS. Cotton Vitellius C.v (Ker, no. 220) the works by Ælfric—including a number of his late compositions—which were added to this manuscript during the first half of the eleventh century are punctuated by only the simple point placed with the greatest regularity at the end of each rhythmical phrase.

[23] See below, p. 362.

Ælfric may have added the sentence *he tobræc ... crist sylf tæhte*, for John's version of the feeding of the 5000, which is the subject of Ælfric's homily, does not mention that Christ handed the bread to the disciples for them to distribute, and some other copies of the homily preserve between *andgite* and *He tobræc* a Latin note originating almost certainly with Ælfric, *Alii euangeliste ferunt quia panes et pisces dominus discipulis distribuisset, discipuli autem ministrauerunt turbis.*[24] At fol. 72v/9 Royal, alone among the extant manuscripts, has the punctuation of a full period after *ungesceadwis* and the following word *and* is written in full, whereas S1 regularly writes *7*. This suggests that Ælfric had interpolated *and byrðenstrang* and the related *And swa hwylce byrðena swa him deoful on besette. þa hi bæron* (fol. 72v/12-13), where again *And* is written in full. At fol. 73v/22 Royal, against all other manuscripts, originally had no punctuation after *bæce* (a *punctus versus* was added later) and the next sentence does not begin with a capital. This suggests that the *bysen* beginning *we willað* and ending *gegearnað* (fol. 74/11) had been an addition on Ælfric's part.[25] Again at fol. 75/18 Royal, against all other manuscripts, originally had no punctuation after *forpærað* (a *punctus versus* was added later) and the next sentence does not begin with a capital. This suggests that Ælfric had interpolated the passage beginning *þa getimode* and ending *belyfað* (fol. 75/25), a comparison of the devil contriving Christ's death with a fish swallowing a baited hook.

The cross-sign, which S2 copied into his text several times,[26] may be other evidence for the way Ælfric's text had been built up, for this scribe was a mechanical copier (as is shown by his inclusion of the discarded ending to homily XXXVIII on fol. 211) and this cross-sign is the one which Ælfric used to mark the insertion in Royal on fol. 105, placing it both at the head of the passage which he added in the

[24] Printed by Thorpe at I: 186/25-6.
[25] This passage is not derived from either of the two sources so far identified for this homily—Bede, *Homeliarum Evangelii Libri II*, hom. II. 3, *CCSL* 122: 200-6, identified by M. Förster, *Anglia* 16 (1894), 1-61, § 78, and Haymo, *Homiliae de Tempore*, hom. LXIII, *PL* 128: 353-8, identified by C. L. Smetana, *Traditio* 17 (1961), 459-60.
[26] See EEMF 13, p. 27.

bottom margin and in the text at the point where the passage was to be interpolated. To evaluate the possible significance of the cross-sign the relationship between Ælfric's subject-matter and his use of sources has to be taken into account, as is the case with punctuation. Professor Cross[27] has examined the subsidiary, amplifying, illustrative passages in homily XX, a homily in which the cross-sign occurs four times in Royal's text, at fols. 100/16, 101/13, 101v/15 and 102v/21. He discusses seven passages (fols. 98/14-98v/8; one which does not now occur in Royal but which clearly formed the contents of a lost slip formerly attached to fol. 99 and related to an insertion mark at fol. 99/18;[28] fols. 100/16-25; 100v/15-19; 100v/23-101/3; 101/13-101v/15; 101v/15-102/16), and he shows that these passages derive from various sources. The passage which was on the lost slip formerly attached to fol. 99 is one in which Ælfric drew an analogy between the three persons of the Trinity and three properties of the sun—its substance, brightness and heat.[29] Together with the sentence which it was intended to precede (*Nis se ælmihtiga god na pryfeald. ac is prynnys;*) it occurs also word-for-word in a very early piece by Ælfric which I take to be an extract from a letter.[30] It has all the appearance of being an addition to homily XX, made by Ælfric either before Royal was written (in which case the scribe accidentally omitted it) or more probably afterwards.[31] This raises the question whether all the other

---

[27] J.E. Cross, 'Ælfric and the Medieval Homiliary—Objection and Contribution', *Scripta minora Regiae Societatis Humaniorum Litterarum Lundensis* (Lund, 1963), pp. 24-34.

[28] The slip was probably not in Ælfric's hand, for the insertion mark is not the cross-sign which Ælfric used on fol. 105; see further, below, n. 54.

[29] Thorpe, I: 282/7-21 (*Seo sunne ... totwæmede.*).

[30] *Ibid.*, II: 606/9-24.

[31] In another of the passages discussed by Professor Cross (fol. 100/16-25) Ælfric uses the same analogy, this time to make the point that it was the Son alone who assumed humanity. At first sight this passage, which is part of Royal's text, would seem to have been composed when the one added on the slip in Royal was already part of the homily. But against this is the insertion in Royal of the words *swa we ær cwædon* at fol. 100/17 which it is natural to suppose were added

passages discussed by Professor Cross were present in the homily all along. The siting of the cross-sign at fol. 101v/15 suggests that it mechanically reproduces one that had been used to mark the point of insertion of an interpolation (cf. fol. 105/21). The passage which follows this sign is one discussed by Professor Cross. So are those that follow two other cross-signs (at fols. 100/16 and 101/13). But the evidence should not be pressed too far in an attempt to identify interpolations precisely or to fix their limits, for mechanical copying may have preserved a sign placed at the head of an inserted passage, or one placed at the point of insertion (in which case, as preserved, it might follow the interpolated passage), or both. What the presence of four cross-signs in Royal's text of homily XX seems to me to support is the general probability that Ælfric had not marshalled all his supplementary, illustrative material for this homily in a single operation at the outset but that he had added suitable passages as he had come across them or called them to mind.

Royal contains indications that details of expression had been altered too. Grammatical revision which had been imperfectly carried out seems to lie behind such hybrid constructions as *þurh ðisne geleafan 7 þurh godum geearnungum* (fol. 103/15-16), with its mixed accusative and dative, and behind such spellings as *namana* (fol. 206v/2).

Much authentic organization and revision of Royal's text took place after the manuscript was written. For instance, sixteen pericope incipits were inserted in it,[32] and it received five additions of

---

as a reference-back when the slip was attached to fol. 99. Ælfric uses the same analogy in a homily for Christmas day which he composed not long after the Second Series. The passage in question (*Ælfric's Lives of Saints*, ed. W.W. Skeat, EETS 76, 82, 94, 114 [1881-1900], no. I/71-9), combining the thought of both the passages in homily XX, has no counterpart in the Latin homily which Ælfric is mainly rendering (a homily extant in Boulogne-sur-Mer MS. 63, fols. 13-18; see Enid M. Raynes, 'MS. Boulogne-sur-Mer 63 and Ælfric', *Medium Ævum* 26 [1957], 65-73) nor in *Twelfth Century Homilies in MS Bodley 343*, ed. A.O. Belfour, vol. 1 (EETS 137 [1909, repr. 1962]), homily IX, Ælfric's partial re-rendering of the same source.

[32] Cf. EEMF 13, pp. 22-3.

substance[33] which do not seem to be making good careless scribal omissions and which all form part of the text in all other copies. There are also four deletions of parts of the text which do not occur in any other copy[34] besides those on fols. 64r-v and 211 already discussed.[35] Many small emendations, substantiated by all other copies, were entered too. There are between seven and eight hundred of them which improve expression or eliminate errors more likely to have arisen during composition than during copying. There are, for instance, numerous short insertions—sometimes of a few words,[36] but mostly of a single word or part of a word (a prefix or the like)—which have a clarifying effect[37] or regularize usage.[38] Some show an attention to fine points of style.[39] Deletions also commonly improve style.[40] Substitutions eliminate misstatements,[41] change wording,[42] alter prepositions, conjunctions, verbal prefixes and so on, improve

---

[33] At fols. 11/18, 99/18 (discussed above, p. 353 and nn. 28-31) and 100/17 (discussed above, n. 31), 105/21, 165/21 and 168v/19 (associated with deletion of some existing text). There is also the note inserted in the bottom margin of fol. 76 by Ælfric (i.e. the same hand as that which entered the cancelling note on fol. 64; see EEMF 13, p. 19, n. 8).

[34] At fols. 78/11, 80v/20-1 (two) and 168v/19-20 (see preceding note).

[35] Above, pp. 345-6 and nn. 2-7.

[36] E.g. at fols. 24v/7, 38/7, 80/9, 137v/22, 149/12, 157v/11, 158/14, 160/8, 165/23 and 176v/21.

[37] Homily XIX, for instance, yields five examples, at fols. 91/20, 91v/4, 95v/4, 95v/5 and 96v/11.

[38] E.g. the insertion of the demonstrative before *hælend* (26 examples) and the insertion of *ðe* at fols. 11/15, 19/24 etc.

[39] E.g. phraseological balance is improved at fols. 15/15, 53v/22, 97v/21 and 173/24.

[40] E.g. at fol. 217/19 if *syððan* goes back to the author.

[41] E.g. at fol. 214v/13 (*sunnan* alt. to *eorðan*).

[42] E.g. at fols. 124/9, 131v/14 (*andwyrde* alt. to *cwæð*), 211/14, 212v/7 and 215/12 (*domes* alt. to *deman*).

word-order,[43] eliminate a great many broken constructions or false concords,[44] and correct numerous grammatical irregularities of many kinds, for instance in the declension of nouns[45] and their gender[46] and in the inflexions of proper names,[47] in the declension of adjectives after demonstratives and possessives,[48] in the form of the relative,[49] in the classes of weak verbs,[50] the cases following verbs[51] and the

---

[43] E.g. at fol. 198/12-13 *us* is brought forward to a better position; at fol. 151/1 the insertion of *þa* before *þancode* necessitated transposing *he* and *þancode*.

[44] E.g. at fol. 55v/23-4 *Swa hwa swa wile beon freond þisre worulde ᛫ þonne bið he geteald* ... is corrected to *Swa hwa swa ...᛫ se bið geteald* ...; at fol. 96/2 *þær bið geþwære sawul. 7 lichama* is corrected to *þær beoð* ...; and at fol. 113v/18 *for þære getacnunge þæt hi 7 ealle cristene menn. sceolon lufian heora nextan swa swa hine sylfne* is corrected to ... *swa swa hi sylfe.*

[45] E.g. at fols. 17v/12, 13 and 16 and 48/4 weak forms of *lufu* are changed to strong ones, at fols. 68/21, 72v/22 and 80v/4 weak forms of *sunu* to strong ones, at fols. 22v/2, 59/21, 59v/19 and 165/2 strong forms of *þeow* to weak ones, and at fol. 188/16 a strong form of *hætu* to a weak one.

[46] The gender of *ærist* is changed from fem. to masc. nine times (e.g. at fol. 78/3, where *ærriste* is alt. to *æristes*), at fols. 5v/17 and 18 that of *wæstm* from fem. to neut., at fol. 9/19 that of *susl* from neut. to fem., at fol. 95v/22 (*þære* alt. to *þam*) that of *lif* from fem. to neut. (unless *þære* was a false concord) and at fol. 100/1 that of *edwist* from neut. to fem.

[47] E.g. at fols. 16/24 and 125/3.

[48] E.g. in homily II strong forms are changed to weak ones at fols. 11v/6, 12v/22 and 13v/7.

[49] E.g. in homily II at fols. 11v/24, 12/21, 13/22 and 13v/14.

[50] At fols. 5v/17 and 56v/10.

[51] E.g. at fols. 137/13, 137v/15 and 138/1 (all *-a* alt. to *-ū*) acc. after *deman* is changed to dat. and at fols. 180v/6 and 182/3 and 6 (first two, *ænne* alt. to *anū*; third, *oþerne* to *oþrū*) acc. after *æswician* to dat. Other references, fols. 19v/20, 36/10 (*hine* alt. to *him*), 54v/2, 54v/6 (*þisne mannan* alt. to *þisum men*), 58/8 (*metes þicgean* alt. to *mete þicgean*), 58/21, 61/6 (*hine* alt. to *him*), 61v/15 (*metes* alt. to

mood of the verb in subordinate clauses,[52] and in cases after prepositions.[53]

It is difficult to detect and analyse all Royal's alterations when examining the manuscript itself, and it becomes still more difficult when one is working from a facsimile, however good, especially when, as is often the case, an alteration involves an erasure. It is not easy to distinguish in a facsimile between a mark left by an erasure and an accidental stain or smudge of which there are a good many in Royal. For instance, in the last eight lines on fol. 5 there is no erasure at *næfre* (1. 18) or *þingum* (1.19) or at the *-o-* of *deofle* (1. 24), but there is an erasure after the final *-a* of *swa swa* (1. 21), the *-l-* of *deofle* (1. 24) is written on top of an erasure of *e* and *ð* is altered by erasure to *d* in *fordón* (1. 25). A further difficulty is to distinguish between the various hands making the entries. Complexity is everywhere. For example, the five substantial added passages listed above, n. 33, were entered in as many hands,[54] at fol. 8v/3 the additions of *-e* to *ælc* and of *-se* to *untrumnes* do not seem to be in the same hand, and on fols. 180-1v two or three hands were responsible for four insertions of *se* before *hælend* (at fols. 180/24, 181/4, 181/22 and 181v/6). Obviously

---

mete), 117v/10, 118/19, 142/12 (*þam folce* alt. to *þæt folc*), 156v/18 and 177v/12 (*biscope* alt. to *biscop*).

[52] Indic. is changed to subj. at fol. 19/16 (*willað* alt. to *willan*) after *gif*, at fol. 54/23 (*biddað* alt. to *biddon*) after *ær þan þe*, at fol. 117v/2 (*onfoð* alt. to *onfon*) after *þæt* (purpose), at fol. 163v/3 (*tobræc* alt. to *tobræce*) after (*het*) *þæt*, at fol. 183/3 (*hebbað* alt. to *hebbon*) after (*bebead*) *þæt* and at fol. 212/5 (*sindon* alt. to *beon*) after (*gedafenað*) *þæt*.

[53] Dat. is changed to acc. after *þurh* (28 examples), *on* (14), *wið* (5), *ongean* (4), *ymbe* (4) and *ofer* (2) and acc. is changed to dat. after *to* (2 examples), *be* (1), *buton* (1) and *mid* (1).

[54] As mentioned in EEMF 13, p. 19, n. 8, I do not think that the added slip, fol. 164v, containing the addition to fol. 165/21, is in Ælfric's hand. I assume also that the hand that wrote the lost slip formerly attached to fol. 99 was the same as the one that wrote *swa we ær cwædon* at fol. 100/17 or at least was different from any other hand entering a substantial addition, since the insertion mark at fol. 99/18 differs from those used in the other cases.

it is impossible to try to identify the hand of an entry at all unless its script contains at least one quite distinctive feature. As a result, the area of doubt is so great among the minor entries that limits cannot be set to the rôle of any particular hand. In my forthcoming edition of the Series, to be published by the Early English Text Society, I offer a complete record of all Royal's alterations nearly contemporary with the writing of the manuscript, classified as entries made—to the best of my belief—by (i) the scribes, (ii) Ælfric and (iii) others.

The manuscript—or at any rate parts of it—seems to have been in Ælfric's hands at a very early stage. Probably he ringed the passage on fol. 64r-v for omission[55] before S2 had corrected it, for some gross scribal errors in it have not been rectified, and similarly some of the alterations Ælfric entered elsewhere (e.g. at fol. 131v/4 and 5) correct errors which we should expect S2 or others[56] who checked his work to have put right if they had not been corrected already. The addition which Ælfric entered in the bottom margin of fol. 105 may have been inserted early too, for it has been corrected in its second line by a hand which may not be Ælfric's.[57] On the other hand, on certain occasions (at fol. 96v/9,[58] probably at fol. 170v/15[59] and perhaps elsewhere) we find Ælfric amending an alteration which had been entered already by someone else. Probably different parts of the manuscript were in his hands at different times and probably the manuscript as a whole passed

---

[55] As the passage was ringed and not crossed out (as the passage on fol. 211 was) it can be assumed that Ælfric did not come upon it already cancelled and merely add a marginal note explaining why he or another on his instructions had cancelled it, but that he encircled the passage when he entered the note.

[56] Correcting hands occur at fols. 99v/14, 114/7 etc.

[57] Substitution of *seo gesihð* for *þu* (or *ða*) *gesihðe*. Also the fact that Ælfric ruled lines for this addition suggests that when he inserted it the manuscript was still in sheets.

[58] The transfer of *ge-* from the end of 1. 8 after the insertion of *ðe*.

[59] The scribe first wrote *7 herodes swor* ...; then *7* was erased and the missing words supplied (clumsily), partly above the line and partly in the margin. Finally another hand, which I take to be Ælfric's, tidied up the correction by erasing the words added above the line and writing *7 herode þæs wifes* in the margin.

through his hands more than once. He seems to have paid particular attention to certain parts of it: for instance, he carefully corrected and revised the second part of homily XXVI (fols. 129v/18-134/15). S2's alterations include some revision (e.g. the marginal addition at fol. 11/18) as distinct from mere correction. It is unlikely that he was an independent originator: probably he transferred revision which was entered in the exemplar after Royal had been copied from it.[60] Additions of substance entered in his hand or in those of others (e.g. the one on the slip, fol. 169) can be assumed to have originated with Ælfric.[61] But what about all the minor corrections and revisions entered in the manuscript in early hands? Were they all the fruits of intense but unsystematic revision on Ælfric's part and did a number of people transfer them to Royal piecemeal from the copy or copies in which Ælfric entered them? Not necessarily, I think. Ælfric may well have let interested friends see the manuscript, and it would have been natural for him—as for any author—to ask qualified readers to correct any mistakes they noticed and to make any improvements they thought fit.[62] The number and character of the hands in which the alterations are entered,[63] and the fact that a few of the alterations in early-looking hands are not absorbed into the text of other manuscripts may be indications that some of Royal's entries are to be explained in this way.

Royal's alterations represent only a stage in the authentic revision

---

[60] It is likely that his insertion of pericope incipits (see EEMF 13, p. 23) is to be explained in the same way.

[61] *Se* had not yet been inserted before *hælend*—as in so many places in Royal—when the phrase at fol. 168v/19 was deleted, as necessitated by the addition of the passage on the slip (fol. 169).

[62] Cf. Sisam, *op. cit.*, p. 179, with reference to Ælfric's gradual revision of his text as witnessed by the extant manuscripts as a whole: 'The facts are best explained if we suppose that Ælfric was constantly retouching the collection or adding to it at the suggestion of friends; and that at any given time he would have a copy by him which embodied these alterations'.

[63] Some of these hands do not look to me like those of trained scribes, e.g. the one referred to as Z's, EEMF 13, p. 19. I accept only the first four examples of this hand cited by Eliason, *ibid.*, n. 7; I reject the fifth, sixth and eighth and regard the seventh as doubtful.

which Ælfric's text was to undergo: many of the processes of change which are begun in Royal were to be carried further and several new processes were to be initiated. Taken together Royal's authenticated changes give Ælfric's text a slightly less revised form than it has in any other copy extant.[64] Presumably it was when Ælfric gave the manuscript away that authorized emendation of it came to an end. Its later alterations show no further contact with the author's text.

Ælfric's prefaces make it clear that he wrote both series of *Catholic Homilies* at Cerne Abbas, in Dorset. He was at Cerne, therefore, when Royal was written, and it seems hardly possible that the manuscript could have been written anywhere else, since at least part of it was in his hands before the second scribe corrected it. The manuscript can be closely dated with some confidence too. Other extant manuscripts show that a text of an early type circulated extensively in the south-east.[65] If, as seems reasonable to suppose, this south-eastern text took its origin from the copy which Ælfric sent to Archbishop Sigeric (itself lost), still other surviving texts derive from two manuscripts (now lost) which must have been produced under Ælfric's supervision between Royal and Sigeric's copy: the two phases in Ælfric's revision which these texts represent—similar to one another but not identical—lie between the point reached by Royal's authentic entries and that of the south-eastern text just mentioned. This multiplication of copies at Cerne would have taken time: resources at so new and small a monastery must have been limited—and the Second Series was in being as a set by the time Ælfric wrote the note on fol. 64 of Royal. Ælfric went to Cerne soon after the monastery was founded there in 987; the Series is arranged, as Dr Sisam has pointed out,[66] in a relative order of fixed and movable feasts which fits the calendars of 989 and 991 but not that of 990; it fits the calendar of 988 also. Again as Dr Sisam has shown,[67] Sigeric's copy was despatched

---

[64] Some obviously faulty readings remain uncorrected in Royal, e.g. *ealle* at fol. 96v/2 where all other copies read *togædere*. Likewise spellings such as *beohtnysse* at fol. 98/24 have not been altered.

[65] Full details of this and the other states of the text will be given in my Early English Text Society edition.

[66] *Op. cit.*, p. 160, n. 1.

[67] *Ibid.*, p. 159.

probably during the first half of 991. It seems likely that it was in 989 that the homilies were first organized as a series[68]—probably at the stage of the first parchment copy taken from the wax tablets. Royal, into which pericope incipits were inserted, cannot have been much later. I would assign its production to the first half of 990 and its revision to the immediately succeeding months.[69]

---

[68] 988 seems rather early for Ælfric to have organized the set as a whole (even if he came to Cerne in 987), but no doubt he composed some of the homilies in that year: for instance, homily XXXVIII was probably the result of two years' growth, preached on the first occasion without a passion and on the second occasion with one (see above, p. 346).

[69] With the help of the Second Series it is possible to refine on this dating with some probability. The wording of Ælfric's note in Royal on fol. 64 shows that at the time he entered it the Second Series (referred to as 'the other book') was already in being as a set and the first part of its homily for mid-Lent Sunday (Thorpe, II: 188-212) was already included in the Series. It has been suggested above, p. 358, that Ælfric entered this note in Royal very soon after the relevant part of the manuscript had been written—that is to say, during the first half of 990. Now this note is more likely to have been occasioned by a homily written in March 990 than by one written a year earlier, so that we may infer that it was towards the end of March 990 that Royal's note became possible—there being also the implication that when the note was entered S1 had written Royal's tenth gathering very recently. Nor should we expect that gathering to have been written much later than the end of March if there was to be time for the completion of Royal and the writing of two other manuscripts by the end of the year.

The supposition that the first part of the Second Series homily for mid-Lent Sunday was composed in March 990 in no way conflicts with the dating evidence of the Series' relative order of fixed and movable feasts. As Dr Sisam has pointed out (*op. cit.*, p. 160, n. 1), there are four relevant points in the Second Series: (i) the second Sunday in Lent precedes St Gregory's Day (12 March); (ii) mid-Lent Sunday follows St Benedict's Day (21 March); (iii) the ninth Sunday after Pentecost precedes St James the Greater's Day (25 July); (iv) the twelfth Sunday after Pentecost precedes the Assumption (15 August). The first

Punctuation

Four marks are used, namely a simple point placed at about mid-height (rather higher by S1, sometimes lower by S2), a *punctus elevatus* (⸵), a *punctus versus* (;) and a *punctus interrogativus* (e.g. at fols. 16v/4 [S1] and 100v/11 [S2]).[70] These marks are used by both main scribes in a well organized way but the density of punctuation is not uniform and there is some unevenness in the distribution of the *punctus elevatus*; for example, as Mr Harlow has pointed out,[71] it does not occur in the first part of homily XXXVI but is regular in the second part. The same marks are used by S3, by Ælfric in entering the addition in the bottom margin of fol. 105 and by the hands that wrote the added passages occupying the slips attached to fols. 164v and 168v, although none of these happened to have occasion to use the *punctus*

---

condition fits the calendar of 989 or that of 991, but not that of 990; the second condition fits the calendar of 990 (next possible year 993), but not that of 989; the third and fourth conditions fit the calendar of 989 (next possible year 992). This may indicate that Ælfric first arranged the Series as a set in 989, perhaps the second half of the year (points (iii) and (iv)), and completed its arrangement in 990 (point (ii)) and perhaps 991 (point (i)). Probably it was in 992 that the Series was sufficiently ready to go to Sigeric—not more than a year after he was sent the First Series, as Dr Sisam has said (*ibid.*, pp. 159-60). On this chronology either the first part of the mid-Lent homily or the Benedict homily was composed as late as 990—or both of them were—and neither was composed later.

There is also the fact that the first part of the mid-Lent homily is not written in Ælfric's alliterative style. This likewise suggests that its composition was not as late as 991, for Ælfric's use of the alliterative style probably began in that year with the Cuthbert homily for an occasion earlier than mid-Lent Sunday. It is likely, however, on this evidence, that it was in 991 that the partly alliterative second part of the mid-Lent homily (Thorpe, II: 212-24) was added to the first part.

[70] This terminology was in use at any rate later in the Middle Ages.

[71] *Op. cit.*, p. 6.

interrogativus. Here and there the original punctuation has been rendered doubtful by alteration. In particular the punctuation of homilies XI, XIII and XIV has been disturbed.

The point and *punctus elevatus* are used within the sentence, the *punctus versus* is used at the close of the sentence and after words introducing direct speech,[72] and the *punctus interrogativus* at the close of most questions, the other questions being ended by the *punctus versus*. A new sentence normally, but not invariably, opens with a capital. The *punctus versus* is used regularly at the close of a rubric, pericope incipit or quotation. A special use of the point is before and after the word *ǽ*. Occasionally there is a point after a numeral or abbreviation in a rubric.[73]

Royal is, I believe, the earliest manuscript of vernacular literature in which the *punctus elevatus* occurs as original punctuation. In a paper some years ago[74] I propounded the view that the system of punctuation which we find in Royal had its origins in liturgical manuscripts and that the marks were there used to indicate musical cadences varying the recitation note of Gospels, Lessons, Epistles, Prayers, Collects, Blessings and Psalms at the points of rest, the phraseological divisions of these texts being the *commata, cola* and *periodi* traditional to Latin grammar and the cadences being a conventional form of the natural inflexions of the human voice. From this source of influence, I maintained, there became available to literature a system of punctuation which indicated to the reader inflexions of the voice[75] appropriate to the traditional phraseological

---

[72] E.g. ... *7 him to cwæð; Ealra þæra þinga* ... (fol. 5v/13-14).

[73] In the text, numbers are expressed by words.

[74] *Liturgical Influence on Punctuation in Late Old English and Early Middle English Manuscripts* (Occasional Papers, no. 1, printed for the Department of Anglo-Saxon, Cambridge, 1952; reprinted as Old English Newsletter *Subsidia* 4, CEMERS, SUNY-Binghamton, 1980).

[75] Professor R. Willard had earlier related Ælfric's punctuation to intonation in describing and transcribing the punctuation of all the extant copies of the Second Series homily for the first Sunday in Lent; see 'The Punctuation and Capitalization of Ælfric's Homily for the First Sunday in Lent', *The University of Texas Studies in English* 29 (1950), 1-32.

divisions, the simple point at the close of a *comma* signifying a lowering of the voice, the *punctus elevatus* at the close of a *colon* signifying a raising, the *punctus versus* at the close of a period signifying the lowering of the voice and the *punctus interrogativus* signifying the inflexion of a question. If this was the theory, each mark, I pointed out, was associated in practice with particular grammatical constructions and particular stylistic effects; for instance, the *punctus elevatus* commonly divided a sentence into two balanced members. Mr Harlow, as a result of a detailed study of the punctuation of five homilies of the First Series of *Catholic Homilies*,[76] as recorded in Royal and five other manuscripts, and of two homilies of the Second Series, has concluded that the punctuation's primary rôle is to indicate pauses,[77] the placing of the marks representing a compromise between grammatical and rhetorical considerations greatly in favour of the latter.[78] The *punctus elevatus* he sees as primarily a mark of a more important pause than that indicated by a simple point, the pause being more important either for syntactic reasons or because it divides members that are in contrast or parallel stylistically.[79]

---

[76] Homilies V, IX, XIII, XXIII and XXXVI (second part only).

[77] *Op. cit.*, p. 3 etc.

[78] *Ibid.*, p. 2 etc.

[79] *Ibid.*, pp. 13-16.

from *The Old English Illustrated Hexateuch*

The Production of
An Illustrated Version

Peter Clemoes

The Old English prose text of the Hexateuch was compiled probably early in the eleventh century by combining Ælfric's translation of some portions, made for other purposes, with an anonymous translation of the rest. Ælfric may never have known that his work was used in this way. By the earliest stage to which our extant copies witness, the text had already acquired serious defects. The production of an illustrated version took place separately at a later stage still, employing a text which by then had acquired further errors peculiar to itself.

The first need of an artist who was intending to produce an illustrated version of this Old English Hexateuch and who was not merely following an existing cycle of pictures[1] must have been to choose the subjects that he was going to portray. Comparison of a short sequence of the illustrations in B (chosen at random)[2] and the corresponding part of BL Royal 1.E.vii[3] suggests that this choice was influenced by the brief episodic chapter divisions of a Latin

---

[1] See *The Old English Illustrated Hexateuch*, ed. C.R. Dodwell and Peter Clemoes, EEMF 18 (Copenhagen, 1974), pp. 66-7.

[2] B designates London, British Library, MS. Cotton Claudius B.iv, the sole surviving copy of this illustrated version.

[3] London, British Library, MS. Royal 1.E.vii and viii form the only surviving Latin bible of late Anglo-Saxon provenance (as distinct from psalters and gospel books); see, further, *The Old English Illustrated Hexateuch*, p. 43, n. 2.

bible. Chapter 30 in the Royal manuscript's list of capitula at the head of Numbers, corresponding to 11.24-9 in the Vulgate numbering, is described thus: 'Tulit dominus ab spiritu moysi et posuit super septuaginta uiros et prophetauerunt et de eldad et medad qui remanserant in castris et prophetabant'. In B the portion of text occupying the last six lines on 115r consists of Numbers 11.24-5 and is followed, at the top of 115v, by an illustration of God transferring the spirit of prophecy from Moses to the seventy elders, and the portion of text between the two pictures on 115v consists of 11.26-30 and is followed by an illustration of Eldad and Meldad prophesying in the camp and of Moses being told of this. The next chapter in the Royal manuscript, 31, corresponding to 11.30-4 in the Vulgate, has this description: 'Misit dominus regem coturnicum in castra et percussit ex populo uiginti tria milia uirorum'. In B the portion of text beginning towards the foot of 115v and continuing on 116r consists of 11.31-4 and is followed by an illustration of the Israelites first gathering and drying quails and then stricken by a plague. Chapter 32 in the Royal manuscript, corresponding to the Vulgate's 12.1-15, is described as follows: 'Aaron et maria male locuti sunt de moysen et maria percussa est lepra et fuit extra castra septem diebus'. In B the portion of text beginning at the top of 116v consists of 12.1-15 and is followed by an illustration of Miriam and Aaron criticizing Moses and (probably) of Miriam stricken by leprosy.[4] The likelihood that the capitular organization of the text of a Latin bible played a part not only in the artist's selection of subjects but also in his placing of them in the Old English text deserves to be thoroughly and systematically investigated throughout the Hexateuch. Surprising, on the evidence of B (92r), is the omission of any depiction of the destruction of Pharaoh's host in the Red Sea (Exodus 14.23-8).

A second need for the artist must have been to ascertain from an existing, unillustrated copy of the Old English how much space was needed for the portion of text related to each picture. His next step would have been to design drawings and place them in the text so that each picture followed the passage in which the episode it portrayed was related. His overriding concern at this stage

---

[4] The chronologically earlier event is portrayed on the right and the later on the left. Is the relationship between them thought of as psychological—an event and its cause—rather than temporal? This interesting feature of a number of the illustrations in B would repay examination.

must have been to produce manuscript pages of a known size each of which would end either with enough space for a picture or with a portion of text which would finish at the foot of the page or could be run on to the next one: in other words a page could not end with a portion of text which finished a few lines or so from the bottom. So paramount is this requirement that it may well have governed his way of working from the start, so that he thought in terms of no more than a manuscript page or two at a time while choosing his subjects as well as while judging the amount of space needed for the passages of text and designing and positioning his drawings in relation to these passages so as to end up with the correct lay-out. The artist proceeded to make a manuscript copy of the combined text and pictures, we may suppose, either by acting as his own scribe as well as artist or by drawing his pictures at the appropriate places on the pages and leaving a scribe to copy in the text between, taking it doubtless from a suitably marked-up unillustrated copy.

Examination of B shows how its lay-out was executed. To begin with, pricks were made as a guide for vertical bounding lines and horizontal writing lines. Then the vertical lines only were ruled, so that there was a pair of them on each lateral boundary of the working space on each page. It is clear that these came first, because they control the width of both text and pictures: the text is governed by them in the usual way, while generally the vertical frames of the pictures either coincide with them fully—the inner edge of the frame agreeing with the inner ruling and the outer edge of the frame with the outer ruling—or are related to the rulings in that the inner edge of the frame agrees with the outer ruling or the outer edge of the frame with the inner ruling. The primacy of the verticals is obvious when, as on 49v, they are crooked and the crookedness is followed by both artist and scribe.

All the horizontal lines, however, were not ruled in a single operation: those to mark the top and bottom boundaries of the picture spaces (a pair of lines for each boundary) were ruled at one time and those for the text at another. This is clear on, for instance, 145v, where the pair of lines scored to give the lower picture its upper limit are out of true with the lines of writing above, which are more exactly aligned with the pricks. No doubt the artist ruled the lines he needed and the scribe ruled his. That it was the artist who did so first is shown by, for example, the way the scribe has written the run-on of his last three words on 38v along the outer edge of the upper frame of the lower picture out of true with his lines of writing above.

Where pictures and text come close together we can analyse the relative order of work more precisely. At the top of the picture on 24v, whatever we make of the intrusion of the sword into the text near the beginning of the lines, the scribe's placing of *aweg* at the very end of the second line, separated from the preceding word, seems designed to keep it to the right of the projecting spear, since there is no comparable gap elsewhere in the line. At the end of the second portion of text on 27v the separation of the last two letters of *hlæfdian* from the rest of the word is surely the result, and not the cause, of the protruding gable line below. On 29v the only gap in the last line of text seems to be caused by the axe-head. On 31v the unique type of *g* used twice in the centre of the line immediately above the lower drawing, in contrast to the normal type used earlier in the line, obviates the need for a descender going down into the tiled roof. In addition, the gap between *r* and *h* in *burh* at the beginning of the same line seems without reason if it was not to allow for the angle of the building below. On 34r an otherwise inexplicable gap in the last line of text corresponds to the tip of a sword-blade in the following drawing and in the last line of text on 36r a similar gap, in an even more crowded area of text, is related to the tip of an angel's wing. On 39v the slight splaying of the *y* and *r* in *hyre* in the last full line of text above the upper drawing seems to be due to the point of the spear coming up from below and the same explanation seems to hold good for the gap between *h* and *y* in *hys* in the last line of text on 44r and again for the gap between *ð* and *i* in *ðing* in the last but one line of text above the drawing on 47r. In this last instance the two protruding spears seem also to have influenced the spacing of the last line of text. On 48r the angel's wing extending from the upper drawing is evidently the cause of the unique gap, between *wíc* and *stów*, in the line of text immediately above, and similarly on 60v the gap between *r* and *u* in *buruh*, the last word above the upper picture, seems clearly to be due to the projecting sword-tip. All these examples show that the outline of the drawings in question was probably there before the neighbouring text was written. Equally clearly, on the other hand, in some other cases the frame of the picture, at least as finally drawn, came after the writing of adjacent text: the top frame of the upper picture on 31r, for example, obviously avoids the word run on above it. My interpretation of these two sets of facts is that the writing of the text came after the artist had sketched in the preliminary outline which was the first stage of his work[5] but before he carried out the later stages which included finishing the frame.

My view of the procedure by which B was produced is, then, that first the artist pricked the parchment, ruled the vertical bounding lines and the horizontal lines he needed for the top and bottom boundaries of his pictures and inserted his preliminary sketch in each picture space, that then the scribe ruled the writing lines he needed and wrote the text, and that lastly the artist (or artists) received back the parchment to complete the illustrations. We can watch the scribe at work ruling his lines on fol. 150, for example: on this, the last leaf of its quire, evidently he began by scoring on the verso the lines he required for the text on the lower two-thirds of the page; then on the recto he scored twelve lines at the top of the page for text which is backed by a picture space on the verso, but wrote the eight lines of text at the foot of the page on the ridges coming through from the verso. Where picture backs picture, as at the top of fol. 86, there is normally no ruling on either side. The manuscript is without question a fascinating example of late Anglo-Saxon book production and calls for exhaustive study.

Professor Dodwell points out that B's picture on 24v reflects a scribal error which is in B's text of Genesis 14.9 but not in that of L (Oxford, Bodleian Library, MS. Laud Misc. 509, fols. 1-115v), the only other witness.[6] Is B, then, the manuscript in which text and pictures were first combined? So far as textual evidence is concerned it could be. Each of the sections of text produced by the interspersion of the pictures normally begins in B with a coloured initial.[7] This distribution of coloured initials almost certainly had not been

---

[5] As identified by Professor Dodwell in his analysis, *The Old English Illustrated Hexateuch*, p. 61.

[6] See *ibid.*, p. 71; cf. the illustration on 127v discussed there. For identification of the MSS without illustrations, designated only by sigla, see S.J. Crawford, ed., *The Old English Version of the Heptateuch*, EETS 160 (London, 1922), reprinted with the text of two additional manuscripts transcribed by N.R. Ker (London, 1969).

[7] The second scribe (who wrote 21r-56r) sometimes used a not specially enlarged ink capital instead, notably from 22r (after the lower illustration) to 44r inclusive, but also at the top of 21v and the top of 45r.

applied to the text as far back in the line of transmission leading to B as the point at which the line of transmission leading to N, P[8] diverged from it, for P has a coloured initial at Exodus 29.9 where L has one[9] but B (100v, sixth line below picture) does not. Similarly it is unlikely to have been applied even as far back as the point at which the line of transmission leading to LN (Lincoln, Cathedral MS. 298, no. 2) diverged from that leading to B, since LN, in the part of Numbers for which it is a witness, has no distinguishing feature marking any place at which B has a coloured initial but L has none[10] and at 13.1 LN seems to echo in its slightly larger-than-usual rubricated capital the coloured initial which in L (and in B by normal practice after a picture) marks the beginning of Ælfric's part of the book. Thus neither N, P's text nor LN's is likely to have had an illustrated copy in its pedigree. On this evidence and, in the relevant part of Numbers, on the evidence that the errors which are in B's text but not in LN's are no more than small slips which could arise in a single copying,[11] B, on the textual side, could, but need not, be a direct copy of a manuscript which did not contain illustrations. On the pictorial side too there is inconclusive evidence. It might or might not have been possible to recreate the freshness that the pictures undoubtedly have. And in the nature of things we cannot say whether or not there was any tracing, which would prove that the pictures were copied into B: owing to elasticity in the fibres of the parchment, any shallow grooves left by tracing would have lasted only long enough to act as temporary guides. There is no way of telling whether the scored outlines,

---

[8] N (Ker, *Catalogue*, 404) = two leaves of Exodus now lost, known only from collations in Thwaites's edition of 1698; P = New York, Pierpont Morgan Library, MS. G.63.

[9] See *The Old Illustrated English Hexateuch*, p. 46 and n. 10.

[10] At 10.1, 11.1, 4, 24, 26 and 31, 12.1, 13.21 and 14.36 and 39 and in the word which in B begins 119v.

[11] In 11.5 (B *eorðæpla*, LLN *eorðæppla*); 11.11 (B *geswenctest*, LLN *swenctest*); 11.18 (B *for ðan ðe ge weopon beforan me 7 hi cwædon*, LLN ... *7 cwædon*, Vulg. *ego enim audiui uos dicere*); 13.6 (B *Saphath*, LLN *Saphat*, Vulg. *Saphat*); 13.28 (B *oncnawon magon*, LLN *oncnawan magon*); 13.31 (B *hrymdon ongean Moysen miclum ceorodon*, LLN *hrimdon 7 ongean* ...); and 14.16 (B *mihtæst*, LLN *mihtest*).

which examination through a magnifying glass reveals here and there, followed traced grooves or not.

Nevertheless I believe that we have reasons to think that B was probably not the manuscript in which text and illustrations were originally combined. An artist executing an illustrated version for the first time would have to move forward page by page if he were to finish each page—as we have seen he had to[12]—either with enough space for a picture or with a passage of text to end at the foot of the page or to continue on the next. For an artist working in this way within B's sequence of production the most natural first step would have been to provide pricks in both lateral margins of each page to guide him when ruling the top and bottom boundaries of his picture spaces. Yet this is not what we find in much of B: pricks in the inner margins become regular only with the thirteenth quire; in the first ten quires there is almost none.[13] An artist fixing the boundaries of his picture spaces anywhere within these first ten quires must therefore have been taking his alignment across the width of a full sheet, from the pricks in one of its outer margins to those in the other, though, of course, actually ruling only between the vertical bounding lines of a page. Unless we are to suppose that he took a separate alignment across the sheet for each of its two constituent pages, the implication of the pricking is that for much of the manuscript he ruled the top and bottom boundaries for the pictures on both pages of a sheet as a single operation. If so, he was often dealing simultaneously with two pages which ultimately were not going to be adjacent, as, for example, 37r and 44v, the outside pages of quire 6. We can realize how tricky the artist's task was when we remember that on the blank sheet of parchment facing him in this instance, the page which was to be 44v would have been to the left and the one which was to be 37r would have been to the right, and that he had to place four pictures on these pages, all different in size, at their correct levels, two to each page. This, I submit, would have been impossible unless he was following an existing model, of the same page size, in which text and illustrations were already combined.[14] And there is also to be

---

[12] Above, pp. 366-7.

[13] The only exception, I believe, is fol. 16, of which the recto is all text.

[14] That pricks in the inner margins were not considered essential when a model of this kind was being followed is shown by Cambridge, Corpus Christi College, MS. 23, of English origin and of the second half of the tenth century.

considered the effect of the blocks of colour put in at the stage which Professor Dodwell terms phase two:[15] it is hard to believe that such colour blocking, carried out over a number of pictures at one time and, as on 145v and 146r, partly obliterating the pre-existing outline, would not have robbed an artist of his vision of the pictures unless he had an independent model, at quite an advanced state of finish, to guide him. It seems to me to be the method more of someone producing a further copy (or further copies) than of someone creating an original. But the nearness of B to the first illustrated version is not in question. If our manuscript was indeed produced at St Augustine's, Canterbury, in the second quarter of the eleventh century,[16] there is every likelihood that the pattern manuscript itself was produced there too at much the same time. B, I suggest, is probably the only surviving, unfinished, product of an enterprise at St Augustine's intended to provide more than one copy of this ambitiously creative design. The partnering of vernacular text and pictures that is involved is more likely to have been a response to lay needs than to monastic ones, though hardly, on the evidence of B's quite moderate standards of workmanship, those of a royal or similarly high-ranking patron. The cause of B remaining at St Augustine's[17] may have been precisely that it was never finished.

The first five quires of this manuscript consist of an illustrated version of Prudentius's *Psychomachia* with a lay-out which is very similar to that of our Hexateuch and which, we can safely assume, was copied from an exemplar. In this instance, it is clear, the text was copied in before the pictures were entered and the text was written on lines which, generally speaking, had been ruled in the right areas for it and not where pictures were to go. Since there are no pricks in the inner margins, this selective ruling, based on the lay-out of the exemplar, was given its alignment across the full sheet.

[15] See *The Old English Illustrated Hexateuch*, pp. 62-3.

[16] See *ibid.*, p. 16.

[17] For good reason to think that it was there throughout the Middle Ages, see *ibid.*, p. 15.

The Publication of Alfred's
Pastoral Care

Kenneth Sisam

The evidence on the publication of Alfred's version of Gregory's *Pastoralis* is exceptionally good; and the details are important because two manuscripts of his time are the prime sources for the study of Early West Saxon. These are Oxford, Bodleian Library, MS. Hatton 20, Sweet's[1] H, and London, British Library, MS. Cotton Tiberius B.xi, Sweet's C, which, apart from some charred fragments, is preserved in a transcript made by Junius when the manuscript had already been mutilated at the end. Both were prepared by the King's orders, yet they differ in many details of forms or spellings and in some readings of substance: thus in the famous Prose Preface H reads: 'ðone naman anne we lufodon ðætte we Cristne wæren, ond swiðe feawe ða ðeawas', where C has *hæfdon* for *lufodon*; and in ch. viii H reads: 'for hiera gitsunge hie doð him to leafe ðone cwide ðe Sanctus Paulus cwæð ...' where C has *lade* 'excuse' for *leafe*. In the first of these H's reading *lufodon* may be a mechanical repetition of the preceding *lufodon*, which survived because it made passable sense. The second is clear evidence of intelligent revision before copies were sent to the bishops.

Nothing in Asser's *Life* suggests that Alfred wrote with his own hand. After hearing explanations from Plegmund, Asser, Grimbold, or John the Old Saxon,[2] he would presumably dictate his version piecemeal, at the times he could spare, to one or more scholarly amanuenses, who would give his words the written form they thought

---

[1] Sweet prints both in his edition, EETS 45, 50 (London, 1871-2). K. Jost, *Anglia* 37 (1913), p. 63 ff., has shown that Junius' transcript of C cannot be relied on in some details.

[2] Prose Preface, EETS 45, p. 6.

best. Here the first complication arises. It has been noticed that at the
end of the book (after ch. 50) psalm numbers are usually given when
the psalms are quoted, as if a different clerk were responsible for that
part.[3] Sweet, referring particularly to *e* for *ie ˂ea*, remarks that the
end of the Hatton MS. is on the whole more archaic than the earlier
part,[4] and *ē* for *īē* becomes frequent in the part where the psalms are
numbered. At about the same place, *sua* as alternative to *swa* ceases
to appear,[5] and *ðæra* as alternative to *ðara* becomes common. Such
differences may be due to the first manuscript and not to the scribes of
the Hatton manuscript.[6]

When the translation was complete, the problem of dissemination
arose. If the original would serve for the King's own use—and we
know from Asser §88 that he was content to read in manuscripts that
had no calligraphic elegance—perhaps a dozen more copies would be
needed: up to ten for his bishops, if Dorchester and Hereford were
included; a few more for favoured non-cathedral foundations like
Shaftesbury, where his daughter was abbess, or for helpers like
Grimbold and John. In the early days of his revival of letters it is
unlikely that Alfred would have around him, or at any one place,
enough trained scribes to deal promptly with this and other literary or
administrative copying. So several copies of the text were made at his
literary headquarters (probably Winchester) by scribes of whose
linguistic background nothing is known. At this stage differences
between copies could arise, and modification of the original forms and
spellings is likely.

Some of these copies of the text were sent to other scriptoria for
copying, in order to distribute and speed up the work. According to
the Verse Preface, where the book itself speaks:

---

[3] S. Potter, 'The Old English Pastoral Care', *Trans. Phil. Soc.* for
1947, p. 119 f.

[4] Introduction to his edition, p. xxx.

[5] P.J. Cosijn, *Altwestsächsische Grammatik* (Den Haag, 1883-6) i,
p. 81.

[6] The problem of distinguishing hands other than the main hand in
the text of Hatton 20 is still unsettled. After consulting Mr. Neil Ker,
I am satisfied that what is said above will not be seriously affected by
any demonstrable change of scribe in that MS.

'King Alfred turned every word of me into English, and sent
me to his copyists, south and north, instructing them to
produce more of the same from the pattern-copy, so that he
might send them to his bishops ...'.

In alliterative verse 'send south and north' means 'send in all
directions'; and possibly help was sought in such strong centres as
Worcester under Wærferth and Canterbury under Plegmund. In this
third group of copies there were further opportunities for confusion of
forms and for colouring from dialects. They would be returned to
headquarters with the pattern copies.

It is unlikely that all the copies made at headquarters were sent out
as patterns. At least one would be useful for reference and for making
others. Tiberius B.xi seems to have been produced at headquarters and
retained there. It was not prepared for sending out, because a blank is
left at the beginning of the Prose Preface for the name and title of the
person addressed. It was at headquarters while other copies were being
distributed, for at the beginning of the Prose Preface it contained the
note:

+ Plegmunde arcebiscepe is agifen his boc 7 Swiðulfe biscepe
7 Werferðe biscepe.[7]

'Archbishop Plegmund has been given his copy, and Bishop
Swithulf [of Rochester], and Bishop Wærferth [of Worcester,
who received the Hatton copy]'.

More decisive palaeographical evidence will be noticed later.

When enough copies of the text were assembled at headquarters,
the prose and verse prefaces, containing the King's personal message,
were added there. As the Prose Preface was transcribed, the name and

---

[7] Wanley, *Antiquæ Literaturæ Septentrionalis Liber Alter seu
Humphredi Wanleii Librorum Vett. Septentrionalium, qui in Angliæ
Bibliothecis extant ... Catalogus Historico-Criticus* (Oxford, 1705), p.
217. The special status of Plegmund and Wærferth indicates that these
were the first three copies sent out. Possibly Swithulf was senior to
Wærferth, but his priority may have been due simply to the
convenience of sending to Canterbury and Rochester together.

style of the person for whom the copy was intended were included at the beginning, e.g. in the Hatton manuscript: 'Ælfred kyning hateð gretan Wærferð biscep ...'; and to avoid any confusion after this had been done, the destination was boldly marked on the first page:

+ ÐEOS BOC SCEAL TO WIOGORA CEASTRE
'This copy is to go to Worcester'.[8]

The evidence for this procedure is clear. The prefaces in the Hatton manuscript are on two added leaves conjoined; they are not part of the gathering with which the contents and the text begin; and they are in hands[9] which do not appear in the contents and text. Again, Wanley tells us that in the headquarters copy Tiberius B.xi the prefaces were in a hand different from that of the text,[10] so they were pretty certainly on added leaves.

The question of the hands is interesting. Wanley, who examined the Tiberius manuscript before it was burnt, and made facsimiles, both from it and from Hatton 20, which required careful study of the letter-forms, says that the Hatton prefaces are in a script very like (*proxime accedunt ad*) the text-hand of Tiberius B.xi.[11] Mr. Neil Ker thinks that they are identical, relying not so much on direct comparison with the charred and shrunken fragments as on the identity between the hand of the Hatton Prose Preface and the Kassel Leaf of the *Pastoral*

---

[8] It is uncertain whether the copies were bound before they were sent out; and it is not clear that the texts were checked at headquarters. Certainly Hatton 20 was not corrected by Tiberius B.xi.

[9] The hand of the Verse Preface has distinguishing characteristics. The Tiberius scribe, who wrote in the Prose Preface, was apparently a person of some importance whose time had to be used sparingly.

[10] Catalogue, p. 217: 'utraque præfatio, sicut in Cod. Werferthiano ab aliena manu scripta, Codici præmittitur'. Enough of the charred MS. remains to confirm this difference of hand.

[11] Catalogue, p. 71. For his facsimiles see Hickes's *Thesaurus, Gram. Anglo-Saxonica* (Oxford, 1703-5), pp. 3 and 78.

Care,[12] and on the probability that this Kassel fragment is one of the lost leaves from the end of Tiberius B.xi. After examining the photographs of the Kassel Leaf which he kindly lent me, I accept his view. Even if we have to do with two scribes of identical training, it is reasonably certain that the text of Tiberius B.xi was copied at headquarters, where the scribe or his 'twin' added the Prose Preface to Hatton 20.

But as the prefaces were also added to Tiberius B.xi in a hand different from that of its main text, it is a fair inference that they were not both ready at headquarters when the text was first handed over for multiplication; in other words, that Alfred finished them while copies of the text were being prepared. The thrifty use of time is natural to a great administrator; and certainly he gave much time and reflection to the Prose Preface.[13] He may have worked on it with a special amanuensis, so that the Prose Preface would show forms and spellings differing from those of the main text.

In fact Cosijn noticed that the Tiberius Prose Preface contains forms that do not occur in the main text, and explained them by a change of scribe.[14] But if such forms were mainly due to the latest scribes, the Hatton Prose Preface should agree with the Tiberius text, since the same hand copied both. Generally they do not agree: thus, the Hatton Prose Preface has regularly (7 times) *liorn*- 'learn', which appears only 3 times in the Tiberius main text against 28 *leorn*-, and it has regular *giond* (6 times) which appears only once in the Tiberius main text. Again, when Sievers investigated *io* forms by noting the places where Tiberius and Hatton agree (so that they probably represent a common source), he found that relatively frequent *io* for etymological *eu*, as in *hioldon*, *ðioda*, *bebiode*, distinguished the common source of the Prose Preface from the common source of the main text.[15] The

---

[12] The Kassel Leaf (Kassel, Landesbibliothek, MS. Anhang 19) contains Sweet, p. 385/20 *beæftan* to 387/7 *sumum*. It is printed by H.M. Flasdieck, *Anglia* 42 (1938), p. 208 ff.

[13] See F. Klaeber, *Anglia* 47 (1923), p. 53 ff.

[14] *Altwestsächsische Grammatik*, Pref. p. vi.

[15] *Zum angelsächsischen Vokalismus*, Dekanatsprogramm der phil. Fakultät, Schriften der Universität Leipzig (Leigzig, 1900), p. 42.

discrepancies are accounted for if the Prose Preface was dictated to an amanuensis who was not used, or not much used, for the main text.

I have noticed nothing distinctive in the language of the short Verse Preface, which follows the Prose Preface in the manuscripts. It is matched by a verse epilogue, and may have been intended originally as the only preface to appear in the book. Before the Prose Preface, Tiberius B.xi (which is most likely to preserve traces of the first draft) and Cambridge, University Library, MS. Ii.1.33 have the heading, 'Ðis is seo foresprǣc hu S(ancte) Gregorius ðas boc gedihte þe man Pastoralem nemnað'; 'This is the preface (telling) how St. Gregory composed this book which is called *Pastoralis*'. The heading does not answer at all to the Prose Preface, which has no mention of Gregory and merely names the *Pastoralis*. But it would serve as heading for the Verse Preface, which begins: 'This work Augustine brought from the South across the salt sea to (us) island-dwellers, as God's champion, the pope of Rome, had previously written it. The learned Gregory, in the wisdom of his heart, had considered many good doctrines, the treasure of his mind. So he who was the best of Romans, wisest of men, highest renowned for glorious deeds, won the greatest number of mankind for the Lord of heaven'.[16]   It seems then that the Prose Preface was inserted, in Tiberius B.xi or an earlier draft, between the Verse Preface and its heading. The alternative is that the heading belongs to Gregory's own preface and has been separated from it by successive insertions of the long table of contents and Alfred's Verse and Prose Prefaces. On either explanation it looks as if the inclusion in the book itself of Alfred's famous letter to his bishops was an afterthought, made possible by the interval necessary to produce enough copies of the text.

---

[16] The translation of these clumsy verses is not free from doubt. *Ærendgewrit*, chosen to alliterate with *Agustinus*, means 'a writing carried by a messenger', here the 'work in Latin'. It is likely enough that Augustine brought a copy with him in 597, for Gregory gave his *Pastoralis*, written in 591, to other leaders of the Church; see M. Manitius, *Geschichte der lat. Literatur des Mittelalters i* (Munich, 1911), p. 104. For *ǣr fore*, in *swǣ hit ǣr fore adihtode*, cf. Alfred's prose usage *ǣr beforan*, Orosius 12/30, &c.

Thus the first issue of an Anglo-Saxon book, and even the original copy as it came from the author, may exhibit different usages of form or spelling in different parts. I cannot follow the investigation into the later manuscripts of the *Pastoral Care*, nor are they likely to throw much clear light on the forms and spellings of the earliest copies. Their importance lies in the substantial variants they may contain. London, British Library, MS. Cotton Otho B.ii, now fire-damaged, seems to have been a tenth-century descendant of the copy Alfred sent to Bishop Heahstan of London, whose name is in the Preface. Cambridge, University Library, MS. Ii.2.4, said to be of the mid-eleventh century, has the name of Bishop Wulfsige (of Sherborne) in the Preface. So both these are prima facie independent authorities for the text. Cambridge, Trinity College, MS. 717 (R.5.22), copied rather later in the eleventh century, probably came from Salisbury.[17] It has no preface, and its affiliations are unsettled, though certainly it has been modernized in places. Cambridge, Corpus Christi College, MS. 12, *circa* 1000, has no name in the Preface. It comes from Worcester, yet it is not copied from the original Worcester MS. Hatton 20. Miss M. Ångström[18] has claimed that it derives from Tiberius B.xi(C). Though 62/22 *geswenced* C and Corpus 12: *gescinded* Hatton and the rest,[19] is the only reading she cites that is clear evidence for the relation, it is supported by 52/8 *lade:leafe* already mentioned, where the manuscripts divide in the same way. In the Prose Preface CCCC 12 agrees with C in two good readings: 2/10 'þa ðeowutdomas þe hie Gode don sceoldon', where H and the Cambridge University manuscript omit *don*, and 4/7 *hæfdon*, where H and the Cambridge University manuscript read *lufodon*. Collation of the whole text of

---

[17] Wanley, *Catalogue*, p. 168, argues acutely that Bishop Jewell's letter to Archbishop Parker, expressing inability to identify the author or the work, cannot refer to Cambridge University MS. Ii.2.4 (in which it is now inserted), but would suit Trinity MS. 717, which lacks the preliminary matter.

[18] *Studies in Old English Manuscripts* (Uppsala, 1937), p. 37f.

[19] Professor Simeon Potter has kindly supplied me with the readings of the Cambridge MSS. in the samples quoted. The Prose Preface is printed from the Corpus and Cambridge University MSS. by F. P. Magoun Jr., *Mediaeval Studies* 11 (1949), p. 113ff.

CCCC 12 is needed to establish that it is simply derived from C, of course with errors and unauthoritative variations of its own. If, as seems likely, the relationship is the same throughout, CCCC 12 has special authority for the latter part of the text, which was missing from C when Junius transcribed it before it was burnt. For the part that Junius transcribed, CCCC 12 should serve as a check: thus at 114/3 Junius has *tælwierðe* 'blameworthy', H correctly *stælwierðe* 'serviceable'; and at 158/19 Junius has *on hiera scyldrum* 'on their shoulders', H correctly *on hiera scyldum* 'in their sins': in both places CCCC 12 agrees with H, indicating that C also agreed and that Junius slipped in transcribing it.

Though most of the literary prose texts survive in more than one manuscript, for practical reasons (the difficulty of the task, the advantage of quick publication, an excessive preoccupation with phonology) the conception of a critical text, formed by weighing the authority and merit of the variants, is a refinement that has seldom touched Anglo-Saxon studies.[20] But if a future editor should aim at getting as near as possible to the wording Alfred sent to be multiplied, he would do well to prefer the charred fragments of Tiberius B.xi, the Kassel Leaf, Junius's transcript, and CCCC 12, which between them present a state of the text earlier than that in the Hatton manuscript and the other three. In this connexion one more reading deserves close consideration. At 198/22 C and CCCC 12 have: 'Gif him ðonne weas gebyrige oððe ungewealdes' 'If then he happens by mischance or unintentionally ...': H and the rest read *wealdes* 'intentionally' for *weas*. Though it cannot be decisive where the paraphrase is free, the Latin original (*si quando vero contra eos vel in minimis lingua labitur*) favours *weas*, and so does the English context, since its trend is that to speak against one's lord in any circumstances is a grave matter. But apart from the exceptional status of Tiberius B.xi, the rare word *weas* 'by chance' has the better claim to be original. Outside this passage it occurs many times, usually with *gebyrian*, in Alfred's prose paraphrase

---

[20] For Alfred's *Boethius*, cf. p. 294; for the OE Bede, p. 130; for *Gregory's Dialogues*, p. 229; for Ælfric's *Catholic Homilies*, p. 165 ff; all in Sisam's *Studies in the History of Old English Literature* (Oxford, 1953).

of *De Consolatione*, from which it passes twice into the verse Metres.[21] Otherwise it is recorded only once, from the Bede Glosses of Alfred's time, which are thought to be Kentish.[22] It seems to have been used in a limited circle, possibly under Kentish influences, and to have died out soon after Alfred's day. *Wealdes* in the Hatton tradition, which is suggested both by the form of *weas* and by the following *ungewealdes*, is naturally explained as a contemporary substitution made by somebody who either did not understand *weas* or thought it would be unintelligible to readers.

---

[21] On the authorship of the verse Metres, see note D at p. 293 in Sisam's *Studies*.

[22] Sweet, *The Oldest English Texts*, EETS 83 (London, 1885), 181/54.

Index to Manuscripts

Listed below are references by page number of appearance for each manuscript mentioned within this book. The citations are arranged alphabetically by city and repository. Readers should refer to 'A Preliminary List of Manuscripts Written or Owned in England up to 1100' by Helmut Gneuss, *ASE* 9 (1981), 1-60, for fuller information concerning those MSS with Gneuss numbers cited (in brackets, following the shelf-mark). The index is keyed, as far as possible, to the citations in Gneuss. MSS mentioned in the book may be by shelf-mark, Gneuss number, or, in a few instances, a shorthand title such as 'the Leningrad Bede'. MSS from Trinity College, Cambridge have two shelf-marks, the second in parentheses. Each set is used by different authors in this book.